THE IMAM AND THE INDIAN

THE IMAM AND THE INDIAN

Prose Pieces by

AMITAV GHOSH

RAVI DAYAL Publisher

permanent black

Delhi

Published by
RAVI DAYAL Publisher
51 E Sujan Singh Park, New Delhi 110003
&
PERMANENT BLACK
D 28 Oxford Apartments, 11 I.P. Extension, Delhi 110092

Distributed by
ORIENT LONGMAN LTD
Bangalore Bhubaneshwar Kolkata Chennai
Ernakulam Guwahati Hyderabad Jaipur
Lucknow Mumbai New Delhi Patna

ISBN 81 7530 058 2

First published 2002
First paperback edition 2006
Second impression 2006

Typeset by Astricks, New Delhi 110070, www.astricks.com
Printed at Pauls Press, New Delhi 110020

for Mukho

Acknowledgements

TO THOSE of a taxonomic bent of mind, it may appear that the contents of this collection are heterogeneous enough to require classification under several different headings. I have resisted the temptation to do this in the belief that in the circuitry of the imagination, connections are of greater importance than disjunctions. The pieces are arranged instead in accordance with the circumstances of their writing.

The first five narratives, for example, were all written in short and intensely focused periods of concentration. Looking back on their chronology, it strikes me that it is probably no accident that, with one exception, their dates coincide with gaps between my longer works. The title piece. 'The Imam and the Indian', was written in Delhi, in 1985, in that fallow period that separated my first novel, *The Circle of Reason*, and the second, *The Shadow Lines*. I did not know it then, but the writing of 'The Imam and the Indian' signalled the gestation of another project — my third book, *In an Antique Land* — which I was not to embark on until 1989. The second and third selections, 'Tibetan Dinner' and 'The Four Corners', were written in 1988 in the brief hiatus between *The Shadow Lines* and *In an Antique Land*, while 'The Ghosts of Mrs Gandhi' was written in the period between *The Calcutta Chromosome* and *The Glass Palace*.

The one exception to this pattern is 'An Egyptian in Baghdad' which I wrote in 1990, while working on *In an Antique Land*. It was written in the wake of a deeply disturbing visit to Egypt, shortly before the Gulf War. On returning to the village where I had lived some ten years before — referred to as Nashawy in my later writings on Egypt — I discovered that many of my friends had been trapped on the shores of the Red Sea. I wrote the article, I remember, in a couple of days, while sitting in a leaky Nile felucca that was on its way from Luxor to Edfu. Luxor, usually so crowded with tourists, had the look of an abandoned city and the rumblings of fundamentalist rage were already audible in the eerie gloom. There was very little traffic on the river and we would travel for hours without catching a glimpse of another boat. At sunset the boatmen would moor the felucca near sandbanks and it would sit among the bulrushes, rocking gently, while the cliffs of the valley of Upper Egypt turned crimson in the light of the fading desert sun. I wrote, I still recall, mainly by the light of a torch. Later, this piece was to become the basis of the epilogue of *In an Antique Land.*

The sixth, seventh and eighth selections ('The Human Comedy in Cairo', 'Petrofiction' and 'Empire and Soul') began as book reviews but metamorphosed into something less easily defined. Three articles that follow these ('The Relations of Envy', 'Categories of Labour' and 'The Slave of Ms. H.6') were written for publication in learned journals and are thus armed with the usual academic apparatus — footnotes, bibliographies and the like. That they were all written at times in my life when I happened to be attached to research institutions is probably no accident.

'The Relations Of Envy' and 'Categories of Labour' are based on chapters of the thesis for which I was awarded a D.Phil. (Ph.D.) in Social Anthropology by Oxford University in 1982. The articles were completed however in Trivandrum, at the Centre for Development Studies, where I also wrote the first draft of *The Circle of Reason.* It was largely because of the open-mindedness and goodwill of Dr K.N. Raj that I was able to join the Centre and I remain deeply grateful to Dr Raj and his colleagues for making that opportunity available to me.

Because these two articles were published separately they contain some repetitions of facts and context. I decided not to excise these so that they could be read as they were written, as arguments that are complete in themselves. The spellings of Arabic words and place names differ in the two articles because of the contrasting styles followed by the publications in which they were first printed. For the first publication of 'The Relations Of Envy' I was able to use the system that I believe to be best suited to the transcription of colloquial Arabic.* 'Categories of Labour and the Orientation of the Fellah Economy' on the other hand was edited to follow the more conventional notation. The concurrent reproduction of both methods of transcription will, I hope, serve to alert the reader to the difficulties inherent in representing colloquial Arabic.

For the record, I would like to note that both these articles grew out of certain linguistic conundrums. The first of these ('The Relations Of Envy') resulted from a popular saying in Nashawy: 'It is the rich who envy the poor'. The solution to this paradox, as the persevering reader will discover, is by no means a moral tale. 'Categories of Labour and the Orientation of the Fellah Economy' followed from the responses I would get when I tried to talk to people about the work they were doing in their fields. For example, the question: 'What are you going to do today?' would often receive puzzling answers, such as: 'Today I'm off to co-operate' or 'today I'm just going to help so-and-so'.

'Yes, but what exactly are you *doing*?'

'That *is* what I am doing.'

'But are you going to harvest rice or pick cotton?'

'Oh, so *that's* what you want to know . . .'

This article was my way of working out why, in this instance, verbs denoting certain calibrations of social relationship superseded verbs that referred to technical acts — an order of precedence that was directly contrary to my expectations.

Readers who persevere with these pieces will discover that

* Devised by T.F. Mitchell. See his *An Introduction to Egyptian Colloquial Arabic*, Oxford, 1978.

despite the difference in form and diction, they share with my fiction certain characteristic subjects and concerns: most notably my interest in patterns of work. It was during my stay in Egypt that I learnt that even the most mundane forms of labour can embody an entire metaphysic — a discovery that was to have a profound influence on my novels *The Circle of Reason* and *The Glass Palace*. I can never adequately express my gratitude to those of my friends from Nashawy and Lataifa who taught me this lesson.

'The Relations Of Envy' was published in *Ethnology* while 'Categories of Labour and the Orientation of the Fellah Economy' was included in the festschrift for Dr Peter Lienhardt, my doctoral supervisor at Oxford. I owe Peter Lienhardt a great debt of gratitude: in retrospect, I doubt very much whether I could have brought my doctoral research to a successful conclusion had I worked with anyone else. Peter Lienhardt's method of supervision was revealed to me at our first meeting, which was held, as form dictated, in a pub. After several pints of beer and many hours of pleasant conversation I thought it fit to broach the subject of my proposed research. I asked, not without some hesitation, whether he had any suggestions about what I might read or what avenues of enquiry I might fruitfully pursue. Peter responded with a snort of alarm that blew a crater in the brimming head of his frothing tankard. Too late, I realized that I had committed an unforgivable solecism and would do best to keep my silence. For a while, Peter turned away to gaze into the middle distance, the preferred focal length of the Oxford don. Then at last he spoke: 'I hope you haven't come to me,' he said, in a tone of silky derision, 'expecting to find a *guru* kind of person.'

This was the last time we spoke about scholarly matters — a circumstance that could not have suited me better. I was later to discover that Peter — like his brother Godfrey — was a reluctant anthropologist. His early education was in literature and in his youth he had been an acolyte of the redoubtable F.R. Leavis. He had been weaned away by that most literary of anthropologists, E.E. Evans-Pritchard, but

I suspect that he had never completely reconciled himself to his conversion. On hearing of my first novel, he responded with utter delight: it was as though this new turn in my life had fulfilled a dream of his own.

Although Peter published very little, he was a man of wide experience and considerable linguistic gifts. He was fluent in Arabic, Persian and Swahili, having worked in Kuwait, Sharjah, Isfahan and the island of Kilwa, near Zanzibar. As an advisor to a Gulf sheikh he had even had a hand in the Buraimi dispute. As a supervisor he made it his business to be a clearer of obstacles, bureaucratic and academic, while also providing encouragement, support and frequent restorative meals. His views on the world at large could not have been more different from my own, but this never seemed to matter. He was generous, entertaining, convivial and loyal: he possessed, in short, more than his fair share of those gifts of friendship for which the English are justly praised. I recognize now that it was largely because of his admirable supervisory methods that I was able to complete my doctoral thesis in the unusually short time of two years and four months. Peter died of lung cancer in 1986: if there were patron saints of doctoral supervisors none would be more deserving of canonization than he.

'The Slave of Ms H.6' began as an attempt to work out the implications of the biographical information I had compiled while translating from Judaeo-Arabic, the letters of Abraham Ben Yiju, the twelfth-century North African merchant whose life forms one of the helical strings of the narrative of *In an Antique Land*. I wrote it in 1991–2, while I was a Fellow at the Centre for the Study of Social Sciences in Kolkata. The article benefited hugely from the advice and criticism of my colleagues there and was, in fact, first published as one of the Centre's Working Papers. That the Centre was so welcoming of this unusual project is itself a tribute to the extraordinary catholicism and collegiality of that remarkable institution.

The next five pieces ('The Indian Diaspora', 'The Global

Reservation', 'The Fundamentalist Challenge', 'The March of the Novel through History' and 'The Greatest Sorrow: Times of Joy Recalled in Wretchedness') have this in common that they were originally intended to be spoken rather than read — that is to say, they began as lectures or talks. The process by which they came to be written was thus almost the exact inverse of that which produced narratives such as 'The Imam and the Indian'. Typically, they began as collections of notes and jottings and came to be gradually knitted together over a period of many months, or even, in some cases, several years. 'The March of the Novel' for example began as the Ida Beam Lecture at the University of Iowa in 1996 and evolved very slowly over the next three years. Somewhere along the line it came to be regarded as an essay and was even awarded a prize under that rubric. To my ears, however, it still retains the distinctive sound of the spoken voice, a quality evident in the directness of its address.

The next selection is my translation of Rabindranath Tagore's classic short story, *'Kshudito Pashan'*, a work to which I am greatly attached. As an allegory of the colonial condition, it is a work of extraordinary suggestive power and atmospheric richness. I finished the translation shortly before I began writing *The Calcutta Chromosome* and it was to have a profound influence on that novel, as well as its successor, *The Glass Palace*. Under the title 'Hungry Stone' my translation was also included in the Oxford University Press (New Delhi) edition of the works of Tagore. The editor, Sukanta Chaudhuri, made some valuable revisions and emendations, for which I owe him many thanks. The last piece 'The Ghat of the Only World' was written in memory of a close friend, the poet Agha Shahid Ali, who died on 8 December 2002.

Over the years, the publications of the Ananda Bazar Group have often taken the initiative of printing Bengali translations of my work. Indeed, the idea of publishing a collection of my shorter prose pieces came initially from Ananda Publishers, which issued a similar volume under the title *Bhromi Bismaye* in 2001. I am glad to be afforded this opportunity to thank Badal Basu of Ananda Publishers.

In its present form this compilation is the outcome of the efforts of my publishers, Rukun Advani and Ravi Dayal: to both of them many thanks. My wife, Deborah Baker, assisted at the birth of many of these pieces and my gratitude to her is, as always, beyond measure. I owe thanks also to my children, Lila and Nayan, not least for providing me with the hours of wakefulness in which many of these pieces were written. My friend, Gautam Mukhopadhaya, to whom this collection is dedicated, has been one of the mainstays of my life since my school days. His unfailing support quickened my steps on many of the journeys that figure in this collection. Not the least of the reasons why I am glad to see this collection in print is that it has given me an opportunity to acknowledge my debt to him.

AMITAV GHOSH

Note

'The Imam and the Indian' was first published in *Granta*, 20 (Cambridge), 1986. It was reprinted in *The Best of Granta Travel*, Granta Books, London, 1991, and in *Displacements: Cultural Identities in Question*, ed. Angelika Bammer, Indiana University Press. A Bengali translation, by Partha Chatterjee, was published in *Baromash* in 1991. 'Tibetan Dinner' was published in *Granta*, 25, 1988 and was reprinted in the *Utne Reader*, 3/1/92. 'Four Corners' was published in *Granta*, 26, 1989 and 'An Egyptian in Baghdad', in *Granta*, 34, 1990. 'The Ghosts of Mrs Gandhi' was published in *The New Yorker*, 17 July 1995.

'The Human Comedy in Cairo; a review of the work of Naguib Mahfouz'; 'Petrofiction' and 'Empire and Soul; a review of the

Baburnama' were all published in *The New Republic* (on 7 May 1990; 2 March 1992; 6 and 13 January 1997 respectively).

'The Relations Of Envy', was published in *Ethnology* (Univ. of Pittsburgh Press, 1984) and 'Categories of Labour and the Orientation of the Fellah Economy', in the *The Diversity of the Muslim Community: Anthropological Essays in Memory of Peter Lienhardt*, ed. Dr Ahmed al-Shahi, London, 1987. 'The Slave of Ms. H.6', was published in *Subaltern Studies*, Vol. VII, Oxford University Press, New Delhi, 1992.

'The Diaspora in Indian Culture' first appeared in *Public Culture*, Philadelphia, 1990. 'The Global Reservation' was the Plenary Address at the Annual Meeting of the Society for Cultural Anthropology, held in Washington on 16 May 1993. It was published in *Cultural Anthropology*, Vol. 9, No. 3, August 1994. 'The Fundamentalist Challenge' was first delivered at a seminar on Writers and Religion, organized by William Gass in 1994 at the International Writers Center, Washington University, St. Louis. It was published in the *Wilson Quarterly* in 1995.

I delivered an early version of 'The March of the Novel through History: The Testimony of my Grandfather's Bookcase', as the Ida Beam Public Lecture at the University of Iowa on 27 September 1996. Subsequently, I presented a more complete version as the Arthur Ravenscroft Memorial Lecture at the University of Leeds, England, on 5 March 1997. It was published in the U.K. in *Kunapipi; A Journal of Post-Colonial Writing* (Vol. XIX) and in the U.S. in the *The Kenyon Review* (Vol. XX, No. 2) in 1998. A Bengali rendering under the title, *'Kathashilper Mayay Gatha Ei Basundhara'*, was published in *Desh* the same year. 'The March of the Novel through History: The Testimony of My Grandfather's Bookcase' was awarded a Pushcart Prize in 1999. 'The Greatest Sorrow: Times of Joy Recalled in Wretchedness', was, in an earlier version, the Neelan Thiruchelvam Memorial Lecture for 2001.

'The Hunger of Stones' (a trans. of Rabindranath Tagore's short story *'Kshudhita Pashan'*) was first published in *Civil Lines 2* (New Delhi), 1995. Under the title 'Hungry Stone' it was also included in the Oxford University Press (New Delhi) edition of the works of Tagore, edited by Sukanta Chaudhuri. Excerpts from 'The Ghat of the Only World' were published in *The Nation* of 11 February 2002.

Contents

1 *The Imam and the Indian*

I MET the Imam of the village and Khamees the Rat at about the same time. I don't exactly remember now — it happened more than six years ago — but I think I met the Imam first.

But this is not quite accurate. I didn't really 'meet' the Imam: I inflicted myself upon him. Perhaps that explains what happened.

Still, there was nothing else I could have done. As the man who led the daily prayers in the mosque, he was a leading figure in the village, and since I, a foreigner, had come to live there, he may well for all I knew have been offended had I neglected to pay him a call. Besides, I wanted to meet him; I was intrigued by what I'd heard about him.

People didn't often talk about the Imam in the village, but when they did, they usually spoke of him somewhat dismissively, but also a little wistfully, as they might of some old, half-forgotten thing, like the annual flooding of the Nile. Listening to my friends speak of him, I had an inkling, long before I actually met him, that he already belonged, in a way, to the village's past. I thought I knew this for certain when I heard that apart from being an Imam he was also, by profession, a barber and a healer. People said he knew a great deal about herbs and poultices and the old kind of medicine. This interested me. This was Tradition: I knew that in rural Egypt Imams and other religious figures are often by custom associated with those two professions.

The trouble was that these accomplishments bought the Imam very little credit in the village. The villagers didn't any longer want an Imam who was also a barber and a healer. The older people wanted someone who had studied at al-Azhar and could quote from Jamal ad-Din Afghani and Mohammad Abduh as fluently as he could from the Hadith, and the younger men wanted a fierce, black-bearded orator, someone whose voice would thunder from the mimbar and reveal to them their destiny. No one had time for old-fashioned Imams who made themselves ridiculous by boiling herbs and cutting hair.

Yet Ustad Ahmed, who taught in the village's secondary school and was as well-read a man as I have ever met, often said — and this was not something he said of many people — that the old Imam read a lot. A lot of what? Politics, theology, even popular science . . . that kind of thing.

This made me all the more determined to meet him, and one evening, a few months after I first came to the village, I found my way to his house. He lived in the centre of the village, on the edge of the dusty open square which had the mosque in its middle. This was the oldest part of the village: a maze of low mud huts huddled together like confectionery on a tray, each hut crowned with a billowing, tousled head of straw.

When I knocked on the door the Imam opened it himself. He was a big man, with very bright brown eyes, set deep in a wrinkled, weather-beaten face. Like the room behind him, he was distinctly untidy: his blue jallabeyya was mud-stained and unwashed and his turban had been knotted anyhow around his head. But his beard, short and white and neatly trimmed, was everything a barber's beard should be. Age had been harsh on his face, but there was a certain energy in the way he arched his shoulders, in the clarity of his eyes and in the way he fidgeted constantly, was never still: it was plain that he was a vigorous, restive kind of person.

'Welcome' he said, courteous but unsmiling, and stood aside and waved me in. It was a long dark room, with sloping walls and a very low ceiling. There was a bed in it and a couple of mats but little else, apart from a few, scattered books: everything bore that dull patina of grime which speaks of years of neglect. Later, I learned that the Imam had divorced his first wife and his second had left him, so that now he lived quite alone and had his meals with his son's family who lived across the square.

'Welcome', he said again, formally.

'Welcome to you', I said, giving him the formal response, and then we began on the long, reassuring litany of Arabic phrases of greeting.

'How are you?'

'How are you?'

'You have brought blessings?'

'May God bless you.'

'Welcome.'

'Welcome to you.'

'You have brought light.'

'The light is yours.'

'How are you?'

'How are you?'

He was very polite, very proper. In a moment he produced a kerosene stove and began to brew tea. But even in the performance of that little ritual there was something about him that was guarded, watchful.

'You're the *doktor al-Hindi*,' he said to me at last, 'aren't you? The Indian doctor?'

I nodded, for that was the name the village had given me. Then I told him that I wanted to talk to him about the methods of his system of medicine.

He looked very surprised and for a while he was silent. Then he put his right hand to his heart and began again on the ritual of greetings and responses, but in a markedly different way this time; one that I had learnt to recognize as a means of changing the subject.

'Welcome.'

'Welcome to you.'

'You have brought light.'

'The light is yours.'

And so on.

At the end of it I repeated what I had said.

'Why do you want to hear about *my* herbs?' he retorted. 'Why don't you go back to your country and find out about your own?'

'I will', I said. 'Soon. But right now . . . '

'No, no', he said restlessly. 'Forget about all that; I'm trying to forget about it myself.'

And then I knew that he would never talk to me about his craft, not just because he had taken a dislike to me for some reason of his own, but because his medicines were as discredited in his own eyes as they were in his clients'; because he knew as well as anybody else that the people who came to him now did so only because of old habits; because he bitterly regretted his inherited association with these relics of the past.

'Instead,' he said, 'let me tell you about what I have been learning over the last few years. Then you can go back to your country and tell them all about it.'

He jumped up, his eyes shining, reached under his bed and brought out a glistening new biscuit tin.

'Here!' he said, opening it. 'Look!'

Inside the box was a hypodermic syringe and a couple of glass phials. This is what he had been learning, he told me: the art of mixing and giving injections. And there was a huge market for it too, in the village: everybody wanted injections, for coughs, colds, fevers, whatever. There was a good living in it. He wanted to demonstrate his skill to me right there, on my arm, and when I protested that I wasn't ill, that I didn't need an injection just then, he was offended. 'All right', he said curtly, standing up. 'I have to go to the mosque right now. Perhaps we can talk about this some other day.'

That was the end of my interview, I walked with him to the mosque and there, with an air of calculated finality, he took my hand in his, gave it a perfunctory shake and vanished up the stairs.

Khamees the Rat I met one morning when I was walking through the rice fields that lay behind the village, watching people transplant their seedlings. Everybody I met was cheerful and busy and the flooded rice fields were sparkling in the clear sunlight. If I shut my ears to the language, I thought, and stretch the date palms a bit and give them a few coconuts, I could easily he back somewhere in Bengal.

I was a long way from the village and not quite sure of my bearings, when I spotted a group of people who had finished their work and were sitting on the path, passing around a hookah.

'Ahlan!' a man in a brown jallabeyya called out to me. 'Hullo! Aren't you the Indian *doktor?'*

'Yes', I called back. 'And who're you?'

'He's a rat', someone answered, raising a gale of laughter. 'Don't go anywhere near him.'

'Tell me *ya doktor*,' the Rat said, 'if I get on to my donkey and ride steadily for thirty days will I make it to India?'

'No', I said. 'You wouldn't make it in thirty months.'

'Thirty months!' he said. 'You must have come a long way.'

'Yes.'

'As for me,' he declared, 'I've never even been as far as Alexandria and if I can help it I never will.'

I laughed: it did not occur to me to believe him.

When I first came to that quiet corner of the Nile Delta I had expected to find on that most ancient and most settled of soils a settled and restful people. I couldn't have been more wrong.

The men of the village had all the busy restlessness of airline passengers in a transit lounge. Many of them had worked and travelled in the sheikhdoms of the Persian Gulf, others had been in Libya and Jordan and Syria, some had been to the Yemen as soldiers, others to Saudi Arabia as pilgrims, a few had visited Europe: some of them had passports so thick they opened out like ink-blackened concertinas. And none of this was new: their grandparents and ancestors and relatives had travelled and migrated too, in much the same way as mine had, in the Indian subcontinent — because of wars, or for money and jobs, or perhaps simply because they got tired of living always in one place. You could read the history of this restlessness in the villagers' surnames: they had names which derived from cities in the Levant, from Turkey, from faraway towns in Nubia; it was as though people had drifted here from every corner of the Middle East. The wanderlust of its founders had been ploughed into the soil of the village: it seemed to me sometimes that every man in it was a traveller. Everyone, that is, except Khamees the Rat, and even his surname, as I discovered later, meant 'of Sudan'.

'Well, never mind *ya doktor*,' Khamees said to me now, 'since you're not going to make it back to your country by sundown anyway, why don't you come and sit with us for a while?'

He smiled and moved up to make room for me.

I liked him at once. He was about my age, in the early twenties, scrawny, with a thin, mobile face deeply scorched by the sun. He had that brightness of eye and the quick, slightly sardonic turn to his mouth that I associated with faces in the coffee-houses of universities in Delhi and Calcutta; he seemed to belong to a world of late-night rehearsals and black coffee and lecture rooms, even though, in fact, unlike most people in the village, he was completely illiterate. Later I learned that he was called the Rat — Khamees the Rat — because he was said to gnaw away at things with his tongue, like a rat did with its teeth. He laughed at everything, people said — at his father, the village's patron saint, the village elders, the Imam, everything.

That day he decided to laugh at me.

'All right *ya doktor*', he said to me as soon as I had seated myself. 'Tell me, is it true what they say, that in your country you burn your dead?'

No sooner had he said it than the women of the group clasped their hands to their hearts and muttered in breathless horror: '*Haram! Haram!*'

My heart sank. This was a conversation I usually went through at least once a day and I was desperately tired of it. 'Yes,' I said, 'it's true; some people in my country burn their dead.'

'You mean,' said Khamees in mock horror, 'that you put them on heaps of wood and just light them up?'

'Yes', I said, hoping that he would tire of this sport if I humoured him.

'Why?' he said. 'Is there a shortage of kindling in your country?'

'No,' I said helplessly, 'you don't understand.' Somewhere in the limitless riches of the Arabic language a word such as 'cremate' must exist, but if it does, I never succeeded in finding it. Instead, for lack of any other, I had to use the word 'burn'. That was unfortunate, for 'burn' was the word for what happened to wood and straw and the eternally damned.

Khamees the Rat turned to his spellbound listeners. 'I'll tell you why they do it', he said. 'They do it so that their bodies can't be punished after the Day of Judgement.'

Everybody burst into wonderstruck laughter. 'Why, how clever', cried one of the younger girls. 'What a good idea! We ought to start doing it ourselves. That way we can do exactly what we like and when we die and the Day of Judgement comes, there'll be nothing there to judge.'

Khamees had got his laugh. Now he gestured to them to be quiet again.

'All right then *ya doktor*', he said. 'Tell me something else: is it true that you are a Magian? That in your country everybody worships cows? Is it true that the other day when you were walking through the fields you saw a man beating a cow and you were so upset that you burst into tears and ran back to your room?'

'No, it's not true', I said, but without much hope: I had heard this story before and knew that there was nothing I could say which would effectively give it the lie. 'You're wrong. In my country people beat their cows all the time; I promise you.'

I could see that no one believed me.

'Everything's upside-down in their country', said a dark, aquiline young woman who, I was told later, was Khamees's wife. 'Tell us *ya doktor:* in your country, do you have crops and fields and canals like we do?'

'Yes,' I said, 'we have crops and fields, but we don't always have canals. In some parts of my country they aren't needed because it rains all the year around.'

'Ya salám',she cried, striking her forehead with the heel of her palm. 'Do you hear that, oh you people? Oh, the Protector, oh, the Lord! It rains all the year round in his country.'

She had gone pale with amazement. 'So tell us then,' she demanded, 'do you have night and day like we do?'

'Shut up woman', said Khamees. 'Of course they don't. It's day all the time over there, didn't you know? They arranged it like that so that they wouldn't have to spend any money on lamps.'

We all laughed, and then someone pointed to a baby lying in the shade of a tree swaddled in a sheet of cloth. 'That's Khamees's baby', I was told. 'He was born last month.'

'That's wonderful', I said. 'Khamees must be very happy.' Khamees gave a cry of delight. 'The Indian knows I'm happy because I've had a son', he said to the others. 'He understands that people are happy when they have children: he's not as upside-down as we thought.'

He slapped me on the knee and lit up the hookah and from that moment we were friends.

One evening, perhaps a month or so after I first met Khamees, he and his brothers and I were walking back to the village from the fields when he spotted the old Imam sitting on the steps that led to the mosque.

'Listen,' he said to me, 'you know the old Imam, don't you? I saw you talking to him once.'

'Yes,' I said, 'I talked to him once.'

'My wife's ill,' Khamees said, 'I want the Imam to come to my house to give her an injection. He won't come if I ask him, he doesn't like me. You go and ask.'

'He doesn't like me either', I said.

'Never mind', Khamees insisted. 'He'll come if you ask him — he knows you're a foreigner. He'll listen to you.'

While Khamees waited on the edge of the square with his brothers I went across to the Imam. I could tell that he had seen me — and Khamees — from a long way off, that he knew I was crossing the square to talk to him. But he would not look in my direction. Instead, he pretended to be deep in conversation with a man who was sitting beside him, an elderly and pious shopkeeper whom I knew slightly.

When I reached them I said 'Good evening' very pointedly to the Imam. He could not ignore me any longer then, but his response was short and curt, and he turned back at once to resume his conversation.

The old shopkeeper was embarrassed now, for he was a courteous, gracious man in the way that seemed to come so naturally to the elders of the village. 'Please sit down', he said to me. 'Do sit. Shall we get you a chair?'

Then he turned to the Imam and said, slightly puzzled: 'You know the Indian *doktor*, don't you? He's come all the way from India to be a student at the University of Alexandria.'

'I know him', said the Imam. 'He came around to ask me questions. But as for this student business, I don't know. What's he going to study? He doesn't even write in Arabic.'

'Well,' said the shopkeeper judiciously, 'that's true; but after all he writes his own languages and he knows English.'

'Oh those', said the Imam. 'What's the use of *those* languages? They're the easiest languages in the world. Anyone can write those.'

He turned to face me for the first time. His eyes were very bright and his mouth was twitching with anger. 'Tell me,' he said, 'why do you worship cows?'

I was so taken aback that I began to stammer. The Imam ignored me. He turned to the old shopkeeper and said: 'That's what they do in his country — did you know? — they worship cows.'

He shot me a glance from the corner of his eyes. 'And shall I tell you what else they do?' he said to the shopkeeper.

He let the question hang for a moment. And then, very loudly, he hissed: 'They burn their dead.'

The shopkeeper recoiled as though he had been slapped. His hands flew to his mouth. 'Oh God!' he muttered. '*Ya Allah*.'

'That's what they do', said the Imam. 'They burn their dead.'

Then suddenly he turned to me and said, very rapidly: 'Why do you allow it? Can't you see that it's a primitive and backward custom? Are you savages that you permit something like that? Look at you: you've had some kind of education; you should know better. How will your country ever progress if you carry on doing these things? You've even been to the West; you've seen how advanced they are. Now tell me: have you ever seen them burning their dead?'

The Imam was shouting now and a circle of young men and boys had gathered around us. Under the pressure of their interested eyes my tongue began to trip, even on syllables I thought I had mastered. I found myself growing angry — as much with my own incompetence as the Imam.

'Yes, they do burn their dead in the West', I managed to say somehow. I raised my voice too now. 'They have special electric furnaces meant just for that.'

The Imam could see that he had stung me. He turned away and laughed. 'He's lying', he said to the crowd. 'They don't burn their dead in the West. They're not an ignorant people. They're advanced, they're educated, they have science, they have guns and tanks and bombs.'

'We have them too!' I shouted back at him. I was as confused now as I was angry. 'In my country we have all those things too', I said to the crowd. 'We have guns and tanks and bombs. And they're better than anything you have — we're way ahead of you.'

The Imam could no longer disguise his anger. 'I tell you, he's lying', he said. 'Our guns and bombs are much better than theirs. Ours are second only to the West's.'

'It's you who's lying', I said. 'You know nothing about this.

Ours are much better. Why, in my country we've even had a nuclear explosion. You won't be able to match that in a hundred years.'

So there we were, the Imam and I, delegates from two superseded civilizations vying with each other to lay claim to the violence of the West.

At that moment, despite the vast gap that lay between us. we understood each other perfectly. We were both travelling, he and I: we were travelling in the West. The only difference was that I had actually been there, in person: I could have told him about the ancient English university I had won a scholarship to, about punk dons with safety pins in their mortarboards, about superhighways and sex shops and Picasso. But none of it would have mattered. We would have known, both of us, that all that was mere fluff: at the bottom, for him as for me and millions and millions of people on the landmasses around us, the West meant only this — science and tanks and guns and bombs.

And we recognized too the inescapability of these things, their strength, their power — evident in nothing so much as this: that even for him, a man of God, and for me, a student of the 'humane' sciences, they had usurped the place of all other languages of argument. He knew, just as I did, that he could no longer say to me, as Ibn Battuta might have when he travelled to India in the fourteenth century: 'You should do this or that because it is right or good or because, God wills it so.' He could not have said it because that language is dead: those things are no longer sayable; they sound absurd. Instead he had had, of necessity, to use that other language, so universal that it extended equally to him, an old-fashioned village Imam, and great leaders at SALT conferences: he had had to say to me: 'You ought not to do this because otherwise you will not have guns and tanks and bombs.'

Since he was a man of God his was the greater defeat.

For a moment then I was desperately envious. The Imam would not have said any of those things to me had I been a Westerner. He would not have dared. Whether I wanted it or not, I would have had around me the protective aura of an inherited expertise in the technology of violence. That aura would have surrounded me, I thought, with a sheet of clear glass, like a bullet-proof screen; or perhaps it would have worked as a talisman, like a press card, armed with which I could have gone off to what were said to be the most terrible places in the world that month, to gaze and wonder. And then perhaps I too would one day have had enough material for a book which would have had for its epigraph the line, *The horror! The horror!* — for the virtue of a sheet of glass is that it does not require one to look within.

But that still leaves Khamees the Rat waiting on the edge of the square.

In the end it was he and his brothers who led me away from the Imam. They took me home with them, and there, while Khamees's wife cooked dinner for us — she was not so ill after all — Khamees said to me: 'Do not be upset, *ya doktor*. Forget about all those guns and things. I'll tell you what: *I'll* come to visit you in your country, even though I've never been anywhere. I'll come all the way.'

He slipped a finger under his skull-cap and scratched his head, thinking hard.

Then he added: 'But if I die, you must bury me.'

2 *Tibetan Dinner*

It was a while before the others at the table had finished pointing out the celebrities who had come to the restaurant for the gala benefit: the Broadway actresses, the Seventh Avenue designers, and the world's most famous rock star's most famous ex-wife, a woman to whom fame belonged like logic to a syllogism, axiomatically. Before the list was quite done, I caught a glimpse of something, a flash of saffron at the other end of the room, and I had to turn and look again.

Peering through a thicket of reed-necked women, I saw that I'd been right: yes, it was a monk in saffron robes, it really was a Buddhist monk — Tibetan, I was almost sure. He was sitting at the head of a table on the far side of the room, spectral in the glow of the restaurant's discreetly hidden lighting. But he was real. His robes were real robes; not drag, not a costume. He was in his early middle age, with clerically cropped hair and a pitted, wind-ravaged face. He happened to look up and noticed me staring at him. He looked surprised to see me: his chopsticks described a slow interrogative arc as they curled up to his mouth.

I was no less surprised to see him: he was probably a little less out of place among the dinner-jackets and designer diamonds than I, in my desert boots and sweater, but only marginally so.

He glanced at me again, and I looked quickly down at my plate. On it sat three dumplings decorated with slivers of vegetables. The dumplings looked oddly familiar, but I couldn't quite place them.

'Who were you looking at?' said the friend who'd taken

me there, an American writer and actress who had spent a long time in India and, in gratitude to the subcontinent, had undertaken to show me the sights of New York.

I gestured foolishly with a lacquered chopstick,

She laughed. 'Well, of course', she said. 'It's his show; he probably organized the whole thing. Didn't you know?'

I didn't know. All I'd been told was that this was the event of the week in New York, very possibly even the month (it wasn't a busy month): a benefit dinner at Indo-Chine, the in-est restaurant in Manhattan — one which had in fact defied every canon of in-ism by being in for almost a whole year, and which therefore had to be seen now if at all, before the tourists from Alabama got to it. My scepticism about the in-ness of the event had been dispelled by the tide of paparazzi we'd had to breast on our way in.

Laughing at my astonishment, she said, 'Didn't I tell you? It's a benefit for the Tibetan cause.'

More astonished still, I said, 'Which Tibetan cause?'

'The Tibetan cause', someone said vaguely, picking at a curl of something indeterminately vegetal that had been carved into a flower shape. It was explained to me then that the benefit was being hosted by a celebrated Hollywood star; a young actor who, having risen to fame through his portrayal of the initiation rites of an American officer, had afterwards converted to Tibetan Buddhism and found so much fulfilment in it he was reported to have sworn that he would put Tibet on the world map, make it a household word in the US, like Maalox or Lysol.

'The odd thing is,' said my friend, 'that he really is very sincere about this: he really isn't like those radical chic cynics of the sixties and seventies. He's not an intellectual, and he probably doesn't know much about Tibet, but he wants to do what little he can. They have to raise money for their schools and so on, and the truth is that no one in New York is going to reach into their pockets unless they can sit at dinner with rock stars' ex-wives. It's not his fault. He's probably doing what they want him to do.'

I looked at the Tibetan monk again. He was being talked to by an improbably distinguished man in a dinner jacket. He caught my eye, and nodded, smiling, as he bit into a dumpling.

Suddenly I remembered what the dumpling was. It was a Tibetan *mo-mo*, but stuffed with salmon and asparagus and such like instead of the usual bits of pork and fat. I sat back to marvel at the one dumpling left on my plate. It seemed a historic bit of food: one of the first genuine morsels of Tibetan *nouvelle cuisine*.

The last time I'd eaten a *mo-mo* was as an undergraduate, in Delhi.

A community of Tibetan refugees had built shacks along the Grand Trunk Road, not far from the university. The shacks were fragile but tenacious, built out of bits of wood, tin and corrugated iron. During the monsoons they would cover the roofs with sheets of tarpaulin and plastic, and weigh them down with bricks and stones. Often the bricks would be washed away and the sheets of plastic would be left flapping in the wind like gigantic prayer-flags. Some of the refugees served *mo-mo*, noodles and *chhang*, the milky Tibetan rice beer, on tables they had knocked together out of discarded crates. Their food was very popular among the drivers who frequented that part of the Grand Trunk Road.

In the university, it was something of a ritual to go to these shacks after an examination. We would drink huge quantities of *chhang* — it was very dilute, so you had to drink jugs of it — and eat noodle soup and *mo-mos*. The *mo-mos* were very simple there: bits of gristle and meat wrapped and boiled in thick skins of flour. They tasted of very little until you dipped them into the red sauce that came with them.

The food was cooked and served by elderly Tibetans; the young people were usually away, working. Communicating with them wasn't easy for the older people rarely knew any but the most functional Hindi.

As we drank our jugs of *chhang*, a fog of mystery would descend on the windy, lamp-lit interiors of the shacks. We would look at the ruddy, weathered faces of the women as they filled our jugs out of the rusty oil-drums in which they brewed the beer, and try to imagine the journey they had made: from their chilly, thin-aired plateau 15,000 feet above sea-level, across the passes of the high Himalayas, down into that steamy slum, floating on a bog of refuse and oil-slicks on the outskirts of Delhi.

Everyone who went there got drunk. You couldn't help doing so — it was hard to be in the presence of so terrible a displacement.

It was an unlikely place, but Tibetans seem to have a talent for surviving on unlikely terrain. Ever since the Chinese invasion of Tibet, dozens of colonies of Tibetan refugees have sprung up all over India. Many of them run thriving businesses in woollen goods, often in the most unexpected places. In Trivandrum, near the southernmost tip of India, where the temperature rarely drops below eighty degrees Fahrenheit and people either wear the thinnest of cottons or go bare-bodied, there are a number of Tibetan stalls in the marketplace, all piled high with woollen scarves and sweaters. They always seem to have more customers than they can handle.

Once, going past the Jama Masjid in Delhi in a bus on a scorching June day, I noticed a Tibetan stall tucked in between the sugar-cane juice vendors. Two middle-aged women dressed in heavy Tibetan *bakus* were sitting in it, knitting. The stall was stacked with the usual brightly coloured woollen goods. The women were smiling cheerfully as they bargained with their customers in sign language and broken Hindi. A small crowd had gathered around them, as though in tribute to their courage and resilience.

I found myself looking around the restaurant, involuntarily, for another Indian face, someone who had been properly invited, unlike me. I suppose I was looking for some acknowledgement, not of a debt, but of a shared history, a gesture towards the those hundreds of sweaters in Trivandrum. I couldn't see any. (Later someone said they'd seen a woman in a sari, but they couldn't be sure; it might have been a Somali robe — this was, after all, New York.)

When I next caught the monk's eye, his smile seemed a little guilty: the hospitality of a poor nation must have seemed dispensable compared to the charity of a rich one. Or perhaps he was merely bewildered. It cannot be easy to celebrate the commodification of one's own suffering.

But I couldn't help feeling that if the lama, like the actor, really wanted to make Tibet a household word in the western world, he wasn't setting about it the right way. He'd probably have done better if he'd turned it into an acronym, like TriBeCa or ComSubPac. And sold the rights to it to a line of detergents or even perhaps a breakfast cereal.

TiBet (where the Cause is): doesn't sound too bad, marketable even.

3 *Four Corners*

IT BECOMES impossible to ignore the Four Corners once Route 160 enters Colorado's Montezuma County: chevroned signposts spring regularly out of the sand and scrub, urging you towards it. Even if you had never heard of it before, did not know that it is the only point in the USA where four states meet, you are soon curious: it begins to seem like a major station, a Golgotha or Gethsemane, on this well-worn tourist pilgrimage.

The size and sleekness of the trailers and travelling homes heading towards it are eloquent of its significance. These are not the trailers you have grown accustomed to seeing in small towns in the South and Midwest — those shiny aluminium goldfish bowls which sit parked in backyards until the ball game in the next town, when they get hitched on to pick-up trucks and towed out to the ball park to serve as adjuncts for tail-gate parties. Not these; these are no ordinary trailers, they are Recreational Vehicles (RVs) — if not quite palaces, then certainly midtown condos, on wheels,

You only get a real idea of how big they are when you try to pass one on a two-lane road in a Honda Civic which lost its fifth gear 8,000 miles ago. Before you are past the master bedroom, are barely abreast of the breakfast nook, that blind curve that seemed so far away when you decided to make a break for it is suddenly right upon you.

It teaches you respect.

Their owners' imaginations are the only limits on the luxuries those RVs may be made to contain.

Once, on a desolate stretch of road in the deserts of western

Utah, I watched an RV pull into a sand-blown Rest Area, right beside my battered Honda Civic. It was almost as long as a supermarket truck and the air around it was sharp with the smell of its newness. A woman with white, curly hair stuck her head out of a window, tried the air, and said something cheerful to someone inside, over the hum of the air-conditioning. A moment later, the door opened, a flight of stairs clicked magically into place under it, and she stepped out, throwing a wave and a cheery 'How you doin'?' in my direction. She was carrying a couple of chairs and a rack of magazines. Her husband climbed out too, and in companionable silence they pulled an awning out of the side of the vehicle and unrolled a ten-foot length of artificial turf under it. She waved again, after the chair, the magazine rack, a pot of geraniums and a vase with an ikebana-ed orchid had been properly arranged on the patch of green. 'I call this my bower', she said, smiling. 'Join us for cakes and coffee?'

Never had a wilderness seemed so utterly vanquished.

Often those RVs have striking names: Winnebago, Itasca . . . The names of the dispossessed tribes of the Americas hold a peculiar allure for the marketing executives of automobile companies. Pontiac, Cherokee — so many tribes are commemorated in forms of transport. It is not a mere matter of fashion that so many of the cars that flash past on the highways carry those names, breathing them into the air like the inscriptions on prayer wheels. This tradition of naming has a long provenance: did not Kit Carson himself, the scourge of the Navajo, name his favourite horse Apache?

There are many of them on Route 160, those memorials to the first peoples of the Americas, bearing number-plates from places thousands of miles away — New York, Georgia, Alaska, Ontario. Having come this far, everybody wants to see the only point where four states meet.

There cannot be many places in the world quite as beautiful as the stretch of desert, mountain and canyon that sprawls over the borders of the four states of Colorado, Utah, New Mexico and Arizona. For the people who inhabited it at the time of the European conquest — the Diné, who came to be known as the Navajo — it was Diné Bikéyah, the country of the Diné, a land into which the First Beings climbed from the Underworlds through a female reed. To them it was the Fourth World, known as the Glittering.

Route 160 runs through some of the most spectacular parts of the Glittering World: around the caves and canyons of Mesa Verde, and through the spectacular mesas that border on Monument Valley. Curiously, its one dull stretch comes when it dips south of the little town of Cortez and heads towards the Four Corners monument. The landscape turns scraggy and undecided, not quite desert and not quite prairie, knotted with dull grey-green scrub, and desert scarred by a few shallow ravines and low cliffs.

That is why it is impossible to miss the Four Corners monument.

It springs up out of nowhere, perched atop nothing, framed by the only stretch of dull country in the region. There is nothing remotely picturesque about its surroundings — no buttes, no mesas, not even a salience of rock or an undulation in the plain. With the greatest effort of the imagination it would not be possible to persuade oneself that this may once have been, like so many places in the Glittering World, a haunt of the Spider Woman or the Talking God or the Hero Twins. Legends of that kind need visible metaphors — wind-scarred buttes or lava fields — to attach themselves to the landscape. For the Four Corners monument the landscape does not exist: it sits squatly on the scrub, like a thumb-tack in a map, unbudging in its secular disenchantedness.

There is something majestic and yet uneasy about the absoluteness of its indifference to this landscape and its topography. It is simply a point where two notional straight lines intersect: a line of latitude, thirty-seven degrees North, and a line of longitude, 109 degrees and two minutes West, the thirty-second degree of longitude west of Washington.

These two straight lines form the boundaries between the four states. These lines have nothing whatever to do with the Glittering World; their very straightness is testimony to a belief in the unpeopledness of this land — they slice through the *tabula rasa* of the New World leaving it crafted in their own image, enchanted with a new enchantment, the magic of Euclidean geometry.

The centre of the Glittering World was Diné Tah, which lay around Largo Canyon, about eighty miles south-east of the Four Corners monument. To the Navajo it was the sacred heartland of their country. The first time they left it *en masse* was in the 1860s after Colonel Kit Carson and the US Army reduced them to starvation by scorching the earth of their Glittering World. Kit Carson felt no personal animosity towards the Navajo. He is said to have commented once: 'I've seen as much of 'em as any white man livin', and I can't help but pity 'em. They'll all soon be gone anyhow.' He was an unlettered man, given to expressing himself plainly. Unlike him, his commanding officer, General James H. Carleton, had had the benefits of an education. He was therefore able to phrase the matter more dispassionately, clothed in the mellow light of current trends in science and theology: 'In their appointed time He wills that one race of men — as in races of lower animals — shall disappear off the face of the earth and give place to another race. . . . The races of the Mammoths and Mastodons, and great Sloths, came and passed away: the Red Man of America is passing away.'

The Navajo were forced to march to an 'experimental' camp at the Bosque Redondo. It was soon clear, however, that the experiment was not going to work, and in 1868 a commission headed by General William T. Sherman was sent to New Mexico to decide what was to be done with the Navajo. Addressing the commission, the Navajo leader, Barboncito, said: 'When the Navajo were first created, four mountains and four rivers were pointed out to us, inside of which we should live, that was to be our country and was given to us by the first woman of the Navajo tribe.' Later, he said to the General: 'I am speaking to you now as if I was speaking to a spirit and I wish you to tell me when you are going to take us to our country.' They were permitted to return later the same year. Of their return, Manuelito, the most renowned of the Navajo war chiefs, said afterwards: 'We felt like talking to the ground, we loved it so.' They were back in Diné Bikéyah, where every butte and mesa pointed to the sacred centre of Diné Tah.

The Four Corners monument evokes a centre too, in its own way. But that central point, the point from which its line of longitude takes its westerly orientation; that central zero degree from which its distance can be so exactly calculated, lies in another landscape, on another continent — far away in Greenwich, England. It is that distant place that the monument unwittingly celebrates.

The monument itself is modest by the standards of monuments in the United States. There is a wide, paved plaza, with plenty of parking space for cars and RVs. On the peripheries there are rows of stalls, manned by people from the neighbouring Ute and Navajo reservations.

In the centre of the plaza is a square cement platform, fenced off by aluminium railings. There is a state flag on each side of the square and towering above them a flag of the United States of America, on an eagle-topped mast. Two straight lines are etched into the cement; they intersect neatly at the centre of the platform. Somebody has thoughtfully provided a small observation post, at one end of the square. There would be little point, after all, in taking pictures of the Four Corners if you couldn't see the two lines intersect. And to get them properly into your frame you have to be above ground level.

You have to queue, both for your turn at the observation post and to get into the centre of the platform. If there are two of you, you have to queue twice at each end, unless you can get somebody to oblige you by taking your picture (and that is easy enough for there are no friendlier people in the world than American tourists). But queuing is no great trial anyway, even in the desert heat, for everyone is good-humoured and it is not long before you find yourself engaged in comparing notes on camp-grounds and motels with everyone around you.

There is a good-natured spirit of competition among the people who walk into the centre of the cement platform: everyone tries to be just a little original when posing for their photographs. A young couple kiss, their lips above the centre and each of their feet in a different state. Another couple pose, more modestly, with one foot on each state and their arms around each others' shoulders. Six middle-aged women distribute themselves between the states, holding hands. An elderly gentleman in Bermuda shorts lets himself slowly down on to his hands and knees and poses with an extremity on each state and his belly-button at the centre. This sets something of a trend; a couple of middle-aged women follow suit. In the end a pretty, teenage girl carries the day by striking a balletic pose on one leg, her toes dead centre on the point where the lines intersect.

Men from the reservations lounge about in the shade of the stalls, around the edges of the plaza. Some rev their cars, huge, lumbering old Chevrolets and Buicks, startling the tourists. A boy, bored, drives into the scrub, sending whirlwinds of sand shooting into the sky. Others sit behind their stalls, selling 'Indian' jewellery and blankets and Navajo Fry Bread. When evening comes and the flow of tourists dwindles, they will pack the contents of their stalls into their cars and go home to their reservations. No one stays the night here; there is nothing to stay for — the attractions of the place are wholly unworldly.

They will be back early next morning: the cars and RVs start arriving soon after dawn, their occupants eager to absorb what they can of the magic of the spectacle of two straight lines intersecting.

4 An Egyptian in Baghdad

THE LAST time I spoke to Nabeel was over a year ago. He was in Baghdad. I was in New York. It wasn't easy getting through. The directory listed a code for Baghdad, but after days of trying, all I'd got was a recorded message telling me that the number I'd dialled didn't exist.

In the end I had to book a call with the operator. She took a while, but eventually there was a voice at the other end, speaking in the blunt, rounded Arabic of Iraq: 'Yes? Who is it?'

Nabeel's familv had told me that he was working as an assistant in a photographer's shop. The owner was an Iraqi and Nabeel had been working for him since 1986, when he left his village in Egypt and went to Iraq. There was a telephone in the shop and the owner was relatively kind, a relatively kind Iraqi, and he allowed Nabeel to receive calls.

I imagined him as a big, paunchy man, Nabeel's boss, sitting at the end of a counter, behind a cash box, with the telephone beside him and a Kodacolor poster of a snow-clad mountain on the wall above. He was wearing a blue *gallabeyyaa* and a white lace cap; he had a carefully trimmed moustache and a pair of sun-glasses in his breast pocket. The telephone beside him was of the old-fashioned kind, black and heavy, and it had a brass lock fastened in its dial. The boss kept the key, and Nabeel and the other assistants had to ask for it when they wanted to make a call. It was late at night in New York, so it had to be morning in Baghdad. The shop must just have opened. They had probably had no customers yet.

'Is Nabeel there?' I asked.

'Who?' said the voice.

'Nabeel Idris Badawy', I said. 'The Egyptian.'

He grunted. *'Wa min inta?'* he said. 'And who're you?'

'I'm a friend of his', I said. 'Tell him it's his friend from India. He'll know.'

'What's that?' he said. 'From where?'

'From India, *ya raiyis*', I said. 'Could you tell him? And quickly if you please, for I'm calling from America.'

'From America?' he shouted down the line. 'But you said you're Indian?'

'Yes, I am — I'm just in America on a visit. Nabeel quickly, if you please, *ya raiyis* . . . '

I heard him shout across the room: '*Ya* Nabeel, somebody wants to talk to you, some Indian or something . . . '

I could tell from Nabeel's first words of greeting that my call had taken him completely by surprise. It was only natural. Eight years had passed since I'd left his village. He and his family had befriended me when I was living there in 1980 and 1981, doing research. I was then in my mid-twenties; Nabeel was a few years younger. We had become close friends, and for the first few years after I'd left, we had written letters back and forth, between India and Egypt. But then he had gone to do his National Service, in the army, and he'd stopped writing. In time I had stopped writing too. He had no way of knowing that I would be in the US on a visit that year. Until a few weeks ago I hadn't known that he was in Baghdad. I knew now because I had just been to Egypt and had visited his village and his family.

'Nabeel's not here *ya* Amitab', his sister-in-law, Fawzia, had said to me, once she recovered from the shock of seeing me at the door. 'He's not in the village — he's gone to Iraq.'

Ushering me in she fussed about distractedly, pumping her kerosene stove, fetching tea and sugar. She was a pretty, good-humoured woman who had always made me welcome in their house. I had been in the village when she was married to Nabeel's elder brother Aly.

'Nabeel left about two years ago', she said. 'He went with his cousin Ismail, do you remember him?'

I did. He was Nabeel's best friend as well as his cousin, although they could not have been more different. Ismail was lively, energetic, always ready with a joke or a pun; Nabeel, on the other hand, was thoughtful and serious, with a marked disinclination for vigorous activity of any kind. When he made his way down the lanes of the village it was in a stately, considered kind of way, in marked contrast to the caperings of his cousin.

'They left for Iraq soon after they finished their National Service', said Fawzia. 'They went to make money.'

They had rented a room in Baghdad with some other young men from the village, she said, and they all lived and cooked and ate together. She had taught Nabeel ind Ismail to cook a few things before they left, so they managed all right. Ismail was a construction labourer. There was good money to be had in construction; Nabeel earned less as a photographer's assistant, but he liked his job. Ismail had been trying to get him to go into construction, but Nabeel wasn't interested.

'You know him', she said, laughing. 'He always wanted a job where he wouldn't have to get his clothes dirty.'

Later, when her husband Aly had come home from the fields, and we had all had dinner, she gave me the number of the shop in Baghdad. Once every couple of months or so she and Nabeel's brothers would make a trip to a post office in a nearby town and telephone him in Baghdad.

'It costs a lot,' she said, 'but you can hear him like he was in the next house.'

Nabeel couldn't telephone them of course, but now and again he would speak into a cassette recorder and send them a tape. He and his brothers had all been through high school; Nabeel himself even had a college degree. But they still found the spoken word more reassuring than the written.

'You must hear his voice on the machine', said Aly and produced a tape. He placed it carefully inside a huge cassette-recorder-cum-radio and we gathered around to listen. Nabeel's voice was very solemn, and he was speaking like a Cairene, almost as though he'd forgotten the village dialect.

'Does he always talk like that now?' I asked Fawzia.

'Oh no', she laughed. 'He's talking like that because it's a cassette. On the telephone he sounds just like he used to.'

Nabeel said almost nothing about himself and his life in Iraq, just that he was well, and that his salary had gone up. He listed in detail the names of all the people he wanted them to convey his greetings to — members of his lineage, people in the village, his school friends. Then he told them about everyone from the village who was in Iraq — that so-and-so was well, that someone had moved to another city and that someone else was about to go home. For the rest he gave his family precise instructions about what they were to do with the money he was sending them; about the additions they were to make to the house, exactly how the rooms should look, how much they should spend on the floors, the windows, the roof. His brothers listened, rapt, though they must have heard the tape through several times already.

Later, Aly wrote down Nabeel's address for me. It consisted of a number on a numbered street in 'New Baghdad'. I pictured to myself an urban development project of the kind that flourishes in the arid hinterlands of Cairo and New Delhi — straight, treeless streets and blocks of yellow buildings divided into 'Pockets', 'Phases' and 'Zones'.

'You must telephone him', one of Nabeel's younger brothers said. 'He'll be so pleased. Do you know, he's kept all your letters, wrapped in a plastic bag? He still talks of you, a lot. Tell me, didn't you once say to him . . .'

And then he recounted, almost word-for-word, a conversation I had once had with Nabeel. It was about something trivial, about my college in Delhi, but for some reason I had written it down in my diary, that very day, while it was still fresh in memory. I had read through my diaries of that time again, recently. That was why I knew that Nabeel's brother had repeated that conversation, or at least a part of it, almost verbatim, in near exact detail. I was amazed. It seemed to me an impossible, deeply moving defiance of time and the laws of hearsay and memory.

'You can be sure that I will telephone him', I said to Nabeel's brother. 'I'll telephone him soon, from America.'

'You must tell him that we are well and that he should send another cassette.'

'Won't he be surprised,' said Fawzia, 'when he hears Amitab's voice on the phone? He'll think someone's playing a joke on him.'

'We'll write and tell him', said Aly. 'We'll write tomorrow so he won't be surprised. We'll tell him that you're going to phone him from America.'

But they hadn't written: the surprise in Nabeel's voice as he greeted me over the phone was proof of that. And I, for my part, even though I had the advantage, was almost as amazed as Nabeel, though for a different reason. When I was living in their village, in 1980 and '81, Nabeel and Ismail had had very definite plans for their immediate future: they wanted salaried jobs in the Agriculture Ministry. It would not have occurred to any of us then to think that within a few years they would both be abroad and that I would be able to speak to them on the phone from thousands of miles away.

There was only one telephone in the village then. It had never worked as far as anyone knew. It was not meant to — it was really a badge of office, a sceptre. It belonged to the government, and it resided in the house of the village headman. When a headman was voted out in the local elections, the telephone was ritually removed from his house and taken to the victor's. It was carried at the head of a procession, accompanied by drums and gunshots, as though it were a saint's relics. 'We carried the telephone that year', people would say, meaning 'we swept the elections'.

Nabeel's family was one of the poorest in the village — and the village was not by any means prosperous. Few families in the village had more than five *feddans* of land, but most had one or two. Nabeel's family had none at all. That was one of the reasons why he and his brothers had all got an education: schools and colleges were free, and they had no land to claim their time.

Nabeel lived with his parents in a three-room adobe hut, along with Aly and Fawzia and their three other brothers. Aly worked in the fields, for a daily wage, when there was work to be had; their father carried a tiny salary as a village watchman. He was a small, frail man with sunken cheeks and watery grey eyes. As a watchman he had the possession of a gun, an ancient Enfield, that was kept in a locked chest under his bed. He said that he'd last had occasion to use it some fifteen years ago when somebody spotted a gang of thieves running through Hassan Bassiuni's cornfields. The thieves had escaped but the gun had mowed down half the field — it was really very much like a blunderbuss. He was very proud of it. Once when a fire broke out in Shahata Hammoudah's house and everyone was busy doing what they could, I noticed Nabeel's father running in the opposite direction. When I next looked around he was standing at attention in front of the burning house, holding his gun, smiling benignly.

Nabeel's mother, a dark, fine-boned woman, secretly despaired of her husband. 'He's been defeated by the world', she would say sometimes. 'There's no one to stand beside Nabeel and his brothers except themselves.'

Now, eight years later, Nabeel's father and mother were both dead. 'And the saddest thing,' Fawzia said to me, 'is that they didn't live to see how things have changed for us.'

The three mud-walled rooms were gone now. In their place was a bungalow, or at least, its skeleton — four or five rooms, in a largely unfinished state, but built of brick and cement and entirely habitable. There was provision for a bathroom, a kitchen, a living-room, as well as another entire apartment upstairs, exactly like the one below. That was where Nabeel would live once he was married, Fawzia said to me. She, for her part, was content: in her house she now had a television set, a cassette recorder, and a washing-machine.

It wasn't just her life that had changed. When I first came to the village in 1980, there were only three or four television sets there, and they belonged to the handful of men who owned fifteen to twenty *feddans* of land, the richest men in the village. Those men still had their fifteen to twenty *feddans* of land and their black-and-white television sets. It was the families who had once been thought of as the poor folk of the village whose homes were now full of all the best-known brand names in Japan — television sets, washing-machines, kitchen appliances, cameras . . . I could not have begun to imagine a change on this scale when I left the village in 1981. If I had not witnessed it with my own eyes I would not have believed it possible.

It was a kind of revolution, but it had happened a long way away. It had been created entirely by the young men who had gone to work in Iraq, once that country began to experience severe labour shortages because of its war with Iran. They were carried along by a great wave of migration. In the late eighties there were estimated to be between two and three million Egyptians in Iraq. Nobody knew for sure: the wave had surged out of the country too quickly to be measured. All of Nabeel's contemporaries were gone now — all the young men with high-school educations and no jobs and no land and nothing to do but play football and lounge around the water-taps when the girls went to fetch water in the evenings. Some of the old men used to say that they would all go to the bad. But in the end it was they who had transformed the village.

'It's we who've been the real gainers in the war', one of the village schoolteachers said to me, while I was walking down the lanes, gaping at all the newly built houses and buildings. 'The Iraqis are doing all the fighting, it's they who're dying. The Arab countries are paying them to break the back of Khomeini's Islamic revolution. For them it's a matter of survival. But in the mean time, while Iraqis are dying, others are making money. But it won't last — that money's tainted, and the price is going to be paid later, some day.'

The young men who'd left were paying a price already. 'Life is really hard there', their families said. 'You never know what's going to happen, from day to day.' And they would tell stories about fights, about lone Egyptians being attacked on the streets, about men being forced to work inhuman hours, about how the Iraqi women would look at Egyptian men from their windows, because so many of their own men were dead, and how it always led to trouble because the Iraqis would find out and kill both the woman and the Egyptian.

'How does Nabeel like it in Iraq?' I asked his brother Aly.

'He's fine', said Aly. 'He's all right.'

'How do you know?'

'That's what he says on the cassettes,' he said, 'I'm sure he's all right.'

'I hope so', I said.

He was frowning now. 'God knows', he said. 'People say life is hard out there.'

Nabeel could not tell me as much over the telephone, with his boss listening. But he was well, he said, and so was his cousin Ismail, and they were managing fine, living with their relatives and friends from back home. In turn he asked me about India, my job, my family. Then I heard a noise down the line; it sounded like another voice in the same room. Nabeel broke off to say, 'Coming, just a moment.'

I said quickly: 'I'm going back to India soon. I'll try and visit you on the way.'

'We'll be expecting you', he said. In the background I could hear the voice again, louder now.

'You'd better go now', I said.

'I'll tell Ismail you're coming', he said hurriedly. 'We'll wait for you.'

But the year passed and the visit eluded me.

2

It was exactly three weeks since Saddam Hussein had invaded Kuwait, and miraculously, Abu-Ali, the old shopkeeper, was on his feet. That was how he happened to see me as I walked down the road past his window.

Nabeel's village was just a mile and a half away and I was on my way there when Abu-Ali sent a child running after me. Abu-Ali's house was where the asphalt road ended and the dirt track began. Taxi drivers would not go any further.

Now Abu-Ali was standing by the window again cradling a radio, twiddling the knob. He had always behaved as though all the village's worries had fallen on his shoulders. Now it looked as though he had taken on all of Egypt's.

The radio was a big one, with a built-in cassette recorder, but in Abu-Ali's huge, swollen hands it seemed as slim and fragile as an advanced model of a calculator. It spat out a medley of electronic sounds as the pointer flashed across its face. But the sounds were lost; the noise in the room was already deafening. Abu-Ali's cousin's daughter was getting married next door. A crowd of women and children had gathered in the lane, outside their house. A boy was beating a tin wash-basin with a spoon and the women and children were clapping in time, and chanting: *'Ya rumman, ya rumman'*, singing of the bride as the bloom of a pomegranate.

At intervals Abu-Ali rose from his bed, went to the window, glared at the women and children outside, shuffled back and collapsed on to his bed again. This was an astonishing feat. When I first knew him years ago, he was already so fat that he found it near impossible to leave his bed. Now he was fatter still. Every time he stood up his belly surged away from him, like backwash leaving a beach. It was pure greed, his neighbours had always said, he ate the way other people force-fed geese, he could eat two chickens and a pot of rice at one sitting. And now that there was all this Iraqi money in his house, that was exactly what he did sometimes — ate two whole chickens and a pot of rice, right after the midday prayers.

'Ate it', muttered Abu-Ali, shuffling across the room yet again. 'The son of a bitch just ate it like it was a chicken's liver. Saw a tasty little morsel and just swallowed it.'

He sounded envious: an appetite was something he could understand.

'So what do you expect?' someone said. The room was quite full now: several men had stopped by to see Abu-Ali on their way to the wedding. 'What was Kuwait but a tasty little morsel cooked up by the British and sucked dry by the Americans?'

'Just ate it!' Abu-Ali twirled the knob of the radio sending the pointer screeching through a succession of stations. 'BBC, BBC,' he muttered, 'where's that son-of-a-bitch BBC?'

A distant, haranguing voice suddenly burst out of the radio, screaming shrilly. Abu-Ali started back in surprise, almost dropping the radio. 'Who's this son of a bitch now?'

'That's Damascus', said someone.

'No it's those son-of-a-bitch Americans broadcasting in Arabic', said someone else.

'No it's Riyadh', said Abu-Ali. 'It sounds like a Saudi.'

'Riyadh is where he should have gone', said another man. 'But he didn't: stopped too soon. It's those Saudi sons of bitches who should have been fixed.'

I jogged the elbow of the man sitting next to me. I knew him well once; he used to teach in a nearby school. Now he was teaching in the Yemen; he'd come home on a visit, intending to leave once the summer holidays ended. But his wife wouldn't let him go; she had four children to bring up and she was not going to let him vanish into a war zone.

'Do you know if Nabeel Badawy is back from Iraq yet?' I asked him.

'Nabeel?' he said. He'd been looking distracted, anxious, ever since he came into the room. Now he looked as though he'd been dazed by the noise and the cigarette smoke. The man next to him had his arm firmly in his grasp, he was shouting into his other ear, his voice hoarse.

'The worst sons of bitches, the most ungrateful, do you know who they are?' he shouted.

'Nabeel Idris Badawy', I said insistently. 'You remember him?'

'The Palestinians', shouted the man, hoarsely. 'The worst sons of bitches.'

'Nabeel Idris Badawy', I repeated. 'From Nashawy?'

'From Nashawy?' said the schoolteacher. 'How many wars have we fought for them, you tell me? Haven't I lost my own brother?'

'Nabeel Idris Mustafa Badawy', said the schoolteacher jubilantly, his voice rising to a shout. 'He was in Iraq; my nephew told me.'

'Them and the Israelis, God forsake them, the sons of bitches. In the end they're always at the bottom of everything.'

'I know Nabeel's in Iraq', I shouted back. 'But do you know if he's back yet'?'

He thought for a moment and then shook his head. 'No,' he said, 'I can't tell you. There are so many boys over there, you know, it's impossible to keep track. Mabrouk Hussein is still there you know, my own nephew. You remember him? And there are others from this village — there's Fahmy and Abusa and . . . '

He began to repeat the names, as everyone else who had come into the room had done. The village was a very small one, no more than 350 souls, just a hamlet really. I knew it well when I lived in the area. At that time only one man from the village was abroad; he taught Arabic in a school in Zaire. But over the last few years more than a dozen of its young men had left. Most had gone to Iraq, a couple to Jordan (it was almost the same thing). Several had returned since the beginning of the year, but five still remained, trapped in Iraq. People said their names over and over again, as though to conjure them out of Iraq, back to the village: Mabrouk, who used to keep goal; Abusa — 'The Frown' — who never smiled; Fahmy, who used to ride out to the fields, on a sheep. I remembered them coming to visit me in the evenings, full of questions: 'What do you grow in India? Do you have schools? Do you have weddings? Rain? An army?' They were very young. None of them had ever been further than the local town. The machines with which they were most familiar were their *kababis* — the Persian wheels their cattle drove, round and round for hours every day, to water their fields. Mabrouk had once come running to my room, hugely excited, and dragged me away to his house to see the brand new water-pump his family had bought. It was very important for him and his family that I take a look at it, for like all the pumps in the area, it was from India (the generic name for water pump was *makana hindi*, 'the Indian machine'). No matter that I had said, time after time, that I knew nothing about water-pumps, I was always asked for an opinion when somebody bought one.

This one was exactly like the others: a big green machine with a spout, and an exhaust pipe. They had hung an old shoe on the spout and stuck an incense stick in the exhaust pipe to protect it from the evil eye. I knocked on the spout with my knuckles, and patted its diesel tank in a well-informed kind of way. 'What do you think?' Mabrouk's father said, 'Is it all right?'

I knocked a little harder, frowning.

He was anxious now: 'So, what do you think?'

I smiled: 'It's a very good one — excellent.'

There was a sigh of relief: 'Get the Indian doctor some tea.'

Mabrouk had shaken my hand: 'I knew you would be able to tell . . .'

And now Mabrouk was in the immediate vicinity of chemical and nuclear weapons, within a few minutes' striking distance of the world's most advanced machinery. It would be he who would have to pay the price of the violence that was invented in quiet, pastoral laboratories in Heidelberg and Berkeley.

'Do you think the Americans are ever going to leave the sacred land?' a young man said at the top of his voice. People fell silent listening. Outside, the clapping seemed suddenly louder; the girls' voices more insistent.

'Never', he shouted. 'Never — they're never going to leave the sacred places. Now that they're there, they're going to stay till the end of time. The've finally achieved what they'd never managed in a thousand years of history. And who's responsible? The Saudis — the sons of bitches.'

'Ya rumman, ya rumman!' the beat was growing faster, the spoons were drumming out a crescendo on the wash-basins. Glancing out of the window I saw three young men walking down the lane. They had all recently returned from Iraq. Abu-Ali's youngest son was among them. The girls stole looks at them as they walked past, singing at the tops of their voices. They were hoping perhaps that they'd stop and join in the singing and dancing, as young men used to. But these three youths walked straight past them. They had small, derisory smiles under their clipped moustaches. They were embarrassed at the sight of their sisters and cousins drumming out a beat on wash-basins while waiting for a groom who was going to arrive in a pick-up truck. They had grown accustomed to seeing weddings with big bands and hired BMWs. They were savvy, street-smart, in some ways — some of them could recite the prices of the best brand-name goods as though they'd memorized a catalogue. They could tell you what counted as a good price for anything ranging from a pair of Nike shoes to a video camera. If you'd paid a piastre more, you'd been had, someone had 'laughed at you'. The girls were going to be disappointed. These young men were not going to tie up their *gallabeyyas* and dance to the rhythm of dented wash-basins.

'Why'd you think the Americans and the British have always supported those son-of-a-bitch sheikhs?' my friend the schoolteacher said. 'Why do you think? Because it was the easiest way to get back all the money they spent on oil — it all went straight back to their casinos and hotels. And they knew some day they would be able to get back here through those sheikhs, the sons of bitches.'

The girls were beginning to irritate Abu-Ali. He shuffled up to the window and yelled: 'Will you stop that noise? Can't you see we're trying to listen to the news on the radio?'

His voice was legendary: it shook the mud floor. The girls stopped their singing, for a moment, taken by surprise. But soon they started again, softly at first, and then louder, gradually. The wedding had been planned a year ago, long before the invasion. They'd been looking forward to it for a long time; they had no wish whatever to forgo one of their few diversions.

'Didn't I tell you to stop that noise?' Abu-Ali ran out of breath, mopped his forehead.

'He's been like this ever since the invasion,' the schoolteacher whispered to me, 'taken it personally.'

In fact Abu-Ali had been lucky. His three sons, who'd all spent long periods of time in Iraq, were back in Egypt now. The youngest had come back just a month before the invasion. 'People say that God was watching over him', his mother had said to me when I went into the house to see her. 'They say "you should praise God for bringing him back in time" — as though I didn't know it.'

Abu-Ali had bought a Datsun pick-up truck with his sons' earnings. It was making good money now, ferrying goods between the nearby towns and villages. He had also built apartments for his sons, all of them expensively furnished with the heavy, gilded furniture that was favoured in rural Egypt. Still, there was one more thing he wanted. A car. He had been just about ready to send two of his sons back to Iraq when the war broke out. He'd even bought the tickets.

'That Saddam Hussein,' he said, 'how could anyone know he'd do this?'

I could have told him of a conversation I'd recorded in my diary on 30 September 1980, when I was living down the road in Nashawy. It was a conversation with one of Nabeel's cousins, a bright young medical student, about the Iran-Iraq war:

> I asked him whether he thought that after the war Saddam Hussein was going to emerge as the strong man of the Middle East. He said no, he never would, because Egypt's army was the strongest in the Middle East, and perhaps in the world; because Egypt's soldiers were the best in the world!

I could still remember thinking about that exclamation mark.

'That Saddam Hüssein,' snarled Abu-Ali, 'I want to kill him.'

His youngest son came into the room and was amazed to see me. After the greetings were over he said: 'Do you know. I used to work for Indians in Iraq? But they were a different kind of Indian — Shia Muslims, Bohras. I used to work in a hotel they ran in Kerbala. It's a great pilgrimage centre you know.'

I was startled: I had only very recently met a group of Bohra Muslims. On my way to Cairo, from Calcutta, I'd had to stop at Amman airport, to catch a connecting flight. I'd met them at the airport. They'd been stranded in Kerbala for several days after the invasion. They'd been very worried, because some members of their party had American and British passports. But when they got to the border it had been all right, the guards had let them through without a word. 'We're Muslims,' they said, 'so it didn't matter.' In Kerbala they'd stayed in a Bohra hotel they'd said — very well run, clean, comfortable. It was an odd coincidence.

'Why did you come through Jordan at a time like this?' he asked. I explained that the trip had been arranged a long time back.

'I travelled through Jordan too once', he said. 'It was a nice place then. But look at it now. Have you seen the pictures on the TV news? They're frightening. That man . . .'

'I want to kill that Saddam Hussein', bellowed his father. 'He's spoilt everything.' The thought of that lost car was sawing into his flesh.

'This war's going to be a disaster', said his son, shaking his head. But he had a look of relief on his face: at least his father wouldn't be able to send him back there now.

'Did you ever come across Nabeel in Iraq?' I asked.

'Nabeel?' he repeated after me. 'Nabeel who?'

'Nabeel Idris Mustafa Badawy', I said. 'From Nashawy.'

He thought for a moment and shook his head: 'No. I didn't

even know he was there. It's a big country and there are so many Egyptians there . . .'

A pick-up truck drew up outside in a flurry of horns. The wash-basins began to crash together, the women began to ululate. The groom had arrived. Abu-Ali paid no notice. He was shouting: '. . . he doesn't know how much harm he's doing to his country. . .'

Many of the men in the room went rushing out to receive the groom. I slipped out with them, unnoticed. Abu-Ali was still shouting: 'he has to be killed, as soon as possible.'

Everywhere in Egypt people seemed to be talking of killing. In the taxi out from Cairo, the six passengers had all agreed that Saddam had to be killed. But then somebody had added: 'And what about the Man here? Hasn't he got to go first?' This met with a chorus of approval: 'He's going to die, the Man'; '. . . and if someone wants to kill him, he can count on me for help.'

Never before in Egypt, had I heard ordinary people so much as criticize their President in public, amongst strangers, far less talk of killing him, even if only metaphorically. I looked out of the window, half-expecting the driver to stop the taxi. But soon enough he too was talking of killing — the Iraqis, the Americans, Palestinians, Israelis, Saudis . . .

It was as though the whole country had been startled suddenly out of sleep and fallen out of bed, fists clenched, swinging wildly at everything in sight.

The fact is that it has been a long sleep and on the whole the dreams have been good. So good, that in the dreamtime Egypt has floated away from earth into the upper atmosphere.

For the last few years the principal sources of Egypt's national income have been these: the repatriated earnings of its workers abroad, Western aid and tourism. Oil and fees from the Suez Canal follow, but not close behind. Life above ground — where most countries have their economies — has contributed increasingly little. A few decades ago Egypt used to grow enough food to feed itself and export some too. Since then, in exactly the period in which India and China have gone from dependency to self-sufficiency in food, Egypt has reached a point where it has to import as much as seventy per cent of its grain. To pay for its food it needs foreign exchange. And so tourism has become a desperately serious business, a matter of economic survival.

Minds are hard at work thinking of ways to make Egypt ever more attractive to tourists, ever more fantastic. A year or so ago they hit upon the idea of turning a town into an opera set. Luxor, they decided — the ancient Thebes — would be just the right setting for Verdi's *Aïda*. It needed a fair bit of work to turn a real town and some real ancient Egyptian ruins into an Italian's fantasy of ancient Egypt, but they did a thorough job. Luxor got new roads, new hotels, and miles of brand new wharfs along the east bank of the Nile. The wharfs are now lined with steamers, often two or three deep: great, floating hotels, several storeys high with many decks of cabins, as well as restaurants. Bars, saunas, gyms, swimming-pools. They bring ever-increasing numbers of tourists to Luxor. Last year Egypt had about two million tourists. Almost every single one of them passed through Luxor.

A very large proportion of the tourists come in the steamers. They are taken to the ruins and back again in air-conditioned coaches. The adventurous few take horse-drawn carriages. All the petty difficulties and irritations of travelling in Egypt have been done away with, the only Egyptians the tourists ever encounter are tour guides and waiters (the number is not negligible).

Outside the temple in Karnak is a large notice, prominently displayed. It catches the eye because it is entirely in Arabic. The notices at the monuments are usually in several languages — Arabic, English, French and sometimes even in German. But in more ways than one, this notice is not like the others. It contains a list of do's and don'ts for Egyptian visitors — don't make a noise, don't climb the monuments. It ends by exhorting them to behave in a manner 'appropriate to Egyptian culture'.

I read it carefully. It makes me think of my aunt in Calcutta, who wanted her money back after visiting the lion sanctuary at the Gir forest in Gujarat. 'Why,' she yelled at the travel agent, 'they were just sleeping, lying in the dust like lizards. Shouldn't someone tell them that they've got to behave like lions?'

I think of stealing the notice, but the tourist police are watching. It seems to me like an icon of the contemporary Middle East: something inestimably precious is found under the earth, and immediately everybody on top is expected to adjust their behaviour accordingly. In this case the pipeline doesn't take anything away, it brings people in, and whisks them through, hermetically sealed.

In the evenings, when the cool breeze blows in from the Nile, the people of Luxor gather on the promenade along the river front. The steamers are brilliantly lit. They are a bit like glass cases at an aquarium: they seem to display entire cross-sections of an ecological niche. The strollers lean over the railings and watch: there's a honeymooning couple, peering nervously from behind the curtains of their cabin, people sitting at the bar, a trim old lady pumping away at a cycling machine, the waiters, watching television. The best time to watch the steamers is dinner time. The tourists file up the stairs, out of the bars and into the dining-room. They sit at their tables, and then the lights are dimmed. Suddenly 'folkloristic troupes' appear, dressed in embroidered fustans, and break into dance. The tourists put down their cutlery and watch the dancers. The strollers lean forward and watch the tourists. Egyptians watching foreigners watching Egyptians dance.

What if the strollers burst into dance, I ask myself. What then?

In the mean while the steamers help to keep Egypt's economy afloat. But it would take only one well-aimed blow to push it under — something that would at one stroke send large numbers of Egyptian workers back from the Gulf, put a stop to tourism, and halt the flow of ships through the Suez

Canal: something just like the invasion of Kuwait, for example.

On the other hand there would be an increase in Western aid. The seven billion dollar debt for armaments might be cancelled (as it has been). There would be no need for an economy any more. The fantasies of military strength would become real. The whole country would be a weapon, supported by the world outside. Just like Iraq was, for so many years.

3

Fawzia was standing at the door of the new house, she saw me as I turned the corner. 'Nabeel's not back yet, *ya* Amitab', she said the moment she saw me. 'He's still over there, in Iraq, and here we are sitting here and waiting.'

'Have you had any news from him? A letter?'

'No, nothing', she said, leading me into their house. 'Nothing at all. The last time we had news of him was when Ismail came back two months ago.'

'Ismail's back?'

'Praise be to God', she smiled. 'He's back in good health and everything.'

'Where is he?' I said, looking around. 'Can you send for him?'

'Of course', she said. 'He's just around the corner, sitting at home. He hasn't found a job yet — does odd jobs here and there, but most of the time he has nothing to do. I'll send for him right now.'

I looked around while I waited. Something seemed to have interrupted the work on their house. When I'd last seen it I had had the impression that it would be completed in a matter of months. But now, a year and half later, the floor was still just a platform of packed earth and gravel. The tiles had not been laid yet, and nor had the walls been plastered or painted.

'Hamdulillah al-salama', Ismail was at the door, laughing, his hand extended. 'Why didn't you come?' he said, as soon

as the greetings were over. 'You remember that day you telephoned from America? Nabeel telephoned me soon after he'd spoken to you. He just picked up the phone and called me where I was working. He told me that you'd said that you were going to visit us. We expected you, for a long time. We made space in our room, and thought of all the places we'd show you. But you know, Nabeel's boss, the shop-owner? He got really upset — he didn't like it a bit that Nabeel had got a long distance call from America.'

'Why didn't Nabeel come back with you? What news of him?'

'He wanted to come back. In fact he had thought that he would. But then he decided to stay for a few more months, make a little more money, so that they could finish building this house. You see how it's still half-finished — all the money was used up. Prices have gone up this last year, everything costs more.'

'And besides,' said Fawzia, 'what would Nabeel do back here? Look at Ismail — just sitting at home, no job, nothing to do . . . '

Ismail shrugged. 'But still, he wanted to come back. He's been there three years. It's more than most, and it's aged him. You'd see what I mean if you saw him. He looks much older. Life's not easy out there.'

'What do you mean?'

'The Iraqis, you know', he pulled a face. 'They're wild; all those years of war have made them a little like animals. They come back from the army for a few days at a time, and they go wild, fighting on the streets, drinking. Egyptians never go out on the streets there at night: if some drunken Iraqis came across you they would kill you, just like that, and nobody would even know, for they'd throw away your papers. It's happened, happens all the time. They blame us you see, they say: "You've taken our jobs and our money and grown rich while we're fighting and dying." '

'What about Saddam Hussein?'

'Saddam Hussein!' he rolled his eyes. 'You have to be

careful when you breathe that name out there — there are spies everywhere, at every corner, listening. One word about Saddam and you're gone, dead. In those ways it's terrible out there though of course there's the money. But still, you can't live long out there, it's impossible. Did you hear what happened during the World Cup?'

Earlier in the year Egypt had played a football match with Algeria, to decide which team would play in the World Cup. Egypt had won and Egyptians everywhere had gone wild with joy. In Iraq the hundreds of thousands of Egyptians who lived packed together, all of them young, all of them male, with no families, children, wives, nothing to do but stare at their newly bought television sets — they had exploded out of their rooms and into the streets in a delirium of joy. Their football team had restored to them that self-respect that their cassette recorders and television sets had somehow failed to bring. To the Iraqis, who have never had anything like a normal political life, probably never seen crowds except at pilgrimages, the massed ranks of Egyptians must have seemed like the coming of Armageddon. They responded by attacking them on the streets, often with firearms — well-trained in war, they fell upon the jubilant unarmed crowds of Egyptian workers.

'You can't imagine what it was like', said Ismail. He had tears in his eyes. 'It was then that I decided to leave. Nabeel decided to leave as well, but of course he always needed to think a long time about everything. At the last minute he thought he'd stay just a little bit longer . . . '

A little later we went to his house to watch the news on the colour television he had brought back with him. It sat perched on its packing case, in the centre of the room, gleaming new, with chickens roosting on a nest of straw beside it. Soon the news started and we saw footage from Jordan: thousands and thousands of men, some in trousers, some in *gallabeyyas*, some carrying their television sets on their backs, some crying out for a drink of water, stretching all the way from the horizon to the Red Sea, standing on the beach as though waiting for the water to part.

There were more than a dozen of us in the room now. We were crowded around the television set, watching carefully, minutely, looking at every face we could see. But there was nothing to be seen except crowds: Nabeel had vanished into the pages of the epic exodus.

5 *The Ghosts of Mrs Gandhi*

NOWHERE ELSE in the world did the year 1984 fulfil its apocalyptic portents as it did in India. Separatist violence in the Punjab; the military attack on the great Sikh temple of Amritsar; the assassination of the Prime Minister, Mrs Indira Gandhi; riots in several cities; the gas disaster in Bhopal — the events followed relentlessly on each other. There were days in 1984 when it took courage to open the New Delhi papers in the morning

Of the year's many catastrophes, the sectarian violence following Gandhi's death had the greatest effect on my life. Looking back, I see that the experiences of that period were profoundly important to my development as a writer, so much so that I have never attempted to write about them until now.

At the time, I was living in a part of New Delhi called Defence Colony — a neighbourhood of large, labyrinthine houses, with little self-contained warrens of servants' rooms tucked away on roof tops and above garages. When I lived there, those rooms had come to house a floating population of the young and straitened — journalists, copywriters, minor executives, and university people like myself. We battened upon this wealthy enclave like mites in a honeycomb spreading from rooftop to rooftop, our ramshackle lives curtained from our landlords by chiffon-draped washing lines and thickets of TV aerials.

I was twenty-eight. The city I considered home was Calcutta, but New Delhi was where I had spent all my adult life except for a few years away in England and Egypt. I had returned to India two years before, upon completing a doctorate at Oxford, and recently found a teaching job at Delhi University. But it was in the privacy of my baking rooftop hutch that my real life was lived. I was writing my first novel, in the classic fashion, perched in a garret.

On the morning of 31 October, the day of Mrs Gandhi's death, I caught a bus to Delhi University as usual, at about half-past nine. From where I lived, it took an hour and a half: a long commute, but not an exceptional one for New Delhi. The assassination had occurred shortly before, just a few miles away, but I had no knowledge of this when I boarded the bus. Nor did I notice anything untoward at any point during the ninety-minute journey. But the news, travelling by word of mouth, raced my bus to the university.

When I walked into the grounds, I saw not the usual boisterous, Frisbee-throwing crowd of students but small groups of people standing intently around transistor radios. A young man detached himself from one of the huddles and approached me, his mouth twisted into the tight-lipped, knowing smile that seems always to accompany the gambit 'Have you heard . . . ?'

The campus was humming, he said. No one knew for sure, but it was being said that Mrs Gandhi had been shot. The word was that she had been assassinated by two Sikh bodyguards, in revenge for her having sent troops to raid the Sikhs' Golden Temple of Amritsar earlier that year.

Just before stepping into the lecture room, I heard a report on All India Radio, the national network: Mrs Gandhi had been rushed to hospital after an attempted assassination.

Nothing stopped: the momentum of the daily routine carried things forward. I went into a classroom and began my lecture, but not many students had shown up and those who had were distracted and distant; there was a lot of fidgeting.

Halfway through the class, I looked out through the room's single, slit-like window. The sunlight lay bright on the lawn below and on the trees beyond. It was the time of year when Delhi was at its best, crisp and cool, its abundant greenery freshly watered by the recently retreated monsoons, its skies washed sparkling clean. By the time I turned back, I had forgotten what I was saying and had to reach for my notes.

My unsteadiness surprised me. I was not an uncritical admirer of Mrs Gandhi. Her brief period of semi-dictatorial rule in the mid-seventies was still alive in my memory. But the ghastliness of her murder was a sudden reminder of the very real qualities that had been taken for granted: her fortitude, her dignity, her physical courage, her endurance.

Yet it was not just grief I felt at that moment. Rather, it was a sense of something slipping loose, of a mooring coming untied somewhere within.

The first reliable report of Mrs Gandhi's death was broadcast from Karachi, by Pakistan's official radio network, at around 1:30 p.m. On All India Radio, regular broadcasts had been replaced by music.

I left the university in the late afternoon with a friend, Hari Sen, who lived at the other end of the city. I needed to make a long-distance phone call, and he had offered to let me use his family's telephone.

To get to Hari's house, we had to change buses at Connaught Place, the elegant circular arcade that lies at the geographical heart of Delhi, linking the old city with the new. As the bus swung around the periphery of the arcade, I noticed that the shops, stalls, and eateries were beginning to shut down, even though it was still afternoon.

Our next bus was not quite full, which was unusual. Just as it was pulling out, a man ran out of an office and jumped on. He was middle-aged and dressed in shirt and trousers, evidently an employee in one of the nearby government buildings. He was a Sikh, but I scarcely noticed this at the time.

He probably jumped on without giving the matter any thought, this being his regular, daily bus. But, as it happened, on this day no choice could have been more unfortunate, for the route of the bus went past the hospital where Indira Gandhi's body then lay. Certain loyalists in her party had begun inciting the crowds gathered there to seek revenge. The motorcade of Giani Zail Singh, the President of the Republic, a Sikh, had already been attacked by a mob.

None of this was known to us then, and we would never have suspected it: violence had never been directed at the Sikhs in Delhi.

As the bus made its way down New Delhi's broad, tree-lined avenues, official-looking cars, with outriders and escorts, overtook us, speeding toward the hospital. As we drew nearer, it became evident that a large number of people had gathered there. But this was no ordinary crowd: it seemed to consist mostly of red-eyed young men in half-unbuttoned shirts. It was now that I noticed that my Sikh fellow-passenger was showing signs of increasing anxiety, sometimes standing up to look out, sometimes glancing out the door. It was too late to get off the bus; thugs were everywhere. The bands of young men grew more and more menacing as we approached the hospital. There was a watchfulness about them; some were armed with steel rods and bicycle chains; others had fanned out across the busy road and were stopping cars and buses.

A stout woman in a sari sitting across the aisle from me was the first to understand what was going on. Rising to her feet, she gestured urgently at the Sikh, who was sitting hunched in his seat. She hissed at him in Hindi, telling him to get down and keep out of sight.

The man started in surprise and squeezed himself into the narrow footspace between the seats. Minutes later, our bus was intercepted by a group of young men dressed in bright, sharp synthetics. Several had bicycle chains wrapped around their wrists. They ran along beside the bus as it slowed to a halt. We heard them call out to the driver through the open door, asking if there were any Sikhs on the bus.

The driver shook his head. No, he said there were no Sikhs on the bus.

A few rows ahead of me, the crouching, turbaned figure had gone completely still. Outside, some of the young men were jumping up to look through the windows, asking if there were any Sikhs on the bus. There was no anger in their voices; that was the most chilling thing of all.

No, someone said, and immediately other voices picked up the refrain. Soon all the passengers were shaking their heads and saying, No, no, let us go now, we have to get home

Eventually, the thugs stepped back and waved us through. Nobody said a word as we sped away down Ring Road.

Hari Sen lived in one of New Delhi's recently developed residential colonies. It was called Safdarjang Enclave, and it was neatly and solidly middle-class, a neighbourhood of aspirations rather than opulence. Like most such New Delhi suburbs, the area had a mixed population: Sikhs were well represented.

A long street ran from end to end of the neighbourhood, like the spine of a comb, with parallel side streets running off it. Hari lived at the end of one of those streets, in a fairly typical, big, one-storey bungalow. The house next door, however, was much grander and uncharacteristically daring in design. An angular structure, it was perched rakishly on stilts. Mr Bawa, the owner, was an elderly Sikh who had spent a long time abroad, working with various international organizations. For several years, he had resided in South-east Asia; thus the stilts.

Hari lived with his family in a household so large and eccentric that it had come to be known among his friends as Macondo, after Gabriel Garcia Marquez's magical village. On this occasion, however, only his mother and teenage sister were at home. I decided to stay over.

It was a very bright morning. When I stepped out into the sunshine, I came upon a sight that I could never have imagined. In every direction, columns of smoke rose slowly into a limpid sky. Sikh houses and businesses were burning. The fires were so carefully targeted that they created an effect quite different from that of a general conflagration: it was like looking upward into the vault of some vast pillared hall.

The columns of smoke increased in number even as I stood outside watching. Some were burning a short distance away. I spoke to a passerby and learned that several nearby Sikh houses had been looted and set on fire that morning. The mob had started at the far end of the colony and was working its way in our direction. Hindus and Muslims who had sheltered or defended Sikhs were also being attacked; their houses were being looted and burned.

It was still and quiet, eerily so. The usual sounds of rush-hour traffic were absent. But every so often we heard a speeding car or a motorcycle on the main street. Later, we discovered that these mysterious speeding vehicles were instrumental in directing the carnage that was taking place. Protected by certain politicians, 'organizers' were zooming around the city, assembling 'mobs' and transporting them to Sikh-owned houses and shops.

Apparently, the transportation was provided free. A civil-rights report published shortly afterward stated that this phase of the violence 'began with the arrival of groups of armed young people in tempo vans, scooters, motorcycles or trucks', and went on to say, 'With cans of petrol they went around the localities and systematically set fire to Sikh houses, shops and gurdwaras. . . . The targets were primarily young Sikhs. They were dragged out, beaten up and then burnt alive. . . . In all the affected spots, a calculated attempt to terrorize the people was evident in the common tendency among the assailants to burn alive the Sikhs on public roads.'

Fire was everywhere; it was the day's motif. Throughout the city, Sikh houses were being looted and then set on fire, often with their occupants still inside.

A survivor — a woman who lost her husband and three sons — offered the following account to Veena Das, a Delhi sociologist: 'Some people, the neighbours, one of my relatives, said it would be better if we hid in an abandoned house near by. So my husband took our three sons and hid there. We locked the house from outside, but there was treachery in people's hearts. Someone must have told the crowd. They baited him to come out. Then they poured kerosene on that house. They burnt them alive. When I went there that night, the bodies of my sons were on the loft — huddled together.'

Over the next few days, some twenty-five hundred people died in Delhi alone. Thousands more died in other cities. The total death toll will never be known. The dead were overwhelmingly Sikh men. Entire neighbourhoods were gutted; tens of thousands of people were left homeless.

Like many other members of my generation, I grew up believing that mass-slaughter of the kind that accompanied the Partition of India and Pakistan, in 1947, could never happen again. But that morning, in the city of Delhi, the violence had reached the same level of intensity.

As Hari and I stood staring into the smoke-streaked sky, Mrs Sen, Hari's mother, was thinking of matters closer at hand. She was about fifty, a tall, graceful woman with a gentle, soft-spoken manner. In an understated way, she was also deeply religious, a devout Hindu. When she heard what was happening, she picked up the phone and called Mr and Mrs Bawa, the elderly Sikh couple next door, to let them know that they were welcome to come over. She met with an unexpected response: an awkward silence. Mrs Bawa thought she was joking, and wasn't sure whether to be amused or not.

Toward midday, Mrs Sen received a phone call: the mob was now in the immediate neighbourhood, advancing systematically from street to street. Hari decided that it was time to go over and have a talk with the Bawas. I went along.

Mr Bawa proved to be a small, slight man. Although he was casually dressed, his turban was neatly tied and his beard was carefully combed and bound. He was puzzled by our visit. After a polite greeting, he asked what he could do for us. It fell to Hari to explain.

Mr Bawa had heard about Indira Gandhi's assassination, of course, and he knew that there had been some trouble. But he could not understand why these 'disturbances' should impinge on him or his wife. He had no more sympathy for the Sikh terrorists than we did; his revulsion at the assassination was, if anything, even greater than ours. Not only was his commitment to India and the Indian state absolute but it was evident from his bearing that he belonged to the country's ruling élite.

How do you explain to someone who has spent a lifetime cocooned in privilege that a potentially terminal rent has appeared in the wrappings? We found ourselves faltering. Mr Bawa could not bring himself to believe that a mob might attack him.

By the time we left it was Mr Bawa who was mouthing reassurances. He sent us off with jovial pats on our backs. He did not actually say 'Buck up', but his manner said it for him.

We were confident that the government would soon act to stop the violence. In India, there is a drill associated with civil disturbances: a curfew is declared; paramilitary units are deployed; in extreme cases, the Army marches to the stricken areas. No city in India is better equipped to perform this drill than New Delhi, with its huge security apparatus. We later learned that in some cities — Calcutta, for example — the state authorities did act promptly to prevent violence. But in New Delhi and in much of northern India — hour followed hour without a response. Every few minutes, we turned to the radio, hoping to hear that the Army had been ordered out. All we heard was mournful music and descriptions of Mrs Gandhi's lying in state; of the comings and goings of dignitaries, foreign and national. The bulletins could have been messages from another planet.

As the afternoon progressed, we continued to hear reports of the mob's steady advance. Before long, it had reached the next alley; we could hear the voices; the smoke was everywhere. There was still no sign of the Army or the police.

Hari again called Mr Bawa, and now, with the flames visible from his windows, he was more receptive. He agreed to come over with his wife, just for a short while. But there was a problem: How? The two properties were separated by a shoulder-high wall, so it was impossible to walk from one house to the other except along the street.

I spotted a few of the thugs already at the end of the street. We could hear the occasional motorcycle, cruising slowly up and down. The Bawas could not risk stepping out into the street. They would be seen; the sun had dipped low in the sky, but it was still light. Mr Bawa balked at the thought of climbing over the wall; it seemed an insuperable obstacle at his age. But eventually Hari persuaded him to try.

We went to wait for them at the back of the Sen's house — in a spot that was well-sheltered from the street. The mob seemed terrifyingly close, the Bawas reckless in their tardiness. A long time passed before the elderly couple finally appeared, hurrying toward us.

Mr Bawa had changed before leaving the house: he was neatly dressed, dapper, even — in blazer and cravat. Mrs Bawa, a small, matronly woman, was dressed in a salwar and kameez. Their cook was with them, and it was with his assistance that they made it over the wall. The cook, who was Hindu, then returned to the house to stand guard.

Hari led the Bawas into the drawing room, where Mrs Sen was waiting, dressed in a chiffon sari. The room was large and well appointed, its walls hung with a rare and beautiful set of miniatures. With the curtains now drawn and the lamps lit, it was warm and welcoming. But all that lay between us and the mob in the street was a row of curtained French windows and a garden wall .

Mrs Sen greeted the elderly couple with folded hands as they came in. The three seated themselves in an intimate circle, and soon a silver tea tray appeared. Instantly, all constraint evaporated, and, to the tinkling of porcelain, the conversation turned to the staples of New Delhi drawing-room chatter.

I could not bring myself to sit down. I stood in the corridor, distracted, looking outside through the front entrance.

A couple of scouts on motorcycles had drawn up next door. They had dismounted and were inspecting the house, walking in among the concrete stilts, looking up into the house. Somehow, they got wind of the cook's presence and called him out.

The cook was very frightened. He was surrounded by thugs thrusting knives in his face and shouting questions. It was dark, and some were carrying kerosene torches. Wasn't it true, they shouted, that his employers were Sikhs? Where were they? Were they hiding inside? Who owned the house — Hindus or Sikhs?

Hari and I hid behind the wall between the two houses and listened to the interrogation. Our fates depended on this lone, frightened man. We had no idea what he would do: of how secure the Bawas were of his loyalties, or whether he might seek revenge for some past slight by revealing their whereabouts. If he did, both houses would burn.

Although stuttering in terror, the cook held his own. Yes, he said, yes, his employers were Sikhs, but they'd left town; there was no one in the house. No, the house didn't belong to them; they were renting from a Hindu.

He succeeded in persuading most of the thugs, but a few eyed the surrounding houses suspiciously. Some appeared at the steel gates in front of us, rattling the bars.

We went up and positioned ourselves at the gates. I remember a strange sense of disconnection as I walked down the driveway, as though I were watching myself from somewhere very distant.

We took hold of the gates and shouted back: Get away! You have no business here! There's no one inside! The house is empty.

To our surprise they began to drift away, one by one.

Just before this, I had stepped into the house to see how Mrs Sen and the Bawas were faring. The thugs were clearly audible in the lamplit drawing room; only a thin curtain shielded the interior from their view.

My memory of what I saw in the drawing room is uncannily vivid. Mrs Sen had a smile on her face as she poured a cup of tea for Mr Bawa. Beside her, Mrs Bawa in a firm, unwavering voice was comparing the domestic situations in New Delhi and Manila.

I was awed by their courage.

The next morning, I heard about a protest that was being organized at the large compound of a relief agency. When I arrived a meeting was already underway, a gathering of seventy or eighty people.

The mood was sombre. Some of the people spoke about neighbourhoods that had been taken over by vengeful mobs. They described countless murders — many by setting the victims alight — as well as terrible destruction; the burning of Sikh temples, the looting of Sikh schools, the razing of Sikh homes and shops. The violence was worse than I had imagined. It was declared at the meeting that an effective initial tactic would be to march into one of the badly affected neighbourhoods and confront the rioters directly.

The group had grown to about a hundred and fifty men and women, among them Swami Agnivesh, a Hindu ascetic; Ravi Chopra, a scientist and environmentalist; and a handful of opposition politicians, including Chandra Shekhar, who became Prime Minister for a brief period several years later.

The group was pitifully small by the standards of a city where crowds of several hundred thousand were routinely mustered for political rallies. Nevertheless, the members rose to their feet and began to march.

Years before, I had read a passage by V.S. Naipaul which has stayed with me ever since. I have never been able to find it again, so this account is from memory. In his incomparable prose Naipaul describes a demonstration. He is in a hotel room, somewhere in Africa or South America; he looks down and sees people marching past. To his surprise, the sight fills him with an obscure longing, a kind of melancholy; he is aware of a wish to go out, to join, to merge his concerns with theirs. Yet he knows he never will; it is simply not in his nature to join crowds.

For many years I read everything of Naipaul's I could lay my hands on; I couldn't have enough of him. I read him with the intimate, appalled attention that one reserves for one's most skilful interlocutors. It was he who first made it possible for me to think of myself as a writer, working in English.

I remembered that passage because I believed that I, too, was not a joiner, and in Naipaul's pitiless mirror I thought I had seen an aspect of myself rendered visible. Yet as this forlorn little group marched out of the shelter of the compound I did not hesitate for a moment: without a second thought, I joined.

The march headed first for Lajpat Nagar, a busy commercial area, a mile or so away. I knew the area. Though it was in New Delhi, its streets resembled the older parts of the city, where small cramped shops tended to spill out on to the footpaths.

We were shouting slogans as we marched: hoary Gandhian staples of peace and brotherhood from half a century before. Then, suddenly, we were confronted with a starkly familiar spectacle, an image of twentieth-century urban horror: burned-out cars, their ransacked interiors visible through smashed windows; debris and rubble everywhere. Blackened pots had been strewn along the street. A cinema had been gutted, and the charred faces of film stars stared out at us from half-burned posters.

As I think back to that march, my memory breaks down, details dissolve. I recently telephoned some friends who had been there. Their memories are similar to mine in only one respect: they, too, clung to one scene while successfully ridding their minds of the rest.

The scene my memory preserved is of a moment when it seemed inevitable that we would be attacked.

Rounding a corner, we found ourselves facing a crowd that was larger and more determined-looking than any other crowds we had encountered. On each previous occasion, we had prevailed by marching at the thugs and engaging them directly, in dialogues that turned quickly into extended shouting matches. In every instance, we had succeeded in facing them down. But this particular mob was intent on confrontation. As its members advanced on us, brandishing knives and steel rods, we stopped. Our voices grew louder as they came toward us; a kind of rapture descended on us, exhilaration in anticipation of a climax. We braced for the attack, leaning forward as though into a wind.

And then something happened that I have never completely understood. Nothing was said; there was no signal, nor was there any break in the rhythm of our chanting. But suddenly all the women in our group — and the women made up more than half of the groups numbers — stepped out and surrounded the men; their saris and kameezes became a thin, fluttering barrier, a wall around us. They turned to face the approaching men, challenging them, daring them to attack.

The thugs took a few more more steps toward us and then faltered, confused. A moment later, they were gone.

The march ended at the walled compound where it had started. In the next couple of hours an organization was created, the Nagarik Ekta Manch, or Citizens' Unity Front, and its work — to bring relief to the injured and the bereft, to shelter the homeless — began the next morning. Food and clothing were needed, and camps had to be established to accommodate the thousands of people with nowhere to sleep. And by the next day we were overwhelmed — literally. The large compound was crowded with vanloads of blankets, secondhand clothing, shoes, and sacks of flour, sugar, and tea. Previously hardnosed, unsentimental businessmen sent cars and trucks. There was barely room to move.

My own role was slight. For a few weeks, I worked with a team from Delhi University, distributing supplies in the slums and working-class neighbourhoods that had been worst hit by the rioting. Then I returned to my desk.

In time, inevitably, most of the Front's volunteers returned to their everyday lives. But some members — most notably the women involved in the running of refugee camps — continued to work for years afterward with Sikh women and children who had been rendered homeless. Lalita Ramdas, Veena Das, Mita Bose, Radha Kumar: these women, each one an accomplished professional, gave up years of their time to repair the enormous damage that had been done in a matter of two or three days.

The Front also formed a team to investigate the riots. I briefly considered joining, but then decided that an investigation would be a waste of time because the politicians capable of inciting violence were unlikely to heed a tiny group of concerned citizens.

I was wrong. A document eventually produced by this team — a slim pamphlet entitled 'Who Are the Guilty?' — has become a classic, a searing indictment of the politicians who encouraged the riots and the police who allowed the rioters to have their way.

Over the years the Indian government has compensated some of the survivors of the 1984 violence and resettled some of the homeless. One gap remains: to this day, no instigator of the riots has been charged. But the pressure on the government has never gone away, and it continues to grow every year, the nails hammered in by that slim document dig just a little deeper.

The pamphlets and others that followed are testaments to the only humane possibility available to people who live in multi-ethnic, multi-religious societies like those of the Indian subcontinent. Human-rights documents such as 'Who Are the Guilty?' are essential to the process of broadening civil institutions: they are the weapons with which society asserts itself against a state that runs criminally amok, as this one did in Delhi in November of 1984.

It is heartening that sanity prevails today in the Punjab. But not elsewhere. In Bombay, local government officials want to stop buildings from being painted green — a colour associated with the Muslim religion. And hundreds of Muslims have been deported from the city's slums — in at least one case for committing an offense no graver than reading a Bengali newspaper. It is imperative that governments ensure that those who instigate mass violence do not go unpunished.

The Bosnian writer Dzevad Karahasan, in a remarkable essay called 'Literature and War' (published last year in his collection *Sarajevo, Exodus of a City*) makes a startling connection between modern literary aestheticism and the contemporary world's indifference to violence: 'The decision to perceive literally everything as an aesthetic phenomenon — completely sidestepping questions about goodness and truth — is an artistic decision. That decision started in the realm of art, and went on to become characteristic of the contemporary world.'

When I went back to my desk in November of 1984, I found myself confronting decisions about writing that I had never faced before. How was I to write about what I had seen without reducing it to mere spectacle? My next novel was bound to be influenced by my experiences, but I could see no way of writing directly about those events without re-creating them as a panorama of violence — 'an aesthetic phenomenon', as Karahasan was to call it. At the time, the idea seemed obscene and futile; of much greater importance were factual reports of the testimony of the victims. But these were already being done by people who were, I knew, more competent than I could be.

Within a few months, I started my novel, which I eventually called *The Shadow Lines* — a book that led me backward in time to earlier memories of riots, ones witnessed in childhood. It became a book not about any one event but about the meaning of such events and their effects on the individuals who live through them.

And until now I have never really written about what I saw in November of 1984. I am not alone; several others who took part in that march went on to publish books, yet nobody, so far as I know, has ever written about it except in passing.

There are good reasons for this, not least the politics of the situation, which leave so little room for the writer. The riots were generated by a cycle of violence, involving the terrorists in the Punjab, on the one hand, and the Indian government, on the other. To write carelessly, in such a way as to appear to endorse terrorism or repression, can add easily to the problem: and in such incendiary circumstances, words cost lives, and it is only appropriate that those who deal in words should pay scrupulous attention to what they say. It is only appropriate that they should find themselves inhibited.

But there is also a simpler explanation. Before I could set down a word, I had to resolve a dilemma, between being a writer and being a citizen. As a writer, I had only one obvious subject: the violence. From the news report, or the latest film or novel, we have come to expect the bloody detail or the elegantly staged conflagration that closes a chapter or effects a climax. But it is worth asking if the very obviousness of this subject arises out of our modern conventions of representation; within the dominant aesthetic of our time — the aesthetic of what Karahasan calls 'indifference' — it is all too easy to present violence as an apocalyptic spectacle, while the resistance to it can as easily figure as mere sentimentality, or, worse, as pathetic or absurd.

Writers don't join crowds — Naipaul and so many others teach us that. But what do you do when the constitutional authority fails to act? You join and in joining bear all the responsibilities and obligations and guilt that joining represents. My experience of the violence was overwhelmingly and memorably of the resistance to it. When I think of the women staring down the mob, I am not filled with a writerly wonder. I am reminded of my gratitude for being saved from injury. What I saw at first hand — and not merely on that march but on the bus, in Hari's house, in the huge compound that filled with essential goods — was not the horror of violence but the affirmation of humanity: in each case, I witnessed the risks that perfectly ordinary people are willing to take for one another.

When I now read descriptions of troubled parts of the world, in which violence appears primordial and inevitable, a fate to which masses of people are largely resigned, I find myself asking, Is that all there was to it? Or is it possible that the authors of these descriptions failed to find a form — or a style or a voice or a plot — that could accommodate both violence *and* the civilized willed response to it?

The truth is that the commonest response to violence is one of repugnance and that a significant number of people everywhere try to oppose it in whatever ways they can. That these efforts rarely appear in accounts of violence is not surprising: they are too undramatic. For those who participate in them, they are often hard to write about for the very reasons that so long delayed my own account of 1984.

'Let us not fool ourselves', Karhasan writes. 'The world is written first — the holy books say, that it was created in words — and all that happens in it, happens in language first.'

It is when we think of the world the aesthetic of indifference might bring into being that we recognize the urgency of remembering the stories we have not written.

6 *The Human Comedy in Cairo*

1

IN EGYPT, the news that the writer Naguib Mahfouz was awarded the Nobel Prize in 1989 was greeted with the kind of jubilation that Egyptians usually reserve for soccer victories. Even though the fundamentalists sounded an ominous note, most people in Cairo were overjoyed. Months later everybody was still full of it. People would tell anecdotes about how the good news had reached Mahfouz. Swedish efficiency has met its match in Cairo's telephones: the news had broken over the wires before the committee (or whatever) could get through to Mahfouz. He was asleep, taking his afternoon siesta (no, it was early in the morning, and he just hadn't woken up yet), when his wife woke him and told him matter-of-factly that somebody wanted to congratulate him for winning the Nobel (no, it was she who wanted to congratulate him, didn't you see the story in . . .).

The stories were on everyone's lips: tales of national pride and collective hope. Mahfouz has a large following in Egypt and is personally popular: he is everybody's slightly eccentric but successful uncle, a modest, generous, kindly man, who has spent over thirty years working as a civil servant. The rest of the Arab world was enthusiastic, too, including the people of some countries who had their own favourite contestants (it had long been rumoured that an Arab writer would soon win the prize). The award to Mahfouz was clearly a recognition of the achievements of Arabic literature, and even if it was several decades overdue, the Arab world in general responded to it with pride.

It would have been interesting, at that moment of elation, if some enterprising pollster had taken it into his head to put two questions to a representative sample of the reading public in the Arab world. The first question being: 'Do you think Naguib Mahfouz is the most interesting, innovative, or imaginative writer in Arabic today?' And the second: 'Do you think that Naguib Mahfouz is the most appropriate candidate for the Nobel Prize for literature in the Arab world today?' It is my guess that the answer to the first question would have been largely 'no', and the answer to the second would have been generally 'yes'.

In the gap between that 'no' and that 'yes' falls the award itself, and the extraordinary power it carries in countries like Egypt and India — old civilizations, trying hard to undo their supersession in the modern world. Once, in my own city of Calcutta, in the gaudy heat of May, stuck in a crowded bus in a traffic jam, I overheard an unexpectedly literary conversation. A sweat-soaked commuter, on his way back from a hard day's work, missed his grip on the overhead rail and dropped his briefcase on his toe. A dam seemed to burst: he began to complain loudly about the traffic, the roads, the fumes, the uncollected garbage. One of his neighbours turned to him and said sharply: 'What are you complaining about? Rabindranath Tagore won the Nobel Prize for literature in 1913, and wasn't he from Calcutta?' At this very moment someone stuck in a bus or a share-taxi in Tahrir or Shubra or some other traffic-logged part of Cairo is almost certainly saying the same thing about Mahfouz. Thus does Stockholm regulate the traffic in Calcutta and Cairo.

In the United States, Mahfouz met with another kind of approval on the occasion of his triumph. The second paragraph of the *New York Times* story on Mahfouz's Nobel, carried on the front page, quoted Israelis declaring Mahfouz's politics to be perfectly acceptable. His work, his concerns, and his subjects came a poor second to this other aspect of his newsworthiness.

For a prize of such power, the ordinary standards of

judgement that apply to books are held in suspension. What matters is that the writer's work be adequately canonical, which is to say, massive, serious, and somehow a part of 'world literature'. If Mahfouz won on these counts, his was the victory of the decathlete, achieved by a slow accumulation of points rather than by a spectacular show of brilliance in a single event. To date, Mahfouz has written some thirty-five novels and twelve volumes of short stories, as well as several plays and screenplays; he is said to be widely read in philosophy and French literature; and he is credited with introducing absurdism and the stream of consciousness technique into Arabic literature. Whatever your opinion about any particular book of his, there can be no denying the weight of Mahfouz's contribution to modern Arabic literature. Thus the general popularity of the award.

2

Mahfouz was born in Cairo in 1911. His father was a minor functionary in the government, and he grew up in the heart of the old city: the crowded district that lies beyond the ancient university of al-Azhar and the mausoleum of the Prophet's grandson, Sayidna Hussein. In the years of Mahfouz's childhood, it was an area where respectable families of modest means, struggling to put their children through school, lived above thriving little shops and businesses and looked out through their dusty windows at medieval mosques, hospitals, and religious schools. This is the world that Mahfouz has made peculiarly his own: a distinctively Cairene world of minor civil servants striving to make ends meet on their salaries, to push their children one rung higher on the civil service ladder while keeping up appearances against the pretensions of pushy grocers and arriviste café owners. No matter that this kind of person has moved out of the neighbourhood (as did Mahfouz's family): their hopes and their anxieties remain much the same.

These are the people of Mahfouz's imaginative universes —

a small, distinctive group within the tumult of modern Egypt. Rural Egypt, which occupied so much of the imaginations of Mahfouz's most illustrious predecessors and contemporaries, never intrudes on his world. Indeed, it is almost artificially excluded. His characters never even have friends or relatives in the countryside, as they almost certainly would in the 'real' world. This needs saying, if only because Mahfouz's world is sometimes said to be a microcosm of Egypt. If this is so, it is surely only in that special sense in which the sansculottes of Paris were somehow a little more 'the People' than the peasants of the Midi.

Much of the interest of Mahfouz lies in his avenue of entry into the world of his characters. He takes the most secret, the least accessible, route: the family. Of course, the family is one of the territories the novel has most successfully claimed for itself everywhere; all around the world there are novelists who, like Mahfouz, build their books on families and their histories, on the endless cycle of birth, marriage, and death. But in Mahfouz's hands, in the world of his People, this invitation into the family has an extra dimension of excitement.

In Egypt, and more generally in the Arab world, as in many conservative, traditional societies, the family is a secret, curtained world, protected from the gaze of outsiders by walls and courtyards, by veils and laws of silence. To be taken past those doors, into the forbidden space of failed marriages and secret desires, the areas that lie most heavily curtained under the genteel ethic of family propriety — and to be introduced into this by the most public of artefacts, a printed book — is to prepare oneself for the pleasurable tingle of the illicit. And once past that curtain, Mahfouz's reader discovers, with guilty delight, a quiet murmur of furtive gropings, dissatisfaction, and despair that confirms everything he has ever suspected about his neighbours. This is Mahfouz's particular talent: he has a fine instinct for discovering the fears, the prejudices, and the suspicions of his People, and serving them back to them as fiction.

In his hands, the intricacies of family relationships become a kind of second language, with which he demonstrates to his readers the dangers that lurk at the margins of their world. These are predicaments that they can all too readily imagine, since they form the nightmare Other-life that gives their respectability its meaning. This is a world in which sisters become prostitutes to help their brothers become 'respectable employees', where fathers who drink encounter their sons in brothels, where ambition is always unscrupulous and young men who look above their station come to a sticky end, where boys who are allowed to stay out too late are plunged 'deep into sin and addiction' and eventually end up in a region that can only be described as Mahfouz's Underworld.

That underworld is a landscape often encountered in his work, always sketched with portentous hints and suggestions, a region of pure fantasy, dank with the 'odour of putrefaction', whose inhabitants always drink themselves into stupors, smoke hashish, fondle bosomy singers, and traffic vaguely in drugs. It is through devices such as these that Mahfouz invites his reader to marvel at the decay of the world as it should be. It is a sentiment that his People are only too willing to take to heart, oppressed as they are by the prospect of poverty and social decline on the one hand, and on the other by the images of wealth that they associate with those who control money and power in their societies.

The predicament is not peculiarly Egyptian. I can think of at least two eminent writers in Calcutta whose plots and material are uncannily similar to Mahfouz's (though Mahfouz is the more skilful practitioner of the craft). This is the kind of fiction that grows out of the sensibility of literate, urban, 'salaried employees' — who, caught between a vast sink of poverty and tiny, impenetrable enclaves of wealth, begin to look for some kind of meaning and authenticity in what they see as their own traditions of respectable gentility. That is their cruellest delusion, for their gentility has very little to do with the traditions of Egypt or India, Islam or Hinduism, and everything to do with Victorianism.

Much of Mahfouz's work seethes with the indignation that grows out of this particular sensibility, indignation at the corruption that allows the unscrupulous to grow rich while decent people labour to earn an honest wage. But indignation is about all it is. Its sources are not interesting enough to give it the fire of real rage or even the anger of outraged morality. Mahfouz has written some quasi-mystical parables, but he is not essentially a religious writer. Indeed, the Arab thinker whose name occurs most frequently in his work is Abu'l 'Ala al-Ma'arri, a medieval freethinker and rationalist. And although Mahfouz has written political satires, he is not essentially a political writer, either. In his books politics and history generally serve as part of the background and mise-en-scène.

If there is something suspect, in the end, even about Mahfouz's indignation, it is probably because it never appears to be turned against his people's own ethic of respectability. His mother figures are impossibly good and forbearing, and girls who leave the sanctuary of the home and go out to work all too often fall prey to temptation. At its best, Mahfouz's work has some of the texture and the richness of detail of the nineteenth-century masters whose influence he acknowledges — Balzac, Tolstoy, Flaubert — but even at its bleakest and most melancholy (as in *The Beginning and the End*) his writing never approximates real tragedy. Its pathos seems to spring almost entirely from a sense of violated gentility. Even for a writer with Mahfouz's skill, it is hard to create tragedy out of the scramble for respectability.

It is in the observation of the small details on which the edifices of respectability are constructed that Mahfouz is really acute about his society. Those are the details that need footnoting in this selection of translations — not the 'sights and smells of Cairo', as his editors have all too predictably assumed. What the foreign reader needs explained is the real meaning of what it is to be a 'salaried employee' in Egypt, the importance of the baccalaureate examinations, what it is to be an eighth-grade functionary. These are arcane and peculiarly Egyptian details, although they have nothing to do with the Egypt of the Pharaohs or Mamelukes, or with anything particularly exotic. But it is those details that make up the fabric of respectable, middle-class life in Egypt, and it is Mahfouz's singular gift that he is able to transform them into the stuff of fiction.

3

The American University in Cairo Press has long been doing a difficult and thankless job in making good writing in Arabic available in English translation. With Mahfouz's Nobel Prize, and the sale of rights to their translations, their efforts have been richly rewarded. It is to be hoped that more and still better translations will be forthcoming soon, so that a wider spectrum of modern Arabic writing will receive the kind of attention it deserves. The four novels published by Doubleday are revised versions of the original American University in Cairo translations. Two of them were written in Mahfouz's early 'realistic' period. *The Beginning and the End* is the melancholy but compelling story of a family pauperized by a sudden death. *Palace Walk* is the first book of Mahfouz's Cairene trilogy, written in 1956–7, in which each book is named after a street in the old city. The trilogy, which charts the history of a Cairene family during the period between the Wars, is a chronicle of the changes that occurred in Egyptian society over that period.

Palace Walk sets the stage for the later books; it is a depiction of what went before the changes, so to speak. The central figure in the book is a patriarch of rather extreme convictions: he has never once, in their decades-old marriage, allowed his wife to leave the house. This is a condition with which she is entirely satisfied, for she reveres her husband, except for one small thing — she longs to visit the mausoleum of Sayidna Hussein, which is down the road. One day one of her sons persuades her to venture out. She does, and for her pains she is struck by a motor car. (Why do such terrible things happen, in Mahfouz's work, to women who leave their houses?) Worse still, the wrathful patriarch, upon discovering her dereliction, packs her off to her mother's, where she languishes, wringing her hands, until he summons her back. In the end, however, the turmoil of Egyptian politics — the last part of the book is set in the period of the 1919 riots against the British presence in Egypt — catches up with the apparently invincible patriarch and leaves him a broken man.

The novel has the feel of the sort of stories people tell about the Old Days, when they want their children to marvel at how much the world has come on since then. In a sense, of course, it is exactly that: Mahfouz was a very young child in the years in which his book is set, and his family had already moved out of the old part of the city. There are some perceptive observations about the psychology of patriarchy — there is a wonderful scene, for example, in which the patriarch's son, a brave and ardent nationalist, finds himself reduced to a quaking heap by the tone of his father's voice. But the reader would be better able to savour those moments, perhaps, if Mahfouz's sympathy with the patriarch were not so patent, if the book were not so pervaded by nostalgia for a time when Men were Men.

The other two novels, *The Thief and the Dogs* (1961) and *Wedding Song* (1981), date from Mahfouz's later period, which was less realistic and more experimental, and they are, frankly, awful. When the spirit moves Mahfouz to be technically adventurous, it also tends to push him away from his accustomed material, leaving him stranded in various exotic enclaves of society. *Wedding Song* is set among a group of raffish theatre people who Drink, Gamble, Take Drugs, and Have Sex (the underworld, again). A particularly disreputable couple has a son who is an idealistic young man; appalled by the lasciviousness and the immorality of his parents' circle, he exposes them in a play before staging his own death. The *Thief and the Dogs* is about . . . well it's about an idealistic sort of fellow who becomes a thief because he is shocked by how rich some people are.

Unfortunately for Doubleday, and fortunately for English readers, the most delightful of Mahfouz's translated works, *Midaq Alley*, has long been available in a good translation by Trevor Le Gassick. It has recently been reissued by the Quality Paperback Book Club, and it is more worth reading than any of Doubleday's four. The novel is set in Mahfouz's familiar world — in a street in the old city — but it lacks the portentousness of some of his other work. It is written tongue-in-cheek, almost as self-parody, and it brims with moments of pure delight.

For instance: the homosexual café owner Kirsha — inevitably of dark and sullen aspect — is interrupted by his wife while entertaining a youth in his café. His wife marches up to the boy and screams: 'Do you want to ruin my home, you rake and son of rakes. . . . Who am I? Don't you know me? I am your fellow-wife . . . ' The boy escapes, and she turns upon her protesting husband and shouts, in a 'voice loud enough to crumble the walls of the café': 'Shut your mouth! You are the . . . lavatory around here, you scarecrow, you disgrace, you rat-bag!' Among the awestruck spectators is the baker's wife, who regularly beats her husband. She turns to him now and remarks: 'You're always moaning about your bad luck and asking why you're the only husband who is beaten! Did you see how even your betters are beaten?' But eventually Kirsha has his say as well. 'Oh you miserable pair, why on earth should the government punish anyone who kills off people like you?' His son declares that he wants to leave home and live in a place where houses have electricity. 'Electricity?' retorts Kirsha. 'Thanks be to God that your mother, for all her scandals, has at least kept our house safe from electricity!'

The inhabitants of this alley are a world away from the mythologized patriarch and his family on Palace Walk.

4

The Nobel Prize has had an unhappy consequence for Mahfouz. Soon after the announcement, possibly as a result of the Rushdie crisis, he began to receive death threats from Islamic fundamentalists. At issue was a book he wrote in 1959 called (in its English translation) *Children of Gebelawi*. It was an allegorical novel, in which three of the principal characters were said to represent the prophets Moses, Jesus, and Muhammad. The *'ulema*, the Muslim doctors of theology and religious law, declared Mahfouz's book to be offensive to Islam. The book was never published in Arabic in Egypt, and for a while Mahfouz stopped writing altogether. But there were more books in time, and the controversy was largely forgotten — until the threats began.

An epoch passed in the Middle East between the late fifties and the late eighties. There is a world of difference between a group of learned scholars pronouncing an anathema and the death threats issued by bands of young men barely out of college. The evolution of the Mahfouz controversy is one very small indication of how dramatically the Middle East has changed within the life-time of his own generation.

In Mahfouz's youth, Islam had been largely sidelined as a political ideology. In Turkey, Ataturk, with the power of the army behind him, appeared intent on pushing everything religious into the wings. During his college years in the late twenties and early thirties, the principal intellectual influence on Mahfouz was a group of nationalists who had set themselves the task of creating a national culture for Egypt that would be distinctively Egyptian. The path they took lay in emphasizing Egypt's Pharaonic and Hellenistic roots, to the point of disavowing all connections with the Arab and Islamic world. It was a time when everything was thinkable in Egypt and nothing was blasphemy.

If *Children of Gebelawi* had been written in those years, it would probably have passed without comment: every writer in Egypt, it would seem, was writing an allegory of some kind. But the book was written in the late fifties, when the political and religious climate in the Middle East had been profoundly altered by the establishment of Israel and then by the Nasserite revolution in Egypt. In Egypt, Islam acquired a new vitality and assertiveness, and the religious establishment was keen to remind everybody of that fact. But even then the *'ulema* followed procedure in condemning the book. There were no calls for bloodshed or retribution: just a clear message that those who persisted in the intellectual habits of the thirties would now have to contend with the doctors of religious law and their followers.

But now even the learned doctors are being slowly consumed by the fires that were kindled at that time. They have not the remotest connection with the bearded young men who now speak in the name of Islam in Egypt: they have themselves been declared unbelievers, pagans — even the most learned of the shaikhs at al-Azhar, for centuries the theological centre of Sunni Islam. In 1977 one of their number, Mohammad al-Dhahabi, a religious scholar and a minister of the government department in the Ministry of Religious Endowments, where Mahfouz worked for much of his life, was kidnapped and killed by a fundamentalist group called the Society of Muslims. At the subsequent trial, conducted by the army, the presiding general in so many words declared the *'ulema* incompetent.

The scholars' only recourse now is to call the preachings of the fundamentalists un-Islamic, as indeed they are by scholastic standards. The Society of Muslims have effectively scorned Muslim history: they have rejected all of medieval Muslim scholarship, including the great jurists who set up the four major schools of Islamic law, and they have also claimed the right to interpret the Koran. A century ago it is they who would have been counted the blasphemers, and any one of their current claims would probably have cost them their lives. They have, in effect, vacated the whole concept of Islam as we know it: for Islam is a history, as well as a doctrine and a practice. Yet today, for millions of Muslims in Egypt and elsewhere, it is they, and not the *shaikhs* of al-Azhar, who are the true Muslims.

The power of the fundamentalists has grown so phenomenally in Egypt over the last few years that they are now in a position to fight pitched battles with the police. Every so often they even claim to have 'liberated' parts of Cairo and some other cities. Why, then, should these fundamentalists revive the charges brought against Mahfouz by their enemies, the learned doctors of religion? It must be the first matter on which they have been in agreement with them in several years. Mahfouz's book is evidently a pretext: their hostility almost certainly stems from his public support of the Camp David accords.

In responding to the threats against him, Mahfouz has shown an exemplary courage. Despite the ominous drift of the political life of his city, he has turned down the government's offer of bodyguards and has refused to change his life in any way. For the time being he appears to have faced down his enemies and shamed them into leaving him alone. In doing so, he has demonstrated the kind of heroism that is both the most necessary and the most rare in his volatile corner of the world: the quiet kind.

7 *Petrofiction*
The Oil Encounter and the Novel

IF THE Spice Trade has any twentieth-century equivalent, it can only be the oil industry. In its economic and strategic value, as well as its ability to generate far-flung political, military, and cultural encounters, oil is clearly the only commodity that can serve as an analogy for pepper. In all matters technical, of course, the comparison is weighted grossly in favour of oil. But in at least one domain it is the Spice Trade that can claim the clear advantage: in the quality of the literature that it nurtured.

Within a few decades of the discovery of the sea route to India, the Portuguese poet Luis de Camoes, had produced the *Lusiads*, the epic poem that chronicled Vasco da Gama's voyage and in effect conjured Portugal into literary nationhood. The Oil Encounter on the other hand, has produced scarcely a single work of note. In English, for example, it has generated little apart from some more or less second-rate travel literature and a vast amount of academic ephemera — nothing remotely of the quality or the intellectual distinction of the travelogues and narratives produced by such sixteenth-century Portuguese writers as Duarte Barbosa, Tomé Pires, and Gaspar Correia. As for an epic poem, the very idea is ludicrous: to the principal protagonists in the Oil Encounter (which means in effect, America and Americans on the one hand and the peoples of the Arabian Peninsula and the Persian Gulf on the other), the history of oil is a matter of embarrassment verging on the unspeakable, the pornographic. It is perhaps the one cultural issue on which the two sides are in complete agreement.

Still, if the Oil Encounter has proved barren, it is surely through no fault of its own. It would be hard to imagine a story that is equal in drama, or in historical resonance. Consider its Livingstonian beginnings: the Westerner with his caravan-loads of machines and instruments thrusting himself unannounced upon small isolated communities, deep within some of the most hostile environments on earth. And think of the post-modern present: city-states where virtually everyone is a 'foreigner'; admixtures of peoples and cultures on a scale never before envisaged; vicious systems of helotry juxtaposed with unparalleled wealth; deserts transformed by technology, and military devastation on an apocalyptic scale.

It is a story that evokes horror, sympathy, guilt, rage, and a great deal else, depending on the listener's situation. The one thing that can be said of it with absolute certainty is that no one anywhere who has any thought either for his conscience or his self-preservation can afford to ignore it. So why, when there is so much to write about, has this encounter proved so imaginatively sterile?

On the American side, the answers are not far to seek. To a great many Americans, oil smells bad. It reeks of unavoidable overseas entanglements, a worrisome foreign dependency, economic uncertainty, risky and expensive military enterprises; of thouands of dead civilians and children and all the troublesome questions that lie buried in their graves. Bad enough at street level, the smell of oil gets a lot worse by the time it seeps into those rooms where serious fiction is written and read. It acquires more than just a whiff of that deep suspicion of the Arab and Muslim worlds that wafts through so much of American intellectual life. And to make things still worse, it begins to smell of pollution and environmental hazards. It reeks, it stinks, it becomes a Problem that can be written about only in the language of Solutions.

But there are other reasons why there isn't a Great American Oil Novel, and some of them lie hidden within the institutions that shape American writing today. It would be hard indeed to imagine the writing school that could teach its graduates to find their way through the uncharted firmaments of the Oil Encounter. In a way, the professionalization of fiction has had much the same effect in America as it had in Britain in another, imperial age: as though in precise counterpoint to the increasing geographical elasticity of the country's involvements, its fictional gaze has turned inward, becoming ever more introspective, ever more concentrated upon its own self-definition. In other words, it has fastened upon a stock of themes and subjects, each of which is accompanied by a well-tested pedagogic technology. Try and imagine a major American writer taking on the Oil Encounter. The idea is literally inconceivable. It isn't fair, of course, to point the finger at American writers. There isn't very much they could write about: neither they nor anyone else really knows anything at all about the human experiences that surround the production of oil. A great deal has been invested in ensuring the muteness of the Oil Encounter: on the American (or Western) side, through regimes of strict corporate secrecy; on the Arab side, by the physical and demographic separation of oil installations and their workers from the indigenous population.

It is no accident then that the genre of 'My Days in the Gulf' has yet to be invented. Most Western oilmen of this generation have no reason to be anything other than silent about their working lives. Their working experience of the Middle East is culturally a nullity, lived out largely within portable versions of Western suburbia.

In some ways the story is oddly similar on the Arab side, except that there it is a quirk of geography — of geology, to be exact — that is largely to blame for oil's literary barrenness. Perversely, oil chose to be discovered in precisely those parts of the Middle East that have been the most marginal in the development of modern Arab culture and literature — on the outermost peripheries of such literary centres as Cairo and Beirut.

Until quite recently, the littoral of the Gulf was considered an outlying region within the Arab world, a kind of frontier whose inhabitants' worth lay more in their virtuous simplicity than in their cultural aspirations. The slight curl of the lip that inevitably accompanies an attitude of that kind has become, if anything, a good deal more pronounced now that many Arab writers from Egypt and Lebanon — countries with faltering economies but rich literary traditions — are constrained to earn their livelihood in the Gulf. As a result, young Arab writers are no more likely to write about the Oil Encounter than are their Western counterparts. No matter how long they have lived in the Gulf or in Libya, when it comes to the practice of fiction they generally prefer to return to the familiar territories staked out by their literary forebears. There are, of course, some notable exceptions (such as the Palestinian writer Ghassan Kanafani's remarkable story 'Men in the Sun'), but otherwise the Gulf serves all too often as a metaphor for corruption and decadence; a surrogate for the expression of the resentment that so many in the Arab world feel toward the regimes that rule the oil kingdoms.

In fact, very few people anywhere write about the Oil Encounter. The silence extends much further than the Arabic- or English-speaking worlds. Take Bengali, a language deeply addicted to the travelogue as a genre. Every year several dozen accounts of travel in America, Europe, China, and so on are published in Bengali, along with innumerable short stories and novels about expatriates in New Jersey, California, and various parts of Europe. Yet the hundreds of thousands of Bengali-speaking people who live and work in the oil kingdoms scarcely ever merit literary attention — or any kind of interest, for that matter.

As one of the few who have tried to write about the floating world of oil, I can bear witness to its slipperiness, to the ways in which it tends to trip fiction into incoherence. In the end, perhaps, it is the craft of writing itself — or rather writing as we know it today — that is responsible for the muteness of the Oil Encounter. The experiences that oil has generated run counter to many of the historical imperatives that have shaped writing over the last couple of centuries and given it its distinctive forms. The territory of oil is bafflingly multilingual, for example, while the novel, with its conventions of naturalistic dialogue, is most at home within monolingual speech communities (within nation-states, in other words). Equally, the novel is never more comfortable than when it is luxuriating in a 'sense of place', revelling in its unique power to evoke mood and atmosphere. But the experiences associated with oil are lived out within a space that is no place at all, a world that is intrinsically displaced, heterogeneous, and international. It is a world that poses a radical challenge not merely to the practice of writing as we know it, but to much of modern culture: to such notions as the idea of distinguishable and distant civilizations, or recognizable and separate 'societies'. It is a world whose closest analogues are medieval, not modern — which is probably why it has proved so successful in eluding the gaze of contemporary global culture. The truth is that we do not yet possess the form that can give the Oil Encounter a literary expression.

For this reason alone, *Cities of Salt*, the Jordanian writer Abdelrahman Munif's monumental five-part cycle of novels dealing with the history of oil, ought to be regarded as a work of immense significance. It so happens that the first novel in the cycle is also in many ways a wonderful work of fiction, perhaps even in parts a great one. Peter Theroux's excellent English translation of this novel was published a few years ago under the eponymous title *Cities of Salt*, and now its successor, *The Trench*, has appeared.

Munif's prose is extremely difficult to translate, being rich in ambiguities and unfamiliar dialectical usages, and so Theroux deserves to be commended for his translations — especially of the first book, where he has done a wonderful job. He is scrupulously faithful to both the letter and the spirit of the original, while sacrificing nothing in readability. Where Theroux has intervened, it is in what would appear to be the relatively unimportant matters of punctuation and typography. (He has numbered each chapter, though the Arabic text does not really have chapters at all, but merely extended breaks between pages; and he has also eliminated Munif's favourite device of punctuation, a sentence or paragraph that ends with two period points rather than one, to indicate indeterminacy, inconclusivity, what you will . . .) These changes are slight enough, but they have the overall affect of producing a text that is much more 'naturalistic' than the original. One day a professor of comparative literature somewhere will have fun using Theroux's translations to document the changes in protocol that texts undergo in being shaped to conform to different cultural expectations.

The Arabic title of Munif's first novel has the connotation of 'the wilderness', or 'the desert', and it begins with what is possibly the best and most detailed account of that mythical event, a First Encounter, in fiction — all the better for being, for once, glimpsed from the wrong end of the telescope. The novel opens, appropriately, on an oasis whose name identifies it as the source, or the beginning: Wadi al-Uyoun, an 'outpouring of green in the harsh, obdurate desert'. To the caravans that occasionally pass through it, as to its inhabitants, the wadi is an 'earthly paradise', and to none more so than one Miteb al-Hathal ('the Troublemaker'), an elder of a tribe called al-Atoum:

> Left to himself to talk about Wadi al-Uyoun, Miteb al-Hathal would go on in a way no one could believe, for he could not confine himself to the good air and the sweetness of the water . . . or to the magnificent nights; he would tell stories which in some cases dated back to the days of Noah, or so said the old men.

But unsettling portents begin to intrude upon this earthly paradise. One evening at sunset, one of Miteb's sons returns from watering the family's livestock and tells his father of the arrival of 'three foreigners with two marsh Arabs, and they speak Arabic' — 'People say they came to look for water.' But when Miteb goes to find out for himself, he sees them going to 'places no one dreamed of going', collecting 'unthinkable things', and writing 'things no one understood', and he comes to the conclusion that 'they certainly didn't come for water — they want something else. But what could they possibly want? What is there in this dry desert besides dust, sand and starvation?'

The people of the wadi hear the foreigners asking questions 'about dialects, about tribes and their disputes, about religion and sects, about the rocks, the winds and the rainy season'; they listen to them quoting from the Koran and repeating the Muslim profession of faith; and they begin to 'wonder among themselves if these were jinn, because people like these who knew all those things and spoke Arabic yet never prayed were not Muslims and could not be normal humans'. Reading the portents, Miteb the Troublemaker senses that something terrible is about to befall the wadi and its people, but he knows neither what it is nor how to prevent it. Then suddenly, to everyone's relief, the foreigners leave, and the wadi settles back, just a trifle uneasily, to its old ways.

But soon enough the strangers come back. They are no longer unspecified 'foreigners' but Americans, and they are everywhere, digging, collecting and handing out 'coins of English and Arab gold'. Their liberality soon wins them friends in the wadi, but even the closest of their accomplices is utterly bewildered by their doings; 'nothing was stranger than their morning prayers: they began by kicking their legs and raising their arms in the air, moving their bodies to the left and right, and then touching their toes until they were panting and drenched with sweat'. Then a number of 'yellow iron hulks' arrive, adding to the bewilderment of the wadi's inhabitants: 'Could a man approach them without injury?

What were they for and how did they behave — did they eat like animals or not?' Fearing the worst, the people of the wadi go to their emir to protest, only to be told that the Americans have 'come from the ends of the earth to help us' — because ' "There are oceans of blessings under this soil." '

The protests are quickly suppressed, Miteb and other troublemakers are threatened with death, and before long the wadi's orchards and dwellings are demolished by the 'yellow iron hulks'. After the flattening of his beloved wadi, Miteb mounts his white Omani she-camel and vanishes into the hills, becoming a prophetic spectral figure who emerges only occasionally from the desert to cry doom and to strike terror into those who collaborate with the oil-men. As for Miteb's family and the rest of the wadi's inhabitants, they are quickly carried away by passing camel caravans. A number of them set out for a coastal settlement called Harran ('the Over-heated'), where the new oil installations are to be built, a 'cluster of low mud houses' — a place evidently very much as Doha and Kuwait were only a few decades ago.

The rest of Munif's narrative centres upon the early stages of Harran's transformation: the construction of the first roads, the gradual influx of people, the building of the oil installations, the port and the emir's palace. Working in shifts, the newly arrived Arab workers and their American overseers slowly conjure two new townships into being, Arab Harran and American Harran. Every evening, after the day's work is done, the men drift home

> to the two sector like streams coursing down a slope, one broad and one small, the Americans to their camp and the Arabs to theirs, the Americans to their swimming pool, where their racket could be heard in the nearby barracks behind the barbed wire. When silence fell the workers guessed the Americans had gone into their air-conditioned rooms whose thick curtains shut everything out: sunlight, dust, flies, and Arabs.

Soon Harran no longer quite belongs to its people, and

the single most important episode in the building of the new city has little to do with them. It is the story of an R-and-R ship that pays the city a brief visit for the benefit of the Americans living in the yet unfinished oiltown:

> The astonished people of Harran approached [the ship] imperceptibly, step by step, like sleepwalkers. They could not believe their eyes and ears. Had there ever been anything like this ship, this huge and magnificent? Where else in the world were there women like these, who resembled both milk and figs in their tanned whiteness? Was it possible that men could shamelessly walk around with women, with no fear of others? Were these their wives, or sweethearts, or something else?

For a whole day and night, the inhabitants of Harran watch the Americans of the oiltown disporting themselves with the newly arrived women, and by the time the ship finally leaves 'the men's balls are ready to burst'. This event eventually comes to mark the beginning of the history of this city of salt:

> This day gave Harran a birth date, recording when and how it was built, for most people have no memory of Harran before that day. Even its own natives, who had lived there since the arrival of the first frightening group of Americans and watched with terror the realignment of the town's shoreline and hills — the Harranis, born and bred there, saddened by the destruction of their houses, recalling the old sorrows of lost travellers and the dead — remembered the day the ship came better than any other day, with fear, awe, and surprise. It was practically the only date they remembered.

The most sustained wrong note in *Cities of Salt* is reserved for its conclusion. The novel ends with a dramatic confrontation between the old Harran and the new: between a world where the emir sat in coffee-houses and gossiped with the Bedouin, where everybody had time for everyone else and no one was ever so ill that they needed remedies that were sold for money, and a universe in which Mr Middleton of the oil company holds their livelihoods in his hands, where to the newly arrived Lebanese doctor Subhi al-Mahmilji ('physician and surgeon, specialist in internal and venereal diseases, Universities of Berlin and Vienna') charges huge fees for the smallest service, where the emir spies on the townspeople with a telescope and needs a cadre of secret police to tell him what they are thinking. 'Everyday it's gotten worse', says one long-time resident of Harran, pointing toward the American enclave: 'I told you, I told every one of you, the Americans are the disease, they're the root of the problem and what's happened now is nothing compared to what they have in store for us.'

The matter comes to a head when a series of events — a killing by the secret police, sightings of the troublemaking Miteb, the laying-off of twenty-three workers — prompts the workers of Harran to invent spontaneously the notion of the strike. They stop working and march through the town chanting:

> . . . The pipeline was built by beasts of prey,
> We will safeguard our rights,
> The Americans do not own it,
> This land is our land.

Then, led by two of Miteb the Troublemaker's sons, they storm the oil installation, sweeping aside the emir's secret police and the oil company's guards, and rescue some of their fellow workers who'd been trapped inside. And the book ends with an unequivocal triumph for the workers: the half-crazed emir flees the city after ordering the oil company to reinstate its sacked employees.

It is not hard to see why Munif would succumb to the temptation to end his book on an optimistic note. His is a devastatingly painful story; a slow, roundabout recounting of the almost accidental humiliation of one people by another. There is very little bitterness in Munif's telling of it. Its effectiveness lies rather in the gradual accumulation of detail. Munif's American oilmen are neither rapacious nor heartless.

On the contrary, they are eager, businesslike, and curious. When invited to an Arab wedding they ask 'about everything, about words, clothing and food, about the names of the bridegroom and his bride and whether they had known each other before, and if they had ever met. . . . Every small thing excited the Americans' amazement.' It is not through direct confrontation that the Harranis met their humiliation. Quite the opposite. Theirs is the indignity of not being taken seriously at all, of being regarded as an obstacle on the scale of a minor technical snag in the process of drilling for oil.

Better than any other, Munif's method shows us why so many people in the Middle East are moved to clutch at straws to regain some measure of self-respect for themselves; why so many Saudis, for example, felt the humiliation of Iraq's army almost as their own. But in fact the story is even grimmer than Munif's version of it, and the ending he chooses is founded in pure wish-fulfilment. It probably has more to do with its author's own history than with the story of oil in the Gulf.

Abdelrahman Munif was born in 1933, into a family of Saudi Arabian origin settled in Jordan. (He was later stripped of his Saudi citizenship for political reasons.) He studied in Baghdad and Cairo, and went on to earn a Ph.D. in oil economics at the University of Belgrade — back in the days of Titoite socialism, when books written by Progressive writers always ended in working-class victories. Since then Munif's working life has been spent mainly in the oil industry in the Middle East, albeit in a rather sequestered corner of it: he has occupied important positions in the Syrian Oil Company, and he has served as editor in chief of an Iraqi journal called *Oil and Development*.

No one, in other words, is in a better position than Munif to know that the final episode in his story is nothing more than an escapist fantasy. He must certainly be aware that the work forces of the international oil companies in the Arabian peninsula have never succeeded in becoming politically effective.

When they showed signs of restiveness in the 1950s, they were ruthlessly and very effectively suppressed by their rulers, with the help of the oil companies. Over the last couple of decades, the powers-that-be in the oil sheikhdoms (and who knows exactly who they are) have followed a careful strategy for keeping their workers quiescent: they have held the Arab component of their work forces at a strictly regulated numerical level, while importing large numbers of migrants from several of the poorer countries of Asia.

The policy has proved magically effective in the short run. It has created a class of workers who, being separated from the indigenous population (and from each other) by barriers of culture and language, are politically passive in a way that a predominantly Arab work force could never be within the Arab-speaking world — a class that is all the more amenable to control for living perpetually under the threat of deportation. It is, in fact, a class of helots, with virtually no rights at all, and its members are often subjected to the most hideous kinds of physical abuse. Their experience makes a mockery of human rights rhetoric that accompanied the Gulf War; the fact that the war has effected no changes in the labour policies of the oil sheikhdoms is proof in the eyes of millions of people in Asia and Africa that the 'new world order' is designed to defend the rights of certain people at the expense of others.

Thus the story of the real consequences of the sort of political restiveness that Munif describes in *Cities of Salt* is not likely to warm the heart quite as cozily as the ending he gives his novel. But if Munif can be accused of naïveté on this score, he must still be given credit for seeing that the workplace, where democracy is said to begin, is the site where the foundations of contemporary authoritarianism in the oil sheikhdoms were laid.

Today it is a commonplace in the Western media that aspirations toward democracy in the Arabian peninsula are a part of the fallout of changes ushered in by oil and the consequent breakdown of 'traditional' society. In fact, in several instances exactly the opposite is true: oil and the developments it has bought in its wake have been directly responsible for the suppression of whatever democratic aspirations and tendencies there were within the region.

Certain parts of the Gulf such as Bahrain, whose commercial importance far predates the discovery of oil, have long possessed sizeable groups of businessmen, professionals, and skilled workers — a stratum not unlike a middle class. On the whole, that class shared the ideology of the nationalist movements of various nearby countries such as India, Egypt, and Iran. It was their liberal aspirations that became the victims of oil's most bizarre, most murderous creation: the petro-despot, dressed in a snowy *dishdasha* and armed with state-of-the-art weaponry — the creature whose gestation and birth Munif sets out to chronicle in the second volume of the *Cities of Salt* cycle, *The Trench*.

Unfortunately *The Trench* comes as a great disappointment. The narrative now moves away from Harran to a city in the interior called Mooran ('the Changeable'), which serves as the seat of the country's ruling dynasty. With the move to the capital, the focus of the narrative now shifts to the country's rulers.

The story of *The Trench* is common enough in the oil sheikhdoms of the Arabian peninsula; it begins with the accession to power of a sultan by the name of Khazael and it ends with his deposition, when he is removed from the throne by rival factions within the royal family. Munif describes the transformations that occur during Sultan Khazael's reign by following the career of one of his chief advisers, a doctor called Subhi al-Mahmilji (who earlier played an important part in the creation of the new Harran). The story has great potential, but Munif's voice does not prove equal to the demands of the narrative. It loses the note of wonder, of detached and reverential curiosity, that lent such magic to parts of *Cities of Salt*, while gaining neither the volume nor the richness of colouring that its material demands.

Instead Munif shifts to satire, and the change proves disastrous. He makes a valiant attempt — not for nothing are his books banned in various countries on the Arabian peninsula — but satire has no hope of success when directed against figures like Sultan Khazael and his family. No one, certainly no mere writer of fiction, could hope to satirize the royal families of the Arabian peninsula with a greater breadth of imagination than they do themselves. As countless newspaper reports can prove, factual accounts of their doings are well able to beggar the fictional imagination. Indeed, in the eyes of the world at large, Arab and non-Arab, the oil sheikh scarcely exists except as a caricature; he is the late twentieth century's most potent symbol of decadence, hypocrisy, and corruption. He pre-empts the very possibility of satire. Of course, it isn't always so. The compulsions and the absurdities of an earlier generation of oil sheikhs had their roots in a genuinely tragic history of predicament. But those very real dilemmas are reduced to caricature in Munif's Sultan Khazael.

Even where it is successful, moreover, Munif's satire is founded ultimately upon a kind of nostalgia, a romantic hearkening back to a pristine, unspoiled past. It is not merely Americans from the oil companies who are the intruders here: every 'foreigner' is to some degree an interloper in Harran and Mooran. As a result, Munif is led to ignore those very elements of the history of the oil kingdoms that ought to inspire his curiousity, the extraordinary admixtures of cultures, peoples, and languages that have resulted from the Oil Encounter.

Workers from other parts of Asia hardly figure at all in Munif's story. When they do it is either as stereotypes (a Pakistani doctor in *Cities of Salt* bears the name Muhammad Jinnah) or as faceless crowds, a massed symbol of chaos: 'Once Harran had been a city of fishermen and travellers coming home, but now it belonged to no one; its people were featureless, of all varieties and yet strangely unvaried. They were all of humanity and yet no one at all, an assemblage of languages, accents, colours and religions.' The irony of *The Trench* is that in the end it leaves its writer a prisoner of his intended victim. Once Munif moves away from the earliest stages of the Oil Encounter, where each side's roles and attributes and identities are clearly assigned, to a more complicated reality — to the crowded, multilingual, culturally polyphonic present of the Arabian peninsula — he is unable to free himself from the prison house of xenophobia, bigotry and racism that was created by precisely such figures as his Sultan Khazael. In its failure, *The Trench* provides still one more lesson in the difficulties that the experience of oil presents for the novelistic imagination.

8 *Empire and Soul:*
a review of The Baburnama

THE BABURNAMA is the autobiography of India's first Mughal emperor, Zahiruddin Mohammad Babur (1483–1530), and it is one of the true marvels of the medieval world. It belongs with that tiny handful of the world's literary masterpieces that can accurately be described as unique: works that are without precedent and without imitators. In the Western tradition, the military memoir has a pedigree that goes back to Xenophon and Julius Caesar. But Babur had no such antecedents available to him. As Wheeler M. Thackston, his most recent translator, notes: 'Babur's memoirs are the first — and until relatively recent times, the only — true autobiography in Islamic literature.' In setting out to write an autobiography, Babur did something that very few writers have done. He invented a form out of whole cloth.

Babur's true literary peers, in this sense, are such epochal figures as Lady Murasaki and Cervantes. But this writer was also the founder of a great empire: Babur was Pizarro *and* Cervantes. What made him pen this immense book? (It numbered 382 folio pages in the original.) And how on earth did he find the time? Between the moment that he gained his first kingdom, at the age of twelve, and his death, thirty-five years later, there seems scarcely to have been a quiet day in Babur's life.

His first kingdom was the only one for which he did not have to risk his life: he inherited it from his father, a scion of a dynasty that was far richer in aspiring rulers than in actual thrones. Babur took a matter-of-fact view of his father: 'He was short in stature, had a round beard and a fleshy face, and was fat. . . . He used to drink a lot. Later in life he held drinking parties once or twice a week. He was fun to be with in a gathering and was good at reciting poetry for his companions. He grew rather fond of *ma'jun* [a narcotic] and under its influence would lose his head. He was of a scrappy temperament and had many scars and brands to show for it.' Though scarcely a model parent, Babur's father, Umar-Shaykh Mirza, was the very soul of docility compared to the rest of his family. More or less the first thought that occurs to Babur on hearing of his father's death is to flee to the mountains so that 'at least I would not fall captive and . . . go to one of my uncles.' Of one of his uncles, Babur writes: 'He never missed the five daily prayers, even when he was drinking. . . . He was a good drinker. Once he started drinking, he drank continually for twenty or thirty days, but when he stopped he did not drink again for the same amount of time.' And of another uncle: 'He was addicted to vice and debauchery. He drank wine continually. He kept a lot of catamites, and in his realm wherever there was a comely, beardless youth, he did everything he could to turn him into a catamite.'

Predictably, Babur's uncles and cousins descended upon his territories soon after he had acceded to the throne. Not to be outdone, Babur counter-attacked. At the age of thirteen he led an army to Samarkand, to join a clutch of cousins and second cousins who were taking advantage of another relative's absence to lay siege to the fabled city. After a siege of seven months, Babur succeeded in having himself crowned the ruler of Samarkand. He was to rule the city for no more than a hundred days, but in many ways this was the defining moment of Babur's life. He was to besiege, conquer and lose Samarkand many times over before he was finally driven southward. But up to the end of his life, even when he had conquered a realm far vaster, richer and more promising than those that had been taken from him, he still pined for his lost city.

For Babur, Samarkand was the epitome of civilization, the centre of the world's urbanity and the fountainhead of all culture. He won a sizeable chunk of India, the land whose riches had triggered Europe's Age of Exploration, but all he really wanted was Samarkand. His link with Samarkand was, in the first instance, familial. His ancestor Timur Lang (1336–1404), known to the West as Tamerlane, had made Samarkand the capital of a vast empire and built it into a great centre of art and literature. For Babur, as for his innumerable Timurid uncles and cousins, to rule Samarkand was to claim succession to their glorious ancestor, the guarantor of their own titles to rule.

The idea of conquering empires was a part of Babur's family heritage. He traced his descent not just to Timur Lang, but also to Jenghis Khan. The story of Babur's kingdom-seeking adolescence and youth has its genesis ultimately in that epochal churning of peoples and cultures that was set in motion by Jenghis Khan (1167–1227) in the thirteenth century. Jenghis Khan's descendants evidently inherited his remarkable cultural and social adaptability. In the course of his life, the old man had become increasingly Sinicized, and had developed an interest in Buddhism and Confucianism. He seems to have had little empathy for the traditions of western Asia; certainly the Muslims and Christians of those regions never encountered a more determined enemy. Within a generation or two, however, Jenghis Khan's descendants took on the cultural and religious (if not linguistic) colourings of the regions that they ruled. One of his grandsons, Kubilai Khan, became emperor of China and a cornerstone of the Confucian order, while another grandson became the Sultan of Persia and a Muslim.

Babur traced his lineage to Jenghis Khan's second son, Chagatay. When the worlds that Jenghis Khan conquered came to be divided among his progeny, Chagatay inherited Central Asia, a region in which Islam was the principal religion, and Persian the language of cultural prestige. Chagatay's inheritance soon fragmented into a number of warring principalities, but he bequeathed his name not just to a realm, but also to a lineage and a language: eastern Turkish, the tongue whose greatest literary exponent Babur was to become.

Central Asia was briefly reunited by Amir Timur, an extra-dynastic usurper who nonetheless thought it politic to lay claim to the legacy of the Great Khan by marrying a Jenghisid princess. His descendants, however, fought each other with the usual courtly relish of medieval princelings. By the time of Babur's birth, the valleys and the steppes of Central Asia teemed with Timurid princes in search of realms to rule. Such was the magic of the Timurid-Jenghisid pedigree that nobody who owned it ever seems to have forfeited the right to a throne.

From the age of twelve onward, Babur(like his innumerable cousins and uncles) took it for granted that he was born to rule. Ruling was in a sense a job, a calling, the only thing he knew how to do, the only thing he could conceive of doing. Even at times when he possessed little more than his horse and the clothes on his back, he and the members of his tiny entourage took it for granted that a kingdom would somehow transpire, if not in this district then in the next. Babur was reluctantly pushed into southeastern Afghanistan and eventually into northern India. These were not his realms of choice; but they were better than the prospect of being an unemployed king.

The instrument of Babur's misery in his early kingdom-seeking years was a chief called Shaybani ('Wormwood') Khan (1451–1510), an Uzbek and a hereditary enemy. The wheel that Jenghis Khan had set in motion had now come full circle: just as his armies had displaced other Turco-Mongol groups, pushing them further and further to the south and the west, so now Babur and his cousins found themselves facing a people who had decided to create their own moment of destiny. With the methodical precision of a cherry-picker, Shaybani Khan plucked Babur and his fellow Timurids off, one by one, driving them steadily before him. 'For nearly 140 years the capital Samarkand had been in our family', writes Babur. 'Then came the Uzbeks, the foreign foe from God knows where, and took over.'

Babur was too close to the events to notice, but there were some marvellous symmetries to these centuries-long processes of migration in Central Asia, to these patterns of encroachment and displacement, of the sudden ascendancy of a nation or a dynasty, of the rise and decline of glittering cities such as Bukhara and Samarkand, Ghazni and Herat. Some of these symmetries even seeped into Babur's life. In much the same way as Shaybani Khan, the Uzbek, was harrying Babur, Jenghis Khan had once pursued a young warrior-poet, one whose life was perhaps even more colourful than Babur's.

The name of the Great Khan's prey was Jalal al-din. He was the heir-presumptive of the kingdom of Khwarazm, centred in the region between the Caspian and Aral Seas. Jenghis Khan had a special grudge against the king of Khwarazm, and after seizing the kingdom he sent a detachment of his swiftest riders to hunt down its ruling family. In what must count as one of the most amazing escapes in history, the fourteen-year-old Jalal al-din rode without a break — for forty days, circling through the deserts, steppes and mountains of Iran and Afghanistan, managing somehow to stay ahead of the great Mongol general Jebe, known even among his fast-riding peoples as 'The Arrow'. Jenghis Khan finally hunted Jalal al-din to a place from which no escape seemed possible, a gorge above the upper Indus. But there again Jalal al-din succeeded in evading the Khan: he spurred his horse over the cliff and into the river, more than a hundred feet below. Legend has it that the pursuer called off the chase, summoned his entourage and pointed to the young prince swimming in the torrent below. 'There,' said Jenghis Khan, who knew about these things, 'goes a brave man.'

He would have said no less for his own descendant. Babur was nothing if not brave. On one occasion in *The Baburnama*, he takes on a hundred men more or less single-handedly. 'Sultan-Ahmad Tambal was standing, maintaining his position with around a hundred men . . . shouting, "Strike! Strike!" . . . At that point three men were left with me. . . . I shot an arrow I had in my thumb ring. . . . When I had another arrow on the string, I went forward. The other three remained behind.' There are times, though, when he glimpses the end of the road. Led into a trap by an old retainer, he writes: 'Suddenly I felt odd. There is nothing worse in the world than fear for one's life. . . . I felt I could endure no more. I rose and went to a corner of the orchard. I thought to myself that whether one lived to a hundred or a thousand in the end one had to die. . . . I readied myself for death.' Minutes later, help arrives.

Often Babur is in despair. His nineteenth year proves to be a hard one: 'During this period in Tashkent I endured much hardship and misery. I had no realm — and no hope of any realm — to rule. Most of my liege men had departed. The few who were left were too wretched to move about with me. . . . Finally I had had all I could take of homelessness and alienation. "With such difficulties," I said to myself, "it would be better to go off on my own so long as I am alive, and with such deprivation and wretchedness it would be better for me to go off to wherever my feet will carry me, even to the ends of the earth." ' But in the end, stoically, he resigns himself to the difficult business of finding a realm: 'When one has pretensions to rule and a desire for conquest, one cannot sit back and just watch if events don't go right once or twice.'

Eventually, our hero's perseverance pays off. In 1504, 'at the beginning of my twenty-third year [when] I first put a razor to my face', moving ever southward, staying one step ahead of the Uzbeks, he stumbles upon the kingdom of Kabul and he decides to seize it for himself. His new realm is full of surprises: 'Eleven or twelve dialects are spoken in Kabul Province: Arabic, Persian, Turkish, Mongolian, Hindi. . . . It is not known if there are so many different peoples and languages in any other province.' Slowly, inevitably, his attention is drawn to the vast subcontinent on the far side of the mountains. He observes, speculatively, that 'four roads lead [to Kabul] from Hindusthan'. But his principal ambitions are still directed toward Samarkand. He even succeeds in briefly recapturing the city of his dreams, only to find himself expelled from it yet again shortly afterwards. With his northern options closed, he turns to the south.

Through all his adventures, Babur kept writing, mainly poetry. Even as he flees from the Uzbeks, he finds time to carve a verse on rock beside a spring. 'Like us many have spoken over this spring / but they were gone in the twinkling of an eye, / We conquered the world with bravery and might, / but we did not take it with us to the grave.' It is a commentary on our times that to us it seems odd, or at least unexpected, that a warrior and a statesman should devote his attention to intricate questions of scansion and metrics. But Babur came from a long line of literary rulers; some of the greatest works of Persian literature were composed in the court of his great-grandfather Amir Timur.

Still, the literary ambitions of Babur's ancestors usually stopped at connoisseurship, patronage and the occasional composition of a *divan*, the collection of poems that was expected of every man of good breeding. Babur did indeed compose several collections of poems, but he was the only man of his line to embark on a work of extended prose. In addition, he did it not in Persian, the literary language of his court, but in Chagatay Turkish, the domestic demotic of his family.

To read *The Baburnama* is to ask oneself again and again what could possibly have prompted a man in Babur's position to write his memoirs. Autobiography was not a form that flourished in Asia, certainly not in Central Asia, where Babur's roots lay. As for the Indian subcontinent, I know of only one autobiography written there before the nineteenth century: a brief account of the life of a merchant. The closest Babur comes to explaining his motives is this: 'I have simply written the truth. I do not intend by what I have written to compliment myself. I have simply set down exactly what happened. Since I have made it a point in this history to write the truth of every matter and to set down no more than the reality of every event, as a consequence I have reported every good and evil I have seen of father and brother and set down the actuality of every fault and virtue of relative and stranger. May the reader excuse me; may the listener take me not to task.'

But he may have come closer to the truth in his first poem, a *ghazal*, written at the age of eighteen: 'Other than my own soul I never found a faithful friend / Other than my own heart I never found a confidant.' It may have been a sense of loneliness, or apartness, that compelled Babur to set down these reflections on his life; and it was probably the intimacy of that endeavour that led him to choose his domestic language over the courtly diction that was generally used in his circle. The memoir that he produced, as a result, was anything but the usual chronicle of affairs of state and battles lost and won. Written centuries before the discovery of the Self, *The Baburnama* is, astonishingly, a narrative of self-discovery.

The tone of the work is disarmingly trusting and confiding. In its self-revelation, it yields nothing to the confessional memoir of the 1990s. Babur does not neglect to record the sexual hesitancies of his first marriage: 'since it was my first marriage I was bashful, I went to her only once every ten, fifteen, or twenty days.' And he writes lyrically about an adolescent infatuation with a boy: 'before this experience I had never felt a desire for anyone, nor did I listen to talk of love and affection or speak of such things.' His evaluations of his relatives and his contemporaries are so frank and unguarded as to suggest that he did not expect his memoirs to be widely circulated.

He writes no less trenchantly about women than men: as friends or adversaries, they were evidently a formidable force in his life. The women in his book are strong-willed and independent; they declare their own agency without hesitation, in matters political and personal. We see Babur at critical moments going into the women's quarters to ask advice; we read about the delinquency of a widowed aunt who gives away her son's kingdom to none other than the dreaded Uzbek, Shaybani Khan, in the hope of winning his love ('in her lust to get a husband, that wretched, feebleminded woman brought destruction on her son'); and about another aunt who was so domineering that her husband dared not 'go to any of his other wives'. We hear of powerful princes being swiftly dispatched by ambitious concubines. We even learn of women who took the initiative in courting Babur. The contemporary Muslim fundamentalists who would carry Afghanistan back to an idealized past in which women never stepped out of the house would do well to have a look at this classic of Islamic life in their part of the world. They would find that the Middle Ages were not quite what they imagine them to be.

Babur is at his most self-revelatory in his description of his drinking life. He came from a hard-drinking line, though he was twenty-nine before he touched his first drink: 'In my childhood I had no desire for wine, for I was unaware of the enjoyment of it. Occasionally my father had offered me some, but I had made excuses. After my father's death I was abstinent. . . . Later, with the desires of young manhood and the promptings of the carnal soul, when I had an inclination for wine, nobody offered — no one even knew that I was interested.' Then, at a party in the city of Herat, in south-western Afghanistan, his nobles offered him wine. 'It crossed my mind,' writes Babur, 'that since they were making such proposals, and here we had come to a fabulous city like Herat, where all the implements of pleasure and revelry were present, and all the devices of entertainment and enjoyment were close at hand, if I didn't drink now, when would I? Deliberating thus with myself, I resolved to make the leap.' This was the beginning of a twenty-year love affair with wine. Babur seems to have dedicated much of his time in Afghanistan to the pursuit of wine and *ma'jun*.

Again, so much for Afghan fundamentalism. Babur provides us with a meticulous record of the parties of his Kabul years. 'At midday we rode off on an excursion, got on a boat, and drank spirits. . . . We drank on the boat until late that night, left the boat roaring drunk, and got on our horses. I took a torch in my hand and, reeling to one side and then the other, let the horse gallop free-reined along the riverbank all the way to the camp. I must have been really drunk. The next morning they told me that I had come galloping into camp holding a torch. I didn't remember a thing, except that when I got to my tent I vomited a lot.' And so things went, until he led his fifth, and final, expedition into India. Shortly before a decisive battle, Babur made a spectacular gesture: he took a public oath of temperance.

The cellars in his camp were emptied into the sand, and he personally broke his sumptuous gold and silver wineglasses and goblets and distributed the pieces to the poor. Three weeks later, he led his army into battle against a massive force assembled by Rana Sangram Singh (popularly known as Rana Sanga), then the most powerful Rajput ruler in north India. Babur prevailed. He did not find temperance easy, though he consoled himself liberally with *ma'jun*. 'Everybody regrets drinking and then takes the oath', he wrote. 'But I have taken the oath and now regret it.' Yet he was true to his oath: he never drank again.

In the course of the two decades that he spent in Kabul, Babur led four expeditions into India. His fifth and final campaign was launched in October, 1525. It had a characteristically light-hearted beginning: 'We mostly drank and had morning draughts on drinking days.' Between marches Babur and his nobles wrote poetry, collected obscene jokes and gave chase to the occasional rhinoceros.

Delhi was then in the control of the Lodi Sultans, a dynasty of Afghan Muslim rulers who had done a great deal to enrich the architectural heritage of the capital. (Their memory is enshrined today in New Delhi's Lodi Gardens, one of the world's loveliest urban parks.) Despite internal dissensions, the Lodis managed to field an army of 100,000 men and 1,000 elephants against Babur's paltry force of 12,000. The armies met on 20 April 1526, at the historic battlefield of Panipat, a few miles north of Delhi. Despite the odds, Babur routed the Lodi Sultan and took possession of Delhi.

With the defeat of Rana Sanga's Rajput coalition the next year, Babur secured his hold on northern India. There were skirmishes and minor battles to be fought, but for the most part Babur busied himself in distributing the spoils to his followers and retainers, and in making detailed observations on his new kingdom. With his usual curiosity, he made extensive enquiries about the natural history of northern India, and on the beliefs and the customs of its inhabitants. It is clear from Babur's notes that he found much that did not please him: the place was too hot, its fruit was unfamiliar, its peoples were bafflingly unlike any he had ever known. But then Babur was never very easy to please, especially where people were concerned; his was a tribal world, and his loyalties and pride were largely invested in his kinsmen and his lineage. For most of those who fell outside that circle — Afghans, Shias, Uzbeks, Indians and so on — he reserved a curiously unprejudiced dislike.

A strain of deep melancholy runs through the last pages of the *The Baburnama*, as though he had come to realize that ruling his new kingdom would entail permanent exile from the landscapes of his childhood. 'Our concern for going thence [to Kabul] is limitless and overwhelming', he wrote to a friend the year before his death. 'How can one forget the pleasures of that country? Especially when abstaining from drinking, how can one forget a licit pleasure like melons and grapes? Recently a melon was brought and as I cut it and ate it I was oddly affected. I wept the whole time I was eating it.' His Indian victories seem to have left Babur with the feeling that his life's work was over. Homesickness, nostalgia and abstinence evidently combined to rob him of his will to live.

Of the many stories told about Babur, none is more wonderful than that of his death. In 1530, Humayun, Babur's beloved eldest son and heir-apparent, was stricken by a fever. He was brought immediately to Babur's court at Agra; but despite the best efforts of the royal physicians, his condition steadily worsened. Driven to despair, Babur consulted a man of religion, who told him that the remedy 'was to give in alms the most valuable thing one had and to seek a cure from God'. Babur is said to have replied: 'I am the most valuable thing that Humayun possesses; than me he has no better thing; I shall make myself a sacrifice for him. May God the Creator accept it.'

Greatly distressed, Babur's courtiers and friends tried to explain that the sage had meant that he should give away money, or gold, or a piece of property. Humayun possessed a priceless diamond, they said, which could be sold and the proceeds given to the poor. Babur would not hear of it. 'What value has worldly wealth?' he is quoted as having said. 'And how can it be a redemption for Humayun? I myself shall be his sacrifice.' He walked three times around Humayun's bed, praying: 'O God! If a life may be exchanged for a life, I who am Babur, I give my life and my being for a Humayun.' A few minutes later, he cried: 'We have borne it away, we have borne it away.' And sure enough, from that moment Babur began to sicken, while Humayun grew slowly well. Babur died near Agra on 21 December 1530. He left orders for his body to be buried in Kabul.

As a writer, an intellectual and a soldier, Babur stood very far above the men of his time. As a ruler, on the other hand, his ideas never extended much beyond those he had absorbed from his cousins and his uncles in his kingdom-seeking days in the steppes. The model of governance that he brought to his Indian empire was essentially the one that he imbibed in his early youth on the steppe, where the business of ruling entailed little more than knocking a rival off his perch and taking his place. Babur had little interest in creating instruments of government. As a result, he left behind a throne that stood on very weak supports. Within ten years of his death, his son Humayun was driven out of India by Sher Shah Suri, a soldier of extraordinary talent and vision. Born in the eastern province of Bihar, into a relatively humble Muslim family, Sher Shah created a bureaucratic and administrative machine of remarkable complexity. He was to rule in Delhi for only five years, but on his death in 1545 he left behind a sound administrative infrastructure. In 1555, Humayun invaded northern India with the help of the Shah of Persia, and conquered Delhi once again from Sher Shah's unworthy heirs. It was probably fortunate for the Mughal dynasty that Humayun did not linger long on his throne. He died within a few months of entering Delhi, stumbling down a steep staircase, while under the influence. It fell to Babur's grandson Akbar, then a boy of thirteen, to take the throne.

Akbar (1542–1605) proved to be one of the greatest rulers in the history of the Indian subcontinent. He appears to have had a profound understanding of Indian institutions of kingship, and particularly of the concept of the 'universal ruler'. He proved adept at incorporating the many different religious, linguistic and dynastic traditions of his empire into the culture of his court. He even synthesized various Muslim and Hindu traditions into a religion of his own devising, the *Din-i-Ilahi*, a creed that was, not unpredictably, centred on himself. Although the new religion never quite caught on, Akbar still enjoyed an exceptionally long reign. The aura of legitimacy that he left behind was to sustain Mughal rule for more than a century.

History is notoriously not about the past. In recent years,

extremist Hindus in India have succeeded in creating a firestorm of political controversy by exhuming aspects of Mughal history. In 1992, in a matter of hours, a well-organized Hindu mob tore down a sixteenth-century mosque in the city of Ayodhya, creating one of the most serious crises in the history of the Indian Republic. Named after Babur, the mosque was known as the Babri Masjid. It was the contention of the Hindu zealots that the mosque stood on the site of a Hindu temple dedicated to Lord Rama, the divine hero of the *Ramayana* epic. A political and archaeological controversy over the site still rages, with politicians and scholars weighing in on both sides.

The Baburnama leaves no doubt that its writer was, in his own distinctive way, a devout and occasionally militant Muslim. In his autobiography Babur repeatedly announces his intention of destroying Hindu temples and images. These declarations were clearly intended, in part, to garner support among local Indian Muslims. So far as actually building mosques and demolishing temples, Babur's declarations were almost certainly greatly in excess of his real intentions. Still, if he had indeed erected mosques on the sites of temples (and there is no clear evidence that he did), he would have done no more than Hindu rulers had themselves done centuries earlier. Archaeological evidence indicates that many important Hindu temples are built upon earlier Buddhist sites; the great Krishna temple of Mathura, for example, stands on what was probably a Buddhist monastery.

Despite Babur's protestations of religious zeal, it is clear from the pages of his autobiography that he was no bigot. Hindus evidently frequented his court, and many Hindus entered his service. The Sikhs — who were to become dedicated adversaries of the Mughal state in the seventeenth century — have long cherished a story, preserved in their scriptural tradition, about an encounter between Babur and Guru Nanak, the founder of their faith. In the process of sacking a town in the Punjab, Babur's soldiers are said to have imprisoned Guru Nanak and one of his disciples. Learning of a miracle performed by the Guru, Babur visited him in prison. Such was the presence of the Guru that Babur is said to have fallen at his feet and cried: 'On the face of this faqir one sees God himself.'

In any event, it is beyond dispute that Babur's descendants presided over a virtually unprecedented efflorescence in Hindu religious activity. Hinduism as we know it today, especially the Hinduism of north India, was essentially shaped in the early years of Mughal rule, often with the active participation and support of the rulers and their officials and feudatories. The *Ramcharitmanas* for example, the version of the *Ramayana* that was to be canonized as the central text of north Indian devotional practice, was composed in Akbar's reign by the great saint-poet Tulsidas.

Mughal rule also coincided with a great renaissance in Krishnaite theology. It was in this period that Rupa Goswamy and other disciples of the Bengali mystic Chaitanya Mahaprabhu rediscovered and mapped out the sacred geography of the Krishna legend. The region consecrated to Krishna lies between Agra and Delhi, the two principal centres of Mughal power in the sixteenth century. The road connecting these two imperial cities runs right past the sacred sites of this area. It has frequently been observed that the Mughals could easily have persecuted the Hindu saints and pilgrims who were then engaged in rediscovering those sites had they wished to. But, far from suppressing the burgeoning activity in that area, Akbar and his nobles actively supported it.

The Hindu generals and officials of Akbar's court built several of the most important temples in this area, with Akbar's active encouragement. Akbar was personally responsible for sustaining some of these temples; he granted land and revenue in perpetuity to no less than thirty-five of them. Indeed, Hinduism would scarcely be recognizable today if Krishnaite theology and Krishna-devotion had been actively suppressed in the sixteenth century. As a living practice, contemporary Hinduism would not be what it is if not for the practices initiated under Mughal rule. The sad irony is that the Hindu fanatics who destroyed the Babri Mosque were attacking a symbol of the very accommodations that made their own faith possible.

The last ruler in Babur's dynastic line was the tragic Bahadur Shah Zafar (1775–1862), who was crowned in Delhi at a time when the British had already taken control of most of northern India. The last emperor ruled over little more than his own palace, yet it was in his name that millions of people across India rose in a desperate, failed bid to expel the British in 1857. In the bloody aftermath, Bahadur Shah was exiled to Rangoon, where he died. On a visit to Rangoon earlier this year, I learned that the current Indian Ambassador to Burma, a Christian career diplomat from the north-eastern state of Mizoram, had taken the initiative to restore and to refurbish Bahadur Shah's modest burial-place. I can think of no more appropriate tribute to the imaginative power of the Mughal order.

Wheeler M. Thackston's splendidly illustrated translation of *The Baburnama* is the third English translation of the work. The first, by William Erskine, appeared in 1826, and the second, the famous version by Annette Beveridge, was published between 1912 and 1921. For all her literary talents, Annette Beveridge was not a professional scholar, and Thackston, who is a professor of Near Eastern languages at Harvard, does not mince his words in his criticism of her translation. It reads, he declares, 'like a student's effort — all the words have been looked up in the dictionary and put together'.

Clearly Thackston is something of a Babur himself, to tilt so blithely at a work that earned the admiration of E.M. Forster's generation. Having myself first encountered *The Baburnama* as a schoolboy, in the Beveridge translation, I was initially outraged at Thackston's easy dismissal of his predecessor. Comparing key passages, however, I found that

Thackston had, on the whole, fulfilled his promise of a more 'fluent, idiomatic and colloquial' rendition. If anything, he has fulfilled it too well. A sentence that Beveridge renders as 'Stay here while I look along the Gava road' becomes, in Thackston's translation, 'You stay here. . . . I'll go check out the Gava road.' But then I know of no rule that requires that Babur sound more like an Edwardian gentleman than a Connecticut mallrat.

In his useful and informative introduction, Thackston informs us that 'Mughal' is a misnomer for the dynasty that Babur founded. Babur and his descendants identified themselves as 'Gurkani', or sons-in-law, the Timurids having married into the line of Jenghis Khan. For Babur, the word 'Mughal' denoted various 'quasi-Buddhistic, quasi-shamanistic' groups and tribes in the remoter parts of Central Asia. And his loathing of Mughals surpassed even his detestation of Uzbeks, Shias, Afghans and assorted infidels. 'Havoc and destruction,' writes Babur, 'have always emanated from the Mughal nation. Up to the present date they have rebelled against me five times — not from any particular impropriety on my part, for they have often done the same with their own khans.' Yet it is probably too late to entertain objections to 'Mogul' as a title for powerful rulers. Are we likely ever to open *The New York Times* and find Eisner or Turner referred to as gurkanis?

Misnamed or not, Babur's dynasty became a synonym for magnificence. For over a century, official histories, British and Indian, have contrived to make the Mughal period a paradigm of Indian statehood. The governments of post-Independence India and Pakistan, like the British colonial regime before them, have striven to appropriate aspects of Mughal symbolism. To this day, the Prime Ministers of India deliver their annual Independence Day address from the ramparts of the Mughal fort in Delhi. But the Mughals have not been well-served by this official attention, at home or abroad. Having been credited with all the artistic and cultural achievements of 'medieval India', they now tend also to attract more than their share of the blame for the perceived failures of that time. It is in the nature of symbols of official grandiosity that they sometimes become the focus of frustrations that ought to be directed elsewhere. This exaggerated political emphasis on the Mughals probably contributed to the escalation of the Babri Mosque controversy.

In fact, the Mughal empire never covered the whole of the Indian subcontinent. In its most brilliant period, it had barely a toehold in the Deccan peninsula. The later Mughals tried hard to extend their domains, but their southern border tended to snap up like a rubber band every time they took a finger off its edge. Aurangzeb, the last of the six great Mughals, who ruled from 1659 to 1707, effectively doomed the empire by over-extending it in the south.

In the long view, the Mughal period was no more than a lucky time-out, a magnificent hallucination whose end had been conceived even before it was born. The truth is that, while Babur was fighting his epic battles in the Indo-Gangetic plain, the future of the subcontinent was being decided in a series of much smaller engagements on the west coast, where various kings and rulers were fighting the Portuguese. For the Indian subcontinent as a whole, the decisive battle of the sixteenth century was probably not Babur's engagement at Panipat (as I was taught in school and college), but rather the battle of Diu.

It was there, in 1509, that a Portuguese fleet attacked and defeated the combined naval forces of the Muslim ruler of Gujarat, the Hindu king of Calicut, and the Sultan of Egypt. On the occasion of his victory, the Portuguese viceroy Dom Francisco de Alameida gave the moral of the outcome: 'As long as you may be powerful at sea, you will hold India as yours; and if you do not possess this power, little will avail you a fortress on the shore.' He was very prescient. To the Mughals fell the thankless task of tending the fortress on the shore.

Babur either had no knowledge of the Portuguese presence in western India or he thought them beneath notice. He never so much as mentions them, though by the time he was seated on the throne of Delhi the Portuguese had already founded a major settlement on the west coast in Goa. Babur remained, to the end, a child of the steppes. Having never seen the sea, he could scarcely be expected to possess an appreciation of naval power. Babur's descendants had the advantage of him: they extended their domains all the way to both coasts. Yet they too, to a degree that is quite baffling, had their gaze turned resolutely inland. Their emissaries to Persia generally took the difficult and dangerous overland route rather than the much easier seagoing one. It is hard to imagine a greater handicap for rulers who would have to contend with an age of maritime power. The saddest aspect of Babur's brief Indian sojourn is that he died without seeing the greatest gift that the subcontinent could have given him: the open ocean. What would he have made of it, this endlessly questing, insatiably curious man of the steppes? We can only wonder.

9 *The Relations of Envy in an Egyptian Village*[1]

ALTHOUGH BELIEFS and practices related to the evil eye are almost certainly as common as witchcraft or sorcery, they have received much less attention from anthropologists. Folklorists on the other hand, have collected a good deal of material on the subject (Dorson 1968: 417), but much of it is inventorial in its perspective; objects, artefacts and practices believed to ward off the evil eye are simply listed without reference to their social context (e.g., Burne 1902; Rouse 1895; Simpson 1915). As a result, it sometimes appears as if Evil Eye beliefs have no internal coherence and represent little more than a generalized fear of evil.

One of the reasons why evil eye beliefs appear to be formless, sociologically speaking, is that the relations which underlie them are far less obvious than those which are associated with, for example, witchcraft. As Spooner (1970) points out, evil eye practices do not lead to public accusations, and so they do not yield the clear patterns of relationship which accusations, involving as they do accusers and accused, necessarily do.

Yet evil eye beliefs do have their own systematic logic, and they too are oriented by specific relations. But these relations differ radically from those which underlie witchcraft and other forms of directed malevolence. The fact that envy is always thought to be the motive force behind the evil eye indicates the nature of the difference between evil eye practices and other forms of directed malevolence. Envy necessarily springs from a situation of asymmetry or imbalance; as a social phenomenon it follows upon certain kinds of division in society. Therefore it cannot be said of evil eye beliefs, as it can of Azande witchcraft, that it is a 'function of personal relations' (Evans-Pritchard 1937: 106); the relations which determine it are part of a wider order of society. This article argues that in the village studied, the beliefs and practices which constitute the evil eye are enmeshed with the conditions of production and the villagers' representation of the dynamics of their own economy.

In the village of Naçaawy ijjadiida (Naçaawy)[2] as in other parts of Egypt and the Middle East (cf. Spooner 1970; Sessions 1898; Burns 1902; Ammar 1954; Granqvist 1947; Simpson 1915; Rouse 1895), people believe that envy (*ḥasad*)[3], working through the agency of the glance (*naẓar*), has efficient action and can destroy or harm the objects or people against which it is directed. The word *ḥasad* is used both as a noun (envy, or the evil eye), and as a verb (to envy, to cast the evil eye); the act of envying and its action are taken to be synonymous. Here, I will translate *ḥasad* as envy, but the connection is important.

The Village

The material I present was collected during a year's fieldwork, between 1980 and 1981, in Egypt's western Delta province of Beḥeira. The field work was done largely in the village (*balad*), Naçaawy ijjadiida, which has a population of about 1,700 living in 215 households. The people of the village are divided into a large number of agnatic families (*'aailaat*; sing. *'aaila*), of which the Badawy is the largest; almost a third of the village.

There is a continuous chain of habitation all around Naçaawy and it is difficult to see where Naçaawy begins and other settlements end. Yet, socially if not spatially, the boundaries of each settlement in the area are clearly drawn.

Each settlement has a guest house (*maḍiafa*). When a member of the settlement dies, each household sends a tray of food and a male representative (usually the head of the household) to the guest house, and the assembled men eat a collective meal there. The same pattern repeats itself on certain other occasions. The meals mark the boundaries of each settlement, for the village membership of a household is determined by which guest house it sends its tray to.

The meals are also displays of communal solidarity; the collective breaking of bread affirms the unity of the households of the village. The people of Naçaawy often say of their village, 'we are one' (*iḥna kullena waaḥid*). Every family in the village has married into every other and every individual in the village can trace a relationship, usually through a number of different routes, to every other. The villagers say they are tied by affinity (*muṣaahara*). If a man from the village kills someone from another village, the village as a whole hosts feasts of reconciliation in their guest house and the elders of the village negotiate and arrange the compensatory payments.[4] Therefore the villagers say of themselves, 'we are one killing' (*iḥna gutl waaḥid*) and 'we are one force' (*iḥna inḍamm waaḥid*).

Nonetheless, the villagers linguistically distinguish between two groups in the village — the 'comfortable people' (*naas mabsuuṭa*) and the 'needy people' (*naas ġalaaba*). The distinction between the two is not sharply defined and many villagers will call themselves comfortable in one context and needy in another. On the whole, however, the 'comfortable people' are the landholding fellahin[5] and the 'needy' include the landless agricultural workers of the village, those fellahin who own very little land, and some poor craftsmen and traders. This division is not tied to that of family. Most families have some 'comfortable' as well as 'needy' people, though some families are more prosperous than others. Among the 'comfortable people', the villagers distinguish some seven or eight families, the largest landholders in the village, who are spoken of as *jamaa'at ilmullaak* (the group of proprietors) which may be translated as 'the well-to-do'.

These divisions, in no sense a contradiction of what has been said above, can be properly understood only in the context of the villagers' sense of community. In part this sentiment is possible, despite the recognized social divisions in the village, because there are no institutional relationships of property between the villagers. Few villagers are tenants of other people in the village; those villagers who lease their land do so mainly for convenience. Landholding households in Naçaawy usually cultivate their own land and lease land only when constrained by circumstances; as for example, when a man dies leaving only minor children. Such land is usually rented to close relatives. Tenancy agreements concluded between the villagers are generally to the advantage of the tenant when compared to similar agreements concluded with urban landlords. Rented land in Naçaawy is paid for with money or for a share of the produce. A cash arrangement is to the tenant's advantage, for Egyptian land reform laws ensure that rents are nominal and that tenants have absolute security of tenure. Under sharecropping agreements, at least half the produce of the land has to be paid to the landlord. Since such agreements are often informal, the landlord may evict the tenant whenever he pleases. Only about eighteen of the 475.8 feddans[6] cultivated by people from Naçaawy are rented on tenancy agreements between villagers, and only a third of these is sharecropped. Urban landlords, on the other hand, own 145 feddans of the land cultivated by the villagers, of which 54 per cent is sharecropped.

That almost a third (31 per cent) of village land is rented from absentee landlords, indicates that tenancy is common to the richest as well as the poorest of the fellahin in Naçaawy. Even the largest landholders in the village cultivate rented land. There are eight households in the village which hold more than nine feddans. Together they hold about 100 feddans, of which 44 are rented. The households I have called the well-to-do, are so only relative to the people of the same village and the surrounding countryside. Though many people in Naçaawy have a better standard of living than parts of the urban population, nobody permanently resident in the village can be considered well-off by global or urban Egyptian standards.

Altogether, two-thirds of the households in the village hold land in one way or another; about 28 per cent of the total area cultivated by the villagers is owned and cultivated by the same households, 23 per cent rented land, and 18.5 per cent is sharecropped. The rest consists of land distributed after the land reforms of 1952. Naçaawy is situated close to what once was one of the largest estates in Egypt. The estate land was distributed among the people of the area during the land reforms so that about a quarter of the households in the village today hold 'reform' (*aṣlaah*) land. About a sixth of the households of the village are supported by landless agricultural workers; there are a few shopkeepers and petty traders.

Despite the divisions of family income, and status, when the villagers say 'we are one', they express a certain truth. No household in the village subsists solely on rent, no household is wholly dependent economically on another, and only one man in the village is permanently in the employ of a household not his own. Even the most prosperous households in the village share with the poorest the fact of being tenants. Relations of tenancy exist not between the villagers, but between the village as a whole and urban landlords.

All the villagers also share the same dialect and the same cultural ethos, which distinguishes them from the people of the cities. Ammar (1954: 39-40) noted of Silwa village in Aswan province that 'the feeling of egalitarianism is so striking in this community that any schematic class division is difficult to apply to its social structure . . . irrespective of their landholdings, they all eat from their hand-produce . . . they live in similar dwellings. . . . Members of each sex dress more or less alike. . . . Strengthening the sense of egalitarianism [is] the sense of brotherhood amongst Muslims enjoined upon them by the Koran.' All this is equally true of Naçaawy; the divisions of income and family are a counterpoint to the real sense of equality and community in the village. This sense of equality, as Ammar (1954) notes, is directly related to

Islamic practice. The villagers say of the whole Islamic world (the *umma*) as they say of the village, 'we are one'. But the nearer excludes the further and, for the villagers, Naçaawy itself stands as a metaphor for the *umma*. Every villager's equality with every other villager constitutes the living practice of Islamic brotherhood. The villagers' image of their community is metaphorically true; in relation to other similar communities and in relation to the cities they are indeed one.

Envy and The Evil Eye

As a set of beliefs, *ḥasad* is of central importance to the daily lives of people in Naçaawy; the fear of envy and of being thought envious regulates an enormous area of village life. There are certain paths in the village that people try to avoid, at the cost of long detours, for they lead past the houses of those known to be envious. When walking, people are careful to keep their eyes averted from the interiors of other houses, lest they be thought envious. Windows are usually small and set high. Doors, the vulnerable points of a house, are almost invariably plastered with impressions of the open palm (*xamsa wi ximaisa*), which all over the Middle East serves as a charm against envy (Rouse 1895; Simpson 1915). When anyone admires an object which belongs to another household, he is careful to begin by saying, 'May the Lord increase your goods' (*rubbena yiziid 'aleik ilxair*), or a similar phrase.

Envy also functions as a general explanatory rubric by providing a means of representing chance and unwelcome happenings to the understanding. When someone falls ill, in addition to seeing a doctor, his family calls in a *ragwi* (one who breaks spells) as added insurance. The villagers have no doubts about the efficient powers of envy. The harmful effects of the envious glance are accepted as an article of faith; people say that it is mentioned in the Koran.

The beliefs and practices surrounding envv and witchcraft (*suḥuur*) are very different in Naçaawy; envy surrounds the everyday life of the villagers while witchcraft is an extraordinary phenomenon. In Naçaawy, witchcraft occurs principally in situations connected with marriage and affinity. Wives divorced against their will (as for barrenness) and girls jilted by their lovers are often said to resort to sorcery. One of the characteristic circumstances in witchcraft is said to occur is within the large household, where several married brothers live together, and it is usually attributed to jealousy between the brothers' wives (*salaaif*). That witchcraft occurs within households is important. It suggests that witchcraft stems from relations between individuals, rather than those within the group as a whole. As we shall see, the patterns of envy are different, for envy always occurs between households, never within them. Although witchcraft and envy are both related to beliefs in directed malevolence, they differ so far as the relationships which direct them and the tensions from which they arise are concerned. Here, I shall deal with only certain typical patterns of envy.

While the incidents of envy in the village, petty and major, are figuratively innumerable, they do not occur at random. Rather, certain clear patterns emerge from the countless tales. There is one clear distinction among them. Some deal with the physical and other attributes of certain individuals who, because of their looks, their skill in dancing, their deportment, and so on, think themselves envied, often without apparent foundation. In such cases, envy seems to be a means of articulating the psychological states of some people in the form of personal envy. This differs from the social envy to which every household in the village is subject under certain circumstances, and which is the main concern of this article.

Livestock

The villagers believe that the principal focus of envy is livestock (*bahaaim*). The greatest concentration of stories about envy deal with livestock, cows and buffaloes in particular. The fellahin usually keep their livestock in pens (*zaraaib*, sing. *zariiba*) deep in the interiors of their houses (cf. Lozach and Hug 1930: 32). Houses in Naçaawy, especially the traditional mud-brick houses (*duur*, sing. *daar*) of the fellahin, are built around courtyards, and have front and back entrances. Every house has a guest room (*mandara*) next to the front entrance, facing the lane or street. This room is the public part of the house and is separated from the interior by the courtyard, which is rarely crossed by people not of that household. The rear entrance, which usually leads out from the *zariiba* to a back lane, is also rarely used by outsiders. Throughout the Middle East, this pattern of architecture, with the *ḥariim* (sanctuary) deep within the interior of a house, seems to seclude women from the gaze of male strangers. But, in marked contrast to other parts of the Arab world, there is little segregation of women in this area of Egypt. Women are never veiled and they converse freely with men and sit with them in the guest room (cf. Antoun 1968: 675-6).

The veiled, secret interior of the house in Naçaawy consists of the *zariiba*, where livestock is kept secluded from prying, envious eyes. Village houses are designed and constructed to prevent people of one household from looking into the *zariiba* of another. Should anyone happen to glance into another household's *zariiba*, it would be considered ill-mannered and suspicious if he did not immediately say: 'In the name of God, the Merciful, the Compassionate' (*bismillah irraḥmaan irraḥiim*), to show that he intended no harm to the livestock. Calves bought to be fattened and sold sometimes never leave the *zariiba* until the day they are spirited off to the market, early in the morning when no one can see them. Mature cows and draught animals are too large to keep permanently in the *zariiba*, but when they are taken out their owners often hang around their necks charms, like old leather shoes, which foil envious glances. It is when they are with livestock that people are most careful to avoid the houses of those who are known for their enviousness. As we shall see in the next section, livestock plays a vital part in the fellah's understanding and conduct of his economy.

Livestock: Productive Capital

The pattern of cultivation in the village is of two types; there are crops grown for sustenance, literally 'for the household' (*lil-bait*), and other crops which are grown for cash. The first category includes rice, wheat, maize,[7] vegetables, and alfalfa. Cash crops are principally cotton and occasionally a special kind of watermelon grown for its savoury seeds.

The distinction is not self-evident. The fellahin grow rice and wheat primarily for sustenance because the self-sufficiency of the household is important to them as a principle, not simply because economic necessities make it incumbent upon them to do so. When the fellahin have a choice between making a profit from growing a crop for the market and growing a variety of crops for the household, they invariably choose the latter, selecting self-sufficiency in food over profit in the market. For example, within the cycle of rotation enforced by the agricultural co-operative in the village, the fellahin are free in summer to plant either maize or vegetables on one part of their land. Most fellahin choose to sow a large part of their land with maize because most of the local bread is made from maize flour. If, instead, they opted for market gardening they could easily make handsome profits, for vegetables fetch a good price in the market while maize flour is cheap and readily available in the village. Yet, no substantial fellah ever chooses this pattern of cropping. They choose, instead, to plant a large quantity of maize precisely so that their households will not have to buy grain in the market. Ammar (1954: 33) notes in Silwa that 'it is believed that bread made out of home grown crops is more lasting and sufficing than that made out of seeds bought at the market, as there is more *baraka* —holiness and sufficiency — in the former kind. . . . "From where are you going to eat?" is a question invariably asked by the villagers of any of them who entertains the idea of growing cotton on the small farm.' The fellahin in Naçaawy hold the same view.

The ways in which cotton and other crops are cultivated

are markedly different. Cotton is grown purely for gain, and its cultivation is marked by an intense effort to make the greatest possible profit from it. The easygoing camaraderie of rice and wheat harvests contrasts markedly with the nervous intensity of cotton-picking. All exchanges connected with cotton are monetary. Hired workers, and camel owners, who usually take their payment in kind during the rice and wheat harvests, always take cash for cotton-picking.

A distinct schema emerges from the fellah's pattern of cultivation. Grain and vegetables provide, in principle, a base of self-sufficiency to every household; cotton, through the money it brings in, provides the dynamic element in the household economy. In the fellah's view, cash in itself is unproductive; it is of greatest use when it is involved in the generation of more wealth. Thus the fellah household does its best in every way to reduce its cash expenses. Given the pattern of cultivation in the village, the land-holding household needs to spend little. It grows its own grain and vegetables, it keeps some domestic birds, guinea-pigs, and rabbits for meat, it pays no rent for its dwelling, and the fields provide fuel in the form of straw and firewood from dry cotton plants. The average household rarely has to pay for labour; the everyday work of cultivation is done by its members and, when a great deal of help is needed, fellah households share labour. Even at the busiest times, most households need hire only a few workers, if any. For everyday needs, most households only have to buy items such as sugar, tea, oil, spices and kerosene. The principal cash expenses of a fellah household consist of gifts to sisters and daughters married outside the village, life-crisis ceremonies and, for the very prosperous, the pilgrimage to Mecca.

It is not just saving cash but putting it to work to generate more money that the fellahin consider important. Significantly, when the villagers exchange cash gifts, the exchange is always geared towards return, if not increase. Thus, for example, the gifts of cash given at weddings (*nuguuṭ*) are meticulously recorded by the receiver and reciprocated, ideally with an addition, when an opportunity presents itself. It is thought meaningless to give a gift of this kind if there is no possibility of return; such money is said to have gone (*raaḥ*), to be lost to the giver. A gift should carry with it the promise of generation and increase.

For the fellahin, livestock represent the ideal pattern of investment. Whenever the fellahin have cash, apart from the little they keep aside for household expenditure, they buy livestock. When they need substantial sums, as for marriages, they sell a cow or a buffalo, but they never let cash lie idle. Having bought a cow or a calf, a household will feed and fatten it (*yiallafu*) for six months to a year and, with luck, sell it for a handsome profit to a butcher or a livestock dealer. In this fashion, people sometimes double their initial investment and plough the returns back into livestock. For the fellahin a healthy cow or cow-buffalo is the image of material increase for it bears calves, which may be sold in the market, and gives milk.

This pattern of investment has deep roots in the folklore of the area. The landless of the village say that 'the money brought by cotton stays in the hands [of the fellahin]' (*ilgirç bitaa' goṭn biyistanna fi yidehum*), for with that money they can invest in livestock. The implicit contrast is with the landless who, because their households do not have the produce of land to sustain them, have to spend their cash on everyday necessities, and are thereby deprived of the means of investment. But they, too, have a similar vision of betterment and invest what little they have in ducks, chickens, goats, and sheep. It is a practice among parents of little girls to put aside a duckling or a gosling as her property in the hope that, with time and a series of lucky sales, it will 'grow' into a cow or calf, which she will be able to sell at the time of her marriage.

The principal orientation in the fellah economy lies in the drive towards enrichment through dealing in livestock. Other aspects of their economy are subordinated to this end. In the winter, for example, the fellahin have a choice between planting alfalfa (*bersiim*), peas, or beans on part of their land. Peas and beans fetch high prices on the market while alfalfa can easily be bought in the village at that time. But every fellah household treats alfalfa as the first priority, for self-sufficiency in alfalfa is thought to be the first step towards a successful trade in livestock.

The fellahin value livestock far more as an investment than for its uses. Though cows and buffaloes are used as draught animals, many fellahin today are buying petrol powered water-pumps and most now rent tractors to plough their land. One reason they give for this is that ploughing and drawing water tends to tire cows and buffaloes and reduce their market value or render them incapable of breeding.

Although the fellahin believe that buying livestock is the most profitable direction of investment, not all fellahin who invest in livestock profit from it. In fact, astuteness and luck are required to be able to profit from livestock, for cattle-dealing is a risky business. Cattle often contract diseases, some fall into canals and cripple themselves, some promising-looking calves refuse to fatten themselves, and the market is often treacherous. If livestock in Naçaawy is surrounded by a great deal of care and anxiety, it is partly because it is so vulnerable to chance. Livestock is thought the best investment not because it is actually the quickest way to make money; the fellahin invest in livestock because livestock represents to them the idea of material increase. The growth of a calf over six months or a cow's pregnancy is a symbol for the growth of their own fortunes.

Livestock is not the primary focus of envy. in Naçaawy because of its market value. Every fellah family owns things which are more valuable than a cow or buffalo (e.g., jewellery, the elaborate kitchen utensils and crockery which accompanies marriages, transistor radios and some television sets). Although these inanimate items are not thought of as objects of envy, it does not mean that people believe them to be safe from malicious glances, for anything may be harmed by envy. But only livestock is worth envying. So, while livestock is kept hidden in the recesses of the house, television sets and radios are displayed prominently in guest rooms. Crockery, often the pride of a household, is the most public of possessions in Naçaawy, and every household sends its best crockery to the guest house every time a collective meal is held there. In fact, these material objects are expressly meant for display, while no household would think of showing off its livestock. Curiously, television sets, jewellery, crockery, etc. are not thought of as the principal objects of envy even though common sense would lead us to suppose that it is precisely such symbols of status and well-being which would attract malice.

That livestock is the principal target becomes apparent in the details of stories about envy. A young fellah related the following episode:

> Once I was taking our cows past Umm Fulaan's house, which is on the way to our house. Umm Fulaan has bad eyes (*'ain wahç*) and as I was going past her house she envied (*ḥasadit*) one of our cows. She leant over to look at the udders (*bizza*) of the cow. She stared at it very hard. After that the cow would give no milk. I try not to go past her house now.

Another story is told by a caretaker of the local primary school:

> A long time ago we had a nanny goat (*maa'iza*) which had many kids and gave us milk. It supplied one bowl of milk every day. We kept it in our house so nobody would see it, but one day a neighbour's wife noticed it. Our neighbours are well-off people with many cows and buffaloes, some of which were milked. But the next day she came to our house and asked for some of our goat's milk, even though they are rich and have plenty of livestock while we are poor and had only our goat. She envied the goat and, sure enough, when we tried to milk the goat it gave only blood. She had envied it well.

In many stories about the envying of livestock, the person who casts the malicious glance is said to look at the udders of the cow, buffalo or goat. Or else it is the fecundity of the animal which is said to be affected by envy. The stories pinpoint the real focus of envy; the possibility of increase. Radios, television sets, jewellery, and crockery do not represent this possibility for they are part of a process of consumption. In themselves, they can do nothing; they neither increase nor produce. The only machines which are sometimes said to attract envy are water-wheels (*kabaabiis*, sing. *kabbaas*) and water-pumps (*makanat arrayy* or *makana hindi*). They, too, are part of a process of production. But, for the villagers, livestock amounts to a representation of the ideas of growth and increase.

Envy and the Fixed Order of Relations

People in Naçaawy have a precise idea of the economic standing of every household in the village and, upon certain occasions, the differences in economic ability are taken into account. When people in the village make contributions to joint ventures, like public Koran readings, every household in the village contributes according to its standing. The principle which regulates this aspect of the villagers' relations with each other is contained in a phrase, 'everybody [according] to their ability' (*kull waaḥid 'ala gaddu*). So, for joint ventures, the well-to-do pay more and the needy pay less, each according to their ability. In like fashion, households contribute gifts of money at marriages. The same principle is applied to bride-price. Similarly those who share a water-wheel are allocated time in proportion to the amount of land they have to water. The villagers say the principle is the same, but here it has the different connotation of 'everybody according to their need'. The principle is perhaps better translated as 'everybody to what they have' or 'everybody to their lot'.

In its application, the principle fixes the positions of households relative to each other. Envy, which is itself a relation and not a series of disconnected incidents, is a reflex of this principle. Objects which are central to the relation of envy are those which represent the possibilities of increase and betterment for individual households, and thereby challenge this fixed order of relations. A household's livestock is believed to be the primary focus of envy directed against it because livestock represents the principal means whereby a household may change its relationship vis-à-vis other households in the village.

A household's improvement of its position in Naçaawy need not be at the expense of other households in the village; the economy of Naçaawy is not a zero-sum game. Households which improve their position do so by trading on the open market or by producing more, so the expense of their betterment is not borne by others in the village. In Naçaawy, it is when one household believes itself to possess the wherewithal to change its position relative to the others that it thinks itself to be subject to envy.

Foster (1972: 170–1) argues that the have-nots envy the haves, that 'envy is generally of superiors'. Lykiardopoulos (1981) argues that prominence and power attract envy. None of this is true of Naçaawy. There, any household may believe itself to be subject to envy, for it is not the absolute characteristics of a household which are envied but the possibility of a change in its position. So, for example, land, which is part of the fixed and predictable order of relations in the village, is never envied. Since there are very few sales of land in the area, land is part of the order from which the fixed set of relations in the village are deduced. The distribution of land is contained within the principle of 'everybody to their lot'. Livestock, because it is ringed with the unpredictable — for the poor man's cow may bear healthy calves year in, year out, while the rich man's languishes sterile — lies at the heart of relations of envy. In fact, the well-to-do of the village are thought to be less vulnerable to envy than others because their positions are less fluid than those of other households.

Other standard forms of envy in Naçaawy adhere to this pattern. One common figure in village envy stories is that of the man who works too hard. This is a figure frequently encountered, for everybody in Naçaawy would like to raise their standard of living and most households work single-mindedly at doing so. People are full of schemes for making money — making bricks, running bicycle-rental businesses, trading in eggs, etc. — though these are incidental to the main pattern of investment in livestock. The following story is illustrative:

> My brother was a barber. When he left for Iraq, I decided to take over his barbering. But I also continued with my house plastering. At the same time, I had another job; I would find workers for people who wanted them [to build houses, etc.]. I was very busy doing these three things. Then some people began to say, 'What's the matter, Mohammad? You're running about making money. What will you do with all this money? It is more than you need.' One day, while plastering a house, the owner said the same thing to me. Soon after, I fell off the scaffolding and had to be taken to a hospital. After that, I gave up my two other jobs and kept to plastering.

In Naçaawy, camels are the most productive of all animals, though only a handful of houses possess one. People say, 'a camel is like a feddan', for by carrying grain, cotton, and firewood a camel can make a lot of money for its owner. When a camel is seen carrying many loads, jealous people are believed to say, 'What's the matter? Is this camel going to carry a whole hamlet or what? This is more than the owner needs.'

The expressions, 'this is more than he needs' and 'this is too much for him' (*da yaama 'aleih* or *da kiṭiir 'aleih*), are the effective parts of envy statements, and reflect the principle of 'everybody to their lot'. For just as everybody knows the economic standing of every household in the village, they also know the needs which accompany it. 'This is too much for you', implies an attempt to exceed those limits.

In Nacaawy people frequently cite children as a target of envy.[8] A mother who gives birth to a boy after bearing several girls, usually keeps the new-born child's sex secret, or says that the child is a girl. Women sometimes dress their baby boys as girls for a long time, so that they may not be envied.

For their parents, male children are a living promise of future increase and prosperity. This is not because boys are better liked. On the contrary, many individuals prefer girls and find greater happiness in their female children, for the relations between male children and their parents, destined as they are to live in the same household, are often very tense. Given the rule of patrilocal residence, girls can do very little for their parents' social well-being, whatever they may do for their individual happiness. A woman's husband does not owe her parents labour or monetary support, and a married woman's household and social fortunes are different from those of her parents. A son, on the other hand, is part of his parents' household and adds to its fortunes in every way.

Some kinds of food (*akl*) are also believed to be particularly subject to envy, as the following story told by a young man of a trading family indicates:

> Once we had slaughtered a duck. One of our neighbours saw us eating it and asked us if we were going to eat the whole duck. She said, 'It will be too much for you.' When we began to eat, we found the meat full of worms and we could not eat the duck. We gave it away to another house, and then it was all right; they could eat it.

Another young man related:

> Once my father was going to Alexandria to meet my uncle. Whenever he goes there, he takes country bread (*fiṭiir baladi*) with him, so he told my mother to make some. When they were making it, some people came and said, 'This is a lot. It is more than you need. What are you going to do with all this?' The bread turned out to be bad.

The foods of envy are almost always meat, fish or bread. They, more than other kinds of food, are believed to give strength. In busy seasons, meals served to men working on the fields always have meat or fish, usually the latter. Meat also occupies the central place in meals and it is always distributed at the table by the seniormost person present (cf. Ammar 1954). Bread, on the other hand, is substance itself; it is well known that the Egyptian word for bread, *'aiç*, also signifies life. That rice and vegetables, which often form the main parts of a meal, are not thought to be objects of envy is significant. Bread and meat, unlike rice or sweetmeats, are identified in themselves with strength and substance.

Envy and Households

Livestock, food, and children are only the symbols through which envy is focused; the objects do not attract envy in themselves. Nobody in Naçaawy would believe that a stray cow or a buffalo, whose owner is unknown, could attract envy. The real target of envy is always a household; livestock and other objects of envy are only the sights through which envy is aimed. The belief that envied food is spoilt only for members of the envied household, and is perfectly edible if given away, is evidence of this.

Morally and economically, households (*bait*, pl. *biyuut*) are the fundamental social units of Naçaawy. Production of all kinds is organized by them. Fellah households hold their land in common and it is cultivated with the collective labour of every member of the household. When a household splits, its land always is divided at the same time. Households of craftsmen own their tools in common and work together; when their household is divided, the tools are divided with it. The division of a household in Naçaawy signifies the birth of two new moral and productive entities in the village; it means another tray sent to the guest house for collective meals, and another group which will work its land together. The household has a common purse and its goods are jointly owned. No distinctions are recognized within the household; the fortunes of the whole household rise or fall together. So, it is said, brothers are the first to envy each other, but only after their original household has been divided.

Sometimes households think themselves envied but are unable to name the envier even after attempts at divination. It sometimes appears that envy centres on one household and that it is not a relationship at all since there is no second party. But, as I have argued, envy responds to the possibility of change in a household's position within the whole village and not simply in relation to one or two households. The fact that the envier is often unknown is a corollary of this; for in such cases the origin of the envy lies not in a single household or person but in the village as a whole. It appears that even when a household does suspect someone in particular, the suspect — unlike the directly hostile figure of witchcraft suspect — is actually a symbol representing the set of relations within the village. This is possibly why, in contrast to the more immediate relationships of witchcraft, evil eye beliefs have the appearance of being a general 'fear of evil influence' (Spooner 1970: 311), and why there are no accusations in evil eye practices; the relation of envy does not obtain between two points, but between one point and an entire set of others.

Envious People

Even though the figure of the envious person is symbolic, there are certain people who are more often suspect than others. They form two classes: (1) those who occupy a certain position in the village or who attract suspicion because of their physical characteristics; and (2) those who stand in a specific relation with a household. The first group is thought to be envious by the entire village. As far as the second group is concerned, each household has a different set of people who stand in a position of envy in relation to it.

The agent of envy is the glance (*naẓar*), but the only kind of glance which is said to have efficient action is the resentful or malicious glance (*naẓar ḥigd*), which springs from a core of hatred and resentment (*ḥigd*). Anybody may be full of malice or hatred on particular occasions or towards particular people, and so anybody may occasionally cause harm through envy. But there are people in the village who are known to be particularly full of spite, and their glances are said to be dangerous to everyone at all times. These people are known as the 'envious' (*ḥussaad*, sing. *ḥaasid*). Although they are treated with some caution, they are not shunned or stigmatized. Some of them are said to be envious because of facial peculiarities or deformities, especially those relating to the eye. The others are all from the well-to-do or relatively prosperous households of the village, which is no mere coincidence.

Villagers say that it is always the rich man (*ilġani*) who envies the poor (*ilfagiir*), and proverbs state, 'The owner of a camel envies the owner of a goat' (*abu jamal biyiḥsid abu jadiya*), and 'The strong envy the weak' (*ilgaadir biyiḥsid iḍḍa'iif*). It is said that to become rich a man must have cunning (*ṣaṭaara*). He must be able to outwit others in his dealings in livestock. He has to save money (*yiwaffar filuus*) for a long time, during which he must deny himself and his family everything that people in the village enjoy. He becomes a miser (*baxiil*); when he sees a stranger pass his doorway, such a man is never heard to shout 'please come in' (*itfaḍḍal*), nor does he serve tea or food to his guests. Thus, as a man grows rich, his personality changes (*nifsu titaġayyar*) and he comes to be filled with hatred and resentment against everyone around him.

It is believed that another way of becoming rich is to find hidden treasure (*yilagi lageyyaat*), that a long time ago people used to put all their money in boxes and pots and bury them in their fields or hide them in their houses. Now, after buying a house from another family a man may find something hidden away and forgotten, or he may stumble upon a cache while ploughing his fields. Whenever someone in the area buys something thought to be beyond his means, everybody wonders whether he has found a hoard of money or gold.[9]

The poor are also said to envy those better off than themselves, but it is the envy of the rich that is feared because the latter have substance and power. 'The rich are more listened to than the poor' (*ilġani masmuu' 'an ilfagiir*) is meant literally, and just as their voices are stronger, so too is their malice believed to be more effective. This does not mean that everyone in well-to-do households is thought of as envious or malicious; it is only a particular person in such households who is singled out. The villagers' representation of wealth does not apply to particular individuals; rather, it is a representation of the condition itself and, to some degree, every well-to-do household is surrounded with the aura which comes from that state. To be rich is to be set apart; to be full of resentment against others. It is the well-to-do of the village who are thought to be the enforcers of the principle of 'everybody to their lot', which is the regulating idea of the relations to envy. Envy is their means to prevent others from aspiring to become like them and of keeping others in their place. If envy arises whenever a household thinks it has the means of changing its position within the determinate set of relations in the village, it is the well-to-do of the village who stand as the defenders of the determinacy of those relations and, so, as the most likely agents of envy.

The second category of the envious, those to whom a household bears a specific relation, are a different embodiment of the same principle. If envy surrounds the possibility of a challenge to the fixed relations in the village, the likelihood of envy increases with the degree of determinacy of particular relationships. So, for example, neighbours (*jiraan*) are thought to be among the most envious. It is because of neighbours that one must be most careful to protect livestock and domestic animals. There are many stories about the lengths to which people will go to thwart the envy of their neighbours, like the one about the old woman who puts some of her chickens out where everybody can see them and regularly berates them in full public view for not laying eggs. She has other chickens secreted away on her roof, and at night she stealthily collects their eggs. But not stealthily enough, for everybody in her neighbourhood knows about her doings. Of course, the principal problem with neighbours in Naçaawy is that they know all about each others households.

It is precisely because everybody in the village knows everything about everyone else that envy is possible. Strangers are not thought of as likely agents of envy as they are elsewhere (Spooner 1970: 313), because in Naçaawy envy is a relationship between the individual household and the community. The ties of community and the degree to which a fixed relationship between households is expected to endure over time are strongest between neighbours, so they too expect each other to be envious. Again, it is the richer neighbour who is thought to be the more envious. People in Naçaawy pity those who live next to the well-to-do.

Brothers and close relatives are also said to be fiercely envious of each other (cf. Ammar 1954: 61). Once brothers have separated their households they are the first to cast envious glances at each other. It is also believed that the brother who has done better than the others is most likely to envy them. The same is said of the children of brothers (*'iyaal 'amm*). Clearly, these relations involve the greatest number of mutual obligations, the closest associations, and the greatest expectations of equality, especially since, in Islamic law, brothers inherit equally. It is when that axis of the relationship appears to be threatened that the likelihood of envy arises.[10]

Discussion

The constantly heard statement 'we are one', in all its ambiguity, lies at the heart of envy in Naçaawy. First, by drawing the boundaries of the village in relation to the outside world, it demarcates the essential sphere within which envy operates. Envy is possible as a mode of relationship in Naçaawy because of the villagers' sense of equality and oneness and, as I have noted, in relation to the outside world this sense of equality has real foundations. No one in Naçaawy lives off rents. There are no long-standing relationships of tenancy between the villagers, and the most prosperous fellah in Naçaawy, though vastly better off than the poorest, still has to work on the land. The real relations of dependency and subordination lie between the village as a whole and the landlords of the cities. These landlords would never be thought of in terms of envy, even when they come to stay in the village, for they fall outside the categories of the community. For the villagers, their relations with the landlords are of a clearly political kind. But even within Naçaawy it is only a matter of time before a few households cross the shadowy boundary into those regions where political relations replace those of envy.

At the same time, the statement 'we are one', by the emphasis with which it is stated and by its form as an assertion, betrays its recognition of its own negation. Evil eye representations luxuriate around precisely this contradiction; between an asserted equality and objective conditions which make its realization impossible. The contradiction is located in the control of land and the organization of production by households. The villagers' egalitarian ethic is ultimately irreconcilable with a mode of organizing production which is geared towards continuous accumulation in households (e.g., in livestock). The essence of the contradiction is property. Envy in Naçaawy takes the form it does because the ownership of productive resources is vested in households and because the subdivision of property turns brothers and cousins into competitors in production.

On a different scale the same tension between an asserted equality and real inequality lies at the heart of Islamic society. In a way, it provides the dynamic for many of the political upheavals in the Islamic world; it is no coincidence that some egalitarian quasi-socialist movements in the Islamic world are also identified with movements for religious purification. But elsewhere, as in Naçaawy, the contradiction cannot be resolved until it is recognized.

Notes

1. The field research on which this article is based was financed by the Inlaks Foundation. I thank Dr Aly Issa and the Dept. of Anthropology, of the Faculty of Arts, Alexandria, for their generous assistance. Some of the material presented here derives from my D.Phil. dissertation at the University of Oxford. I am grateful to Dr Peter Lienhardt, who supervised the dissertation, and Dr Emrys Peters, who examined it, for their comments and suggestions. The article is a revised version of a paper read at a seminar of the Centre for Development Studies, Trivandrum, and I would like to thank Dr Geeta Sen, Mihir Shah and my other colleagues for their suggestions.
2. The names of the village and the families are pseudonyms.
3. I have followed Mitchell's system of transcription (Mitchell 1978),

with a few modifications. The symbol ç represents the sound sh (as in shirt), corresponding to the letter *çiin*, ġ represents the *ġain*, and the conventional ' the *'ain*. In the dialect of the area studied the *jiim* is pronounced j, not g, and the *qaaf*, g, is not the glottal stop used in urban Egypt. The village dialect also differs from the urban in the conjugation of verbs in the first person singular and plural and on several other points of usage. Words of Arabic origin which appear in the *Oxford English Dictionary* have not been transcribed, though I have changed the *OED* spelling of 'fellaheen' to 'fellahin'.

4. Only close male kin (patrilineally related to the killer), however, are liable to be killed in retaliation.
5. In the village, *fellaḥiin* generally refers to those farmers who hold some land.
6. A feddan is equal to 1.038 acres.
7. Parts of the rice, wheat and maize crops are also given to the agricultural co-operative as payment for fertilizer, insecticides, etc.
8. Ethnographic accounts of the Arab world often suggest that children are the principal objects of envy; probably because ethnographers (e.g. Ammar 1954; Granqvist 1947) come across evil eye beliefs while investigating child rearing practices. If one puts a question such as 'What is likely to attract envy?' to the Naçaawy villagers, children usually come about halfway down the list, while livestock is almost invariably the first to be mentioned.
9. Ibn Khaldun (1978: 301) thought treasure-hunting a problem serious enough to merit prolonged comment: 'Many weak minded persons in cities hope to discover property under the surface of the earth and to make some profit from it. They believe that all the property of the nations of the past was stored underground and sealed with magic talismans.' And, 'The occurrence of finds and treasures in Egypt is explained by the fact that Egypt was in the possession of the Copts for two thousand or more years. Their dead were buried with their possessions of gold, silver, precious stones and pearls. . . . Because of the existence of [treasures in graves] the Egyptians have been concerned with the search for treasures and their discovery' (Ibn Khaldun 1978: 303–4). In Nacaawy, 'finding treasure' is simply a metaphor for absolute chance in economic life.
10. Pocock (1973: 39) ascribes envy between kin in a Gujarati village to expectations of equality. For an altogether different context of such beliefs, see Reminick's (1974) account of evil eye beliefs among the Amhara of Ethiopia.

Bibliography

Ammar, H., *Growing up in an Egyptian Village*, London, 1954.

Antoun, R.T., 'On the Modesty of Women in Arab Muslim Villages: A Study in the Accommodation of Traditions', *American Anthropologist* 70: 671–93, 1968.

Burne, C.S., 'Charm against the Evil Eye', *Folklore* 13: 202, 1902.

Dorson, R.M., *The British Folklorists: A History*, Chicago,1968.

Evans-Pritchard, E.E., *Witchcraft, Oracles and Magic among the Azande*, Oxford, 1937.

Foster, G.M., 'The Anatomy of Envy: A Study of Symbolic Behaviour', *Current Anthropology* 13: 165–86, 1972.

Granqvist, H., *Birth and Childhood among the Arabs*, Helsinki, 1947.

Ibn Khaldun, *The Muqaddimah* (trans. F. Rosenthal and ed. N. J. Dawood), London, 1978.

Lozach, J., and G. Hug, *L'habitat rural en Egypte*, publications de la Societe Royale de Geographie d'Egypte, Cairo, 1930.

Lykiardopoulos, A., 'The Evil Eye: Towards an Exhaustive Study', *Folklore* 92: 221–9, 1981.

Mitchell, T.F., *An Introduction to Egyptian Colloquial Arabic*, Oxford, 1978.

Pocock, D.F., *Mind, Body and Wealth*, Oxford, 1973.

Reminick, R.A., 'The Evil Eye Belief among the Amhara of Ethiopia', *Ethnology* 13: 279–90, 1974.

Rouse, W.H.D., 'Notes from Syria', *Folklore* 6: 172–5, 1895.

Sessions, F., 'Some Syrian Folklore Notes Gathered on Mount Lebanon', *Folklore* 9: 3–19, 1898.

Simpson,H., 'Some Algerian Superstitions Noted among the Shawia Berbers of the Aures Mountains and their Nomad Neighbors', *Folklore* 26: 225–54, 1915.

Spooner, B., 'The Evil Eye in the Middle East', *Witchcraft Confessions and Accusations*, ed. M. Douglas, pp. 311–15, London, 1970.

10 Categories of Labour and the Orientation of the Fellah Economy

ANY FORM of sustained production demands a systematic organization of processes of work, especially if the production of large surpluses is involved. Although, self-evidently, this is no less true of agrarian societies than it is of the industrial, this fact is often overlooked in empirical accounts of agricultural communities, possibly because the staggered rhythms of agricultural work contrast poorly with the immediately visible tautness of the production line. But agrarian rhythms of work have their own equally exacting organizational demands, for they transfer into the axis of time the interlocking of functions which the production line achieves in space. In this sense agrarian forms of work organization and discipline are no less rigorous than the industrial. Yet we are comparatively ignorant of these forms. So much so that it has almost come to be assumed that beyond the household there is virtually no organization of work in agrarian societies.[1]

In general, anthropological and ethnological accounts of production in non-industrial societies have tended to concentrate on technology and techniques (i.e., 'material culture'). As a result much more material is available, for example, on technology in agrarian societies, seen both as a system of meanings and representations as well as a set of material constraints, than there is on the organization of work.[2]

Two likely reasons for this disparity suggest themselves immediately. One is that anthropologists and ethnologists, being themselves usually members of industrial societies, have, on the whole, been guided by the image of the production line — in which work is reduced in a very simple and dramatic way to the performance of certain technical acts — in the description of labour processes in non-industrial societies. The second, which is a corollary of the first, is that their accounts have been founded on an implicit assumption that forms of work are ultimately reducible to technology. Or, in other words, it has been assumed that the description of a technical system is more or less exhaustive of the whole process of labour.

It is of course self-evident that all processes of work are critically related to technology: all technologies generate certain material requirements which must be met if that technology is to operate at all. However, in most cases these requirements can be satisfied by a very wide variety of social combinations. The constraints of technology, therefore, can only tell us what must be done; they can tell us nothing, or very little, about those who do it, what their relations are, or how they are organized, and these relations constitute the process of work no less critically than individual technical acts. Yet, the privileged position accorded to technology and techniques in the description of work processes means that the totality of relations which properly constitute a system of labour often comes to be excluded from the account by the assumptions which surround the notion of work.

In this paper I have attempted to describe the structure of social relationships which constitutes the labour process among a community of fellahin[3] in the north-western corner of the Nile Delta. The system of production in this area is neither an archaism nor a threatened form of life; on the contrary, it is an extremely versatile and efficient form of agriculture which over the last century, has responded swiftly to global changes and in the process transformed itself so that today, in terms of yield per acre, it is arguably the most productive form of agriculture in the world. However, it is the argument of this paper that the structure of labour in this community is a means of both resisting and appropriating some of the forms of relationship which have come to be synonymous with 'modernity', and that finally, the system as a whole constitutes a commentary on the very nature of social relations.

1

The material presented here was collected in the course of a year's fieldwork, conducted between 1980 and 1981,[4] in a village, *balad*, and a nearbv hamlet, *'izba*, in the governorate of Beheira in north-western Egypt. The village, Nashawy al-Jadida,[5] then had a population of about 1,700 souls, living in 215 households. The people of the village are divided into a number of agnatic 'families', *'ā'ilat* (sing. *'ā'ila*), of which the Badawi is the largest, adding up to almost a third of the village.

The village is situated close to what was once one of the largest estates in Egypt. The estate was distributed among the people of the area during the land reforms which followed the 'revolution' of 1952. About a quarter of the total area cultivated by the villagers is owned by households in the village, a little less than half is either rented or sharecropped, and the rest is land that has been redistributed by the government under various programmes. Today about two-thirds of the households in the village hold land in one way or another, about one-sixth are landless and derive their income mainly from agricultural labour, and the rest make their livings from crafts, trades, shopkeeping, etc.

About 30 per cent of the total area cultivated by the villagers is owned by urban landlords. This land is let to the villagers under rent or sharecropping agreements. Very few households in the village own more than ten feddans[6] and most landholding households have only about four. Most households own only a fraction of their total landholdings. Even the largest landholders cultivate a large part of their landholdings under tenancy and sharecropping agreements, and in this the richest fellahin in the village are in the same situation as the poorest. There are few tenancy agreements between the villagers and those that exist are mainly to the advantage of the tenant compared to similar agreements between villagers and urban landlords. Villagers let out land only when they are constrained by circumstances. These are usually demographic rather than strictly economic circumstances: for example, a widow with minor children usually has no option but to let out her land. Such land is usually let to close relatives.

Thus, even though there are important economic differences within the village, there are no permanent relations of tenancy between the villagers. The landlords from whom the villagers rent land for long periods are all absentee who live in various Egyptian and even European cities. Equally significant is the fact that there is only one man in the village who is permanently in the employ of another household. Thus the villagers often say of themselves 'we are all one' and this is at least metaphorically true, for none of the economic disparities of the village are at all significant when compared to the vast gap between the villagers and the landlords of the city.

The hamlet of Laṭaifa, which is about fifteen minutes' walk from Nashawy has a population of about 220, all of whom are members of one family, *'ā'ila*. All the households in the hamlet own land (between two and seven feddans) and the economic differences between them are slight. The people of Laṭaifa are linked by a particularly strong ethic of family unity.

2

It is a striking feature of life in the area around Nashawy that people place an enormous value on their labour power. It is commonly said in the area: 'No one works for nothing here', *maḥaddish ba-yishtaghal balāsh hina*, and this is an evident truth. No one rushes to unburden friends or relatives of heavy loads — that too is labour of a kind and people are much more willing to dispense hospitality than lend a shoulder out of turn. The attitude is so marked that it is common to see little children bargaining furiously over their wages for some small task. It is folk wisdom in Nashawy that nothing is free, that nothing is given without return, and if this is true of material objects it is no less true of the sweat of one's brow.

The care that the people of this area take to safeguard their labour power is, at least in part, a product of a more general set of representations which regulate the relationship between individuals and society. For example: although people here are familiar with the classical terminology of succession in Islamic law, a person's inheritance is spoken of as his or her *ḥagg* (classical Arabic *ḥaqq*). In this context the word is used in the sense of 'right' but the scope of its meanings also covers the notions of 'justice' and 'truth'. In the context of inheritance the notion of *ḥagg* refers to an individual's rightful due, or what is owed to him by the past.[7]

The word *ḥagg* is also commonly used in the sense of 'price'. Thus 'the price of tea' for example is *ḥagg ishshayy*. But, used in this way the term implies more than a mere monetary equivalence in a system of such equivalences. Rather, it indicates what an object can command by virtue of its inherent worth. Thus a man's blood-money and a woman's bride-wealth are also spoken of as their *ḥagg*. *Ḥagg* is the central judicial concept in feuds and disputes in the area. All disputes therefore concern 'right' in the triple sense of truth, justice and individual right. Thus, for example, a dispute, whether it is over inheritance (*ḥagg*), blood-money (*ḥagg*), or bride-wealth (*ḥagg*), is equally concerned with individual rights, as well as truth and justice.

Thus, in Nashawy the notion of *ḥagg* is the fulcrum of the relationship between individuals and society; it defines not only that which is due to them but also the store they set on themselves and what they think of their own worth. The man who stands up for his rights is said to be a man whose 'blood is heavy', *dammu tāgil*; a man to be feared and respected if not loved. In contrast, the man who is incapable of claiming his rightful due is one whose 'blood is light', *dammu khafif*, an entertaining man perhaps, but lightweight and of little account in the world. The same accounting extends to an individual's labour power. A man or woman's 'sweat', *'arag*, is an integral and valuable part of his or her person. A man who gives his labour away too easily, therefore, is a man who sets little value by himself.

This awareness of the value of an individual's labour power is all the more acute for the fact that the fellahin have long had a monetary standard for evaluating their capacity for labour. The introduction of cotton into Egypt in the 1820s had the effect of rapidly monetizing the economy (Mabro: 7). This phenomenon did not limit itself to the urban economy but rapidly filtered into rural areas. Today in Nashawy all goods and services can be bought for money, and all transactions in the local shops and weekly markets are in cash. The introduction of cash crops also tied the Egyptian economy into the world market in the first part of the nineteenth century, so that by the 1860s Egyptian agriculture was responding to the fluctuations caused in the world market by the American Civil War and the subsequent fall in American cotton production (Baer 1962: 21: Mabro: 7). For the same reason new methods of agricultural organization were introduced very early into Egypt. The large estates of pre-revolutionary Egypt, unlike Russian or Sicilian estates, were organized on highly efficient, capitalistic lines, often employing the most advanced forms of technology then available (Mabro: 62). So the Egyptian fellahin, especially those who lived in close proximity to large, efficient landed estates, as did the people of Nashawy and Laṭaifa, have long had contacts with advanced agricultural techniques and methods of organization. This accounts at least partly perhaps, for the great eagerness with which the fellahin of the area adopt hybrid seeds, fertilizers, methods of rotation and so on. Today the yield of cotton per acre in the area around Nashawy is almost double the comparable rate in the U.S.A. The people of Nashawy have therefore long been adept at using modern agricultural techniques. Indeed, it might well be said that given their capital constraints, they have used them more skilfully than farmers anywhere else.

Equally, they have been familiar with a monetized economy and monetary standards of reckoning for several generations. Today in Nashawy even young children are aware of exactly how much money a day's labour is worth, how much of that is due to their parents and how much they can keep to themselves. Naturally this has only intensified their awareness of the value of their labour power.

3

Equally, history plays a critical part in the villagers' estimation of the value of their labour, at least in that their collective memory serves as a constant reminder to them of how, in the past, that value was violated.

Before 1952 most of the land around Nashawy belonged to a Pasha's estate. The village was not itself 'tied' to the estate and a few of the villagers, notably the Badawi, owned some land, but the village as a whole derived a large part of its income from the estate. As far as I could ascertain, every household in the village, apart from that of the *'omda* (headman), sent men and children to work for daily wages on the estate. Some villagers also cultivated plots on the estate outside the cotton season. Even those who are among the richest and most important men in the village today, were sent out to work on the estate when they were children.

The experience of working on the estates weighs heavily to this day on the memories of the middle-aged and elderly people of the village: when they talk of the past it is usually of the beatings they were given by the overseers of the estate, of his right to deprive them of their wages if he saw fit, and of how little they were paid for their labours (between three and five piastres for a day's work). There is nothing rosy about the villagers' description of their past. The village headman plays a similar role in the villagers' memories.

The post of the headman had been held by one small branch of the Badawi as far back as anyone can remember, until the last incumbent was defeated by a member of another family a few years ago. The Badawi headmen, whose children have all migrated to cities now, were the largest landowners in the village, and they made free use of their powers[8] to conscript the villagers into cultivating their land. The headman also had the power to recruit men for the Nile corvée and the villagers remember the threat of recruitment being used to extort money.

The villagers ascribe this 'oppression', *ẓulm*, to the general circumstances of the country as they were then. To them the headmen (*il-'omad*), the Pashas (*il-bāshāwāt*) and their estates, the monarchy (*il-malakiyya*), and the imperialists (*il-musta-'mirīn*), form a complete system each part of which is inextricably linked with the others. They say that all of them together enforced the most hateful aspect of their past — being made to work against their will. In their reckoning of time the 'revolution' of 1952 (*as-sowra*) forms a division of epochs almost parallel to that between Islam and the *Jāhiliyya* (the times of ignorance). Today, though they are often critical of the regime, they say 'there is liberty here', *fīh ḥurriyya hina*.

There can be little doubt that the latter sentiment is deeply felt, for it was often stated to me in contexts where it could not have been intended to mislead. This is a matter of some surprise, for the villagers do not necessarily make much use of the conventional freedoms available to them. But for the villagers the liberty they refer to is a real one, for it consists primarily in the freedom to work as they please; in other words, that they cannot be made to work against their will, because, as they say, contrasting the bureaucratic certainties of today with the arbitrariness of the past: 'Everything is official now', *kulla ḥāja rasmī innahārda*. This is not merely an abstract freedom: it concerns the right, of immense importance in their day-to-day lives, to sell or do what they will with their labour. Thus, as the villagers say, today no one works for nothing. When this fieldwork was conducted, the daily wage rate for a man varied between £E 1.50 to £E 3.00 a day, even though the 1952 Agrarian Reform Act stipulated a minimum rate of only sixty piastres. By contrast many salaried employees of the government with university degrees, earn less than £E 30 a month.

4

However, this intense awareness of the value of individual labour power is only one of the dominant elements of the structure that orders the organization of work in Nashawy. The other element is the diametrically opposed principle of 'co-operation', *ta'āwun*. Thus, when the villagers contrast their way of life to life in the cities, they say: 'We all help each other here; it is not as it is in the cities. There is co-operation here', *iḥna bi-nissā 'idu ba'ḍ, mish zayy il-mudun, fīh ta'āwun hina*. The most significant phrase, the one that is most often repeated, is: 'There is co-operation here'. For the villagers the principle of co-operation (*ta'āwun*) — the willingness to work together — is an essential element in their definition of themselves as a community.

So when the inhabitants of a settlement in this area say of their village or hamlet: 'We are all one' (*iḥna kullena wāḥid*), they are not merely mouthing a pious sentiment. In fact, the statement 'we are all one' is the formula which makes the collective life of the village possible and also gives it a sharply defined symbolic form.

In the area around Nashawy, as in many parts of the Middle East, every settlement has a communal hall, usually attached to it mosque, which is known as the 'guest house', *maḍiafa*. When a man or a senior woman dies, every household in his or her settlement sends a tray of food and a representative, usually the head of the household, to the guest house. The food is sent, the villagers say, in order to 'help' the bereaved household in providing hospitality for the guests from other settlements who come to condole on such occasions — hence the term 'guest house'.

This is a form of reasoning, much in evidence in Nashawy's exegesis of its social self, in which the seductive language of practical utility serves to mask a statement that is of an entirely symbolic nature. The truth is that it would actually be considered shameful, *'aib*, in the extreme for a guest from another settlement to remain in the guest house when the meal is actually served. This is, of course, a well-known rule of etiquette and everybody who goes to another settlement to mourn, apart from the stray anthropologist, makes sure that they leave the guest house well before sunset. So the meal that is said to be for mourners from other settlements becomes, in effect, a feast of communion for the whole village, assembled by proxy. The absence of the guest plays a curiously inverted symbolic role in this feast: it is in relation to that figure, the figure of the stranger, *gharīb*, that the village affirms its unity in the face of bereavement.

The same pattern is repeated on a number of other occasions. For example feasts of reconciliation, organized on very similar lines, are sometimes held in the guest house to mark the end of blood feuds. Some settlements also hold collective meals in the guest house to celebrate important religious feasts. Thus, though settlements in this area are often continuous and have no discernible boundaries, socially their borders are clearly drawn: a household belongs to the settlement to the guest house of which it sends its tray.

These feasts constitute the ceremonial representation of the principle 'we are all one'. The principle itself is founded on the belief in the equality and unity all Muslims. The mosque therefore also plays a crucial role in defining the boundaries of a community: every settlement is also a congregation. The villagers often say of the whole of the Islamic world, and indeed of the whole of mankind: 'we are all one'. But the nearer excludes the further, and for its inhabitants the village stands as a metaphor for the whole of the Islamic *umma* and beyond that, of human gregariousness itself.

5

The relationship between these two elements — co-operation on the one hand and the consciousness of the value of individual labour on the other — constitutes the structure which regulates the organization of work in Nashawy. The complex articulation of these two elements generates a range of different categories of labour and it is to the description of these that we shall now turn.

Work and the household: 'pooling' 'and 'service'

The basic unit of production in Nashawy is the household. The members of a household own land in common, cultivate it together and make their purchases out of a common purse. It is usual in the village for married men with grown children to live with their fathers if they are alive. Although households are usually divided after the death of their founding members, there are a few cases in which married men have continued to live in joint households with their brothers after their parents' death.[9] When a household splits, its possessions, including land, are always divided; the division of a household is therefore synonymous with the division of its productive functions.

It is said of the work of brothers, sisters and lineal cousins who live in the same household, that 'they co-operate (with each other)', *bi-yita'āwanū*. The term used for co-operation in this sense, *ta'āwun*, is an overarching category which refers to a whole range of work. At the same time, in certain marked contexts it is also used to refer to a mode of organizing work which is specific to the household. For convenience I shall refer to this form of co-operation — the organization of household labour — as 'pooled' work.

The fact that household labour is classified under the rubric of co-operation is significant: it indicates that though labour is pooled within the household, it is not for that reason undifferentiated. The meaning of pooled labour is best illustrated by the example of women's work.

It has been noted above that the formation of a household in Nashawy is synonymous with the division of property. The laws of the Shari'a give women certain rights in this property since women inherit from their fathers in the ratio of one to two in relation to their brothers. However, Islam recognizes two sources of law. While the Shari'a is the superior of the two, the second, *'urf*, custom, is also recognized as legitimate so long as it does not contradict the law of the Shari'a.

In Nashawy, as in most of rural Egypt, Shari'a law is observed in principle in that women are allotted rights in their father's property in due mathematical proportions. But it is the custom that women do not actually claim their shares. Instead, usually, they formally entrust their land to one of their brothers or patrilateral cousins. Thereafter it is recognized that the productive property of her brother's or cousin's household includes her share, and this gives her certain rights in that household. For example, it entitles her to regular gifts from the produce of that household's land. But perhaps the most important claim it confers is that it gives her the unconditional right to join, and live with dignity, in that household whenever she pleases. So, a woman who has been divorced or widowed for example, always has the option of joining the household to which she has entrusted her share of her father's productive property. Thus, in her lifetime a woman's rights in productive property always remain within her natal household or in some branch of it.

In her marital household a woman's property rights are limited to household goods bought with her bride-wealth; she has no claims on its productive property. By law a woman is entitled only to maintenance, *nafaqa*, which includes food, clothing and lodging, from her husband (Fyzee: 111; Schacht: 167; Pearl: 46, 65–7). In fact, women often turn to their brothers rather than their husbands when they want new clothes, or for financial support when they fall ill. Should a woman be divorced she is entitled to take her household goods back with her.

These two forms of property correspond to two different

forms of labour. In a household where a woman has productive property, she is expected to perform labour which adds to the income of the household. So, for example, in poorer households, divorced, separated and unmarried women who live with their brothers are expected to work for wages, and to contribute to the common income of the household. In better-off households women in such positions are often bought sewing-machines and are expected to earn money for the household by tailoring. These forms of labour are treated as a normal part of the pooling of household labour. The important point is that women in these circumstances are not usually expected to contribute any domestic labour within the household.

In the household of her marriage, however, a woman's work consists of domestic labour. The household's income on the other hand, is the responsibility of her husband and his brothers and sisters. If a man should for some reason become unable to provide for his wife and children, she can legitimately leave him and return to her brothers and later negotiate a divorce. The domestic labour a woman renders her husband and his household is categorized as 'service', *khidma*, and is thereby distinguished from the pooled labour of the natal members of the household.

It sometimes happens that a woman remains with her husband even when he is incapable of maintaining her, and works to earn money for both of them. But in these circumstances her labour is clearly distinguished from pool labour, for her husband will always say of her that 'she [works to] help me' (*heyya bi-tisā'idnī*), in apology for his inability to meet his obligations and recognition of her generosity.

Gender-specific categories, such as 'men's work' and 'women's work', are often used to classify processes of labour in agrarian societies. In the context of the fellah economy it would be misleading to allow a privileged position to categories such as those, based as they are on purely external or functional criteria of classification. For while it is true that there are only certain categories of work that a woman may do among the fellahin, those categories are also subject to a prior principle of classification, so that the work a woman actually does is determined primarily by her relationship to the household in which she is resident, and only secondarily by her gender. According to the nature of that relationship her work is geared to different ends and accompanied by different rights. In this, gender belongs at best to a secondary order of classification: the basic principle which orders women's work as well as men's is the nature of their relationship with the productive property of their households of residence.

Since residence in Nashawy is usually patrilocal, the issue is very straightforwardly resolved for most men: they have shares in the productive property of the households they live in and therefore they work to produce for those households. But the operation of the principle, as always with any rule of social ordering, is seen at its clearest when it is applied to anomalies: in this instance, the few cases in the village in which married men live with their wives' fathers. The men who are in that position naturally have no share in the productive property of their households of residence. But the work they do is the same as that of the other men of the household. However, their work is not considered to be part of that household's pooled labour; instead these men too are said to be rendering 'service', *khidma*. The distinction between the work these men do and the work their wives' brothers do is clearly not based upon the tasks they actually perform. The distinction is based on the fact that they have no share in the household's productive property, and it is in this sense that their labour is formally identified with the labour of a woman in her husband's household. This position is considered shameful, *'aib*, for a man. But the source of this shame does not, I think, lie in an imputation of femininity. Rather, it has its origins in the expropriation of productive labour; in its denial of a man's *ḥagg*. It is worth noting that 'service' is not in itself considered shameful for a man. On the contrary, work that is voluntarily performed in order to maintain the tomb of the village saint, for example, a category of labour that is also classified as 'service', is considered the finest kind of work. But since, within the household, a man does not have the option of rendering 'service', he must perforce contribute productive labour to his wife's father's household, even though he has no share in its productive property. It is this that creates his anomalous position within that household.

Among the fellahin therefore the household consists of a number of people who stand in certain specific relationships with a given piece of productive property. It is the nature of those relationships, rather than gender, which determine what category of work each individual will perform.

To return to pooled labour: the work of the household, which includes work on the fields as well as in the house, is done without any exact reckoning of how much labour is contributed by each member. This is in the nature of such work, for it would be impossible to tot up exact accounts where one man has to feed the cattle and another has to water the fields. Rather, the pooling of labour is a combination of functions under the direction of the head of the household. But this is not to say that individuals in a household are not aware of how much labour they are contributing in relation to the others. In fact, everybody keeps an eye on everybody else to make sure that they do their fair share. Laziness on the part of a senior member is often considered an adequate reason for dividing the household. The work ethic of the household thus also ensures a certain intensity of effort on the part of every member.

The pooling of labour therefore does not imply that individuals are willing to forget the value of their labour in the context of the household; rather, it is a temporary sinking of individual differences for the mutual benefit of those involved. It is significant, for example, that the collective meals of mourning, *ma'āza*, held in the village guest house are also said to be 'co-operation [pooling] for good', *ta'āwun bi-lkhair*. In these ceremonies too the whole village is represented as a unity in which all differences of family and status are temporarily submerged.

'Help'

A second category of co-operative work is help, *musā'ada*, usually extended to neighbours and kin. The distinctive feature of this kind of labour is that formally, at least, it is voluntarily offered. For the most part labour offered as help goes towards building houses; it rarely has to do with cultivation. It is not, however, for that reason any less demanding: house-building in Nashawy is often a very arduous and lengthy business.

Usually when people in Nashawy make bricks or build houses they hire a few workers, some of whom are skilled in these tasks, to work with them, but in addition a large number of neighbours and relatives always come to help. On the whole paid workers and those who come to help do roughly similar work, yet they are always strictly distinguished from each other. Again this distinction clearly has nothing to do with the nature of the work the groups do; the difference lies in their relationships with the owner of the house.

The obligation to help a neighbour or kinsman does not stop at physical labour. A man who is building a house also relies on his kinsmen in the village and his neighbours, to contribute to his project by providing beds and help to feed the hired workers and relatives who come from other villages. This is no mean obligation, for in such circumstances people are expected to provide elaborate and expensive meals.

Some other kinds of labour also fall under the category of help. The odd bit of work a man may do for those whose fields border on to his own is said to be help. Equally the work a man may do occasionally to help his parents-in-law is also considered help. Help is most often contributed to kin by marriage, *nasā'ib*, and neighbours, *jīrān*. It is common to help fathers- and brothers-in-law with house-building, and people often take advantage of such occasions to visit their sisters and daughters.

The essential difference between help and other ways of

organizing work is that it is, in principle, voluntary. The fellahin say, when contrasting help with other such forms, that people are free to choose when they wish to offer help even if they happen to be reciprocating labour that had been previously contributed to them. So, if a man is asked to help on the grounds that he had been helped in the past, he will be within his rights to say that he is too busy or that he has something else to do, though of course this can only be a deferment of his obligation. Naturally therefore, most of the work that is classified as help has to do with occasional jobs like house-building or brick-making. As a system, help cannot cope with everyday tasks or with work which has to be planned and organized over extended periods.

Help is a kind of gift then, and is therefore subject to the general rules of gift-giving. It is voluntary in form, though given in the expectation of eventual, if not immediate or exact return.

'The system of fellowship'

The third mode of organizing labour through co-operation is central to the economic functioning of the area; the fellahin call it the system of fellowship, *tanẓīmat azzimāl.* The system is based on an exact exchange of labour between households, and it functions in seasons in which there is an increased demand for labour. When the members of a landowning household decide to harvest their rice, for instance, they send word to certain relatives, neighbours and friends who then send one or more men from their households to work with them. In turn when those households decide to harvest their rice, the first 'host' household must contribute exactly the amount of labour it received from each of its 'guests'. If one of those households had sent two men, the host household must send two men in return, and so on. So on one day a household acquires a debt of a certain number of working days and pays it off over the rest of the harvesting season.[10]

In large villages each household makes its fellowship

arrangements independently — there are no fixed groups of households which form fellowship units, though closely associated households do, on the whole, tend to have the same partners. In Nashawy there is no set pattern to the constitution of groups of fellows: they consist of varying proportions of lineal and affinal kin, neighbours and friends. In small settlements all the fellah households form a single fellowship unit together.

It is worth emphasizing that the relations of fellowship obtain between households, not individuals. A household may send any of its men to work for its fellows; it is not under an obligation to send a particular man. As a rule each household sends one man to work with its partners. The villagers call this the principle of 'one from every household', *wāḥid min kulla dār*, a principle which also applies to the organization of mourning ceremonies. However, when a household plays host, all the working men of that household go out to work with the fellowship group. When reciprocating labour, the working men of a household take it in turns to go out to work: being from the same unit of production, they are, in that context, interchangeable.

The system of fellowship enforces strictly equal exchange. For example, if one member of a group of fellows has more land than the others, his partners will demand that he hires additional workers when they come to work on his land. The insistence on exact reciprocity is carried down to apparently trivial details. When a group is harvesting rice, for example, the workers are all careful to make sure that they are spaced at regular intervals so that no one has a larger area to cover than the others. This insistence on equal exchange is of course strictly in keeping with the parsimony with which the fellahin approach all matters concerned with labour.

Once entered into functionally, the system of fellowship is obligatory and binding Therefore it is ideally suited to the needs of a system of production based on the household, for it provides a reliable means of making large groups of workers available at times when a single household cannot cope with the work. As such the system of fellowship, unlike the pattern of help exchanges, is necessarily obligatory, since if it were not so it would be impossible for any household to plan ahead. This system permits co-operation over extended periods and in this sense it provides a means of 'banking' labour.

It is the duty of every household which participates in fellowship exchanges to feed those who come to work with them when they play host. These meals are carried out to the fields by the women of the host household in large trays. So, although women do not participate directly in fellowship exchanges, no household can join in these exchanges without the active participation of its women. The system thus calls upon the household in its role of provider as well as producer: every household prides itself on the food it serves to its fellows and people boast at length of the size of the fish or the price of the meat they have served.

Only landholding households participate in the system of fellowship since, self-evidently, landless people would have nothing to gain from the system. However, in large villages most working groups consist of hired workers as well as fellowship partners. In small hamlets workers are rarely hired.

Strictly speaking the system of fellowship consists only of labour exchanges and in its normal functioning it excludes monetary transactions. However, the semantic significance of the system arises precisely from the fact that it is in a closely articulated relationship of contrast with the system of monetary exchanges. Thus, in certain circumstances, for example, when a household is unable for some reason to reciprocate labour on a particular day, it is required to send the sum of money needed to hire a worker for the day. The system of fellowship therefore is not a simple barter system: the workers who participate in it are always aware of the monetary value of their labour and its translatability into corresponding commodities. Rather, the exclusion of monetary transactions from the system in the general run of its functioning adds another dimension of value, a moral one, to these exchanges. The system of fellowship is not therefore only a method of organizing labour: it is also, in the broadest sense, a means of excluding impersonal criteria of value from certain domains of social life.

6

The fourth method of organizing labour in Nashawy falls outside the category of co-operation, *ta'āwun*, and is in direct contrast with it. This category, work, *shughl*, derives from the verbal root *shaghal*, to work, which also produces the derived verbal form *ishtaghal* (to work). Any kind of work that is paid for with money falls under the category of work. The categorization of work therefore has nothing to do with the nature of the work itself for any kind of work can be done for money in Nashawy. However, in general it is the more intensive kinds of agricultural work which offer good daily wages and therefore attract large numbers of hired workers. Many men work for money during the rice-transplanting season and the rice- and wheat-harvesting seasons, but the bulk of the labour for all operations connected with the rice and wheat crops is recruited through fellowship exchanges. It is in relation to the cotton crop that exchanges in money are most evident: in the months of June and July, when the schools are closed, the agricultural co-operatives organize large numbers of children into work forces for picking leaves with worms on them from cotton plants, and pay them a daily wage. A number of men also work as overseers at that time. Later in the season large numbers of workers are needed to pick cotton, and then again most of the workers are hired for daily wages.

There are about thirty-five landless households in Nashawy which live entirely off agricultural wages, and most of the men who work for daily wages belong to these households. These men may be sure of regular employment in the months of April and May, when rice is transplanted, August and September when rice and cotton are harvested, and February, when wheat is harvested and cotton planted. At other times few people need to hire labour, so men who make a living from agricultural wages seek employment in towns and government farms at those times of the year. Almost every fellah household in the village, no matter how much land it holds, sends its children out to earn money by picking cotton. The kind of work women may do for daily wages in Nashawy includes planting cotton and vegetables, and transplanting rice. Women never take part in the actual harvesting of a crop but they do most of the threshing of grains and beans, and they also make hay and straw.

7

The fact that most exchanges connected with cotton, not only those of labour, are conducted in money has partly to do with the functional requirements of the cotton crop since the cultivation of cotton requires a great deal of labour. But equally, unlike other crops, cotton is thought of in straightforwardly monetary terms. It would be simplistic to ascribe this entirely to the bare economic fact that cotton is a cash crop; it is also related to the history of agriculture in Egypt and the fellah's representation of his economy.

The large estates of pre-revolutionary Egypt made their profits principally from a single cash crop. In the Delta this crop was cotton. Consequently, cotton was the only crop organized and supervised by the management of the estate. The fellahin were permitted to cultivate other crops on their own, though a certain proportion of these had to be surrendered to the estate. The agricultural co-operatives founded after 1952 took over some of the purely functional principles of the estates. An agricultural co-operative, *jam'iyya ta'āwuniyya zirā'iyya*, oversees cultivation in a village, *qarya*, which usually consists of a number of settlements spread over a considerable area, and is better likened to a district than to a village as such. While the fellahin who form the membership of the co-operatives individually own their land (within the provisions of the land reform laws), the trained agricultural engineers who staff the co-operatives supervise the rotation of crops, the distribution of fertilizers, spraying of insecticides and so on. These engineers are recruited by the Ministry of Agriculture and they form a link between the co-operatives and the Central government. The co-operatives also provide credit and eventually buy the cotton from the fellahin at set rates.

The staff of the co-operatives organizes and oversees the cultivation of cotton in each village. The cultivation of other crops, such as rice, wheat, alfalfa, maize, and vegetables is much less closely supervised. The co-operatives have rules of rotation for these crops, but within certain classes of crops the individual farmer is free to choose what he will plant. All fellahin take care to grow some wheat, rice, maize, alfalfa and vegetables as far as the pattern of rotation on their lands will allow. Some part of the rice and wheat crops are given to the co-operatives in payment for advances of fertilizers and insecticide. Apart from that, most households keep the bulk of these crops for their own consumption, some sell large amounts in the market, while others sell none at all, depending on the size of their crop relative to the number of people in their households. Every landholding household, however, does its best to keep at least enough wheat, rice and maize to see it through the year. The point is not how much grain or vegetables the fellahin actually sell so much as the fact that they do not see the production of these crops as geared principally 'for the market', *lil-sūg*. Instead, they are said to be 'for the house', *lil-bait*. So while it is common to see women of fellah households selling vegetables in local markets and towns, this is principally because some vegetables have to be harvested at one time. Since the fellahin have no means of storing vegetables for long periods marketing them is simply a means of providing vegetables for the household over the season. With the money made by selling vegetables on one day the household buys vegetables at the weekly market for the rest of the season. As a rule the fellahin around Nashawy do not grow any one vegetable in a quantity large enough to market profitably, with the possible exception of carrots. They grow a little of many different kinds of vegetables in order to give their diet variety. When it comes to vegetables fellahin make up their minds as to what and how much they will plant by considering the needs of their households, not the market. Cotton, on the other hand, is grown exclusively for cash.

The real significance of cultivation 'for the house' is best illustrated by the fellah's choice of crops. For purposes of rotation, agricultural co-operatives divide the land under their jurisdictions into three parts. In summer cotton is compulsorily grown on one of those parts, another is given over to rice, and on the third the individual farmer is permitted to grow rice or vegetables as he pleases. Much of the bread of this region is made from maize flour and fellahin who have the right category of land usually plant maize on the better part of it.

However, if instead they were to grow only vegetables on these plots, they could easily make an overall profit, for many vegetables fetch high prices in the local markets, while maize flour is cheap and easily available. That this is a feasible alternative is recognized: fellahin with very small plots of land who need cash for their day-to-day expenses often go in for this pattern of cropping. But these fellahin lie on the fringe of the peasantry: no substantial fellah would think of buying grain in the market when he could grow it for himself, even if he could thereby make a profit, in monetary terms. As the fellah conceives of his economy, it is wasteful to spend money on everyday needs such as food, and the absolute waste involved in buying maize in the market, would, in his eyes, far outweigh the value of any profit he could make in this fashion.

The fellah household prides itself on its self-sufficiency and its ability to feed itself. Fellahin boast that they always have everything that they wish to eat in their houses, so that they can afford to be generous and hospitable. They contrast this with the lives of people in the cities who, they say, are 'miserly because they have to buy everything for money', *humma bukhala 'aleshān humma bi-yishtarū kulla ḥāja bi-filūs*. Fellah households have everything they need by way of food at home: chickens, ducks, geese, guinea-pigs, pigeons, grain, vegetables, and milk from their cows and buffaloes. They spend very little on fuel, for their fields produce even that in the form of dry cotton plants and straw. The only things they have to buy for daily consumption are tea, sugar, spices and cooking oil, and in their own way all these things assume a special significance simply because they have to be bought with money. When inviting strangers into their houses people say: 'Come and have tea with us: we have sugar', *ta'āla tashrab shayy 'andena; 'andena sukkar*. A man's generosity is judged by the strength of the tea he makes for his guests and the amount of sugar he puts into it. Apart from these things, fellahin only spend cash on life-cycle ceremonies, gifts and visits to sisters and daughters married outside the village and finally, the *ḥajj*, which is the crowning event of every successful fellah's career. The fellahin pity townspeople and others who have to spend money on their daily needs and things temporary. And for the landless the most eloquent sign of their deprivation is the fact that they have to buy grain in the market.

In his study of a village in the Aswan region, at the other end of Egypt, Hamed Ammar noted: 'It is believed that bread made out of home grown crops is more lasting and sufficing than that made out of seeds bought at the market, as there is more *baraka* — holiness and sufficiency — in the former kind. Even those few farmers with comparatively large-sized farms who have recently taken up the cultivation of cash crops like cotton and sugar cane, still reserve the major part of their land for corn . . . "From where are you going to eat?" is a question invariably asked by the villagers of any of them who entertains the idea of growing cotton on the small farm' (Ammar: 33). In much the same way, the fellahin in Nashawy argue that there is no profit in using money from a cash crop to buy grain because, for them, money is a means of material growth and increase, not to be squandered on everyday necessities.

The fact that the fellahin try to avoid spending money on grain, etc. is not so much the result of an absolute shortage of cash as it is the product of a belief in how such cash as is available to them can best be used. They consider that money has been well used only when it has been invested productively. It is significant that often when cash exchanges do occur in Nashawy, as, for example, in the cash contributions that are offered at weddings, *nugūṭ*, they are geared towards return, if not increase. But, for the fellahin, cash in itself is simply a means — it does not grow of itself. For them, the means of enrichment and material growth is thought to be livestock.

Whenever a fellah has some cash to spare he buys a calf, or a young buffalo or even a kid or lamb. If his money falls short he may go into partnership, *ishtarak bīh*, with a relative or a friend, or else he may buy chickens, ducks, guinea-pigs or rabbits instead. Having bought, for example, a calf, he will fatten it for a year, and then sell it for a handsome profit to a butcher or livestock dealer, sometimes doubling the initial investment. With his profit he may buy two more calves, or even a cow, for a cow, or cow-buffalo, is the very image of productivity and material increase for the fellahin.

Parents often put aside a duckling or a gosling for little girls in the hope that through a series of lucky sales it will over time, 'grow' into a calf or cow, which the girl will be able to sell for money at the time of her marriage. Ammar quotes a proverb from Aswan which is exactly similar to several proverbs current in Nashawy: 'My mother gave me a chicken, the chicken bought me a goose, the goose bought me a small goat, the goat bought me a sheep, the sheep bought me a small donkey, the donkey bought me a cow and the cow bought me a *kirat*'[11] (Ammar: 22).

The importance that the fellahin assign to livestock has little to do with the part they play in production. Though cattle and buffaloes are often used as draught animals, as far as possible the fellahin try to hire tractors to do the ploughing, because, they say, ploughing 'tires' an animal and reduces its value — an exhausted cow or buffalo cannot give milk or bear calves. Often when fellahin buy modern water pumps it is in order to spare their livestock the exhausting labour of drawing water with the traditional Persian water-wheels.

The landless of Nashawy say of the fellahin that 'the piastre [which comes from] cotton stays in their hands', *il-girsh bi-ta' guṭn yistanna fī yidehum*, for with that money they buy livestock and with the money they make by selling livestock they buy more land. So, they say, 'land begets land and property begets property', *il-arḍ bi-tajīb arḍ wa-milk bi-yajīb milk.* This constitutes, in effect, a systematic summary of the fellah's domestic economy and the patterns of growth towards which it is oriented: grain and vegetables grown on household land provide sustenance, the cotton crop provides the dynamic element in the circle through cash, the cash is used to buy live- stock, and the livestock is eventually sold in the hope of making enough profit to invest in more land, and so on. However, since land is astronomically expensive in the area, fellahin who do actually profit from this cycle of investment often go on to invest in other enterprises as well — chicken runs, small shops, dairy farming, and, of course, more livestock.

Naturally only a few households do ultimately profit from this pattern of investment, since livestock is notoriously subject to accident and disease. The fellah's belief in livestock as a means of material growth cannot therefore be a result of actual experience for, in all probability, very few households do ultimately make a profit from the process of trading in livestock.

However, the economy of the fellah household is wholly oriented towards this pattern of investment. As we have seen, for the fellahin the conservation of cash is a higher priority than quick profits through variations in the crop cycle. This becomes even clearer when it comes to the cultivation of alfalfa. For the purposes of rotation alfalfa is in the same category of crops as peas and beans. Both peas and beans fetch high prices in the market, while alfalfa is a fodder crop from which the fellah makes no money as such. Alfalfa can also be bought locally so that a fellah could make a profit by growing peas and beans on his land while buying alfalfa from others. But every fellah household prefers to grow its own alfalfa, for the cultivation of alfalfa is thought to be an essential complement to profits through livestock. Winter, the season in which alfalfa is cultivated, is thought to be the season of relative ease and comfort, when alfalfa-fed cattle bear plenty of milk and there is an abundance of cheese and butter in the village. It is then too that cattle are fattened for sale. For all these purposes alfalfa could well be purchased, but for the fellahin, alfalfa bought with money would not possess the quality of sufficiency that a crop grown on household land would have, since it would involve the exchange of cash — even if those exchanges were to result ultimately in a profit for the household.

Given the trajectory of the fellah economy in Nashawy therefore, it is only to be expected that most exchanges connected with cotton will be conducted in cash. Thus, camel owners take their payment in kind when they transport grain or straw, for, they say, there is *baraka*, 'holiness and sufficiency', that way. But when they transport cotton, or even the dry cotton plants used as firewood, they take their payment in cash. Similarly people who work for daily wages usually take their payment in kind when their work has to do with the harvesting or threshing of grain, while they always take cash when they work on the cotton crop.

For a fellah household a sufficiency of labour is thought to be no less important than a sufficiency of food: just as a household ideally ought not to have to buy any grain, so too it ought not to have to spend any money hiring labour. The system of fellowship is in part a function of the constellation of representations, for it provides a means of banking labour that a household may perform labour-intensive tasks without having to spend too much cash.

In general those who hold land do not work for wages; it is the landless who do so and it is they too who have to spend money on grain and vegetables. For that reason the landless are spoken of in Nashawy as *nās ghalāba* (poor, lit. defeated, people). They say of themselves that they are 'weak', *da'īf*, unlike the 'strong', *jāmid*, fellahin or landowning peasants. In terms of the villagers' representation of their household economy this is entirely accurate for the landless are multiply weak: having no land they have to work for money, and with this money they have to buy their daily necessities so that they are deprived of the means of growth. But the objective grounds for this series of identifications are dubious: a landless man working all the year round may earn a considerable amount of money, and may well be in a better economic situation than the small sharecropper. Nevertheless, the landless, in their entanglement in cash exchanges, are seen to be cut off from the cycle of material growth towards which even the poorest of the fellahin can orient the functioning of their households.

8

Thus the system of fellowship articulates the technical and functional requirements of an agricultural cycle with a particular conception of economy and economic growth. This articulation is achieved through a system of exchange, and it is in its aspect as an exchange system that much of its significance lies: as in all such systems the medium is an inseparable part of the message.

In the first place the system of fellowship, like all systems of exchange, can be used both to include and exclude. For those whom it includes — i.e. the bulk of the landholding fellahin — the connotations of the systems are those of fellowship and community.[12] But the system can also he used to exclude or to make a wholly different kind of social statement. Thus, in order to emphasize their sense of separateness from the people who live around them, the tightly-knit lineage of Laṭaifa never enter into fellowship exchanges with people of other settlements, other than close affinal kin. Equally, elsewhere, a few fellah families pointedly refrain from participating in fellowship exchanges. Instead, they hire labour when they need to. The wastage implied in this, in the unspoken language of the fellahin, becomes a kind of conspicuous consumption through which they assert their superiority over others. This is not necessarily a function of their economic position; rather, it is a product of social aspirations.

For those who participate in it, the most important of the many meanings of the system of fellowship is that it permits the functioning of labour processes through co-operative understandings: that is, on the basis of equality, and because of a sense of community which excludes impersonal monetary exchanges. As it demonstrates through its efficiency, systems of labour exchange such as this are not necessarily archaisms doomed to extinction by modernity.[13] Indeed, the system of fellowship can be interpreted as a statement *about* modernity and impersonal forms of relationship. It is precisely in excluding such relationships from a specific domain of social life that it creates its own meaning. In this sense the system of fellowship in Nashawy is a total social fact in an even more complete sense than Mauss intended, for it conjoins the technical appropriation of nature with a form of organizing labour in order to make a statement about society.

9

The categories *ta'āwun* (pooling), *musā'ada* (help), *tanẓīmat azzimāl* (the system of fellowship) and *shughl* (work), together form a systematic whole. However, it must be stressed that I have derived their meanings from usage. The terms do not form rigid categories and the people of the area do not have a systematic exegesis of these categories present in their minds.

The structure as a whole operates at a deeper level than conscious exegesis: the terms are not names but deeds. Thus the terms are almost always encountered in verbal forms — I have referred to them here by their derived nominal forms merely for convenience. Thus *taʿāwun* is a nominal form of the verb *yitaʿāwan* (to co-operate), the verb *yisāʿid*, to help, corresponds to the noun *musāʿada*; and *yishtaghal*, to work, corresponds to the nouns *ishtaghal* or *shughl*. Only fellowship exchanges form a named system as such and are often referred to as *tanẓīmat azzimāl* (the system of fellowship). However, the corresponding verb, *yizmal*, to work as fellows or colleagues, is also frequently used.

The question: 'What are you doing?' when put to a group of, say harvesters, in Nashawy, will frequently meet with a response in which the workers will point to some of their number and say: 'We are [working together as] fellows; they are working for wages', *iḥna bi-nazamalu baʿḍ wa-humma bi-yishtaghalū bi-lijār*. Similarly, people building houses or making bricks often describe their work by saying of a part of their group: 'They are working, while we are helping [our relatives]', *humma bi-yishtaghalū wa-iḥna bi-nisāʿidhum*. Their utterances do not usually constitute the nature of the activity itself as the subject of the description — they do not, for example, say that some of them are cutting rice while others are tying it up in bundles, or that some of them are laying bricks while others are digging the foundation. For them, in certain contexts, the activity and the nature of the group performing it are semantically indistinguishable. In speech, the fact that these identifications are effected through verbs, not nouns, indicates to the listener that the very nature of their actions is different, even when they are 'doing' the same thing. It is impossible to express the same sense in English, because there are no such verbs. Even the circumlocution: 'Some of those who are working with us are relatives and some are hired workers', does not come near to conveying the meaning of the verbal distinctions made in the dialect of the lower Delta. Perhaps the closest the English language comes to expressing the kind of meaning implied in the verbal categories used in Nashawy, is in the distinction, often made in everyday speech, between 'working' and 'helping around the house'.

10

The distinction between 'work' and 'helping around the house' mirrors the absolute separations established by a modern capitalist economy: the separation of productive and private life, of production and reproduction, capital and labour. In such societies all productive labour is identical in its separation from the means of production and in its character as a commodity. Equally, in such societies productive labour is physically and spatially separated from all other kinds of social activity. In these circumstances labour, in its form as a mode of relationship to the means of production, coincides so closely with its form as a physical activity that the identification of the process of work poses no real problem.

In those agrarian societies in which peasant proprietorship is the rule, labour is not reduced to a uniform commodity and therefore can assume an enormous diversity of forms. For the fellah in Nashawy for example, the real division of labour begins not at his place of work but in a series of prior social relationships. An analysis of work in such a society therefore necessarily involves the examination of a whole range of relations and representations. An act of labour in Nashawy is not merely a performance of a technically necessary function: it contains within it both a history and a metaphysic.

Notes

1. Donham makes a number of pertinent remarks on this issue.
2. See, for example, Tyler, and Brown and Van Bolt's articles. There have, of course, been innumerable descriptive studies of ritual and belief in agricultural production, including Maurice and Proux (77–970) and Firth's *The work of the Gods in Tikopia*. The ASA volume (no. 19), *The Social Anthropology of Work*, represents a welcome change of direction.
3. Words of Arabic origin which appear in the *Oxford English Dictionary* have not been transliterated, though I have changed the *OED* spelling of fellaheen to fellahin.

4. I would like to thank the Inlaks Foundation for financing the field research on which this article is based and the Department of Anthropology, Faculty of Arts, Alexandria, for their generous assistance. An earlier version of this paper was presented in the Department of Sociology, Delhi University, and I would like to thank my colleagues in the Department, especially Dr J.P.S. Uberoi, Dr Veena Das and Deepak Mehta for their comments. The field research on which this paper is based was conducted under the supervision of Dr Peter Lienhardt. This paper is an inadequate token of my deep gratitude for his constant encouragement, support and, most of all, his friendship.
5. Hereafter referred to as Nashawy. The names of settlements and families given here are not their actual names.
6. A feddan is equal to 1.038 acres.
7. This usage is not limited to the local dialect. The literary usage of the classical form *ḥaqq* is often similar. See for example Tayyib Salih's novel *Mowsim al-hijra ilā al-shimāl* (9, 51).
8. Baer (1969) provides an excellent account of the powers of the *'omda* and of the history of the institution.
9. Fifty-three of Nashawy's 215 households were 'joint' in that they consisted of at least two nuclear families. Of these 21 consisted of married brothers living together after their fathers' deaths. There are only six households consisting of married brothers living together after both parents' deaths.
10. Methods of organizing labour through systems comparable to help and the system of fellowship have been reported from many parts of the world (Bartels 1975, 1977 [Macha Oromo, southwest Ethiopia]; Stoler: 681 [Java]; Maurice and Proux: 155 [Indo-China]; Berleant-Schiller: 265 [Antigua]; and Reichel-Dolmatoff: 211 [Colombia]. There have been many reports of co-operative labour in the Central Andes [Guillet: 153]). To the best of my knowledge they have not been reported before of Egypt or the Middle East. It seems likely that some forms of co-operative labour exist in every agrarian society, though it is only to be expected that their methods of organization, principles and significance will vary with circumstances.

    There is now an extensive literature on the subject of co-operative labour, and some classifications have been proposed. Of these Erasmus' categories of 'festive' and 'exchange' labour are in widest use. Moore writes of festive labour that it has no 'permanent organization, and work parties are organized ad hoc to undertake specific tasks; persons are attracted to a work party both by relatively lavish provision of food and drink . . . holding a work party rarely implies any obligation on the part of the host to reciprocate . . . if any reciprocity is implied it is only weak . . . (Moore: 272). 'Help' in Nashawy is comparable to 'festive labour' in that it has no permanent organization and does not imply immediate return. However, 'help' and 'festive labour' also differ fundamentally. While in Nashawy meals provided to those who come to help are better than everyday meals, they are not by any means lavish enough to be considered an incentive for contributing labour. 'Festive labour' groups also appear to be open to all who choose to attend, while 'help' groups in Nashawy are formed entirely around personal ties. It is because of these differences that 'help' is comparable in form to a gift. The system of fellowship on the other hand is exactly similar in its operation to many other systems of exchange labour (see Moore: 272).

11. There are 24 *qīrāṭ* to a feddan.
12. Terms which signify fellowship are common in systems of exchange labour. The *dado* groups of the Macha Oromo are composed of *hiriya*. 'The word *hiriya* within context, is best translated by "companion" or "comrade" ' (Bartels 1977: 503). Those who participate in the system of fellowship are called *zumala* (sing. *zamīl*), colleagues or fellows.
13. The imminent demise of systems of exchange labour has often been predicted (see Erasmus 1956 and Moore 1975). Yet, as Guillet notes, exchange labour is evidently flourishing in the Central Andes and elsewhere. He attributes this to the cost-benefit ratios of exchange labour (162). Extrapolating from the example of the third world family firm, he argues that exchange labour is more efficient than wage labour because people work harder where family interests are concerned than they do for an unrelated paymaster (162). In addition, as he phrases it, exchange labour has the 'element of fulfilling one's obligation to engage in social interaction with one's social peers' (163). But Guillet follows Erasmus and Moore in attributing the persistence of exchange labour, in part, to a shortage of money; exchange labour 'does not require the expenditure of scarce cash and one does not have to cover the costs of the subsistence needs of the labourers whom one recruits, as in fully proletarianized wage labour' (162).

Given a certain degree of monetization in the economy, which certainly exists in the Central Andes (Guillet: 157), it appears to me as difficult to prove an absolute shortage of cash as it would be to prove the contrary. The shortage has to be established not in general terms, for it is hardly in dispute that the people of the Central Andes and Egypt are cash-deprived in a global sense, but specifically, in relation to the priorities of production units. To establish the point satisfactorily a great deal of data on household income and expenditure, convertible assets, standard of living and the relative cost of wage labour would have to be produced.

The fellahin, for example, spend a good deal of money on weddings, mortuary rites and so on. Equally, the peasants of the Andes contribute money to the Church (Guillet: 157). Given this, we cannot accept on trust that they have an absolute shortage of cash. It is surely a question of priorities; of how people wish to spend or invest such money as they have. As I have argued, the system of fellowship fits perfectly with the economic orientations of the fellahin because, by minimizing expenditure on labour it leaves the average household free to orient its expenditure in a particular direction. To accept that exchange labour persists mainly because of a cash shortage we would have to be convinced that the average peasant household in these societies would not be able to hire labour even if they were willing to make it a top priority. Secondly, if a household were to send its men out to work as wage-labourers during the harvesting season and then hire a work group for its own fields with their earnings, it would not, if it had a complement of men approximating to the demographic mean, have a new outflow of cash at all. In other words, if they were to replace the social accounting implicit in the system of fellowship with accounts based on cash, the average household would not be a loser — not, at any rate, of cash.

References.

Ammar, H., *Growing up in an Egyptian Village*, London, 1954.

Baer, Gabriel, *A History of Land Ownership in Modern Egypt, 1800–1950*, Oxford, 1962.

—— *Studies in the Social History of Modern Egypt*, Chicago, 1969.

Bartels, L., 'Dado: A form of co-operation between farmers', *Anthropos*, 70: 5/6, pp. 883–925, 1975.

—— 'Dado: A form of co-operation on equal terms among the Macha Oromo of Ethiopia', *Anthropos*, 72: 3/4, pp. 497–513, 1977.

Berleant-Schiller. R., 'Production and division of labour in a West Indian peasant community', *American Ethnologist*, 4: 2, pp. 253–70, 1977.

Brown, M.F. and Van Bolt, M.L., 'Aguaran Jivaro gardening magic in the Alto Rio Mayo, Peru', *Ethnology*, 19: 2, pp. 169–89, 1980.

Donham, Donald L., 'Beyond the domestic mode of production', *Man* n.s. 16: 4, pp. 515–38, 1981.

Erasmus, C., 'Culture, Structure and Process: The occurrence and

disappearance of reciprocal farm labour', *Southwestern Journal of Anthropology*, 12, pp. 444–69, 1956.
Firth, Raymond, *The work of the Gods in Tikopia*, vols. I and II, London, 1940.
Fyzee, Asaf A.A., *Outlines of Muhammadan Law* (3rd edition), London, 1964.
Guillet, D., 'Reciprocal labour and peripheral capitalism in the Central Andes', *Ethnology*, 19: 2, pp. 151–68, 1980.
Mabro, R., *The Egyptian Economy*, Oxford, 1974.
Maurice A. and Proux G.M., *L'Ame du riz*, Extrait du Bulletin de la Societe des Etudes Indochinoises, nouvelle serie, 29: 2–3, Saigon, 1954.
Mauss, M., 'Essai sur le don', in *Sociologie et Anthropologie*, Paris, 1950.
Moore, M.P., 'Co-operative labour in peasant agriculture', *Journal of Peasant Studies*, 2: 3, pp. 270–91, 1975.
Pearl, David, *A textbook of Muslim Law*, London, 1979.
Reichel-Dolmatoff, G. and A., *The people of Aritama*, London, 1961.
Salih, Tayyib, *Mowsim al-hijra ilā al-shimāl*, Beirut, 1981.
Schacht, J., *An Introduction to Islamic Law*, Oxford, 1964.
Stoler, Ann L., 'Rice Harvesting in Kali Loro: a study of class and labour relations in rural Java', *American Ethnologist*, 4: 4, pp. 678–95, 1977.
Tyler, S.A., 'Fields are for planting', *Journal of the Indian Anthropological Society*, 9: 1, pp. 17–38, 1974.
Wallman, Sandra (ed.), *The Social Anthropology of Work*, (A.S.A. Monographs: 19), London, 1979.

11 *The Slave of MS. H.6*

I

THE SLAVE of MS. H.6 was first ushered upon the stage of modern history in 1942.

It was a brief appearance, in the obscurest of theatres; and then too, he was scarcely out of the wings before he was gone again — more a prompter's whisper than a recognizable face in the cast.

This first appearance occured within a short article in the Hebrew journal *Zion*,[1] published in Jerusalem. The article was written by a E. Strauss, and it dealt with new sources for the history of Middle Eastern Jews. It contained, among other things, a transcription in Hebrew characters of a long letter written by a merchant in Aden and sent to a friend and business associate who was then living in the town of Mangalore, on the south-western coast of India. The writer of the letter was called Khalaf ibn Isḥaq; his friend in Mangalore bore the name Abraham ibn Yijū.

Khalaf ibn Isḥaq's letter was written in the summer of the year AD 1148: a moment in history as singular, in a curious way, as that other moment, almost eight hundred years later, when the slave first stepped upon the stage of the contemporary world.[2]

1. *Zion*, n.s. V, 1942, Jerusalem. In the English abstract the article is entitled 'Documents for the Economic and Social History of the Jews of the Near East'. The article includes a transcription in Hebrew characters of Geniza MS. H.6 of the National and University Library, Jerusalem. My translation is based upon Strauss's transcription.

2. Gibb, 1969b: 513.

The very summer that Khalaf ibn Iṣḥaq sent his letter to Mangalore, the Crusaders, led by the German king, Conrad, with his army newly-arrived from Germany suffered a major reverse on the plains near Damascus.[3] The price of this defeat was so great, writes the contemporary Arab historian Ibn al-Athīr, that after the battle 'the German Franks returned to their country, which lies over yonder, beyond Constantinople, and God rid the faithful of this calamity'.[4] A no less critical battle, fought on the plains west of Alexandria, at al-'Alamīn, was to usher in the slave upon his appearance in 1942.

Khalaf ibn Iṣḥaq is probably not ignorant of the events that are taking place at the other end of the peninsula, while he is writing his letter to his friend. He and his fellow merchants in Aden make it their business to keep themselves well-informed. From season to season they follow the fluctuations of the prices of iron, cardamom and pepper in the markets of Cairo. They are always quick to relay news that concerns them to their friends in Malabar.[5]

But in this letter Khalaf ibn Iṣḥaq does not concern himself unduly with politics or warfare. He and his friends usually prefer to leave the carrying of that kind of news to the travelling merchants and seamen who take their letters to India.[6] Here he writes to Ben Yijū[7] about a certain family matter: sending him news of an itinerant and worrisome brother.[8] He goes on to acknowledge receipt of some goods that Ben Yijū has sent him: a shipment of areca nuts; two

3. Berry: 508–10.

4. Maalouf: 150.

5. In T-S 20.137, recto, lines 22-3, a letter sent to Ben Yijū in Mangalore in 1135, an Adenese merchant reports on the state of demand for pepper, and the prices of some other commodities in Cairo that year.

6. In T-S 13 J 7, fol. 27, recto, in a letter sent from Aden to Ben Yijū in Mangalore, probably in the late 1140s, one of their friends remarks: 'As for the news of Egypt, my master will hear it from the traders . . . ' (lines 18–19).

7. I have used the accepted transcription of the Hebrew form of the name here. In general, however, for the sake of convenience, I have transcribed names exactly as they are spelt in the documents.

8. MS. H.6, lines 10–14.

locks of Indian manufacture, and two bowls from a Mangalore brass workshop in which Ben Yijū has an interest.[9] He informs him that he has sent him some presents — 'things which have no price and no value' — 'two jars of sugar, a jar of almonds and two jars of raisins, altogether five jars'.[10]

It is only at the very end of the letter that the slave makes his entry. Khalaf ibn Iṣḥaq, while sending his good wishes to Ben Yijū and his children, mentions him especially, and sends him 'plentiful greetings'.[11]

It is an ordinary trader's letter; the mention of the slave is so brief as to be hardly worth notice. But it happens to come to us from a time when the only people for whom we can even begin to imagine a properly individual human existence are the literate and the consequential: those who have the means to inscribe themselves upon history. The slave of MS. H.6 was none of those things, and it is only because of a series of extraordinary accidents that, in this instance, the barely discernible traces that the humble and the ordinary leave upon the world happen to have been preserved. If this initial mention of his name resounds so loudly eight centuries later, it is surely because it has all the promise of the first murmur of rain in a plague of drought.

In his commentary on the letter, Dr Strauss described the people who figure in it as 'mostly merchants'.[12] That was about all that was known of them then. Dr Strauss was also careful to note that this is the first document of its kind in which the town Mangalore is mentioned.[13]

In 1942 even that had the status of a discovery.[14]

9. MS. H.6, lines 15–16. For Ben Yijū's bronze workshop, see Goitein, 1973: 192. Goitein uses the term 'factory'; to me 'workshop' seems more appropriate.

10. MS. H.6, lines 17–19.

11. MS. H.6, line 23.

12. English abstract, Strauss, 1942.

13. See Strauss, 148–9. I am grateful to Dr Leon Wieseltier for translating the Hebrew sections of the article for me.

14. I would like to thank my colleagues at the Centre for Studies in Social Sciences, Calcutta, for their comments on an earlier version of this paper. I

II

The slave's second appearance occurred twenty-four years later, in a collection of letters written by Jewish traders in the Middle Ages, translated into English by S.D. Goitein.

The slave's role is no less brief here, but this time he has a bigger part in the production: he has earned himself a footnote. His second appearance, like his first, occurs in a letter written by Khalaf ibn Iṣḥaq. But in the twenty-four years that have passed between the two, he has slipped backwards in time: he is ten years younger now. The letter in which his name now appears was written by Khalaf ibn Iṣḥaq in 1138 : Nūr al-Dīn's father, Sultan Zangi, is still alive, busy acquiring cities through well-planned marriages, and the troops of the Byzantine emperor, John Comnenus, have withdrawn northwards after a futile campaign in Syria.[15] But here, even more than later, business weighs heavily on Khalaf ibn Iṣḥaq's mind: a consignment of pepper lost in a shipwreck at the Bāb al-Mandab; cardamom received and silk dispatched to Malabar; accounts for a long list of household goods that Ben Yijū had asked to have sent to Mangalore, complete with an apology for the misadventures of a frying-pan — 'You asked me to buy a frying-pan of stone in a case. Later on, its case broke, whereupon I bought you an iron pan for a niṣāfī, which is, after all, better than a stone pan'.[16]

But for all the merchandise mentioned in it, the letter's spirit is anything but mercenary: it is lit with a warmth that Goitein's translation renders, still alive and glowing, in cold English print. 'I was glad', writes Khalaf ibn Iṣḥaq, 'when I looked at your letter, even before I had taken notice of its content. Then I read it full of happiness and, while studying it, became joyous and cheerful . . . You mentioned, my master, that you were longing for me. Believe me that I feel

---

am grateful in particular to Partha Chatterjee for his many suggestions and criticisms—but most of all for his encouragement and support.

15. Gibb, 1969a: 459.

16. Goitein, 1973: 189.

twice as strongly and even more than what you have described . . .'.[17]

Again the slave's brief entry occurs towards the end of the main body of the text; once more Khalaf ibn Isḥaq sends him 'plentiful greetings', but this time he also mentions him by name. Attached to this mention of his name is a footnote. It explains him as: '(Ibn) Yijū's slave and business agent, a respected member of his household'.[18]

Terse as this is, there is a promise of more to come in Goitein's preface to the book. When this collection appeared, the first two volumes of Goitein's moumental study, *A Mediterranean Society*, had already been published. They had been immediately acknowledged as a landmark in the writing of medieval history. In his preface to the collection of letters, as in many previous publications, Goitein recorded his intention to publish a similar study of the trade between India and the Middle East in the same period. This was to be his *India Book*,[19] the product of a lifetime of scholarly labour. It was to contain his translations of a corpus of several hundred documents relating to the India trade. Thus the eloquent brevity of that one footnote already contains the pledge that some of these documents would contain more material on the life of the slave.

But thirty years after Goitein first announced its gestation, the *India Book*[20] had yet to appear; other pressing concerns had pushed it to the margins of his scholarly programme. It was still under preparation when he died in 1985. The publication of his drafts and notes for the book has been promised, and is still eagerly awaited.[21]

17. Ibid.: 187.

18. Ibid.: 191, fn.

19. The work was also known by other names, such as *India Volume* (Tobi: 365).

20. See Goitein, 1954, and 1980: 43.

21. I would like to thank Dr A. Udovitch, and especially Dr Mark Cohen of Princeton University, for allowing me access to the S.D. Goitein Laboratory for Geniza Research, which is housed in the Department of Near Eastern

The published oeuvre that Goitein left behind is immense; the complete bibliography of his work lists over fifty pages of entries. This oeuvre was, naturally, profoundly informed by his lifelong study of the material for his *India Book.* He had also already published the catalogue numbers of about three hundred documents related to India, including those that concerned Ben Yijū. Other clues to that material lie scattered through his notes and publications like the trail of a wind-blown treasure hunt. It was this trail of clues that provided the beginnings of the research that has led to this narrative: it is to the pioneering labours of S.D. Goitein that the stories of the slave, and his master, Ben Yijū, are most indebted.

In 1966 however, that footnote rang the curtain upon the slave once again. Thus ended his brief career in the modern world, in an obscurity only a shade less dense than that of his earlier life in the medieval.

III

The slave of MS. H.6 owes the preservation of his memory to an epic series of accidents and coincidences. The documents in which he figures are part of an immense trove of manuscripts that were discovered in Cairo in the nineteenth century. They were recovered from a chamber that had been built into the back wall of a medieval synagogue in a quarter

---

Studies at Princeton. Following the Laboratory's terms of functioning, I was allowed to consult only a limited amount of material, and under restrictions concerning the taking of notes, etc. Since Goitein's notes for the *India Book* are still to be published, I have not referred to his datings or any other previously unpublished material. Fortunately the dates of the most important documents have already been published by Goitein and other scholars, and they are adequate for the purposes of this narrative. I owe an additional debt of gratitude to Dr Mark Cohen for his support and encouragement and for the constructive criticism he has so generously proffered throughout my research. I need hardly add however, that he bears no responsibility for the views and opinions expressed in this article.

of Cairo known as Fusṭāṭ, or Old Cairo, which was once the capital of Islamic Egypt.

In the Middle Ages, Jews, like Christians and Muslims, considered it sacrilegious to destroy any written token of the name of God. In Jewish communities it was the custom to deposit all such pieces of writing in an appropriate place until they could be buried on consecrated ground, as a safeguard against the possibility of the desecration of God's name.[22] This custom is observed to this day in some Jewish communities. In effect, the prohibition extended to virtually all their writings, for they would invariably inscribe invocations to God at the head of every sheet of paper.

Synagogues usually had depositories built especially for this purpose, and these chambers were known by the term 'Geniza'.[23] Not all the documents deposited in these chambers had to do with strictly religious matters. The people who used these Genizas would not have countenanced the modern distinction between the 'secular' and the 'religious': for them there was little that fell outside the scope of God's work, no matter whether it had to do with marriage, prayer or porterage contracts.[24] The depositories did in fact contain innumerable scriptural documents, but they were neither religious libraries nor archives: they were places where the members of the congregation would throw all the papers in their possession, including letters, bills, contracts, poems, marriage deeds and so on. Often the same piece of paper would contain several different writings, for paper was expensive in the Middle Ages, and people were thrifty in its use. Thus the Genizas were repositories for documents of every kind: they were, so to speak, the sacrosanct wastebin for most of the writings of their congregations.

Of the innumerable Genizas that once dotted the Middle East, only one has survived intact into modern times. This is the Geniza of the synagogue of the Palestinians in Fusṭāṭ.

22. Kahle: 2.
23. Ibid.: 2.
24. See S.D. Goitein, *Islamic Society*: 248.

Documents were deposited in the Geniza in varying amounts for almost a thousand years, beginning in the eleventh century and ending in the nineteenth. In fact, the document that is thought to be the last to have found its way into the Geniza is a divorce bill written in Bombay in 1879.[25] Most of the documents that relate to the trade with India, however, date from the eleventh and twelfth centuries,[26] a period in which Egypt, under the rule of the Fatimids, assumed the political and economic leadership of the Middle East. Cairo at this time was probably the premier city of the Old World. It was at this time too that the Jewish communities of the Middle East were most active in the India trade. Later, in the thirteenth century, a syndicate of Muslim merchants gradually gained control of the trade, squeezing out other communities.

In its prime, however, the congregation that prayed at the Synagogue of the Palestinians in Fusṭāṭ consisted of an extraordinary gathering of people: in the eleventh and twelfth centuries it probably had no equal in wealth, learning and influence anywhere among the Jewish communities of the world. The great Talmudic scholar Mūsa ibn Maimūn, known to the western world as Moses Maimonides, was one of its members. The twelfth century Hebrew poet, Judah Halevy, is known to have prayed there as well.

Most of the prominent members of the congregation, however, were traders and merchants. And since, in this period, the trade with the east was the motor of the international economy,[27] many of the merchants of the synagogue of Fusṭāṭ were inevitably involved in the India trade. Maimonides himself had a hand in the trade, and his brother Da'ūd is thought to have died on his way to India.[28]

The community was also involved in the merchandizing of eastern products in southern and south-eastern Europe, and many of its members had extensive connections throughout

25. Goitein, 1967: 9.
26. Cf. Goitein, 1973: 4.
27. Goitein, 1973: 6.
28. Goitein, 1973: 207.

the Mediterranean. Indeed several Jewish merchants based in Fusṭāṭ are known to have travelled regularly between Europe, Egypt and India.[29]

The merchants of the congregation were as richly varied in their geographical origins as they were well travelled. They came to Fusṭāṭ from every region of the Arab world: Spain, the Maghreb, Sicily, Iraq, the Levant, and Yemen. The wealthiest and most influential members of the community, in fact, had their origins not in Egypt, but in North Africa, particularly the regions of modern Tunisia and Algeria that were known to the Arab geographers as Ifrīqiya.

For centuries the Cairo Geniza was the repository of much of the written material produced by this uncommonly diverse community. The number of documents deposited in it began to decline progressively after the thirteenth century, and in time the flow nearly stopped altogether. For centuries after that, the Geniza had the good fortune to be forgotten. Rumours of its existence began to leak out to the world in the eighteenth century. The first confirmed reports date to the mid-nineteenth century.[30] These reports started a small-scale race between the Great Powers for the acquisition of the documents. By the turn of the century the documents, many tens of thousands in number, had been dispersed over the globe. They are now referred to collectively as the Geniza Documents. The largest collection by far is that of the Taylor–Schechter Collection in the Cambridge University Library.[31] But there are substantial collections also in Leningrad, Oxford, Budapest, Paris, Vienna, London, Jerusalem and at least two cities in the USA. Ironically, Cairo, which bred and nurtured the documents over so many centuries, has none left today. Nor, until very recently, have Egyptian scholars and politicians concerned themselves with these documents as they have, for example, with the Gnostic Gospels.[32] Deceived perhaps by the

29. Goitein, 1954 and Strauss, 1942.
30. Kahle: 2.
31. Ibid.: 5.
32. Cf. Pagels: xxv.

current divisions of the Middle East, they seem content to excise them from Egypt's history.

The body of documents was so large and their dispersal so haphazard that sections of many manuscripts were divided between several collections. It is only because of the painstaking work of scholars such as S.D. Goitein that some of the connections between these documents have been discovered. Even today, although much labour has been expended on the Geniza collections, it can still truthfully be said that the work on the documents has only just begun.

Amongst the papers of the Geniza, about seventy have been identified, most of them by S.D. Goitein, as being related in one way or another to Abraham Ben Yijū.[33] Some of these are letters sent to him by friends and associates at various points in his travels. The others are letters and a variety of other documents, including poems, accounts, and calendrical calculations, that he wrote himself. Ben Yijū also sometimes acted as a scribe for friends who wished to take advantage of his remarkably clear and elegant handwriting.[34] It is this strikingly distinctive hand that has proved to be the principal means for the identification of his papers.

Many individual fragments of paper contain several different documents — a letter from a friend, for example, with other texts written by Ben Yijū in the margins, or on the reverse side. Paper was scarce and expensive at the time, and in his conservation of it Ben Yijū displayed the care of a craftsman.

Some of the documents relating to Ben Yijū have been published — a few in English translations, and some in Arabic transcriptions. I have myself deciphered and translated several of these documents from the original manuscripts.[35] It is these

33. Goitein, 1973: 186.

34. See Goitein, 1973: 62–5, for a letter written by Ben Yijū in Mangalore, on behalf of one Mahrūz ibn Ya'qūb. The letter was sent to a merchant in Broach.

35. A list of the documents I have referred to in the course of this article is included in the bibliography, under Geniza Documents. I would like to thank the Syndics of the Cambridge University Library for giving me permission to examine and publish excerpts from these documents. I am grateful to

few fragments that provide such material as there is on the life of the slave.

Each of these documents has a story of its own: of travel from Aden and Egypt, to Malabar and Sicily and then back again to Cairo — medieval histories that somersault into a further chronicle of travel and dispersal in modern times. Their history has the baffling elusiveness of lights seen in parallel mirrors: they are both the stuff of history and history itself, as real as a battle or a temple; they are each a living history and a commentary on the writing of history; a mocking aside on how histories are stolen, bought and traded in the marketplace. The story of the slave of MS. H.6 is one tiny spark within the bright lights of this looking-glass chamber, faint, elusive and often jeering.

IV

If I have deferred the naming of the slave it is because his name is one of the few pegs I have on which to hang a history.

The documents in which the slave's name is mentioned, like most of the manuscripts of the Geniza, are written in a language that has come to be known as Judæo-Arabic. This is one of the many varieties of Arabic that came into being when the language of the Arabian peninsula came into contact with other languages after the Islamic expansion in the eighth and ninth centuries.[36] Along with the other peoples

---

Dr Stefan Reif, Director of the Taylor–Schechter Genizah Research Unit, Cambridge, for his encouragement and I owe a particular debt of thanks to Dr Geoffrey Khan, also of the Taylor–Schechter Genizah Research Unit, who guided my first faltering steps in the almost absurdly recondite field of Geniza studies. I would also like to thank Menahem Ben Sasson for his patience with my innumerable queries and for the time he took in going over some of my transcriptions. A separate tribute is due to the staff of the Manuscripts Reading Room of the Cambridge University Library for their unfailing helpfulness and efficiency.

36. Ferguson: 49; Versteegh: 17; Blau: 17.

of the conquered regions, Aramaic-speaking Jews were soon assimilated into the use of Arabic.[37]

Arabic-speaking Jews were using Arabic as a medium of literary expression, at least as early as the tenth century, and by the twelfth century, when Moses Maimonides wrote his *Guide for the Perplexed*, Arabic had become the language in which Middle Eastern Jews discussed their most sacred matters.[38] But this was not quite the language that their Muslim contemporaries used in their writing.[39] Muslims, influenced as they were by the language of the Koran, usually tried to write as close an approximation of the classical language as their abilities permitted. The classical language had no such significance for Jews, of course, and as a result they tended to write in a style that was much closer to the spoken Arabic of their time.[40] At the same time, even when Hebrew had ceased to be the language of communication for Middle Eastern Jews, it had lost none of its scriptural and religious significance, and literate Jews devoted much of their education to the study of Hebrew texts. Sections of these texts would often pour out of their memories, and many of the Judæo-Arabic documents of the Geniza are thickly strewn with Hebrew and Aramaic words and phrases. But usually Hebrew passages occur in the form of scriptural quotations and customary sayings, for not all of those who wrote in Judæo-Arabic knew enough Hebrew to be able to express themselves adequately in it.

The most important difference between Arabic and Judæo-Arabic is also the most immediately noticeable: the latter was written in the Hebrew script. To serve this function, the Hebrew alphabet had to be modified because it possessed fewer characters than the Arabic. So diacritical dots, like those used in Arabic, were introduced, although in

37. See Hirschberg: 149–53 for a fuller treatment of the Arabicization of North African Jews.

38. Blau: 19–25; Hirschberg: 153.

39. Blau: 23.

40 Ibid.

practice the dots were rarely used and single Hebrew symbols often served for two Arabic characters.[41] But the system still proved workable enough to last over a millennium: it was still in use among the Iraqi Jews of Bombay in the nineteenth century.[42]

It is this script, in a sense, that has sealed a vault of mystery upon the slave's name. In Hebrew, as in Arabic, short vowels are not normally indicated in the written language. So the only clue the documents provide to the slave's name is a set of three consonants: B-M-H. The last of these is probably not a consonant at all, but rather the open vowel known in Arabic as the *teh marbūṭa*, often represented by the same symbol. These three characters are all that we have to go on; if they were to be taken at face value they would endow the slave with the puzzling and unlovely name 'Bama' or 'Bamah'.[43]

The first difficulty in looking for a root for this word is that we have no means of knowing what language the slave was named in. It is almost certain that he first came into Ben Yijū's service while Ben Yijū was living on the Malabar coast. But he may well have been brought there from the far rims of the Indian Ocean — from the slave markets of Zanzibar or Berbera, or, like much of the slave population of the Middle East and north India, from the steppes of Asia, and the mountains of the Balkans and the Caucasus. There are some indications that slaves from western Europe were regularly traded in India and China. Ibn Khordadbeh, the ninth-century Persian chronicler, wrote of the Jewish merchants of the time:

> They travel from the west to the east, and from the east to the west . . . From the west they bring eunuchs, female slaves, boys, silk brocades,[44] furs, and swords. They set off from the

41. Ibid.: 34–5, and 134–5, for a more detailed account of the orthography of Judæo-Arabic.

42. Roland: 17.

43. Goitein used the form 'Bama' in *Letters of Medieval Jewish Traders* (1973), but chose 'Bamah' in his article, 'From Aden to India', 1980: 52.

44. Ifrīqiyah was an important centre of silk production at that time. Silk appears to have been one of its principal exports. A treatise entitled *The*

> country of the Franks on the western sea and travel . . . to Sind, India and China. On their way back they carry musk, aloes, camphor and cinnamon, and other products of the eastern countries.[45]

A list of the goods exported from the Maghreb to the East, recorded a century later by the geographer Ibn Hauqāl, includes women of mixed Byzantine-Berber-Muslim origin, and Byzantine and Slavonic boys and slave-girls.[46]

Evidently, slaves from the coast of the Mediterranean, the interior of Europe, and Africa were regularly sold in India and the Far East in the early Middle Ages. But both the accounts I have quoted pre-date the lifetime of the slave of MS. H.6 by centuries. At the time when Khalaf ibn Iṣḥaq was writing of him, the possibility of his having come to the Malabar from Europe was much diminished, for the Crusades had intervened in the mean while, severely disrupting the trade routes of the Mediterranean.

There is a hint, however, that Ben Yijū may have done business with slave-dealers from the Yemeni town of Zabīd. It lies in a couple of sentences in a letter written to him by a correspondent in Aden at some point during his stay in the Malabar. I quote: 'This year the traders (jallāb) have not come here yet from Zabīd . . . because they are staying (home) to celebrate (the feast of) 'Īd. They will only set out after the 'Īd'.[47]

The suggestion lies in the word he used for 'trader'. It is conspicuously not the word that was generally used for that purpose in such letters. The dictionaries list one of the connotations of this other word as 'slave-trader'![48]

If Ben Yijū were indeed waiting for a visit from Yemeni

Description of the Finishing of Silk and its Dyeing in Differing Colours has been preserved in the Geniza. See Hirschberg: 270.

45. Quoted in Reinaud's introduction to the *Géographie d'Aboulféda*, 1848: 58. See also Hirschberg: 252.

46. Quoted by Hirschberg: 252.

47. T-S 20.130, lines 43–6.

48. See, Wehr: 129.

slave-traders, he would be doing nothing untoward for a man of his times and circumstances. Slavery in his era had none of the connotations that European capitalism was to give it after the sixteenth century. It was a common practice for merchants in his position to recruit slaves as business agents and apprentices. These slaves were usually manumitted after a period in service.[49]

It is known for certain that Ben Yijū acquired more than one slave during his residence in Malabar. But if he was actively involved in trading in slaves, this is certainly the only indication of it in the documents — and a nuance in a word's meaning counts as a suggestion of a possibility rather than as proof.

The alternative possibilities for the slave's origins brim over. Yet, it seems to me that there are good reasons for believing that he was in fact from the Indian subcontinent. To begin with, the puzzling characters in the slave's name are themselves an indication that he was not brought to India from the Middle East. Slaves sold in the markets of the Middle East were usually given Arabic names of a distinctive kind — Lu'lu' (Pearl), for example, and Jawhar (Jewel)[50]— names that placed them on the boundaries of ordinary human society. But the slave's name is almost certainly not of Arabic origin and it bears no resemblance to those market names.[51]

The language of the documents provides only one further clue to the mystery of the slave's name: in Judæo-Arabic, as in Arabic, doubled consonants are usually represented only

49. See Hirschberg; 181–3, and Goitein 1962. Assaf notes that an eleventh-century Spanish poet who translated the outstanding works of Hebrew literature was of servile origin (Assaf: 1940). See also section 10 below.

50. Cf. Goitein, 1962.

51. Dr Geoffrey Khan has found the name Bāmah in a third century AH Arabic papyrus, and he interprets it as a rendering of the Coptic Pamei/Pame (personal communication). It is extremely unlikely, however, that the B-M-H of MS. H.6 is intended to represent the same name. In the first place, it is spelt differently. Secondly, all the evidence indicates that the slave who bore the name was acquired by Ben Yijū in India.

by a single character. Since these consonants occur only in the medial position, it is possible that the medial 'M' in B-M-A is a doubled consonant. If that were so it would mean that the letters were intended to represent a word which has roughly the shape B-M-M-A. The first vowel in the word is clearly a short vowel, but we have no indication of which it is. The word could be Bamma, but there are several other possibilities as well.

Professor Goitein suggests a solution to the question of the name in the very footnote in which the slave makes his second appearance. He reports that A.L. Basham, the historian of ancient India, was of the opinion that 'Bama' 'is vernacular for Brahmā'.[52] The suggestion is that the slave's name was derived from the name of the Hindu deity Brahmā.

If this were so it would be in many ways an entirely satisfactory solution. But attractive as it may seem, this possibility is not so much a solution as a second riddle posed in answer to the first.

In the first place, we may be sure that the slave's name as it is represented in the documents is not a misspelling, or a mishearing of the word 'Brahmā'. That deity was well-known to Arab travellers and geographers, and accurate transcriptions of the name Brahmā, and of similar words like Brāhman, had been current in Arabic since the tenth century.[53] Ben Yijū and his friends would almost certainly have been familiar with the word and with the established conventions for spelling it in Arabic. In any case Ben Yijū, who lived in India for seventeen years, would certainly have been able to provide at least as accurate a transcription as, for instance, the traveller Mas'ūdī, who only spent a short time in the

52. Goitein, 1973: 191.

53. The tenth-century Arab geographer Mas'ūdī, for example, who is reported to have lived in Malabar, Sri Lanka and other parts of the subcontinent, mentions these words several times in his encyclopaedic compendium *Meadows of Gold* (*Murūj al-Dhahab*).The words occur also in al-Idrīsī's geographical work, written in the twelfth century, *Kitāb tazha al-mushtāq fi iḥtirāq al-afāq*.

country. We may be sure therefore that whatever the slave's name may have been, it was not Brahmā.

The name — whether it was Bomma, Bamma, or even Bama — may well have been a derivative of Brahmā: indeed it seems almost likely at first glance. But Brahmā is a word of Indo-European, Sanskritic origin, while the slave, if Ben Yijū did in fact acquire him in Mangalore, was probably weaned on a Dravidian language, and given a name current in a Dravidian tongue. If we consider further that in general Sanskritic names in Dravidian-speaking regions tend to be appropriated by the upper castes, while the slave was almost certainly born into one of the lower castes, then the matter becomes more puzzling still. In that apparently simple connection then, there lies a gap caused by historical processes at whose workings we can only begin to guess. And given the sparseness of the sources for the reconstruction of the social history of medieval India, the best we can do is to try to explore that gap with such contemporary tools as come to hand, clumsy though they may seem. We have no choice in the matter, for the name Brahmā is clearly not a solution but a shaky first step, and it has already tipped us over the edge.

V

Six years or so after Ben Yijū took up residence in Mangalore, not far from that city a man was killed while trying to rescue his masters' cattle from raiders. The man's name was Māsaleya Bamma. His masters were known as the 'One Thousand Fighters' and they made a grant of 'wet' land in their servant's memory, and caused an inscription to be carved in stone recording his deed and their commemoration of it. The inscription is dated 15 June 1126, and it was discovered in what appears to have been Māsaleya Bamma's native village, Tilivalli, in Dharwar district, less than two hundred miles in a north-easterly direction from Mangalore.[54] Another

54. Panchamukhi: 71–2.

inscription of the same period records a marriage between one Seṭṭi-Bamma of a merchant family (Vaishya-kula) and a pious woman called Akkanabbe. The inscription was found in Athani *taluka*, Belgaum district, about 380 miles north of Mangalore.[55]

The inscriptions prove beyond all doubt that the name Bamma was a common one in the twelfth century, at least in the region to the immediate north-east of Mangalore.[56] Other inscriptions of the period prove that there was an active cult of Brahmā worship in that area in the same period.[57]

This is worth remarking on, for although the god Brahmā is one of the deities of the Hindu trinity, the active worship of Brahmā is so rare that it has been said 'in Hindu devotion Brahmā has no following at all'.[58] To the best of my knowledge there are no active Brahmā shrines today in the region in which the inscriptions were found. Indeed, there could not be, I was once told by a woman of that area, for had not Brahmā lusted after his own daughter and forced upon her that primal incestuous act of which the world was born?[59]

Yet Brahmā figures regularly as an element in names in that area. Equally, names like Bomma, Bommai and Bommaya are common there, as well as in the region around Mangalore, even today, and in folk etymology they are generally linked to the deity Brahmā.

An attractive chain of reasoning seems to suggest itself: a series of links between the Sanskritic Brahmā and the Bomma of the inscriptions, and between both and the slave of MS. H.6. But that very attractiveness urges caution: the slave was probably born in the vicinity of Mangalore, and, despite the

55. Ibid.: 72–3.

56. See also Desai (45) for mention of a twelfth-century general called 'Brahma or Bamma Daṇḍādhīśa'.

57. An inscription of AD 1030, for example, extols a man for being a 'meditator at the feet of Brahmadeva' (Panchamukhi: 18). See also Bhatt: 358, for other epigraphical references to Brahmā worship in medieval Karnataka.

58. Eck: 202.

59. Cf. O'Flaherty: 33–4.

short distance that separates that region from the east, it is in fact a different ecological, linguisitic and cultural world.

VI

Mangalore sits upon a distinctive geographical formation: the strip of land that runs the length of the western coast of the subcontinent, along the foot of the range of mountains that stands like a wall between the sea and the massif of the Deccan peninsula. It is a thin shaving of land, barely twenty-five kilometres wide for much of its length, sliced into fragments by 114 short rivers which flow almost directly from the mountains into the sea.[60] The part which begins to the immediate south of Bombay and runs as far as Trivandrum in Kerala is an exuberantly green stretch of country with a tropical climate and moderate temperatures. Only a short distance, a few dozen miles, separates this strip of land from the plateau to the east. But between them stand the Sahyādri mountains — the Western Ghats — which serve to wring much of the moisture of the monsoons upon the coast. To the west of the Ghats lies lush, well-watered tropical land with an average annual rainfall that ranges between 300 and 500 cms; to the east is a dry semi-arid zone which receives only 60 to 80 cms of rain every year.[61] The figures are telling enough, but the difference between the two ecological regions is not of a gently graded statistical kind; it is so marked and sudden that it can be seen with the naked eye, from an aeroplane.

All along the lower two-thirds of the coast, a cultural divide accompanies the ecological. At the same time, the coastal strip is not a single cultural region either: it contains several regions which shade gradually into each other, from the Indo-European-speaking region of the Konkan to the Dravidian-language regions of the south. Often, the shores

60. Cf. *Gazetteer of India*: 60–1; Report of the Irrigation Commission, 1972: 254–6.

61. *Gazetteer*, 1973: 67, and Pillai and Kundu: 55.

of the short, wide rivers that shoot out of the Ghats serve both as boundaries and as negotiating tables between these regions. Each of these coastal areas is distinct, but, like a watchmaker's cogs, they are also closely and intricately articulated with each other. Amongst several of the larger castes, for example, there are recognized chains of equivalences which extend from region to region.[62] The regions also have in common the fact that they are all markedly different from their counterparts in the hinterland. The degree of the difference varies at different points: towards the south lie the related regions that are now grouped together as Kerala — an area that has some affinities with its eastern neighbour, Tamilnadu, but is largely a self-contained linguistic and cultural region. Towards the north, in the Konkan, the affinities between the coast and hinterland become more pronounced, although the coast still retains its distinctive identity.[63]

The region around Mangalore forms a kind of multi-jointed hinge: between the northern and southern parts of the coast, and between the seaboard and its eastern hinterland. The region is known as Tuḷunāḍ or Tuḷuva, after the language spoken by a large proportion of its inhabitants, Tuḷu. The Ghats and the Arabian Sea serve as its natural boundaries on the east and west, and the two rivers, the Chandragiri and the Sharāvati, on the south and north.[64] The region is today a part of the state of Karnataka, whose official language is Kannada, but one of its most distinguished historians has remarked: 'the Tuḷu country . . . has retained to this day its geographical identity and has come to form a part of the state of Karnataka purely through an accident of history'.[65]

But in the geography of human history no culture is an island, and the fact is that Tuḷunāḍ is even less so than its neighbour to the south. The Tuḷu language, for instance,

62. Cf. Bhatt: 230; Buchanan: 217 and Ramesh, 1981: 7–8.

63. Cf. Ramesh, 1981: 8.

64. Cf. ibid.: 4 and Buchanan: 213.

65. Ramesh, 1981: 2–3.

which is structurally akin to Kannada, has a rich repertoire of oral traditions, but it does not possess its own script, and so has not developed its own literature.[66] When it is written, it is usually in the Kannada script, and since late antiquity inscriptions in the region have generally been written in Kannada.[67]

For much of its history the region has had a distinct political identity of its own. For twelve centuries or so it was ruled by a single dynasty, the Āḷupa or Āḷuva.[68] The dynasty is first mentioned in Kannada inscriptions of the fifth century AD, but it probably came into power in the first centuries of the Christian era, for Ptolemy, the Alexandrian geographer of the second century AD, identifies the Tuḷuva region as Olokhoira, a term which is widely accepted to be a corruption of Āḷvakhēḏa, 'the land of the Āḷvas'.[69] For most of their history the Āḷupas preserved a certain measure of autonomy for themselves and their principality by judiciously picking allies amongst the various dynasties that followed each other to power in the regions to their immediate east and south: the Çālukyas of Bādāmi, the Rāṣṭrakūṭas, the Pallavas, the Çālukyas of Kalyāṇa, and the Çōḷas.[70] It was in the reign of the Āḷupa king Kavi Āḷupēndra (*c.*1110–*c.*1160) that Ben Yijū came to Mangalore.[71]

In the fourteenth century the Hoysaḷas, after repeated attacks on Tuḷunāḍ from the east, finally dethroned the dynasty.[72] But even afterwards the area kept a certain distinctiveness,

66. Cf. ibid.: 7; Upadhyaya and Upadhyaya:1; and Claus, 1979b: 96.

67. Cf. Ramesh, 1970: 73; Bhatt: 20.

68. The name of this dynasty is also spelt in various inscriptions as Āḷva, Āḷuka, and Āḷapa (cf. Ramesh, 1970: 30, and Bhatt: 25). Following the usage current among historians of the region, I have used the form Āḷupa.

69. Bhatt: 18; Ramesh, 1970: 26.

70. For detailed accounts of the history of the Āḷupas, see Ramesh, 1970; Bhatt: 18–41; and Saletore, 1936.

71. Cf. Ramesh, 1970: 115. Bhatt: 23 dates Kavi Āḷupendra's reign from AD 1115 to 1155.

72. Ramesh, 1970: 138–49; Bhatt: 35–40.

culturally and politically.[73] In effect Tuḷunāḍ was a region in the sense of the word *deśa*, or the French *pays* — 'country' is too loaded a term to use — an area, like many others in the subcontinent, not 'independent' but distinctive and singular, and precisely because of that, enmeshed with its neighbours in an intricate network of differences.

One aspect of this distinctiveness is that this region, in defiance of the views of Indologists, possesses what seems to be a flourishing cult of Brahmā worship. There are said to be several Brahmā shrines in Tuḷunāḍ,[74] and one scholar reports Brahmā to be the central deity in one of the most important Tuḷu folk epics (*pāḍdanas*), the myth of the wronged wife Siri.[75]

But upon closer examination the matter turns out to be more complicated still: the images of the Tuḷu Brahmā, for example, seem unrecognizable. In classical Hindu iconography Brahmā is usually represented as a four-headed, four-armed figure accompanied by a goose.[76] In Tuḷunāḍ, on the other hand, 'Brahmā' is usually represented as a figure seated on a horse, with a sword in hand.[77] These icons look nothing like the finely moulded bronze and stone images of Sanskritic deities that can be seen in Tuḷunāḍ's many large and celebrated temples. Images of the Tuḷu 'Brahmā' are usually carved very simply, in wood, and painted in bright colours.[78] Their most remarkable feature is usually the face: a simple oval

73. For the later history of the region, see Ramesh, 1970; Bhatt: 51–141; and Kamath, 1965.

74. Bhatt: plates 323–6.

75. Bhatt: 26.

76. Cf. Das: 135; Eck: 107–8.

77. Bhatt: 357 writes: 'The Brahma . . . of Tuḷu-nāḍu is represented in the form of a warrior seated on a horse with a sword in hand.' See also plate 325c in Bhatt's *Studies* for an illustration of an unusual bronze icon of the Tuḷu 'Brahmā'.

78. This was pointed out to me by Dr B.A. Viveka Rai of the Department of Kannada at Mangalore University. I am deeply grateful to Dr Rai for this and innumerable other comments and suggestions, for his generosity with his time and his erudition, and for a great many other kindnesses.

shape, dominated by a pair of huge eyes, and long curling moustaches, an image that brings to mind images of hero-figures, both in Tuḷunāḍ and elsewhere.[79] The figures are housed not in temples, as the classical deities usually are, but in small shrines called Brahmā-sthānas.[80] Indeed, all the important temples of Tuḷunāḍ are either Jaina temples, or temples dedicated to the familiar deities of mainstream Hinduism: Śiva, Viṣṇu, Kṛṣṇa, and manifestations of the Devī. To the best of my knowledge there is not a single Brahmā temple in their number.[81]

Upon closer reading, the 'Brahmā' of the Siri folk epic too becomes an increasingly puzzling figure: a personal, often wrathful deity who protects Siri through various trials but eventually punishes her female descendants with a dreadful curse. Siri is herself an unusual kind of female protagonist. Outraged by the preference her husband shows for his mistress, she leaves, taking her child with her, and eventually obtains a divorce and marries again.[82] She would be an improbable symbol of female virtue almost anywhere in India, but she is a key figure in the Tuḷuva pantheon of heroes and heroines. The matter becomes clearer when we learn that she was born into a caste called Bant, for the Bants are one of many Tuḷuva communities whose rules of inheritance are primarily matrilineal.[83] Clearly, the virtues she personifies are not those of the patrilineal mainstream of Indian society.

The cult of Siri is closely related to the principal institution of popular religion in Tuḷunāḍ: a complex of spirit-cults and possession rituals that are known as the cult of *bhūta* worship.[84]

79. See Upadhyaya and Upadhyaya: plate 4, and Bhatt: plate 326b. Bhatt describes the images on plate 323 as Bhūta-Brahmās, but their iconography proves them to be of classical derivation — as a glance at plate 325c shows.

80. Cf. Bhatt: 357.

81. See, for example, Bhatt: plates 329–402. In this long inventory of the temples and icons of Tuḷunāḍ, there is only one representation of Brahmā, a figure carved in wood in whicn Brahmā is depicted in the classical fashion.

82. Bhatt: 26–7.

83. Claus, 1979a: 39.

84. Cf. Bhatt: 359–66.

The sense of the word bhūta in Tuḷu is very different from the meaning the word carries in some other Indian languages. In northern India the word bhūta generally refers to a ghost or a malign presence. Tuḷu bhūtas, on the other hand, though they have their vengeful aspects, are often benign, protective figures, ancestral spirits and heroes who have been assimilated to the ranks of minor deities.[85] Some of the deities of pan-Indian myth have been assimilated into the Bhūta cult, but for the most part the bhūtas are thought of as local, personal deities, and the Tuḷuva villagers speak of them as '"our" gods'.[86] In some ways the bhūtas are comparable to the *yakṣa*s, *gaṇas*, *nāga*s and *devīs* who flourish everywhere in Hindu India.[87] But unlike lesser divinities in most places, the bhūtas of Tuḷunāḍ are worshipped through an elaborate ritual complex with its own legends, festivals and rites, as well as a form of theatre which bears a family resemblance to the more celebrated Yakṣagaṇa and Kathakali styles native to that part of the coast.[88]

The constituency of the cult, so to speak, consists of a certain set of the middle and lower castes of Tuḷunāḍ. These castes cover a wide expanse of the hierarchy, ranging from ruling landlords to untouchables. But by tradition they all play designated rôles in the cult — one provides patronage, another tends the shrines, and some enact the rituals—and in certain ways they all participate in the ethos that makes the culture of Tuḷunāḍ distinctive.[89] Together they form a distinct social group with deep roots in the region, and their shared cultural institutions mark a boundary of sorts between them and the other groups that inhabit Tuḷunāḍ. Tuḷuva Brahmins, for example, who are by tradition said to be immigrants into the region, participate only indirectly and in very limited ways in the Bhūta cult.[90]

85. Nichter: 140; Claus, 1973: 235; Bruckner: 18.
86. Claus, 1973: 232.
87. Cf. Eck: 61.
88. Upadhyaya and Upadhyaya: 12.
89. Nichter: 143.
90. Cf. Bhatt: 237; Nichter: 139.

The most important distinguishing mark of the shared culture of these castes, apart from the Tuḷu language and the Bhūta cult, is a form of succession and inheritance that is governed by what is known as the Aḷiya-santāna law. By the rules of this system of law, men transmit their immovable property, not to their own children, but matrilineally, to their sister's children.[91]

All the castes that participate fully in the Bhūta cult are governed to some degree by rules of matrilineal succession.[92] The Tuḷuva Brahmins, who for the most part do not, are entirely patrilineal.[93] One of the institutions that the matrilineal Tuḷuva castes have in common is a set of loose groupings called *baḷis*, a term that has been translated as 'lineages'.[94] The institution is evidently of some antiquity, for baḷis are mentioned in several early medieval inscriptions. They are exogamous groupings corresponding to the Brahmanical *gotra*s, except that their membership is determined matrilineally.[95] They also bear some resemblance to exogamous totemic groups since, unlike gotras, they derive their names from a wide variety of sources, such as place-names, personal names, names of deities, and so on. The number of such names is considerable: over 130 are mentioned in inscriptions alone.

91. Amongst the Tuḷuva, as with most groups that are characterized as 'matrilineal', these rules apply only to certain categories of property. 'Between, and even to a surprising degree within, the various castes one encounters an array of kinship organization which cannot easily be covered merely by applying the labels patrilineal and matrilineal' (Claus, 1981: 213). Claus quite rightly questions the value of what Needham has called 'nomothetic classifications' such as these. In Claus's view, some Tuḷuva kinship institutions are suggestive of double unilineal descent (Claus, 1981:234). Where I have used the term 'matrilineal' without qualification, it is purely for convenience; the qualifications must be taken for granted.

92. Cf. Nichter: 141.

93. See Claus, 1981: 214. Of course, forms of matrilineal succession are a feature of the organization of many groups on this coast, the most notable being the Nāyar of Kerala who have achieved an unparalleled eminence in the anthropological literature on matrilineality. Some aspects of this literature are discussed at length in Dumont, 1964.

94. Bhatt: 241.

95. Ibid.: 250.

Some of the baḷis were shared amongst the castes, and Bhatt observes that affiliation to the baḷis gave the non-Brahmin Tuḷuva 'a cohesion, a solidarity in society . . .'.[96]

The principal matrilineal Tuḷuva castes (or caste groupings) are the Bants, the Billavas, the Magavīra (who are known variously as Mogheyara, Mogēra, etc.), and the Holeyas. The British administrator Francis Buchanan, who travelled through South Kanara in 1801, just two years after the British took possession of the area, kept detailed records of their relative numbers at that time. At Buchanan's request the collector of the district, a Mr Ravenshaw, provided him with a list of statistics which described the composition of the district's population. Buchanan and Ravenshaw evidently had more faith in the mathematical value of caste than the 'native officers' who collected the information. Buchanan thought the list to be accurate 'with respect to numbers', but he also found it necessary to apologize for the account, while chiding his informants for the hopeless plasticity of their social lives: 'The different castes are detailed in the usual confused manner, with which they are spoken of by the native officers of revenue'.[97]

But for Buchanan caste numbers were power, and he was not deterred. He compiled a formidable inventory which divided the district's total population—of a little less than 400,000—into 122 castes, whose numbers ranged from 5 to 50,000. Of the total, the Bants number 52,819, the Billavas 53,764, the Magavīra 11,082, and the Holeya 52,022.[98] Together, these four castes accounted for about 43 per cent of the district's total population at that time.[99] The proportion does

96. Ibid.: 242.

97. Buchanan: 204.

98. This figure includes all the groups which Buchanan lists as 'Whalliaru' (206–7).

99. The percentage of Tuḷu speakers in the district appears to have stayed reasonably constant, for their numbers were estimated to represent about 47 per cent of the district's total in 1961 — a figure which would, of course, include a large number of Tuḷuva Brahmins (*Karnataka Gazetteer*: 94).

not seem large, but at the time when Buchanan visited South Kanara the district's population had long been swollen by the Konkani immigrants who had been squeezed out of the region of Goa after the Portuguese conquest. Even today the Tuḷuva are in a majority in the southern parts of the district,[100] and it is probably fair to conclude that in the Middle Ages they constituted the bulk of the area's population.

Of the four major Tuḷuva castes, the Bants are the highest ranked and until quite recently they controlled most of the land in Tuḷunāḍ.[101] The earliest epigraphic references to them date only as far back as the tenth and eleventh centuries, but their presence in the area almost certainly goes much further back.[102] As landowners they played a central rôle in the organization of Bhūta-worship, for the cult was closely articulated with gradations of space, each field, village and region being related to a particular spirit or set of spirits.[103] But the actual custodianship of the Bhūta shrines was not in their hands: as a rule the tending of the shrines and the conduct of the rituals were the prerogative of certain Billava sub-castes.[104]

Of the Billavas, Buchanan notes that '(they) pretend to be Sudras, but acknowledge their inferiority to the Bants', and adds that those of them 'who are in easy circumstances burn their dead; those who die poor are buried'.[105] They are often characterized as 'toddy-tappers', like their counterparts in Malabar, the Tiyas, who are also popularly credited with the introduction of coconut farming into south India.[106] They are traditionally associated with the collection of toddy and

100. Claus, 1981: 212.

101. Buchanan: 213; Claus, 1979b:98 and 1981: 213.

102. Bhatt: 233.

103. Cf. Nichter: 142. I would like to thank Fr Alfonsus D'Souza, S.J., of St Aloysius College, Mangalore, a specialist on the religious practices of the district, for pointing out this aspect of the cult to me. For his generosity with his time, and for the kindness and patience with which he introduced me to many other aspects of Tuḷuva religion, I owe him a great debt of gratitude.

104. Brückner: 18.

105. Buchanan: 239.

106. Bhatt: 226.

the distillation of liquor, although the great majority of them are, and probably always have been, cultivators.[107] By tradition they are also associated with the martial arts and the single most famous pair of Tuḷuva heroes, the brothers Kōṭi-Chennaya,[108] are archetypal heroes of the caste who symbolize the often hostile competition between the Billavas and the Bants.[109] A Billava sub-caste called Pūjāri is mainly responsible for the tending of Bhūta shrines and for the conduct of rituals.[110]

The Magavīra were by tradition the fishermen of Tuḷunāḍ.[111] Buchanan writes of this caste: 'They pretend to be Sudras of a pure descent, which is rather doubtful . . . but they acknowledge themselves greatly inferior to the Bants'.[112] By legend and practice they are associated with the sea and seafaring; an association that is celebrated in the Magavīra's own Bhūta cult: the cult of the seafaring spirit, the Bobbariya Bhūta.

The Holeyas were the most disadvantaged of the Tuḷuva castes: Buchanan characterizes them as 'slaves employed in cultivation'.[113] In fact, the term Holeya appears to lump together several quite different groups.[114] Some of these play key rôles in Bhūta-worship, performing special parts in the ritual theatre and possession-ceremonies associated with the cult.[115]

Mention of the Billavas, Magavīras and the Holeyas appears fairly late in the inscriptions. The earliest reference to the Billavas, for example, dates only as far back as the fifteenth century.[116] But this is merely an indication of their

107. Ibid.: 226–8.
108. Cf. Rai:9; Bhatt: 360; and Saletore: 1.
109. Claus, 1979b: 110; Saletore: 460.
110. Bhatt: 227.
111. Saletore: 464; Bhatt: 228–9.
112. Buchanan: 217.
113. Ibid.: 207.
114. Cf. Bhatt: 251–2.
115. Claus, 1979a: 47; 1979b: 113.
116. Bhatt: 228.

lack of social power: there is every reason to suppose that all the major Tuḷuva castes share an equally long history of settlement in the region.

Although the Tuḷuva castes form a distinct social group they do not, of course, live in isolation from the many other castes and communities that inhabit Tuḷunāḍ. Of these one of the largest is that of the Tuḷuva Brahmins. When Buchanan visited Tuḷunāḍ their numbers added up to almost a tenth of the total population of the district.[117]

The Brahmins were the custodians of the pan-Indian Hindu tradition that formed the complementary other half of the folk religion of Tuḷunāḍ. The area has its fair share and more of temples dedicated to the deities of the Sanskritic pantheon, and all of the Tuḷuva castes who had access to those temples participated in the worship of those deities, just as they did in the Bhūta cult. There was, of course, no contradiction in this, for to them the Bhūtas and the Sanskritic deities (*devaru*) represented aspects of divine and supernatural power that shaded imperceptibly into each other.[118]

The Bhūta pantheon has a hierarchy of its own, a pyramid of divinities which has local spirits and lineage ancestors at its base, the Bhūta-heroes of Tuḷuva legend higher up its slopes, and certain deities known as *daivas* at the apex.[119] But perhaps an architectural metaphor is inappropriate here, for these rankings are so fluid that new spirits constantly enter at the bottom while the others are swirled upwards and downwards with the passage of time.[120] At its upper levels this soft-edged edifice fades gently into the clouds of the Sanskritic pantheon, and hidden in those mists there is a good deal of two-way traffic.[121]

It is generally agreed upon that the flow of this traffic was

117. Buchanan: 205.

118. Nichter: 145; Claus, 1973: 232.

119. See Rai: 9; Claus, 1979b: 96; Brückner: 20, 29 and Bhatt: 360.

120. Nichter: 147–9.

121. There is, of course, a symbiotic relationship between folk deities and Sanskritic gods throughout Hindu India. See Eck: 68–9.

directed by Brahmin priests. The landowners and kings of Tuḷunāḍ patronized both forms of worship, and temples and Bhūta-shrines were often built close to each other. Sometimes the landlords would appoint Brahmins to supervise the functioning of both temples and Bhūta-shrines, so even though Brahmins did not officiate at Bhūta rituals they were well-placed to influence the structure of popular religion in the area.[122]

The Brahmins for their part had a complex relationship with the divinities of the Bhūta cult. They treated some Bhūtas as ritually impure and relegated their shrines to the outer courtyards of the temples. Other spirits were co-opted and incorporated into the Brahmanical pantheon.[123] Some lesser Bhūtas were transformed into bodyguards for major gods, while the more important Bhūta deities were given Brahmanical identities or were treated as avatārs of Śiva, Viṣṇu and the Devī.[124] This could not, of course, have been a matter of Brahmiṇ conspiracy. The fact is that the other Tuḷuva castes must have been willing accomplices in the re-definition of their deities, even though some among them may now be inclined to forget that complicity, in the wake of contemporary 'Dravidianist' movements.

The first candidates for Brahmanical co-optation were naturally the gods who stood at the very top of the Bhūta hierarchy, and foremost among these was a god known as Bermeṛu or Bemmeṛu.[125] The final syllable in the name, -ṛu, is an honorific, and the name is properly Berme, Birme or Bemme. It is Berme who watches over the fate of the heroes of the folk-epics and it is to him that their protagonists appeal.[126] In the shrines where he is worshipped, he is depicted as a warrior, seated on a horse, sword in hand. He is, in fact,

122. Cf. Nichter: 143.

123. Ibid.: 141.

124. For a detailed account of the workings of this process, see Nichter's article.

125. Cf. Brückner: 29; Claus, 1979a: 40.

126. Cf. Bhatt: 24; Saletore: 496.

none other than the divinity who is sometimes said to be 'Brahmā'. But so strong is his character that his co-optation has never quite succeeded; for most Tuḷu-speaking people he is still Bermeṛu, and even those who refer to him as Brahmā usually add his other name in parentheses.[127]

In Tuḷu legend the name Berme sometimes occurs as a personal name: the father of the heroine Siri, for example, is known as Berme Alva.[128] Both Berme (Bemme) and his alter ego, Brahmā, are linked in folk philology to a name that is current among the Tuḷuva to this day: Bomma.[129] Whether the philological link is actually tenable or not is probably largely a matter of opinion. What is certain is that cognates of both 'Berme' ('Bemme') and 'Bomma' are closely associated with the naming systems of matrilineal Tuḷuva castes. It can be established beyond reasonable doubt that both those names were current among the Tuḷuva in the Middle Ages, for a Bermera-baḷi, a Bommiya-baḷi and even a Bommi-seṭṭiya-baḷi[130] are among the many matrilineal baḷis mentioned in medieval inscriptions.[131] So, whatever the etymological connection between the words Bomma and Berme/Bemme,[132] it is certain that 'Bomma' was widely in currency as a name-element in Tuḷunāḍ in the Middle Ages.

From that, several related assumptions seem to follow: that

127. Cf. Claus, 1979a: 40; and Prabhu: 25. Bhatt's puzzlement is instructive: 'Although it cannot be easily explained how Brahma who occupies such an exalted position in the Hindu pantheon is assigned such a low and degraded place amongst the devils (*bhūtas*) in Tuḷu-nāḍu, we may hypothetically say that since devil-worship has been, for centuries, the core of the Tuḷuva cult amongst the non-Brahmins, Siva, the Lord of the bhūtas, himself may have been represented being called Brahma.' (356)

128. Cf. Bhatt: 26.

129. Indeed, a nineteenth-century observer even listed a bhūta called Bommartāye (Rev. A. Manner, Tuḷu-Paḍdānaḷu, 1886, quoted by Bhatt, p. 379).

130. I have introduced a hyphen here between the elements Bomm and seṭṭiya.

131. Bhatt: 243; 250-1.

132. There may be none at all, for the Bommiya-baḷi is named after a mythological figure called Bonyannāya (Bhatt: 250).

the letters B-M-A of MS. H.6 are actually intended to be B-M-M-A; and that these in turn are meant to spell Bomma, a name current among the Tuḷuva groups who formed most of the population of the area around Mangalore at the time when Abraham Ben Yijū took up residence there. There is good reason then to believe that the slave of MS. H.6 was called Bomma, and that he was born into one of those matrilineal Tuḷuva castes which have traditionally been linked with Bhūta-worship.

Of course, much of this is founded on the ghost of a letter, the 'm' that may lie locked within the vault of the Geniza's language: on the mere possibility of a doubled consonant, it may be wildly intemperate to make any assumptions at all. But if we were to persist in these rash speculations, we would soon arrive at the threshold of a further problem: the question of finding a caste for Bomma.

There is little to guide us: Bomma throws so tiny a shadow that the Geniza yields only three facts about him that are of use here. The first and most obvious of these is the fact of his slavery. The second, that he undertook a few long journeys by ship, which suggests that he had some acquaintance with sea travel. The third, that he played an important part in Ben Yijū's business, and therefore probably had some acquaintance with trade.

The first of these facts would seem to rule out the Bants, for it is unlikely that a member of the most important landowning community would be sold into slavery. Of the two principal agricultural castes, the Billavas and the Holeyas, the latter seem the more likely possibility, since many of them appear to have been bonded serfs living in conditions of extreme poverty. Yet certain other circumstances make the Magavīra caste likelier still.

In the first place, the Magavīras' affinity for the sea and seafaring is well documented, not merely a matter of customary association. The Portuguese traveller Duarte Barbosa, who travelled along the west coast in the early years of the sixteenth century, writes of 'another sect of people still lower . . . which they call Moguer. . . . These people for the most part get their living at sea, they are mariners and fishermen.'[133] They were also closely associated with the Mapilla Muslims, another seafaring community, and with the Middle Eastern traders who lived on the cities of the coast. Barbosa comments: 'They are some of them very rich men who have got ships with which they navigate, for they gain much money with the Moors.'[134] Their associations with the Muslims and 'Moors' is commemorated in the legend of the Bhūta who is uniquely the Magavīras' own: the Bobbariya Bhūta, who is said to be the spirit of a Muslim mariner and trader who died at sea.[135] No Magavīra settlement is without its Bobbariya shrine: usually a simple pillar and platform of stone, with a wooden mace beside it.[136] None of the communities of Tuḷunāḍ could have better equipped Bomma for the rôle he was eventually to play in Ben Yijū's business than the Magavīra.

We could assume then, if we so wished, that Bomma was of the Magavīra caste, since that seems the likeliest possibility. Yet the exercise may be to no purpose at all: for in dealing with caste, as with schizophrenia, we can never be sure where the fantasies of the analyst end and the plight of the subject begins.

VII

The Geniza documents reveal nothing about how Ben Yijū's path came to cross Bomma's. Ben Yijū may well have written to his correspondents in Aden when Bomma first came into

133. Barbosa: 138. Barbosa's reference to this caste is curious, however, for it occurs in the context of a long description of the 'sects' of the region around Calicut, what Barbosa calls 'the kingdom of Malabar'. The group of Magavīras he encountered were probably a small community of immigrants from nearby Tuḷunād, for he notes that 'there are very few of these in the country . . . ' (138).

134. Barbosa: 138.

135. Upadhyaya and Upadhyaya: 60; Saletore: 461; Prabhu: 143–4.

136. Upadhyaya and Upadhyaya: 60.

his service, for the acquiring of a slave by a trader frequently also meant the introduction of a new employee into the business. But whether he did or not will never be known, for none of the letters Ben Yijū wrote to his friends in Aden ever made their way into the Geniza. What is left of his correspondence with them is as bafflingly one-sided as an overheard telephone conversation: what Ben Yijū had to say in his letters has to be deduced from his friends' responses.

The first positively datable reference to Bomma occurs in a letter sent to Ben Yijū in 1135.[137] Ben Yijū had already been at least three years in Malabar at the time.[138]

The letter is a remarkable one: one of the most unusual in the Geniza. In part it is a letter of complaint. The cause for complaint is Bomma: his behaviour has outraged the morals of Ben Yijū's correspondent. But Ben Yijū's correspondent has also had another, greater shock recently: Aden, where he lives, has been the target of a naval raid. What remains of the letter he wrote to Ben Yijū after the occasion bears the suggestion that Bomma, upon his very first appearance in the Geniza documents, may have been present at the enactment of a full-blooded historical event, more than a thousand miles away from his home in Mangalore.

The man who wrote this letter was a key figure in the trade of the Indian Ocean. His name was Maḍmūn ibn al-Ḥasan ibn Bundār, and he was the *Nagīd* or chief representative of the merchants of Aden.[139] He was a relative of Khalaf ibn Iṣḥaq, the writer of the letter of MS. H.6, and he was also related to Ben Yijū's third regular correspondent in Aden, a merchant and judicial functionary called Yūsuf ibn Abraham ibn Bundār.[140] These three men, Khalaf ibn Iṣḥaq. Yūsuf ibn Abraham and Maḍmūn ibn Bundār, were relatives and had

137. T-S 20.137, recto, and T-S N.S. J1.

138. Ben Yijū arrived in India at some point before 1132. See section VIII below.

139. Maḍmūn ibn Bundār's career is extensively chronicled in the Geniza. See, for example, Goitein, 1973: 177–82, and 1980: 45.

140. One of his letters is reprinted in Goitein, 1973; 192–7.

close connections with one another as well as with a vast network of merchants, both in Aden and far beyond.[141] The threads of their relationships stretched like a cat's cradle across the known world, from Morocco as far as Sumatra:[142] it was a circumstance so dispersed that it almost precluded the notion of exile.

Ben Yijū himself had his origins in the western end of this far-flung world — in the city of Mahdia, which was then one of the premier ports in the region known as Ifrīqiya (North Africa). The material provides very few clues to his early life. What can be gathered of his father, Farḥia, suggests that he was a scholar and religious teacher. He may have dabbled in business like most scholars of his time, but on the whole his family probably lived in modest circumstances. He had four children altogether, three sons, Abraham, Mubashshir and Yūsuf, and one daughter, Barkha.[143]

Abraham Ben Yijū was certainly well enough educated to have become a scholar, like his father, or a man of letters. But instead, early in his life he chose a career in business, either because the circumstances of his family were too straitened to support another scholar, or, more likely, because an adventurer's streak pushed him into it. In a way the choice would have been an obvious one for a young man growing up in a port where merchant vessels from all over the Mediterranean docked regularly. At that time the Jewish merchants of Ifrīqiya were very closely connected with the Indian Ocean trade, so the decision to become a merchant, once taken, would inevitably have led the young Ben Yijū eastwards, first to Egypt and then further still — to Aden and Mangalore in his case.

141. Ibid.: 1973: 192.

142. A merchant from Fusṭāṭ is known to have lived for fifteen years in Sumatra, the furthest point east yet recorded for anyone connected with the Geniza (cf. Goitein, 1967b: 157–8).

143. For the sake of consistency, I have transcribed the names exactly as they are written in the documents. The Hebrew equivalents of Mubashshir and Barkha are Mevasser and Berākha.

Ben Yijū probably first encountered Maḍmūn in Aden, but the first item in their correspondence was written by Maḍmūn when Ben Yijū was already in Malabar.[144] On the evidence of Maḍmūn's early letters, Ben Yijū's relationship with him at that time fell somewhere between that of an agent and junior partner. Ben Yijū may have worked for Maḍmūn in Aden, as an employee or apprentice, and it was probably with Maḍmūn's assistance that he set up his business in Mangalore.

The events that Maḍmūn describes, in the very letter in which he refers to Bomma for the first time, occurred in Aden in 1135. Bomma had probably been sent there to buy goods for Ben Yijū's household. The event was not of any great significance, but it still made an impression deep enough to earn itself a place in a history written a century and a half later.[145] It was nothing more significant than a raid on Aden by a fleet of ships sent by the Amīr of Kīsh (Qaiṣ), a tiny island principality at the mouth of the Straits of Hormuz. The rulers of Kīsh at this time were given to piratical expeditions which spread much alarm up and down the coasts of Africa, India and the Arabian Peninsula. Even distant Cambay, on the west coast of India, had to be fortified against their depredations.[146] The raid to which Bomma may have been a witness was not one of their more successful forays. The defenders of Aden repulsed the raid and the Amīr's fleet had to scurry back to Kīsh as best it could. Still, it threw the city into turmoil and prompted the usually business-like Maḍmūn to compose a long descriptive passage in his letter to Ben Yijū.

This passage has been published in English by Professor Goitein:

144. T-S 20.130. My assumption that this is the first item in Maḍmūn's correspondence with Bin Yijū is based on a comment in the letter (recto, lines 4–5) in which Maḍmūn mentions the hardships of the voyage to India, which suggests that it was a response to a letter by Ben Yijū in which he had complained of an unpleasant journey.

145. Cf. Goitein 1956: 248. The historian was Ibn al-Mujāwir (died 1291).

146. Cf. al-Idrīsī: 59, 153, 171.

> This year, at the beginning of the seafaring time, the son of al-'Amīd , the ruler of Kīsh, sent an expedition against Aden demanding a part of the town, which was refused, whereupon he sent this expedition . . . [The fifteen ships] remained in the haven of Aden [awaiting][147] the incoming ships, but did not enter the city. The people of the city were very much afraid of them, but God did not give them victory or success. Many of them were killed and their ships were thrust with spears and they died of thirst and hunger. The first of the merchants' ships to arrive were the two vessels of the shipmaster Rāmisht. They attacked them but God did not give them victory. As soon as the ships entered the port, they were manned with a great number of regular troops, whereupon the enemy was chased from the port and began to disperse on the sea. Thus God did not give them victory and they made off in the most ignominious way, after having suffered great losses and humiliation . . . [148]

The published passage leaves out the first six lines of the document. They are worth retrieving: they show that despite his still lingering alarm, the memory of the raid was not the uppermost thought on Maḍmūn's mind when he wrote this letter. That honour was reserved for Bomma: he had walked into his office, very drunk, and demanded money.

This is how the lines read: 'And after that he [Bomma] started on other things. He said: Give me more money, [what I have] is not enough. He took 4 months money from me, eight dīnārs. Often, he would come here very drunk, and would not listen to a word I said.'[149] He ends plaintively: 'I do not know what the need was for my Master to send him here.'[150] He does not neglect, later in the same letter, to debit Ben Yijū for the eight dīnārs that he advanced to Bomma.[151]

147. I have substituted the word 'awaiting' here for the Arabic *intaẓarū*, which Goitein translates as 'attending'.

148. Goitein, 1956: 256. The passage is a translation of the document T-S 20.137, recto, lines 9–22.

149. T-S 20.137, recto, lines 1–5.

150. Ibid.: lines 5–6.

151. Ibid.: lines 41–3.

The letter does not provide any indication of whether Bomma was actually present in Aden when the raid occurred. We must assume that he was: the prospect of a troop of Adenese soldiers being cheered into battle by a drunken Bomma is too valuable to be lightly forsaken.

VIII

This raid occurred in 1135, and Maḍmūn's letter was probably written later the same year.[152] This makes it one of the earliest of the reliably dated documents that relate to Ben Yijū's stay in Malabar. But it is not the very earliest. The first of Ben Yijū's documents that has been precisely dated was written on 17 October 1132, in Mangalore.[153] The date is known because it happens to be a legal document and thus takes note of the place where it was written and the day of its writing.

How long Ben Yijū had been in India at the time we can only guess. Certainly he had been there long enough to acquire slaves and set up a household, so it may have been as much as a year or two, which would mean that he had moved to Mangalore in 1130 or 1131.

The acquisition of a male slave would have been commonplace for a foreign merchant setting up in business on the Malabar coast. Contemporary accounts suggest that the rulers and kings of the west coast welcomed foreign traders warmly,[154] and often even provided them with servants and employees in their keenness to attract trade to their cities.

The Persian envoy ʿAbd al-Razzāq al-Samarqandī, who was dispatched, much against his wishes, to the court of Vijaynagar in 1442, had to travel through Malabar on the way. He records that his companions bought some slaves who escaped in the course of their travels. The king of Vijaynagar,

152. Goitein, 1956: 250.
153. Goitein, 1973: 202.
154. See, for example, Idrīsī: 177.

hearing of this, personally made good their losses.[155] Duarte Barbosa, travelling in Malabar sixty or so years later, found that the Zamorin of Calicut 'gave to each [foreign trader] a Nair to guard and serve him, a Chety scribe for his accounts, and to take care of his property, and a broker for his trade'.[156]

Barbosa records that these merchants were known collectively as *pardesis* in Calicut, even though their members included 'Arabs, Persians, Guzarates, Khorasanys, and Decanys . . . '. These were not itinerant traders; they were expatriates who had settled in Malabar for considerable lengths of time: 'they are great merchants, and possess in this place wives and children, and ships for sailing to all parts with all kinds of goods'. The community was large, and so powerful that they even had a court of their own, in which their laws were administered without interference from the Zamorin.[157]

The pardesis' style of life was sumptuous enough to surprise the worldly Persian courtier 'Abd al-Razzāq: 'they dress themselves in magnificent apparel after the manner of the Arabs, and manifest luxury in every particular . . . '[158] Barbosa was no less impressed:

> These are white men and very gentlemanlike and of good appearance, they go well dressed, and adorned with silk stuffs, scarlet cloth, camlets and cottons: their head-dress wrapped around their heads. They have large houses and many servants: they are very luxurious in eating, drinking and sleeping . . .[159]

Barbosa found the 'Moors' present in force at the Zamorin's court, just as Vasco da Gama and 'Abd al-Razzāq had earlier.[160] The rulers of Malabar probably depended a good deal on the resident pardesi merchants for advice on the

155. Major: 29.
156. Barbosa: 148.
157. Ibid.: 147.
158. Major: 17.
159. Barbosa: 148.
160. Major: 19.

conduct of their trade, and for the direction of their relations with countries and rulers overseas.[161]

These accounts were written more than three centuries after Bomma and Ben Yijū's lifetimes, and they describe a place 200 miles down the coast from Mangalore. Yet it is not unlikely that Ben Yijū's way of life in Mangalore was similar to that of the pardesis of Calicut: the foreign merchants had close links with each other up and down the length of the west coast, and they appear to have had shared customs and traditions. It is a curious coincidence, for example, that like Barbosa's pardesis with their Nair and 'Chety' employees, Ben Yijū too did business with a certain Sesu Shetty and had an agent called Nair, as we shall see. Like the pardesis of Calicut, Ben Yijū also had a pronounced taste for certain luxuries. He appears to have been fastidious, for example, in matters of clothing.

The people he lived amongst were by preference generally bare-bodied. 'Abd al-Razzāq notes that most of the people he saw in Malabar 'have the body nearly naked; they wear only bandages around the middle, called lankoutah, which descend from the navel to above the knee'. This was true of men and women alike, and for people of all classes.[162] The markers of social distinction among them appear to have lain mainly in jewellery and ornaments.[163] Bomma, for example, would probably have worn earrings, and maybe even a necklace or chain, as well as a 'bandage around the middle'.

To Ben Yijū and the Middle Eastern merchants, on the other hand, the thought of going bare-bodied would have

161. Their thirst for trade sometimes made them eager to ingratiate themselves with foreign powers. 'Abd al-Razzāq recounts that the Zamorin of Calicut, upon hearing of the power of the Persian king Shah Rukh, sent him presents and the message: 'In this port, on every Friday and every solemn feast day, the Khotbah is celebrated according to the prescribed rules of Islamism. With your majesty's permission, these prayers shall be adorned and honoured by the addition of your name and of your illustrious titles.' Major: 15.

162. Major: 17. 'Abd al-Razzāq also notes that this apparel was common to 'the king and to the beggar'.

163. See Barbosa: 87.

been shocking, at least as far as it concerned themselves. They would have been accustomed to think of clothes as a double layer of modesty for the body, so that the under-robe that cloaked the body's nakedness would itself need to be covered in turn by a further screen of outer clothing. Anything less would have seemed immodest within the terms of their culture. Their heads, in particular, would always have been covered, for in their civilization a covered head was seen as a sign of pious humility.[164]

This does not appear to have been a matter on which Ben Yijū was disposed to compromise. In several letters and accounts we read of the Egyptian robes (*fūṭa*) and fine Alexandrian cloaks (*maqṭā'*)[165] that he imported. Others mention lengths of cloth and kerchiefs which he may have used as turbans.[166] He probably had something of a reputation for being a dapper dresser because one of his correspondents, sending him a shawl from Aden, thought it prudent to extol its qualities: 'I have also for my own part, sent for you . . . a fine new Dibīqi shawl, with nicely worked borders — an appropriate garment for men of eminence'.[167] No matter that in the humidity of Mangalore a turban, robe or shawl would probably take only a week's wearing to grow mildew: Ben Yijū's sense of what he owed himself clearly prevailed over climate and convenience. He was probably never seen on the streets of Mangalore in anything other than a turban and robe of much the same kind that he would have worn in Egypt or Aden. But once he was indoors better sense may have prevailed, inducing him to exchange his robes for a 'bandage around the middle'.

Amongst the many everyday things that Ben Yijū must have missed in India, paper was probably the most important.

164. See Goitein's (1983: 153–9) discussion of attitudes towards clothing as they are represented in the Geniza.

165. Cf. T-S 1080 J 95, recto, lines 8–9; T-S 10 J 9, fol. 24, lines 14–15; T-S 10 J 12, fol. 5, verso, line 9.

166. Cf. T-S 8 J 7, fol. 23, recto margin.

167. T-S 18 J 2, fol. 7, recto, lines 15–18.

In Tuḷunāḍ, as in most parts of India, the material most commonly used for writing was the palm-leaf, and paper was evidently difficult to obtain. Ben Yijū must have asked for paper in every letter to Aden, for packages of these were sent to him with virtually every shipment of cargo. He must have been fussy about the quality of his paper too, for his correspondents often added little notes in their letters to let him know that they had exerted themselves to please him. Maḍmūn, for example, informs him in one of his letters that the three packets of Egyptian Ṭalḥi paper he has sent are 'of faultless quality',[168] and in another he writes of 'two large quires of fine paper, of the Sulṭāni kind — no one knows its like'.[169]

We have reason to be grateful to Maḍmūn for his pains: the paper he sent Ben Yijū was of such unmatched quality that even today, eight hundred years later, after enduring several sea journeys, many of those papers are still in excellent condition and show no sign of the kind of decay that will certainly afflict *these* pages within, at best, a decade. Ben Yijū probably also imported his ink — or else he may have found a vegetable dye that could be used as a substitute. He was no less careful in the husbanding of his supplies of ink than he was with his paper. For his accounts and other throwaway jottings he would water the ink, while for other writings he would use a thick, dark solution, which remains vivid to this day on certain fragments. He probably used a quill to write with, but there is a distant possibility that he may have used an early prototype of a fountain pen. The concept of a pen with an inbuilt reservoir of ink appears to have been current in Egypt as early as the tenth century. The Fatimid Caliph al-Mu'izz is reported to have had one crafted for him, with such success that his secretary was 'able to write in the most elegant script that could possibly be desired . . . '.[170] However, this innovation may not ever have

168. T-S K 25.252, verso, lines 14–15.

169. T-S 18 J 2, fol. 7, recto, lines 19–20. For treatments of the medieval paper industry in the Middle East, see Ashtor, 1977: 266–73, and Goitein, 1961: 189–93.

170. Bosworth: 232.

percolated beyond the Caliph's palace, and it is probably likelier than not that Ben Yijū had to make do with a selection of quills. While writing he would often stop to whittle his pens' nibs as they grew blunt: the change in the texture of his writing can be seen quite clearly — accompanied often by little splutters of ink, of exactly the kind that everybody who has had a pre-ballpoint childhood will remember from the erratic pens of their schooldays.

Ben Yijū liked to indulge himself in other matters too. Much of the kitchenware for his house was imported from Aden — even such things as frying-pans and sieves.[171] He also had crockery, soap, goblets and glasses sent out from the Middle East. He is known to have imported a velvet-like carpet from Gujarat, via Aden, and his mats came all the way from Berbera in Africa.[172] He seems to have been well-known amongst his friends for his love of sweets: they regularly sent him raisins, and sometimes nougat and dates as well. The palm sugar that was produced on the Malabar coast was clearly not to his taste, for his friends appear to have been under instructions to send him cane sugar from the Middle East at every possible opportunity.[173] On one occasion, when Khalaf ibn Iṣḥaq failed in his duty, he even added the apologetic note: 'Your servant looked for sugar, but there is none to be had this year . . . '[174]

Clearly, Abraham Ben Yijū was a man who had a taste for good living.

IX

It would seem to follow that Ben Yijū, no less than the pardesis of Calicut, would aspire to 'large houses and many

171. Cf. T-S 20,137, recto, line 47.

172. Cf. T-S MS. Or. 1081 J3, recto, lines 7–8; & T-S 18 J 2, fol. 7, recto, line 12. For mention of a 'Barūji ṭanfasa', see T-S K 25.252, recto, line 23.

173. The production of cane sugar was a flourishing industry in the Middle East in the twelfth century, Ashtor, 1977.

174. T-S 18 J 5, fol.1, recto, margin.

servants'. It could well be then that he first acquired Bomma as a hand to work in his house and only later took him into his business.

In either case it would have been an easy matter for Ben Yijū to find a slave in Mangalore. Francis Buchanan, before travelling to South Kanara in 1801, asked the collector how many slaves there were in the district, and received the answer: 7,924.[175] By his account, agricultural labourers and men of low caste sometimes sold their sister's children, their heirs by matrilineal descent, to raise money.

Buchanan reckoned that 'a good slave sells for 10 Pagodas, or about 4 guineas'.[176] This meant about 40 rupees, at a time when a hired man's daily rice allowance was worth a little more than an anna, and his yearly wage consisted of about 5½ rupees and the use of a house.[177] In effect, the cost of buying 'a good slave', at Buchanan's valuation, would be only a little more than that of hiring a worker for a year. Buchanan adds that a male slave received about an anna's worth of rice a day, as well as an annual allowance of cloth and a small sum in cash. In addition, a slave's master bore the expenses of his marriage, but his children belonged either to his or his wife's master.[178]

For all its apparent precision, Buchanan's account is puzzling: for example, just a few pages after he notes the number of slaves in the district as 7,924, he describes the Holeya caste as 'slaves employed in cultivation' and enters their number as 47,358.[179] It is as though his usage of the word 'slave' and the institutions he was trying to describe were somehow askew, at odds with each other.

Buchanan was writing at a time when the slave trade was

175. Buchanan: 203.

176. Ibid.: 228.

177. These figures are computed from Buchanan's reckoning of the cost of maintaining a hired worker (p. 227), the cost of rice (p. 243) and the relative value of currencies (p. 219).

178. Buchanan: 228.

179. Ibid.: 207.

one of the pillars of the colonial economy of the Americas, and he, no less that the British officials serving in the Caribbean, would have understood slavery in the modern Western sense, that is, primarily as an economic circumstance, a way of organizing production. But for all their accountant-like precision, that one discrepancy proves that his figures were not equal to the complexity of the circumstances he was trying to describe: his account took the wrong turn somewhere, misled by the signposts of the Enlightenment.

Clearly, what Buchanan called 'slavery' ranged from village-level jajmani relationships of ritual patronage and clientage at one end of the scale, to certain forms of credit at the other, in which pauperized men and women were forced to offer their bodies and labour power to their creditors. It is, of course, well known that until recent times creditors often realized debts of this kind by selling the people who formed their living collateral. It could be that the 47,358 Holeyas of Buchanan's description actually fell into the first category, while the 7,924 'slaves' fell into the second.

People of the second category — 'slaves' sold by their families to realize debts or raise money — appear to have been freely traded in medieval Karnataka. An inscription from the early fifteenth century indicates that 'cattle, slaves and horses' were sold at village fairs.[180] A reference in a twelfth-century Jaina work suggests that some of these slaves were traded outside Karnataka, possibly even abroad.[181] Material from the Geniza suggests that this is more than likely. There is plenty of evidence to prove that Indian men and women were regularly sold in the markets of the Middle East,[182] and, considering the close links that Middle Eastern merchants had with the west coast, it would seem to follow that a large number of those Indian slaves came from that region.

180. Chidanandamurthy: 186.

181. Ibid.: 183.

182. Several documents in the Geniza offer proof that North African Jews, for instance, kept Indian, Slavonic, Byzantine, Libyan and Negro slaves (Hirschberg: 182). See also Assaf, 1940.

It could be that Ben Yijū acquired Bomma at one of the village fairs or markets in which slaves were sold. But the weight of the evidence suggests that Bomma was a kind of apprentice to Ben Yijū, and that he began by doing odd jobs and errands (like travelling to Aden) and worked his way upwards in his business.

Buchanan unfortunately does not supply the Tuḷu or Kannada terms that he renders as 'slave'. The fifteenth-century inscription that mentions slave markets, however, uses the Kannada word *tottu*, which is an ambiguous term, used for servants and hired workers as well as 'slaves'. It might be translated as 'serf', but even that apparently does not do justice to its many connotations. This is inevitable in a way, for the medieval idea of slavery tends to confound contemporary conceptions of both servitude and its mirror image, individual freedom.[183]

To begin with, in many parts of the world, including Egypt and north India, slavery was the principal means of recruitment to positions of power in the state. Secondly, in medieval India and in the Middle East, as in many African societies,[184] slavery appears to have been a means of creating ties of fictive kinship. Wherever kinship played an important organizational rôle in society, there had to be some parallel institution for creating and initiating new ties and alignments: left to itself kinship would be too narrowly bounded a principle — even in a purely demographic sense — to be workable. Often it was 'slavery' that played that rôle, and in its origins it had little resemblance to slavery as it is understood today — although once it came to be penetrated by modern forms of exchange, after the seventeenth and eighteenth centuries, it spelt disaster for the societies that practised it. In the Middle Ages, however, it was often a means of creating quasi-familial bonds. Thus, the merchants of Cairo would often take slaves into their family businesses as 'confidants', but just in case they acquired

183. Cf. Finley, 1980: 58–62. See also, Rosenthal, 1960: 91.
184. See, for example, Evans-Pritchard: 220–5.

too much power within the family, they would free them once their own sons were grown up.[185]

The most elusive aspect of slavery such as this is the part it plays as metaphor, as an instrument of the medieval imagination. It was the principle that shaped much traditional education, for example, as well as forms of apprenticeship in the arts and crafts. It is well known that in many vocations the lines between apprentice, disciple and bondsman were so thin as to be invisible: initiation required aspirants to surrender some part of their freedom to their masters. In the tradition of Hindustani music, for instance, an aspirant enters an *ustād*'s tutelage through a right of passage, the *gandh bandh*, a ceremony that turns the young student into his teacher's *banda*, his bondsman.[186]

It is hardly surprising then that Chidanandamurthy's scholarly account of slavery in medieval Karnataka[187] should draw much of its material not from the standard historical sources but from the work of a poet — a contemporary of Ben Yijū and Bomma — the saint and mystic Basavaṇṇa (*c.* 1106–68).[188] Together with the group of saint-poets known as the Vacanakāras, Basavaṇṇa was to spark a movement of religious pietism and social protest that would burn with a brief but scorching flame in the twelfth and thirteenth centuries. It was one of the Bhakti movements that swept medieval India, the Vīraśaiva movement, centred in Kalyāṇa in northern Karnataka, about three hundred miles or so from Mangalore. It was founded on a quest for the dissolution of all differences of selfhood, wealth, caste and gender in the pursuit of the one, attributeless, 'bodiless god' who, in Ramanujan's wonderful rendering of the Kannada, was the 'lord of the meeting rivers' to Basavaṇṇa and the 'lord white as jasmine' to the woman

185. Goitein, 1973: 13.

186. Cf. Wade: 169.

187. Dr A.K. Viveka Rai very kindly translated this article into English for me.

188. Ramanujan: 61. Cf. Desai: 137, 168.

poet Mahādēviyakka. He was a Śiva who belonged neither to a caste nor to a temple:

> The rich
> will make temples for Śiva.
> What shall I,
> a poor man,
> do?
>
> My legs are pillars,
> the body the shrine,
> the head a cupola
> of gold.[189]

In seeking his lord, Basavaṇṇa becomes his lover's complement, androgynous in the fierceness of his passion:[190]

> I wear these men's clothes
> only for you.
>
> Sometimes I am man,
> sometimes I am woman.
>
> O lord of the meeting rivers
> I'll make wars for you
> but I'll be your devotees' bride.[191]

The metaphor that guides Basavaṇṇa's seeking is that of the 'slave', the tottu of the inscription, in search of his master. Basavaṇṇa is both his lord's lover and his bondsman:

> Don't make me hear all day
> 'Whose man, whose man, whose man is this?'
>
> Let me hear, 'This man is mine, mine,
> this man is mine'.[192]

The imagery would not have been unfamiliar to Ben Yijū. He and his friends were all orthodox, observant Jews, strongly aware of their distinctive religious identity. But they

189. Ramanujan: 88.
190. Cf. ibid.: 29.
191. Ibid.: 87.
192. Ibid.: 70.

were also part of the Arabic-speaking world, and the everyday language of their religious life was one they shared with the Muslims of that region: when they invoke the name of God in their writings it is usually as Allah, and their invocations more often than not take the forms current in Arabic usage, such as *inshā'allāh* and *al-ḥamdu l-illāh*. Distinct though their faith was, it was still a part of the religious world of the Middle East — and that world had been turned on its head by the Sūfis of Islām. Many members of the congregation of the Synagogue of the Palestinians are known to have been powerfully influenced by Sūfism.[193] Abraham Maimonides (1186–1238), the son of the great Talmudist Moses Maimonides, and head of the Jews of Egypt for thirty-two years, even said once that the Sūfis were 'worthier disciples of the Prophets of Israel than were the Jews of his time'.[194]

Most Sūfis would have regarded the Vacanakāras as pantheistic and blasphemous in their desire to merge themselves in their lord. Their own conceptions of extinction (*fanā*) and subsistence (*baqā*) always assumed an utterly transcendant God.[195] Yet they would probably have acknowledged a commonality in the nature of their striving, and they would certainly have seen a likeness in their imagery.

For the Sūfis too the notion of being tied, being held by bonds, is the central metaphor of their collective life. Forms of the Arabic root which expresses that idea r-b-ṭ, 'to bind, tie up', are threaded through their discourse: they range from the brotherhoods called *rabīṭa* to the *murābiṭ* of Morocco and *rabita kurmak*, the Turkish phrase which expresses the tie between the Sūfi Shaikh and his disciples.[196] The Sūfis too drew some of their most powerful images from slavery: metaphors of perfect devotion and love strung together in an imagery of charged spiritual eroticism. Thus, in Sūfi tradition, the eleventh-century Sulṭān, Maḥmūd of Ghaznī, the

193. See, for example, Goitein, 1953–4.
194. Goitein, 1967b: 146.
195. Cf. Schimmel: 141–3.
196. Ibid.: 231, 237.

fearsome and bloodthirsty conqueror of Indian legend — is a symbol of mystical longing because of the perfect love that bound him and his soldier-slave, Ayāz.[197]

The imagery of Basavaṇṇa and the Sūfis hangs suspended far above the workaday world of master craftsmen and apprentices, traders and novice accountants. But even the most mundane institutions have their life-giving myths, and in the setting of the distant frame provided by these, the elements of slavery in those relationships would have appeared not as demeaning bonds, but possibly as ties that were in some small way ennobling — human connections, pledges of commitment, in a relationship that could just as easily have been a matter of daily wages.

Ben Yijū may well have read something of the Sūfis, but Bomma was almost certainly wholly ignorant of Basavaṇṇa's teachings. It was only after his lifetime that Tuḷunāḍ heard rumours of the Vacanakāras, and even then their influence in that area was slight at best. But still, Basavaṇṇa and the Vacanakāras had changed their times by holding in view for a brief while that other image of religious life, the 'anti-structure' that is written on one of the sides of the spinning coin of Hinduism. Bomma too would have had a glimpse of it, for he would certainly have had some acquaintance with that great wealth of popular tradition that has always, and against all odds, kept the shine on that side of the coin.

For his part, Ben Yijū may well have participated in that range of folk practices and syncretic beliefs which have always formed the hidden and subversive counter-image of the orthodox religions of the Middle East: the exorcism cults, the magical rites, the customs of visiting saints' graves, and such like.[198] It was perhaps that no-man's land of inarticulate counter-beliefs that formed a small patch of level ground between Bomma and Ben Yijū — the Bhūta-worshipping,

197. Ibid.: 292.

198. A large number of documents relating to such esoteric and magical cults have survived in the Geniza. See Golb, 1967.

matrilineally-descended Tuḷu, and the orthodox, patriarchal Jew who would seem to have nothing at all in common.

X

The paper that Ben Yijū attested in Mangalore on 17 October 1132 was a legal document granting manumission to a female slave. A second document, related to this one, has also been found in the Geniza. It is written in Ben Yijū's handwriting, on one of the many scraps of paper on which he habitually made notes. It is a draft of a deposition, in formal legal language, backing up a document of manumission. The term used for 'slave' (*amtī*) in the document, an Aramaic word, leaves no doubt that the slave in question was female.[199]

Of the two, the deed of manumission is, of course, the more important, but it is relatively inaccessible, for it is now in the collection of an institute in Leningrad. However, S.D. Goitein gained access to it, and referred to it in several of his works. His dating establishes it as the earliest document from Ben Yijū's stay in India.

It is probably not a coincidence that the earliest surviving record of Ben Yijū's life in India has to do with a woman. Ben Yijū may well have expected to acquire a mistress soon after arriving in Mangalore, for amongst Middle Easterners India bore a reputation as a place notable for the ease of its sexual relations. If Ben Yijū had read Mas'ūdī, for example, he would have learnt that Indian men were accustomed to make 'young slave girls drink and dance for them',[200] and had he known of the works of his contemporary, the Sharīf al-Idrīsī, he would have discovered that in India 'concubinage is permitted between everyone, so long as it is not with married women'.[201] Abū Zeid, listening to travellers' tales in Sirāf in the tenth century, heard a great deal of talk about

199. T-S 12.458 verso, lines 5–13. I would like to thank Geoffrey Khan for translating parts of this document for me.

200. Mas'ūdī: 169.

201. al-Idrīsī: 178.

devadāsīs. 'Let us thank God', he writes, savouring his shock, at the end of a long and accurate account of the institution, 'for the Koran which He has chosen for us and with which He has preserved us from the sins of the infidels.'[202] Many travellers, like the writer of the *Akhbār al-Hind wa al-Ṣīn*, were struck by the number of courtesans in India.[203] The Italian traveller Nicoló Conti, who travelled to India in the early part of the fifteenth century, found that: 'Public women are everywhere to be had, residing in particular houses of their own in all parts of the cities, who attract the men by sweet perfumes and ointments, by their blandishments, beauty and youth; for the Indians are much addicted to licentiousness.'[204]

Ben Yijū's slave girl's name was spelt A-sh-ū.[205] The fact that he chose to manumit her indicates that his intentions towards her were anything but casual. And since he seems to have celebrated the occasion of her manumission with some fanfare, it seems as though he was issuing public notice of a wedding, or betrothal.

Three years later, when Bomma went to Aden, Ben Yijū was already a father. The proof of this lies in the letter which Maḍmūn wrote to him in 1135. Towards the end of the letter, listing the presents he is sending to Ben Yijū, Maḍmūn adds: 'I have also sent a piece of coral for your son Surūr'.[206]

There is no particular reason to connect Ashū's manumission with Ben Yijū's fatherhood, and yet it is difficult not to. Professor Goitein, for one, was persuaded by this coincidence that Ben Yijū had married Ashū, and that Ashū was 'probably beautiful'.[207]

Ashū is not mentioned anywhere else in the entire corpus of documents. Ben Yijū does not once refer to her in his letters

202. See Ferrand: 124.
203. Ibid.: 68.
204. Major: 23.
205. Goitein 1973: 202.
206. T-S N.S. J 1, recto, line 11.
207. Goitein 1973: 202.

or jottings. Nor do his correspondents, who are always careful to greet his children and Bomma, ever mention her or send her their greetings. But this lack may be proof precisely that he did marry her, for only a marriage of that kind — with a slave girl, born outside the community of his faith — could have earned so pointed a silence on the part of his friends.

In Ben Yijū's circle, as among most people in the Middle East, there was a preference for marriages between the children of brothers, and failing that between cousins and relatives.[208] This was a preference that Ben Yijū himself shared fully, as we shall see. That he chose to marry soon after his arrival in India is an indication, in part, that he knew he would not soon be able to return to the Middle East to contract a marriage of that kind. Yet, he could well have married into the large and ancient community of Jews in Malabar. His reasons for not doing so could not have had anything to do with a lack of orthodoxy in their practices. His near-contemporary, the strict and learned Benjamin of Tudela, not a man to suffer heterodoxy lightly, saw much to approve of in this community: 'And throughout the [land] including all the towns there, live several thousand Israelites. The inhabitants are all black, and the Jews are also. The latter are good and benevolent. They know the law of Moses and the prophets, and to a small extent the Talmud and the Halacha.'[209]

But since, despite the obvious alternative, Ben Yijū chose to marry outside the community of his faith, risking the disapproval of his friends, it can only have been because some other consideration overrode all the others. If I hesitate to call it love, it is only because the documents offer no certain proof.

Certainly Ben Yijū's shopping lists do bear the signs of an ardent lover. Some of the clothes he ordered from Aden must

208. Cf. Goitein, 1973: 202, and Falk, 1962–3. For a brief review of the literature on cousin marriage in the Middle East, see Keyser, and for a lengthier account, see chapter II of Ghosh, 1982.

209. Benjamin of Tudela: 120–1.

have been for Ashū; and the Isfahani *kohl* that occasionally figures in his accounts would definitely have been intended for her.[210] As we have seen, he spared no expense on creature comforts for his household.

About Ashū's origins there is only a single clue. It occurs in the accounts Ben Yijū scribbled on the back of Maḍmūn's letter. The line is: '[Owed] to Nair my brother-in-law [*ṣahrī*], one Manarī dīnār'.[211] The evidence is slight, but it leaves little room for doubt that Ben Yijū had married into that caste, so much beloved of modern anthropology: the matrilineal Nairs of Kerala. This is wholly plausible, for references in several inscriptions show that there was a sizable settlement of Nairs in Tuḷunāḍ in that period.[212]

Matrilineality may have been more than he bargained for, because his newly-acquired relatives were soon to prove a sore trial to him.

XI

Bomma was not to remain long in Aden. Unkindly, Maḍmūn sent him back in the same boat that was carrying the letter that complained to Ben Yijū of his servant's revelries. But Maḍmūn's letter does not appear to have excited an excess of wrath in Ben Yijū: Bomma continued to work for him and eventually came to play an important part in the running of his business. Nor does Maḍmūn appear to have borne Bomma a grudge. In his later letters, he is always careful to send his greetings to Bomma.[213] Ben Yijū's other friends in Aden, too, appear to have gladly forgiven Bomma. Within a few years, Khalaf ibn Iṣḥaq was to write of him affectionately as 'brother Bomma' and in the fullness of time he was even to honour him with the respectful title of 'Shaikh'.[214]

210. For his orders of *kohl*, see, for example, T-S 10 J 12, fol. 5, verso, line 10 ('Ispahani *kohl*') & T-S 10 J 9, fol. 24 line 18.

211. T-S 20.137, verso, line 19 (account no. 2).

212. Bhatt: 234–5.

213. See T-S MS. Or. 1081, J3, verso, line 9.

214. Cf. Goitein, 1973; 191 and Strauss: 149 (line 23 'to brother Bomma

But in 1135 Bomma was merely playing the part of courier for his master. Among the things he brought back were several letters written by Maḍmūn. His letter to Ben Yijū contained detailed instructions about what he was to do with them: 'collect all the letters for the people of Mangalore yourself . . . and be careful with them because they contain things I need urgently'.[215] These letters were part of a regular correspondence between him and certain members of the trading communities (Bāniyān) of Mangalore, and in a later letter he even named these correspondents. 'Please deliver most specially to Sesu Shetty (Sūs Sītī)[216] and Kanābtī and Iṣḥāq the Bāniyān my most distinguished greetings and tell them of my affection for them. Inform them that the price of pepper in this coming year will be thirty dīnārs a bahar or more than that, and that of "renewed"iron will not drop below twenty dīnārs'.[217]

What Maḍmūn does not reveal is what language his letters to the Baniyān of Mangalore were written in.

One likely possibility is that the letters were written for Maḍmūn in Arabic by a scribe, and then translated for his correspondents in Mangalore by translators. But, on the other hand, Arabic does not appear to have been widely spoken on the Malabar coast in that period, even by Muslims.[218] The author of the ninth-century *Akhbār al-Hind wa al-Ṣīn*, who had travelled widely throughout the Indian Ocean, was much struck by this: 'One does not know a single Chinese or Indian Muslim or anyone [there] who speaks Arabic'.[219]

The other possibility is that the letters were written in Judæo-Arabic and that Ben Yijū himself translated them orally for the benefit of the 'Bāniyān' of Mangalore. But that

---

especially from me, plentiful greetings'); and T-S 18 J 4, fol.18, recto, line 46, 'and special greetings to Shaikh Bomma'.

215. T-S N.S. J 1 verso, lines 6-8.

216. I am grateful to Dr Viveka Rai for suggesting this interpretation of the Arabic spelling of the name.

217. T-S 18 J 2, fol.7, verso, lines 1-6. See also Goitein 1980; 53.

218. Goitein assumed that Hindu merchants knew Arabic (1973: 65, fn.). But there appears to me to be no indication of this whatever.

219. Ferrand: 71.

raises a further question: what language did he translate them into? He is unlikely to have achieved fluency in Tuḷu in the time he had spent in Mangalore. Nor can it be assumed that the Indian traders of his acquaintance would particularly wish to speak to him in their mother tongues. Modern sociolinguistics has repeatedly demonstrated that in India people often prefer to keep separate the language they use at home, among their kin, and the language in which they deal with the world outside.[220]

A troop of other questions march behind these: in what language did Ben Yijū speak with Ashū? Or with Bomma? Or with the 'Arabs, Persians, Guzarates, Khorasanys, and Decanys' who lived in Malabar and with whom, given the nature of his occupation, he must have had to do business?[221] The questions extend far beyond Ben Yijū's immediate experience. Mangalore was by no means unique in its cosmopolitanism; it was one in a chain of trading ports stretching all the way from Arabia and East Africa to China.[222] Mere common sense suggests that trade in a region as large and as diverse as the Indian Ocean could not conceivably have been conducted in a tongue that was native to any one group of traders: to function at all the language of business within this community would have to be both simple and widely dispersed.

Given what we know about the practices of Arab traders

220. See, for example, Pandit: 11–12.

221. Several accounts comment on the cosmopolitanism of medieval Malabar. See, for example, Benjamin of Tudela's 'Itinerary' (twelfth century) (120–1); the 'Narrative of the Journey of Abd-er Razzak', an account by a fifteenth-century Persian envoy to the court of Vijainagar: 'Calicut is a perfectly secure harbour, which like that of Ormuz, brings together merchants from every country' (Major: 14). The travelogue of the sixteenth-century Portuguese sailor, Duarte Barbosa, describes the varied merchant populations of the towns of Malabar at some length (102–4, 146–8, 149–51, 172, etc.).

222. Several Arab geographers and travellers described the ports that formed the links in the chain of trade that stretched across the Indian Ocean. See, for example, al-Idrīsī: 39–91. Chinese and other sources also mention settlements of Persians, 'Brahmins' and Malayans in Hainan, Canton, etc. (cf. Hourani: 62–72).

in the Mediterranean — the other area in which Arabic came into close contact with Indo-European languages — it seems likely that they used a trading jargon or an elaborated pidgin of some kind. The documents provide very few clues about what the nature of this pidgin may have been. It is worth remarking that while the documents contain several proper names of clearly Dravidian origin — Nambiyar, for example, as well as Nair and Tinbu — as far as I have been able to determine they do not contain any Dravidian words used as common nouns.[223]

On the other hand, words of Persian origin frequently figure in them. These words often appear to be specialized for use in the region of the Indian Ocean: for example, the word *nākhuda*, shipmaster, or *kārdār*, 'foreman'.[224] Similarly, travellers who visited Malabar in the Middle Ages often, curiously enough, used words of clearly north Indian or Persian origin in their descriptions of the region.[225] Thus, for example, Abū Zeyd al-Ḥasan used the term *baykarji* (bairagi) to describe the mendicants of Malabar, Duarte Barbosa writes about pardesis and 'Abd al-Razzāq uses the word 'lankoutah'.[226]

This suggests that Arab travellers in Malabar used a language that was neither Arabic nor the domestic language of the people of the area. Mas'ūdī, the only Arab geographer who has anything to say about the languages of the west coast, provides a possible solution. Mas'ūdī describes one of these languages as Kiriyya, which has been identified, plausibly enough, as Kannada. To the cities of the coast, on the other hand, he attributes a language called Lāriyya. He

223. Cf. Goitein, 1973: 64 for the name 'Tinbu' (Tambi?). The letters NMBIRNI occur in T-S K 25.252, recto, line 13. It was probably intended to spell some form of the name 'Nambiyar'. Bin Yijū's accounts on the verso of T-S 20.137 mention the name 'Nair' as well as two names written as LNGY and LNBY, almost certainly Dravidian forms.

224. Cf. Hourani: 65; Goitein, 1973: 191 fn.; 193.

225. Hourani: 65.

226. Ferrand: 123; Major: 17.

derives the name from what he calls 'The Sea of Lārawi' (*baḥr al-lārawī*), which Nainar has identified as the Laccadive Sea.[227] In Mas'udī's usage the sea that lies off the whole of the west coast is the Lārawī Sea: he specifically names Thana and Cambay in Gujarat, along with several ports in Karnataka, such as Ṣaimūr (identified as the modern Shirur), as lying upon that sea.[228] Since the languages native to those areas were entirely different — indeed of different language families — self-evidently he could not have been referring to the languages native to the peoples of those regions. Instead he is probably referring here to a pidgin used by traders along the entire length of the west coast: following his usage I shall call it Lāriyya. If I am right in supposing that the lexicon of Lāriyya was largely of Perso-Arabic and north Indian derivation, it would seem to follow that Lāriyya could have been the parent pidgin that ultimately gave birth to Urdū.

It is well known that trade languages like Sabir and Lingua Franca were widely used for the purposes of trade in the region of the Mediterranean.[229] It has been suggested that it was these parent pidgins, carried around the world by the Portuguese, that provided the syntactical structure for many of the pidgin and creole languages that developed later in the regions of the Atlantic and Indian Oceans.[230]

But this is surely to ascribe to European intervention a phenomenon that almost certainly preceded it. Considering the volume and extent of trade in the Indian Ocean, it would seem likely that a trade language was already in use there since long before the arrival of the Portuguese.[231] It would follow then that the Portuguese were merely agents in the relexification of pre-existing linguistic structures.

The thought of Ben Yijū, sitting in a Bania's office in Mangalore, translating a letter from Aden into a trade language that

227. Nainar: 95.
228. Ibid.: 95.
229. Versteegh: 114, Whinnom: 296.
230. Cf. Holm: 46.
231. Cf. Versteegh: 115.

could be understood most of the way across the Indian Ocean, is not really difficult to conceive, intriguing though it is. What is hard to imagine is how he and Ashū adapted that commercial pidgin to the uses of the bedroom.

XII

Some time after Bomma returned from his riotous visit to Aden, Ben Yijū had reason to use some unaccustomedly strong language. But it was not Bomma who was the cause of Ben Yijū's displeasure.

Again we have Maḍmūn's 1135 letter to thank for furnishing evidence of this. In the accounts that Ben Yijū wrote on the back of this letter there occurs this short passage: 'The remainder of the account with al-Baṣāra [is] 3 mithqāls. [Still] owed to him by the kādār, may God curse him, [are] 14 mithqāls, for two bahārs of cardamom. He [the kādār] did not deliver the cardamom, so I bought for [al-Baṣāra?] two bahārs from Fandarīna as a substitute, for 17 mithqāls.'[232]

The matter at hand is clear enough: Ben Yijū had given a middleman, the 'kādār', an advance for a consignment of cardamom. He had then covered his risk by making advance sales of the cardamom to some of his business associates. But then, when the kādār pocketed his advance without delivering the cardamom, he found himself with a debt on his hands and no cardamom to show for it; in effect he was caught in the classic bind of the speculator in commodity futures.

Soon the affair of the undelivered cardamom took on international overtones. In the late 1130s Yūsuf ibn Abraham, Ben Yijū's associate in Aden, wrote: 'You, my master, mentioned that you approached the kārdāl gently in order to get something for us back from him. Perhaps you should threaten him that here in Aden we disgrace anyone that owes us something and does not fulfil his commitments . . . If he does not pay, we shall issue an official letter of

232. T-S 20.137, verso, lines 1–4.

censure and send it to him, so that he will become aware of his crime.'[233]

Yūsuf ibn Abraham misspells the middleman's unfamiliar title, both here, and in a later letter, just as Ben Yijū had himself, in his accounts. The word was actually kārdār, 'manager' or 'foreman'.[234] Ben Yijū's other correspondents gave the word its proper spellings in their letters, and Ben Yijū himself was to spell it correctly elsewhere.

Khalaf ibn Iṣḥaq too had reason to write to Ben Yijū about the matter of the kārdār, but he took a different view of the matter. In a letter sent some years after Yūsuf ibn Abraham's, he writes: 'As for the delay in the [delivery of the kārdār's] cardamom, may God curse him, I have spoken to some people about the matter, and they said to me that the cardamom was yours, and we had no share in it. It's a matter [to be decided] between you and the kārdār: deal with this thing individually with him, separately from us.'[235]

There can be no mistaking his meaning: in order to cut his losses Ben Yijū had charged Khalaf ibn Iṣḥaq and Yūsuf ibn Abraham for some part of the money that he had advanced to the kārdār. But he was shrewd enough to leave the powerful Maḍmūn out of his schemes.[236]

The usually indulgent Khalaf ibn Iṣḥaq has a few strong words for this bit of slippery dealing on Ben Yijū's part. 'Your

233. Goitein, 1973; 193. I have substituted the words 'disgrace' and 'censure' for the words 'excommunicate' and 'excommunication'. The words used in the manuscript (T-S 12.320, recto) are two forms of the Arabic root sh-m-t. I am informed by Dr Geoffrey Khan that this is not the root that is normally used to designate excommunication in the Geniza documents; it should be read instead as 'the metathesized form of sh-t-m (to insult, defame), which is used in Maghrebī Arabic. . . . The letter would, therefore, be referring to some form of public defamation, or "rogues gallery" '. (Personal communication.) Goitein probably used the term 'excommunicate' on the assumption that the 'kārdāl' was Jewish. The evidence, as we shall see, suggests otherwise.

234. Goitein, 1973: 193.

235. T-S 18 J 4, fol. 18, recto, lines 26–8.

236. Maḍmūn never mentions the matter in any of his letters to Ben Yijū.

servant sends you things, trusting that you will [use them] to buy [shipments] — he and others too — without asking for sureties of advances . . . [Those] who send you supplies do not ask you to use them as advances for things [they] didn't ask you [to buy].'[237]

The affair of the kārdār's cardamom dragged on for a long time. In a letter written years later, the tenacious Yūsuf ibn Abraham refers to the matter again: 'My master wrote that the kārdāl has not paid him anything, including the six mithqāls that were advanced . . . by him. My master well knows that it was his decision to give the kārdāl the money . . .'[238]

There is only one other reference to the kārdār in the documents. It has no direct bearing on this affair but it does throw some light on it.

The reference occurs in a tiny fragment: a scrap torn from the bottom right-hand corner of a longer sheet of paper. The fragment is badly weathered and pitted with holes. It is covered on both sides with Ben Yijū's unmistakable handwriting. The writing has faded in parts; the recto is barely decipherable. It appears to be a record of one or more shipments of goods. The goods and certain names that occur in the accounts prove that they were written in India. But the text contains no leads at all for the dating of the fragment: all that can be ventured with any certainty on that score is that it was written at some point during Ben Yijū's stay in India — any time between 1131 to 1149.

The reference to the kārdār occurs in the last line but one in the text on the verso. The sentence goes thus: 'Remaining [with me] for Nāīr, the brother of the kārdār, 3 fīlī dirham-.s'[239]

The term 'brother', as it is used here, probably means relative in a general sense rather than sibling. What is curious is that it defines Nāīr, whom we know to have been Ben

237. T-S 18 J 4, fol. 18, recto, lines 29–31. However, the precise meaning of this passage is unclear, and my reading of it must be treated with caution.

238. T-S 12. 235, verso, lines 3–5.

239. T-S N.S. J 10, verso, margin.

Yijū's brother-in-law, by his relationship to the kārdār, and not the reverse.

If we read closely enough between the lines, there seems to be a suggestion implicit in the construction of the sentence: that it was the kārdār who was the link between Ben Yijū and the man he called his brother-in-law, Nāīr. If we were to read closer still, the sentence might even suggest that it was the kārdār who had led Ben Yijū to Ashū. That may have been the reason why Ben Yijū trusted him to the point of making him an advance; or perhaps the kārdār saw his advance as his payment for negotiating the liaison.

XIII

Ben Yijū spent at least seventeen years in India, and for almost all that time he lived in Mangalore. The only other place he is known to have visited for any length of time was a town that was called Jurbattan in Arabic.[240] The town has been identified by Nainar as the modern Srikandapuram. It lies in the foothills of the Ghats, about 150 kms south of Mangalore and about 35 kms inland from Cannanore. It is a small town, surrounded by plantations of cashew and rubber, virtually unknown outside Malabar. Yet in the Middle Ages it must have been one of the best-known places in India, for there are innumerable references to it in the works of the Arab travellers and geographers.[241] Ben Yijū also had connections with another small Malabar town that was well known to the Arabs: a town they called Dahbattān, which has been identified by Nainar as Dharmadam.[242] Another town that Ben Yijū had connections with was 'Fandarīna'—Pantalayini Kollam, near Calicut.[243] Ben Yijū visited all these

240. Khalaf ibn Iṣḥaq writes in a letter: 'Your servant asked about my master, and they said to me he is in Jurbattan with his household and children . . . ' (T-S Misc. Box 25, fragm. 103, recto, lines 25-7.)

241. Cf. Nainar: 41.

242. Nainar: 32; see also Goitein 1973: 188.

243. Nainar: 35.

towns in Malabar, yet in all the time he spent in India he probably never ventured further inland than Srikandapuram.

This appears to have been the general pattern among the pardesi merchants. They evidently saw the west coast as their field of operations and kept themselves to it. Their own networks and links with each other extended all the way up and down the coast, irrespective of political, cultural and linguisitic boundaries, such as there were. Perhaps for that reason, they did not distinguish, as a rule, between the different cultural and political regions of the west coast. Nor, curiously enough, did they distinguish between the coast and the interior:[244] to them the whole land mass was *bilād al-Hind*, 'the country of India'. Thus my use of the adjective 'Indian' for Tuḷunāḍ, and Bomma, is not an anachronism: I am merely following the usage of the documents.

This usage was largely in keeping with the academic geography of the Arabs in which the entire subcontinent, beginning at the eastern border of Sind and extending to Assam (Lakshmipura) and even beyond, was called al-Hind, just as China was known as Ṣīn.[245] But China was, of course, a single political entity: an empire whose subdivisions were provinces of the larger state. India, on the other hand, was divided into several 'independent' kingdoms, large and small. The Arab geographers were well aware of this. In their descriptions of India they were careful to specify the regions and kingdoms of India, and they knew very well that the rulers of these kingdoms were not merely often at war, but that a state of continuous, almost ritual, opposition was an essential part of their political structure. Masʿūdī, for instance, writes: 'The kingdoms of India are continually at war with each other, and are divided by their languages and their beliefs.'[246]

Yet, despite this, they were also insistent that al-Hind had a centre, recognized by all its kings and regions. Over several

244. The Arabic term *malabār* for the southern part of the coast, for example, rarely occurs in the documents.

245. See, for example, Masʿūdī: 163.

246. Ibid.: 163.

centuries Arab geographers and travellers appear to have been in agreement on this subject: the centre of al-Hind, as far as they were concerned, lay in the domains of a king whom they called the Balhāra, whose capital was the city of Mankir.[247]

Nainar has suggested that 'Balhāra' was the Arabic representation of the title Vallabharāja (Supreme King), which was assumed by most of the Çālukyas and Rāṣṭrakūṭas, and that Mankir referred to the city of Malkhed, later in Hyderabad State. But in fact these appellations appear to have been indifferent to the steady turnover of dynasties, kingdoms and capitals in the region, and they may have been used more in a metaphoric than a purely descriptive fashion: as a way of saying that al-Hind had its own idiosyncratic manner of reconciling the one and the many.

In any case, it would seem that Ben Yijū and his fellow merchants knew nothing at all of the great dynasties and kingdoms of India: there is not a single reference to them in the documents. Their contacts with the rulers of the small principalities they lived in were probably the only dealings they ever needed to have with the political structures of the subcontinent.

XIV

Two children were born to Ben Yijū in India: we can only surmise that Ashū was their mother. The first, a son, was named Surūr. Following the custom of the Arab world, Ben Yijū, after the birth of his son, was often called Abū Surūr (Surūr's father) by his friends. His second child was a daughter, to whom he gave the name Sitt al-Dār, 'Lady of the House', a name that is still common in the villages of Egypt today.[248]

In his eighteen years in India, Ben Yijū had gained a wife, children, and at least one slave. His letters and accounts show

247. See Mas'ūdī: 177; al-Idrīsī: 173; and Ferrand: 48.
248. Cf. Goitein, 1973: 202.

that he had also set up a brass workshop in which workers made locks, did repairs and made various objects to order, some of which were exported to Aden. His dealings in pepper, iron, ginger and arecanuts were clearly profitable, and he had obviously built up a considerable fortune. But in all those years he had been totally cut off from the family he had left behind in Ifrīqiya.

Then, in the mid-1140s or so, he had news that his brother Mubashshir had travelled eastwards to join him.[249] Ben Yijū was clearly greatly moved by the news and he made provision for paying his brother's passage from Aden to India. But in the event his hopes came to nothing, for Mubashshir turned back at Egypt and went to Sicily.[250]

Mubashshir's journey happened to coincide with a period of extraordinary turmoil in Ifrīqiya and the Maghreb: a time that was to culminate in the utter destruction of the world of Ben Yijū's youth. Ifrīqiya was repeatedly attacked by Roger II from 1143 onwards. For several years, not a single year went by without a Sicilian attack on the North African coast.[251] There followed a wave of emigration out of North Africa.[252] It was this tide that probably carried the Ben Yijū family to Sicily— unbeknownst to Abraham in Mangalore.

In those very years the Muwaḥḥids (Almohads) were gaining in strength in the Maghreb and advancing steadily eastwards. Between 1145 and 1146 they took the cities of Oran, Tlemcen and the oasis of Sijilmāsa, the hub of the Saharan trade routes. For seven months they tried peaceably

249. T-S 18 J 4, fol. 18, recto, lines 33–5.

250. Cf. Strauss: 149. Altogether there are five documents which refer to Mubashshir. The last of these is MS. H.6 which has been reliably dated by Strauss as having been written in 1148. Since Mubashshir's stay in Egypt does not appear to have been very long, it can be assumed with a fair degree of certainty that the other letters were written in the three- or four-year period immediately preceding 1148. From their contents they can be arranged in the following chronological order: 1. T-S 18 J 4, fol. 18. 2. T-S Misc. Box 25, fragm. 103. 3. T-S 13 J 7, fol. 27. 4. T-S 12.235. 5. MS. H.6 (cf. Strauss).

251. Hirschberg: 120.

252. Wieruszowski: 23.

to convert Sijilmāsa's large Jewish community to Islām. When their efforts went unrewarded, they put a hundred and fifty Jews to the sword. The rest, led by their judge, converted. They were relatively lucky: at about the same time 100,000 Jews and Christians were massacred in Fez and 120,000 in Marrakesh.[253]

Ben Yijū almost certainly knew of the events in his homeland. At the time when Khalaf ibn Iṣḥaq was writing to Ben Yijū in Mangalore, one Solomon Kohen of Fusṭāṭ was writing a letter to his father, a native of Sijilmāsa, in Aden. The letter eventually came to rest in the Geniza:[254] it was addressed to Judah ha-Kohen Sijilmāsī, an important merchant, whose sister was married to Ben Yijū's mentor, Maḍmūn ibn Bundār.[255] Judah ha-Kohen, known as Abū Zikrī, was a frequent visitor to India and happened to be a friend of Ben Yijū's.[256] We need have no doubt that Judah ha-Kohen, upon receiving his son's letter, would have sent word to his friends in India about the events in the land of their birth.

The news must have turned Ben Yijū's thoughts towards North Africa and the Middle East. He had already written to his friends in Aden of his wish to return: 'Every year you speak of coming to Aden,' says Khalaf ibn Iṣḥaq at the end of one of his letters, 'but you never do it.'[257]

Finally, in about 1149, Ben Yijū packed up his bags and moved to Aden, taking all his worldly goods and his two adolescent children with him. The next few years were hard ones for him. The letters he wrote to his brothers, who were both living in Sicily at that time, show that he lost his son

253. Hirschberg: 128.

254. Ibid.: 127.

255. Goitein, 1973: 62.

256. Barely three years before this, he had been stranded in Gujarat after being captured by pirates. On that occasion Ben Yijū had had to help in forwarding him money through the good offices of an Indian shipowner called Tinbu. See Goitein, 1973: 62–5.

257. Strauss, 1942.

while living in Aden. 'Sulīmān and Abraham will tell you of the state I am in', he wrote to his brother Yūsuf. 'I am sick at heart.'[258]

At some point in his stay in the Yemen, probably soon after his son's death, Ben Yijū moved from Aden into the highlands in the interior of the Yemen. He was accorded a position of great respect within his community there and was even called upon to act as a judge in inheritance disputes.[259] But Ben Yijū did not remain long in the highlands: soon enough, he moved back to Egypt and joined the congregation of the Synagogue of the Palestinians in Fusṭāṭ.

Nowhere in Ben Yijū's correspondence with his brothers is Āshū's name ever mentioned; neither he nor they ever refer to her. It seems likely in fact that Āshū had stayed behind in Mangalore when Ben Yijū left for the Middle East.

Ben Yijū spent several years in Egypt, and a dowry list preserved in the Geniza suggests that he celebrated his daughter's wedding there.[260] The list proves that this child of a Nair woman from Malabar eventually married her uncle Yūsuf's son, Surūr.

Ben Yijū himself disappears from the records after his daughter's marriage. His nephews and son-in-law do not mention him in their later letters to each other; nor has the Geniza yet provided any record of his death. In the absence of definite evidence, we are free to imagine the rest of his life as we please. Of the many conceivable endings, the one which is most pleasing to me is the possibility that he returned to Malabar to live out the rest of his life with Āshū.

There is no mention of Bomma in Ben Yijū's letters to his brothers, but Bomma's story is not finished yet.

258. T-S 12,337, recto line 34, and margin.

259. His drafts for three judgements written in this period have been preserved (T-S 10 J 9, fol.24, verso).

260. Cf. Goitein, 1973: 202.

XV

Bomma's story ends in the city of Philadelphia in the United States.

In downtown Philadelphia, housed in a splendidly modern edifice, lies the Annenberg Research Institute: a centre for social and historical research established by a family which has built an immense fortune upon the merchandizing of a popular weekly guide to American television. In the bowels of this building is a great vault, steel-sealed and laser-beamed, equipped with an alarm system that needs no more than a few seconds to mobilize whole fleets of helicopters and police cars.

Within the soundproofed, humidity-controlled interior of this vault are two catafalque-like cabinets. Inside one of these, encased in sheets of clear plastic and acid-free paper, there lies a curious fragment from the Cairo Geniza. It is written in Ben Yijū's writing, but in tiny, crabbed characters, as though the hand that wrote them had turned stiff with age.

The writing on this fragment is so small and faint that it is hard to make sense of the whole of it: only a few words and sentences are decipherable. They reveal the document to be one of Ben Yijū's many sets of accounts. These accounts, however, are quite unlike those he wrote in India: many of them list purchases of various kinds of bread, while in rice-eating Tuḷunāḍ Ben Yijū's accounts usually quoted the price of rice. That, and the mention of certain names, establishes beyond doubt that the document was written in Egypt, probably in Fusṭāṭ.

Hidden in this jumble of scribbled lines, and the lists of various kinds of loaves, there is a mention of a sum of money owed to Bomma.[261] We may be certain therefore that Bomma was with Ben Yijū in Egypt in the mid-1150s. He may even have been a witness to the defeat of the Crusaders' attempts to invade Egypt, and to the accession of Sulṭān Ṣalāḥ al-Dīn.

261. Dropsie Univ. 472.

For all we know, this may be the tip of an iceberg of evidence pointing to Indian involvements in the Crusades.

In Philadelphia then, cared for by the by-products of 'Dallas' and 'Dynasty', and protected by the might of the American police, lies entombed the last testament to the life of Ben Yijū's toddy-loving slave, Bomma, the Bhūta-worshipping fisherman from Tuḷunāḍ.

Bomma, I cannot help feeling, would have been hugely amused.

Geniza Documents

This list includes only such documents as have been referred to in the course of this paper.

Abbreviations

T-S: Taylor-Schechter Collection (Cambridge University Library)
N.S.: New Series

1. T-S 12.235
2. T-S 12.337
3. T-S 12.458
4. T-S 20.130
5. T-S 20.137
6. T-S N.S. J 1
7. T-S N.S. J 10
8. T-S K 25.252
9. T-S 1080 J 95
10. T-S MS. Or. 1081, J3
11. T-S Misc. Box 25, fragm. 103
12. T-S 8 J 7, fol. 23
13. T-S 10 J 9, fol. 24
14. T-S 10 J 12, fol. 5
15. T-S 13 J 7, fol. 27
16. T-S 18 J 2, fol. 7
17. T-S 18 J 4, fol. 18
18. T-S 18 J 5, fol. 1
19. Dropsie Univ. 472.

References

Ashtor, E., 'Levantine Sugar Industry in the Later Middle Ages — An Example of Technological Decline', *Israel Or. Studies*, VII, Tel Aviv University, 1977.

Assaf, S., 'Slavery and Slave Trade in the Middle Ages', pt. 2, *Zion*, n.s., 5th. year, vol. III-IV, Jerusalem, 1940.

Attal, Robert, *A Bibliography of the Writings of Prof. Shlomo Dov Goitein*, Hebrew University, Jerusalem, 1975 (Supplement, 1987).

Barbosa, Duarte, *A Description of the Coasts of East Africa and Malabar in the Beginning of the Sixteenth Century*, trans. from an early Spanish MS. in the Barcelona Library with notes and a preface, by Henry, E.J. Stanley, The Hakluyt Society, London, 1866.

Benjamin of Tudela, *The Itinerary: Travels in the Middle Ages*. Introductions by Michael A. Signer (1983); Marcus Nathan Adler (1907); A. Asher (1840); Joseph Simon, 1983.

Berry, Virginia G., 'The Second Crusade', in K.M. Seton (gen.ed.), *A History of the Crusades*, vol. I (pp.463–512), The University of Wisconsin Press, Madison, 1969.

Bhat, Leela, 'Women in Pāḍdanas', in U.P. Upadhyaya (ed.), *Folk Epics of Tulunad*, 24–34, Udupi, 1986.

Bhatt, P. Gururaja, *Studies in Tuluva History and Culture*, Manipal, Karnataka, 1970.

Blau, J., *Judæo-Arabic*, Clarendon, Oxford, 1965.

Bosworth, C.E., 'A Mediaeval Islamic Prototype of the Fountain Pen?', *Journal of Semitic Studies*, XXVI/2, 1981.

Brückner, Heidrun, 'Bhūta-Worship in Coastal Karnāṭaka: An Oral Tuḷu Myth and Festival Ritual of Jumādi', *Studien zur Indologie und Iranistik*, 13/14, Reinbek, 1987.

Buchanan, Francis, *A Journey through Mysore, Malabar and Canara*, London, 1807.

Chidanandamurthy, M, 'Pagaraṇa mattu itara samprabandhagaḷu.' (*Pagarana and other research papers*), Pustaka Chilume, Mysore, 1984.

Claus, P., 'Possession, Protection and Punishment as Attributes of the Deities in a South Indian Village', *Man in India*, 53, 231–42, 1973.

—— (1979a) 'Spirit Possession and Spirit Mediumship from the

Perspective of Tulu Oral Traditions', *Culture, Medicine & Psychiatry*, 3, 94–129, 1979.

Claus, P., (1979b) 'Mayndaḷa: A Legend and Possession Cult of Tuḷunāḍ', *Asian Folklore Studies*, vol. 38:2, 1979.

—— 'Terminological Aspects of Tuḷu Kinship: Kin Terms, Kin Sets, and Kin Groups of the Matrilineal Castes', *American Studies in the Anthropology of India*, 1981.

Das, Veena, *Structure and Cognition*, Oxford University Press, New Delhi, 1977.

Desai, P.B., *Basaveshwara and His Times*, Karnatak University, Dharwar, 1968.

Dumont, Louis, 'Marriage in India, the Present State of the Question', pt. II, *Contributions to Indian Sociology*, VII, 77–98, 1964.

Eck, Diana L., *Banaras, City of Light*, Routledge & Kegan Paul, London, 1983.

Evans-Pritchard, E.E., *The Nuer*, Oxford, 1940.

Falk, Z.W., 'Endogamy in Israel', *Tarbiz*, 32, Jerusalem, 1962–3.

Ferguson, C.A., 'The Arabic Koiné', in S.H. Al-Ani (ed.), *Readings in Arabic Linguistics*, Bloomington, Indiana, 1978.

Ferrand, G., *Voyage du Marchand Arabe Sulayman en Inde et en Chine*, Paris, 1922.

Finley, M.I., *Ancient Slavery and Modern Ideology*, Chatto & Windus, London, 1980.

The Gazetteer of India, vol. 1, Publications Division, Govt. of India, 1973.

Ghosh, Amitav, 'Kinship in Relation to Economic and Social Organization in an Egyptian Village Community', unpublished D.Phil. thesis, Oxford, 1982.

Gibb, H.A.R., 'Zengi and the Fall of Edessa', in K.M. Seton (gen. ed.), *A History of the Crusades*, vol. II, 449–62, The University of Wisconsin Press, Madison, 1969a.

—— 'The Career of Nūr al-Dīn', in K.M. Seton (gen. ed.), *A History of the Crusades*, vol. 1, 513–27, The University of Wisconsin Press, Madison, 1969b.

Goitein, S.D., 'From the Mediterranean to India: Documents on the trade to India, South Arabia, and East Africa from the eleventh and twelfth centuries', *Speculum*, vol. 29, 181–97, 1954.

—— 'A Jewish Addict to Sufism in the Time of the Nagid David II Maimonides', *Jewish Quarterly Review*, vol. 44, 37–49, 1953–4.

Goitein, S.D., 'Two Eye-Witness Reports on an Expedition of the King of Kīsh (Qaiṣ) against Aden', *Bulletin of the School of African and Oriental Studies*, XVI/2, 247–57, London, 1956.

—— 'The Main Industries of the Mediterranean Area as Reflected in the Records of the Cairo Geniza', *Journal of the Economic and Social History of the Orient*, vol. IV, E.J. Brill, Leiden, 1961.

—— 'Slaves and Slavegirls in the Cairo Geniza Records', *Arabica*, vol. 9, 1–20, 1962.

—— *A Mediterranean Society*, vols I-V, (vol. I 1967, vol. II 1971, vol. III 1978, vol. IV 1983, vol. V 1988), University of California Press.

—— 'Abraham Maimonides and his Pietist Circle', in Alexander Altmann (ed.), *Jewish Medieval and Renaissance Studies*, Harvard University Press, Cambridge, Mass., 1967.

—— *Letters of Medieval Jewish Traders*, Princeton University Press, Princeton, 1973.

—— 'From Aden to India: Specimens of the Correspondence of India Traders of the Twelfth Century', *Journal of the Economic and Social History of the Orient*, vol. XXIII, pts I & II, 1980.

Golb, Norman, 'Aspects of the Historical Background of Jewish Life in Medieval Egypt', in Alexander Altmann (ed.), *Jewish Medieval and Renaissance Studies*, Harvard University Press, Cambridge, Mass., 1967.

H. Hirschberg, *A History of the Jews in North Africa*, trans. M. Eichelberg, E.J. Brill, Leiden, 1974.

Holm, J.A., *Pidgins and Creoles*, vol. 1, Cambridge University Press, Cambridge, 1988.

Hourani, G.F., *Arab Seafaring in the Indian Ocean in Ancient and Early Medieval Times*, Princeton University Press, 1951.

Al-Idrīsī (Muh. b. Muh.), *Kitāb tazha al-mushtāq fi iḥtirāq al-afāq*, (*Géographie d'Edrisi*), ed. & trans. P.A. Jaubert, vol. 1, Paris, 1836.

Kahle, Paul, *The Cairo Geniza*, Oxford University Press, London, 1947.

Kamath, S.U., *Tuluva in Vijayanagar Times, 1336–1646*, unpublished Ph.D. Thesis, Bombay University, 1965.

Karnataka State Gazetteer: South Kanara District, Govt. of Karnataka, Bangalore, 1973.

Keyser, J.M.B., 'The Middle Eastern Case; is there a marriage rule?', *Ethnology*, 13, 293–309.

Maalouf, Amin, *The Crusades through Arab Eyes*, trans. Jon Rothschild, Al Saqi Books, London, 1984.

Masʿūdī, *Murūj al-Dhahab* (*Les Prairies d'Or*), ed. & trans. C. Barbier de Meynard & Pavet de Courteille, vol. 1, Société Asiatique, l'Imprimerie Imperiale, Paris, 1861.

Major, R.H. (ed.), *India in the Fifteenth Century; being a Collection of Narratives of Voyages To India*, includes 'Narrative of the Voyage of Abd-er-Razzak, Ambassador from Shah Rukh, AH 845, AD 1442', trans. from the Persian into French by M. Quatremére, Eng. trans. R.H. Major; 'The Travels of Nicoló Conti in the East in the early part of the Fifteenth Century', trans. J. Winter Jones; 'The Travels of Athanasius Nikitin, a Native of Twer', trans. Count Wielhorsky; 'The Journey of Hieronimo di Santo Stefano', a Genoese, trans. by R.H. Major, Hakluyt Society, London, 1856.

Nainar, S. Muhammad Husayn, *The Knowledge of India Possessed by Arab Geographers down to the 14th Century AD with Special Reference to Southern India*, Madras University Islamic Series, University of Madras, 1942.

Nichter, Mark, 'The Joga and Maya of Tuluva Buta', *Eastern Anthropologist*, vol. 30, no. 2.

O'Flaherty, W.D., *Hindu Myths*, Penguin, London, 1975.

Pagels, Elaine, *The Gnostic Gospels*, Vintage Books, New York, 1989.

Panchamukhi, R.S. (ed.), *Karnataka Inscriptions*, vol. II, Kannada Research Institute, Dharwar, 1951.

Pandit, Prabodh, *India: A Profile in Multilingualism*, Dev Raj Chanana Memorial Lectures, Delhi, 1976.

Pillai, K.G. & D.K. Kundu, 'Fertiliser Use in Southern Plateau and Hills Region', *Fertiliser News*, 35, 6, New Delhi, June 1990.

Prabhu, K. Sanjiva, *Special Study Report on Bhuta Cult in South Kanara District*. Census of India, Series 14, Mysore, 1971.

Rai, B.A. Viveka, 'Pāḍdanas as Folk Epics', in U.P. Upadhyaya (ed.), *Folk Epics of Tulunad*, 9–13, Udupi, 1986.

Ramanujan, A.K., *Speaking of Siva*, Penguin Books, London, 1987.

Ramesh, K.V., *A History of South Kanara*, Karnatak University, Research Publications Series, No. 12, Dharwar, 1970.

—— 'Geographical Factors in Tuḷuva History', Academy Silver Jubilee Lecture, Academy of General Education, Manipal, Karnataka, 1981.

M. Reinaud (trans.), *Géographie d'Aboulféda*, Imprimerie Nationale, Paris, 1848.

Report of the Irrigation Commission 1972, vol. I, pt. 1, Ministry of Irrigation and Power, Govt. of India, New Delhi, 1972.

Roland, Joan G., *Jews in British India: Identity in a Colonial Era*, University Press of New England, Hanover & London, 1989.

Rosenthal, Franz, *The Muslim Concept of Freedom Prior to the Nineteenth Century*, E.J. Brill, Leiden, 1960.

Saletore, B.A., *Ancient Karnataka*, vol. 1, History of Tuluva, Oriental Book Agency, Poona, 1936.

Schimmel, Annemarie, *Mystical Dimensions of Islam*, University of North Carolina Press, Chapel Hill, 1975.

Shaked, S., *A Tentative Bibliography of Geniza Documents*, Mouton & Co., The Hague, 1964.

Strauss (Ashtor), E., 'Documents for the Economic and Social History of the Near East', *Zion*, n.s. V, Jerusalem, 1942.

Tobi, Yosef, 'Poetry and Society in the Works of Abraham ben Halfon (Yemen, 12th Century)', in Reuben Ahroni (ed.), *Bibilical and Other Studies in memory of S.D. Goitein*, Hebrew Annual Review, vol. 9, Dept. of Judaic and Near Eastern Languages and Literatures, Ohio State University, 1985.

Upadhyaya, U.P. & S.P. Upadhyaya (ed.), *Bhuta Worship: Aspects of a Ritualistic Theatre*, Regional Resources Centre for Folk Performing Arts, M.G.M. College, Udupi, Karnataka, 1984.

Versteegh, Kees, *Pidginization and Creolization: The Case of Arabic*, Current Issues in Linguistic Theory, no. 33, Amsterdam, 1984.

Wade, B.C., *Khyāl: Creativity within North India's Classical Music Tradition*, Cambridge University Press, Cambridge, 1984.

Wehr, Hans, *A Dictionary of Modern Written Arabic*, J.M. Cowan (ed.), Spoken Language Services Inc., Ithaca, New York, 1976.

Whinnom, Keith, Lingue France, 'Historical Problems', in A. Valdman (ed.) *Pidgin and Creole Linguistics*, Indiana University Press, Bloomington, 1977.

Wieruszowski, H., 'The Norman Kingdom of Sicily and the Crusades', in K.M. Seton (gen. ed.), *A History of the Crusades*, The University of Wisconsin Press, Madison, 1969.

12 *The Diaspora in Indian Culture*

THE MODERN Indian diaspora — the huge migration from the subcontinent that began in the mid-nineteenth century — is not merely one of the most important demographic dislocations of modern times: it now represents an important force in world culture. The culture of the diaspora is also increasingly a factor within the culture of the Indian subcontinent. This is self-evidently true of its material culture, which now sets the standard for all that is desirable in the metropolitan cities. But the diaspora also counts among its members some of the world's finest writers: to my mind there are no finer writers writing in the English language today than V.S. Naipaul, Salman Rushdie and A. K. Ramanujan. In its own way the literary culture of the diaspora is also an important social and political — and, of course, literary — force within India. One index of this is the sensitivity the State and the Indian political class has shown towards the writers of the diaspora: witness the violence of the State's response to the work of both V.S. Naipaul and Salman Rushdie. Naipaul's *Area of Darkness* (with which I shall be primarily concerned here) and Rushdie's *Satanic Verses* have, in very different ways, provoked controversy and widespread public discussion in India. Both have been banned (though the ban on *Area of Darkness* was lifted long ago). These bans are reprehensible and senseless: the Government of India should know that it cannot deal with ideas through its apparatus of repression. But the response of the State is also, in a way, both curious and comic — for it is not often, after all, that the Indian State springs thus tigerishly into action. Indeed, as the innumerable thousands of people who have pitted their weight against its immovable vastness know only too well, it is often easier to get a response from the Sanchi stupa or the Thar desert. Why then the State's sensitivity to the writing of the diaspora?

We could perhaps ascribe it to the 'colonial mentality' — that complex of ideas and responses with which we are all familiar, and which we are all united in decrying. We would not be wholly wrong, of course: it is certainly true, for example, that the political class of India is much more sensitive to the writing that filters through it from London, than it is to that which comes out of New York. But if the colonial mentality were a sufficient explanation, then one would expect this class to be equally, if not more, sensitive to the writing of Westerners (and we know that once upon a time it was — consider, for example, Mahatma Gandhi's and Tagore's responses to Katherine Mayo's *Mother India*). The literary production of the West on India has, if anything, grown over the last few decades — we have only to think of M.M. Kaye and her imitators to be convinced of that. In addition there is an endless flow of Indo-babble — popular travel writing, journalism, etc. on India. There is also the increasingly large output of those University departments throughout the Western world which are wholly devoted to the study of India. Some of this writing is critical of the Indian State to the point of being vitriolic: take the work of Gunnar Myrdal, for example. But to all of this the Indian State is wholly indifferent: it is merely the work of 'foreigners' who are always going on about something anyway, while Mr Naipaul . . . ? Well, Mr Naipaul is different somehow.

Thus, the 'colonial' hypothesis does not really work: the thickness of the Indian political skin is reserved wholly for the touch of the diasporic 'Indian'. It seems to me that to understand this phenomenon we have to look further — at the curious nature of India's cultural relationship with her diaspora.

We do not adequately acknowledge, I think, the distinctiveness of this relationship. Consider, for example, that historically the relationships between diasporic populations and their mother countries were maintained, at least in part, through the reproduction of political and social institutions. This is true for example of the ancient Greeks; it is true of the Arab expansion, of the Turkish conquests and, of course, of the great Anglo-Saxon migrations of the last two centuries.

But the relationship between modern India and its diasporic population is not an institutional relationship. Inasmuch as they share institutions it is because of their common relationship to the British Empire, and because of a shared history of subjection. The institutional relationships between them, when they exist at all, are all mediated through Britain. But India's relationship with its diaspora is not a mediated relationship: it is experientially a very direct relationship even though its whole history is a chronicle of mediations. And oddly enough, that is why the relationship has lasted even when the institutions have changed — as they did, for example, in Cheddi Jagan's Guyana.

Consider further that those other forms of cultural and social relationships that tie dispersed populations to the mother country are absent here. Take language for example. India exported her unique methods of adapting to linguistic diversity with her migrants. Wherever they went, Indian migrants proved to be linguistically adaptable in ways that British or French or Chinese migrants were not. If anything, the fact of dispersal speeded up the processes of linguistic flux endemic to the subcontinent. As a result the principal language of Mauritius — despite the numerical preponderance of Indian migrants on that island — is not Hindi (which appears at best to have the status of a domestic solidarity language) but a French creole. Similarly, the principal language of Indian migrants in Trinidad and Guyana is creole rather than Hindi. When Shiva Naipaul tells us that he grew up speaking no languages other than English he cannot be telling us the exact truth. He probably grew up speaking the English creole of Trinidad, while acquiring standard English in school — in exactly the same way as his great-grandfather probably grew up speaking Bhojpuri at home while acquiring a more literary version of Hindi either in the *paatshala* or in the marketplace. Thus, India exported with her population, not a language, as other civilizations have done, but a linguistic process — the process of adaptation to heteroglossia.

We are sometimes told that the 'real' bond between India and its diaspora lies in the 'immemorial realities' of caste and kinship. If this argument has any merit at all it would hold only for those groups of migrant Indians who regularly went back to India to marry, as did the Gujaratis of East Africa for example. But, in fact, most groups have, for whatever reasons, usually married within the migrant community (e.g., the Indians of Fiji, Mauritius and the West Indies). Amongst them, presumably their self-sufficiency in this respect would contribute precisely to the severance of their ties with the mother country.

Equally there are no really significant economic links between India and her diaspora (though these links appear to be developing now). Diasporic Indians have always followed their business instincts in investing their money, and those instincts have usually led them away from rather than towards India. The only group of migrants who play a really significant role in India's economy — the workers of the Persian Gulf — are not diasporic at all, properly speaking.

Further, there are no significant political or strategic considerations in the links between India and her diaspora: I take it to be self-evident that India's power and concerns are too localized to be much concerned with the strategic significance of Fiji or Guyana. Nor for that matter are the links primarily religious. As we all know, Hinduism, as well as South Asian Islam, is defined primarily by its patterns of systematic diversity. Hinduism, in particular, simply does not possess that institutional uniformity of practice that bound, for example, the Jewish peoples around the world. Indian Hindu visitors to the West Indies often report that they find little that is familiar in the practice of 'Hindu' West Indians. If anything, India has exported with its diaspora that peculiarly subcontinental tradition of complementary difference that ties its Hindus and Muslims. That is why, perhaps, the elaborately communal calculations that Naipaul describes in *The Suffrage of Elvira* seems so familiar to Indians.

Despite all this, the relationship between India and its diaspora is very real. On at least two occasions — the Uganda crisis and the recent crisis in Fiji — the Indian government did actually resort to real political brinkmanship on behalf of its diaspora. Its efforts may not have amounted to very much in either case — a fact for which the diaspora will probably never forgive it — but the truth is that, given the capabilities of a poor and relatively impotent nation, it did what little it could. The question again is why, for the populations of Uganda and Fiji were not Indian citizens and India owed them no obligations.

When we stop to think about the matter for a moment it becomes apparent, I think, that the relationship between India and the diaspora is a very peculiar, almost inexplicable phenomenon. We tend to take for granted that there is, and should be, a relationship between India and the 'Indians'. But in fact the relationship is a genuine historical anomaly: in the first place because we have to recognize that the links are not those of language, religion, politics or economics. In a sense the links are those of culture, but again of a kind of culture in which the most important cultural institutions as we usually understand them — for example, language and religion — are absent. We are left then with a pill that is very hard to swallow for those of us who were reared in the chill shadow of New Delhi materialism: the simple fact that the links between India and her diaspora are lived within the imagination. It is therefore an epic relationship: an epic without a text, which is all for the better perhaps, for if that text were ever written it would be a shabby, bedraggled, melancholy kind of epic — but still formally, an epic it would have to be. It is because this relationship is so much a relationship of the imagination that the specialists of the imagination — writers — play so important a part within it.

There is another sense in which the relationship is an epic one, and that is in the part that the metaphors of space play in it. As anthropologists and Indologists have shown us, the symbolic spatial structure of India is infinitely reproducible. It can be encapsulated in a microcosm, as in Banaras, and it can be exported wholesale to be reproduced in other countries. It is for that reason, of course, that we have an Ayodhya in Thailand today.

But within the imagination of the modern diaspora these locations manifest themselves in a strikingly different way. The pages of V.S. Naipaul's Trinidad novels are replete with references to the Ganges, to Ayodhya and Kashi. But when the women of his novels speak of the waters of the Ganga, they are not referring to a local river which has taken on the metaphorical role of sacredness in their lives: they are referring to the actual Ganga, across the oceans, far away. They have no choice; they never had the power to give their world its names. Taken across the seas as instruments of a colonial power, they entered a New World that was already named in the image of Old Europe: of York and Amsterdam, Castile and Aragon, the Hebrides and Caledonia. Their new world had no room for the words that lived in their imagination.

And yet those words — and the points in space to which they referred — lived with them, through constant use and repetition in their everyday lives. That is the trouble with an infinitely reproducible space: since it does not refer to actual places it cannot be left behind. The British colonist, for example, knows when he begins his journey that his voyage will separate him from his homeland: that once he is in his new country England will be a point on the far side of the globe, a distant Yoo-Kay, to be spoken of with nostalgia (or dislike), and to be treated as a model in most matters social, political and cultural. For the Indian, India is none of those things: quite the opposite in fact. And yet India can never be distant or separate in quite the same way, simply because the points that constitute it enter so insidiously into the vocabulary of everyday life. Eventually the place and the realities that accompany it vanish from memory and only the words and the geometric diagram remain. The place, India, becomes in fact an empty space, mapped purely by words. And thus V.S. Naipaul's indignation when he discovers that the pure spaces of his childhood are not merely peopled, but overwhelmingly alive.

Just as the spaces of India travel with the migrant, India too has no vocabulary for separating the migrant from India. Consider, for instance, the importance that the notion of the 'colonial' has, both for the British vision of places such as Australia, South Africa and Rhodesia, and for the Australian's understanding of himself. To be 'colonial' is to be imperfectly assimilated into the mother culture; it is to practice a second-hand or simplified — if not simple-minded — version of it. So, as generations of talented Australians have discovered in England, the voice of the 'colonial' is very easily marginalized within the culture of the 'mother country': being imperfectly British, the colonial is simply excluded as a player in the mother culture. It is no coincidence therefore that so many diasporic Indian writers, too, so often choose to write either about India or about Indian communities abroad (just as it is no coincidence, I think, that the first wholly American novel by an Indian, *The Golden Gate*, comes from a non-diasporic Indian). V.S. Naipaul, for instance, has never felt the slightest hesitation in writing novels about places and people — Africa and Africans to take an example — with whom he has only a passing acquaintance. But although he has lived most of his life in England he has written only one novel with a wholly English setting and in which all the characters are English. This novel, *Mr. Stone and the Knight's Companion*, is one his finest; it is also, unusually for a work of Naipaul's, a tender and compassionate novel — inevitably perhaps, for Naipaul is always at his most compassionate when he writes about white people. But the novel went largely unnoticed when it first appeared in England, and even today it remains one of the least known of his works. England is only too willing to celebrate V.S. Naipaul when he writes about the Other World; they find it much harder to take him seriously when he writes of their own — he can never be anything but an imperfect part of it.

It is impossible to be imperfectly Indian. There is no notion comparable to that of the colonial. Were it possible to be an imperfect Indian, everybody in India would be. This is not merely because India has failed to develop a national culture. It is not a lack; it is in itself the form of Indian culture. If there is any one pattern in Indian culture in the broadest sense it is simply this: that the culture seems to be constructed around the proliferation of differences (albeit within certain parameters). To be different in a world of differences is irrevocably to belong. Thus anybody anywhere who has even the most tenuous links with India is Indian; potentially a player within the culture. The mother country simply does not have the cultural means to cut them off.

Another of the interesting features of the cultural representation of space in India is that India has always been constituted as much by the notion of the periphery as it has by the notion of the centre. Thus, to take a Hindu example, the *dhams* at the four points of India play no less important a part in the definition of Hindu sacred space than does Banaras. (For Muslims in Bangladesh and Pakistan, the sacred sites at the centre of the subcontinent — the graves of Nizamuddin Auliya and Moinuddin Chishti — continue to play a vital part in the cycle of ritual and pilgrimage. For Sikhs too, the significance of Patna Sahib lies precisely in that it is not at the centre.)

It seems to me that this notion of the periphery has now expanded to include the diaspora. That is why the opinions of the diaspora are so significant to India: it is that part of itself which is both hostage and representative in the world outside — it is the mirror in which modern India seeks to know itself.

13 The Global Reservation: Notes toward an Ethnography of International Peacekeeping

Of the many dramatic consequences of the end of the Cold War, few have been as notable as the sudden expansion in the international role of the United Nations. Consider for example, that the UN has embarked on almost as many peacekeeping operations in the four years that have passed since 1989, as it did in the four decades that preceded it. The prospects are that in the next few years its peacekeeping activities will expand faster still. In a sense, the very fact of the UN's interventionism is a guarantee of this, for it provides an incentive for conflicts to be taken to the point where intercession becomes inevitable.

It is no coincidence that the majority of the UN's peacekeeping operations to date have been in places that fall within anthropology's traditional domains — in Asia, Africa, and Central America — and there can be little doubt that it is those very areas that will provide most of the locations for the UN missions of the future. In many of these places, peacekeeping operations will inevitably become harbingers of the future, not merely because of their immediate impact on the ebb and flow of politics, but also because they will serve as a political model, as a pattern of order and governance. It is the peculiar power of such models that they produce imaginative — and therefore cultural and political — resonances that reach far beyond the fields where they are first tested: nationalism is one example. It is my belief that the workings of international peacekeeping as we see them today may well contain the elements of another such model, one that will probably be the twentieth century's most important political legacy to the next.

It is probably too early to determine what exactly those elements are; certainly I shall make no attempt to do so here. What follows is rather a set of notes about one such UN exercise: the functioning of the United Nations' Transitional Authority in Cambodia (known universally by the acronym UNTAC).

The peacekeeping mission in Cambodia, which culminated in the countrywide elections of May 1993, was the most ambitious project of its kind ever undertaken by the UN until that time. At one point the total strength of UNTAC stood at over twenty thousand people, drawn from several dozen countries. Its cost — estimated at two billion dollars — far surpassed that of any previous operation.

I spent a month in Cambodia in early 1993. I was researching an article on an entirely different subject, but inevitably I spent a great deal of time with UN officials and volunteers. I would like to think of the notes that follow as an impressionistic contribution to a yet uninvented discipline — the ethnography of international peacekeeping. Or, in other words, an anthropology of the future.

Child of Bureaucracy

The maxim that the UN is a bureaucracy is true in several senses. It is a bureaucracy in the ordering of its procedures, in the manner of its internal organization, and in the sense that neither of the bodies that directs its operations — the Security Council or the General Assembly — are chosen by direct popular vote. A bureaucracy is by definition a hierarchy, and if the UN is an exception, it is only in the sense that, being mothered by all the world's bureaucracies, it is the child of all the world's hierarchies. UNTAC's Indian contingent, for example, was a microcosm of the social and organizational hierarchies that are encapsulated in the Indian bureaucracy

— the divisions between various wings and branches of the civil and armed services, the caste and class differences that determine entry into the army and bureaucracy — and indeed the quotas and reservations that have been enacted by the Indian parliament to offset those differences.

But equally, the UN also replicates the international hierarchies that order the relations between rich and poor, weak and powerful nations. Within UNTAC, it was no secret that certain key administrative positions were reserved for the representatives of a small group of wealthy or powerful countries. If this is worth remarking on, it is surely not because the UN happens to reflect the realities of the world that sustains it. Rather it is because the UN itself, as an organization, has no language to deal with those realities. Born in the period of post-War decolonization, the vocabulary of the UN has always been centred on international egalitarianism. Thus the circumstances of a localized peacekeeping operation today, when a variety of powerful global interests come directly into play, represent a problem for the UN's own organizational culture, since that culture possesses no vocabulary to deal with international hierarchy except for the anodyne terms *perm five* and *donor country*.

For the professional bureaucrat, steeped in principles of Weberian rationality, this asymmetry of power creates contradictions that are difficult to resolve. The training of young Indian or Pakistani or Kenyan bureaucrats, for example, is focused on the notions of the organizational integrity of the bureaucracy and of the necessity to resist the intrusions of political power. For many of them, the fact of working within a hierarchy that is unrelated to a specific function poses a difficult epistemological dilemma.

Thus, several of the UNTAC officials I met appeared to suspect that the lines of command within the organization were not clear, that the real sources of power were not where they appeared to be. Many also complained in private that UNTAC was disorganized, inefficient, corrupt, and incompetent — not, and this is worth remarking on, in its intentions or its methods of realizing them, but precisely as a structure, as an organization.

To me, exactly the opposite seemed to be true. Common sense suggests that any organization that has to deal with people from several dozens of different countries would be ridden with conflicts and confusion. But I came away convinced that considered purely as an organization UNTAC was, in many ways, a remarkably successful body.

One reason for this, I think, is that there are certain organizational advantages (as well as the obvious disadvantages) inherent in the circumstances in which bodies such as UNTAC operate. UNTAC had no difficulty, for example, in creating an absolute separation between itself and the society in which it was functioning: its boundaries were clear and self-evident. UNTAC employees and volunteers were foreigners, protected by a kind of diplomatic immunity, and distinguished by their appearance, their flags, and their cars: whatever their differences with each other, they were never so great as the difference between them and the general mass of Cambodians.

Travelling in Cambodia, I was constantly surprised to discover how much imaginative and classificatory power that distinction was capable of generating. UNTAC personnel often complained that Cambodians seemed wholly incapable of recognizing the differences between them: that, despite their many different nationalities, they were always simply 'UNTAC'. But to me the manifestations of the inverse of that principle seemed no less remarkable.

The Rescuer and the Rescued

Once, for instance, I decided to go to Kompong Thom to look for Pol Pot's family home. Kompong Thom has great military importance, for it straddles the vital middle section of Cambodia: the town itself lies at the strategic heart of the country. Two of the country's most important roadways intersect to the north of the little town. One of them leads directly to Thailand and has long been one of the most hotly contested highways in Cambodia. The point where the two roads meet is guarded by an old army encampment. Here, in this strategic hub, this centre of centres, looking for Pol Pot's ancestral home, inevitably, I came across someone from mine. He was a Bangladeshi sergeant, a large, friendly man with a bushy moustache; we had an ancestral district in common, in Bangladesh, and the unexpectedness of this discovery — at the edge of a Cambodian minefield — linked us immediately in a ridiculously intimate kind of bonhomie.

The sergeant and his colleagues were teaching a group of Cambodian soldiers professional de-mining techniques. My new-found friend and his colleagues had been trained as sappers and engineers, but none of them had ever seen or worked in a minefield that had been laid with intent to kill, so to speak. For their Cambodian charges on the other hand, mines were a commonplace hazard of everyday life, like spiders or snakes.

This irony was not lost on the Bangladeshi sergeant. 'They think nothing of laying mines', he said, in trenchant Bengali. 'They scatter them about like popped rice. Often they mine their own doorstep before going to bed, to keep thieves out. They mine their cars, their television sets, even their vegetable patches. They don't care who gets killed; life really has no value here.'

In the time they had spent at Kompong Thom, the sergeant and his colleagues had become friends with several Cambodian members of their team. But the better they got to know them the more hopeless the country's situation appeared. This despite the fact that Cambodians in general had a standard of living that would be considered enviable by most people in Bangladesh or India; despite the fact that Kompong Thom — for all that it had been on the battlefront for decades — was neater and better-ordered than any provincial town in the subcontinent; despite the fact that the sergeant was himself from a country that had suffered the ravages of a bloody civil war in the early seventies.

'They're working hard here because they're getting paid in dollars', the sergeant said. 'For them it's all dollars, dollars, dollars. Sometimes, at the end of the day, we have to hand out a couple of dollars from our own pockets to get them to finish the day's work.'

He laughed: 'It's their own country, and we have to pay them to make it safe. What I wonder is: what will they do when we're gone?'

He waved good-naturedly at his Cambodian trainees, and they waved back, bobbing their heads, smiling, and bowing. Both sides were working hard at their jobs, the expert and the amateur, the feckless and the responsible, the doughty rescuer and the hapless rescued: everybody was taking his role seriously. I told the sergeant what a friend of mine, a long-time resident, had said, in Phnom Penh: that Cambodia was a country that was actually only fifteen years old; that it had managed remarkably well considering that it had been built up almost from scratch after the fall of the genocidal Pol Pot regime in 1979 and that, too, in a situation of near-complete international isolation. Europe and Japan had received massive amounts of aid after the Second World War. But Cambodia, which had been subjected to one of the heaviest bombings in the history of war and had then had to live through a bloody and destructive revolution, got virtually nothing. Yet Cambodians had made do with what they had. But the sergeant was looking for large-scale proofs of progress — roads, a functioning postal system, 'Projects', 'Schemes', 'Plans' — and their lack rendered meaningless those tiny, cumulative efforts by which individuals and families reclaim their lives — a shutter repaired, a class taught, a palm-tree tended — and which are no longer noticeable once they are done since they sink into the order of normalcy, where they belong, and cease to be acts of affirmation and hope. He was the smallest of cogs in the vast machinery of UNTAC, but no less than the international bureaucrats in Phnom Penh, his vision of the country was organized around his part in saving it from itself.

Managing Diversity

I was to hear echoes of the sergeant's views again and again while talking to UNTAC personnel — people of different culture, gender, class, and race. They made a doubly forceful impression because I was all too well aware that an entirely different set of perceptions were possible in similar circumstances. For of course, UNTAC was not the first diverse group of foreigners to arrive in Cambodia. Small groups of relief workers have been living in Phnom Penh and other parts of the country for more than a decade now. Some of their members arrived soon after the Pol Pot regime was driven out of power in 1979. They witnessed the devastation that was left behind, and many of them have a great deal of respect for what Cambodians have achieved in the last ten years with the limited resources at their disposal. Their views were an indicator that the opinions I so often heard from UNTAC personnel were reflections of an organizational culture — that they marked the boundaries of a group that had been assembled for very specific reasons.

For its own part, UNTAC was not behindhand in the policing of its own boundaries. Its volunteers were required to sign two different pledges of secrecy, and all employees were forbidden to talk to the press without prior clearance from headquarters. Indeed, for an apostolic emissary of democracy, UNTAC was a remarkably secretive organization.

For example, allegations of misconduct involving UNTAC personnel were not infrequent. Some were evidently well founded. I quote a passage here from a document written by an UNTAC employee for internal circulation only:[1] 'A Bulgarian UNTAC soldier . . . was standing in the doorway of [a] hotel [in Phnom Penh]. He was drunk. An old man, over seventy years old, came up to the soldier to beg some money. As the old beggar joined his palms and raised them, the soldier grabbed him by the shirtfront. He pushed the old man on to his knees, unzipped his fly, and started pissing on him.' When

UNTAC's police arrived, the document continues, the soldier was sent back to his base: that was it.

Problems of law and order are unavoidable of course, where such large numbers of people are involved. But instead of dealing with these problems openly, UNTAC generally chose to conceal them, and journalists were discouraged from making enquiries.

An American correspondent who tried to follow up on some of these stories was harassed to the point where she had to threaten a lawsuit. Although she was one of the most respected journalists in the city, when she talked about the matter, it was in hushed voices: she had to be careful, she said; UNTAC officials had already tried to pressure her agency into firing her for what they described as 'negative reporting'. Journalists who ran afoul of the UNTAC press office often found their access to information drying up. Her access was already very restricted; if it were cut off altogether, it would become impossible for her to function in Phnom Penh. The threat implicit in that situation was enough to make her careful to avoid further confrontations.

Within its own boundaries, UNTAC was very successful in motivating its personnel and creating an ethic of organizational loyalty. Its most important achievement — the registering of voters — was primarily the result of the spirit and dedication of thousands of young volunteers who fanned out across the country, often living and working in very difficult circumstances.

That UNTAC was able to generate this kind of motivation came as a surprise to some of the volunteers themselves, who had doubted that so disparate a group could be made to function efficiently. But of course, as colonial armies have demonstrated over and over again in the last couple of centuries, diversity of origin is never in itself a hindrance to organizational efficiency. Diversity, it is worth recalling, is not the same thing as difference and, if properly managed, can easily be transformed into its mirror image, homogeneity.

In a body such as UNTAC, corporate loyalty appears to

be a function of the maintenance of organizational boundaries; of the creation and management of a set of clear distinctions between the peacekeeping force and the local population. This is, in my opinion, one of the organizational strategies that determines the success or failure of a peacekeeping operation (and the UN's Cambodia operation was, in its own estimation, counted as a success). In Somalia on the other hand, the organizational boundaries of the UN's peacekeeping mission appear to have broken down. This happened largely because one of the major constituent units happened to belong to the former colonial power, Italy, and thus possessed an extensive network of independent contacts with the local population, which it attempted to develop and cultivate.

Quite possibly, the Italian contingent in Somalia was attempting to emulate a different organizational style: that of the independent humanitarian relief mission or 'Non-Governmental Organization' (NGO), whose success lies precisely in creating credible links with the local population. By contrast, the success or failure of a UN operation appears to depend largely on the efficacy of the barriers between itself and the people of the region where it is located.

It is probably no accident, therefore, that a sharp division has arisen over the last couple of years between relief missions and NGOs, on the one hand, and the UN, on the other, with both trying strenuously to distance themselves from each other. The style of functioning of relief missions and NGOs is based on assumptions that were widely held in the era of decolonization which followed the end of the Second World War: conceptions that owed a great deal in turn to anthropology. The UN's current peacekeeping missions — even though they make a claim to global legitimacy on much the same humanitarian grounds as the relief missions — are in fact an entirely different phenomenon, whose assumptions and principles have yet to be adumbrated.

Arbiter of Ethnicity

One of UNTAC's most secretive units was a group called the Strategic Investigation Team. The team derived its function from a clause in UNTAC's mandate which required it to verify the withdrawal of all foreign forces from Cambodia. The phrase 'foreign forces' was in fact a euphemism for Vietnamese, and the work of the Strategic Investigation Team lay principally in investigating allegations about the presence of Vietnamese soldiers on Cambodian soil.

The task was unusually difficult because it led inevitably to an infinite regress of begged questions — among them many that belong with those vast imponderables whose answers are being sought with blood and bullets all over the world today: questions of nationality and ethnicity, difference, belonging, and freedom. Those issues were posed with a particular urgency by the Khmer Rouge in Cambodia, for they refused to cooperate in the peace process on the grounds that there were two or three million armed Vietnamese in Cambodia. The fact that the UN found absolutely no evidence to support this did not deter them from making that claim. As far as they were concerned, every Vietnamese in Cambodia counted as a soldier in disguise, no matter whether male or female, child or adult, no matter whether they belonged to the long-settled Vietnamese minority in Phnom Penh, whether they were construction labourers attracted by the UNTAC-created housing boom or transhumant fishermen who had travelled up the Mekong in observance of an ancient pattern of seasonal migration.

The term disguise, with its connotations of hidden identity and masking, has a charged meaning in the rhetoric of the current leadership of the Khmer Rouge: it embodies the ultimate pathology of nationalist thought, where the national and racial Other becomes so pervasive, so omnipresent, that he is no longer distinguishable from the Self except in death. When Pol Pot and his clique held power, in the Democratic Kampuchea of the late seventies, their final bloodiest purges were directed against their own eastern-zone cadres, on the grounds that they were 'Khmer bodies with Vietnamese minds.'

Today those genocidal conceptions play a greater part than ever in the ideology of the Khmer Rouge. A defector who surrendered to UN officials a few months before the elections used the following words to describe his political training with the Khmer Rouge:

> As far as the Vietnamese are concerned, whenever we meet them we must kill them, whether they are militaries or civilians, because they are not ordinary civilians but soldiers disguised as civilians. We must kill them, whether they are men, women, or children, there is no distinction, they are enemies. Children are not militaries but if they are born or grow up in Cambodia, when they will be adult, they will consider Cambodian land as theirs. So we make no distinction. As to women, they give birth to Vietnamese children.[2]

The Khmer Rouge carried out several massacres of civilians after the arrival of UNTAC, most of them directed against small communities of Vietnamese fishermen. The personnel who staffed UNTAC's Strategic Investigation Teams, military officers for the most part, were not given to pondering the implications of their duties. Even less were they inclined to discuss those duties with outsiders. But it so happened that I struck up a friendship with an officer who was serving in the team — I shall call him T.C. By inclination T.C. was no less tight-lipped than his colleagues, but he sometimes found it hard to turn his mind entirely from the assignments he had to perform during the day. For he, too, was from a part of the world where dilemmas of the kind that he was required to resolve in the performance of his duties were posed in bloody and bewildering forms. He was not unaware of the possibility that, at some point in the future, people he knew at home might also have their fates decided by a young officer from a distant continent who would have to make decisions about their linguistic or ethnic identity.

It was he, not I, who first used the analogy of ethnic cleansing.

Many of the reports his office received about people alleged to be Vietnamese were clearly denunciations intended to settle scores between neighbours and within families. As far as his team was concerned, the mere fact of an individual's ethnicity was irrelevant: UNTAC was concerned solely with foreign military personnel — not with economic migrants, nor with people of Vietnamese or Chinese origin who had been born in Cambodia.

The problem was that in a country with a drafted army, like Vietnam, most able-bodied men had done military service at some point and could, at a stretch, be described as soldiers, even if they happened to have come to Phnom Penh to work in a restaurant or at a construction site. Besides, like every army, the Vietnamese had left behind a number of deserters and stragglers. Some of these had married Khmer women and begun working on the land.

On one occasion, T.C. and his team travelled to a village deep in the countryside to investigate a report that seemed to be well documented. But upon talking to the man in question, T.C. began to have doubts. The man denied being Vietnamese; he spoke fluent Khmer, and he was married to a Khmer woman. He was very poor; he lived with his wife and children in a tumbledown, thatch-walled shack, and he supported them by working on the land. Reluctant to add to their evident misery, T.C., a family man himself, was all too willing to believe him. But the man broke down under interrogation. He admitted to being Vietnamese and to having come into the country with the army. But he was not a soldier, he insisted; he had worked as an interpreter for the army, and he had decided to stay behind in his wife's village after the army withdrew. T.C. would have been glad to accept his story at face value, for by this time his wife and children had begun to weep. But then, on a tip from some people in the village, his team searched the man's hut and found a gun. The man claimed that he had only acquired it recently, for self-defence, because he had begun to worry about his family's safety in the aftermath of the recent attacks on the Vietnamese. At this point, however, there was nothing T.C. could do; he had to take him in. After months of investigation, this was the closest he had come to discovering a Vietnamese soldier in disguise.

At the end of the story, T.C. commented, 'And I would easily have taken him for Khmer if our language expert hadn't been present. He's very good at picking out Vietnamese.' That was how I learnt that an 'expert' in linguistics had conducted the interrogation. I was immediately curious, because I had been told by many knowledgeable people that it is often impossible to tell the difference between ethnic Khmer and Vietnamese, even for Cambodians. A UN report quotes a Cambodian who asked an UNTAC officer whether there was a machine that could identify a person's ethnicity and was disappointed to hear that there was not.[3]

I was very keen to discover what manner of expert it was who had the job of filling in for that machine, and after some effort I contrived to arrange a meeting with him. I do not know exactly what I had expected, but it was certainly not the person it turned out to be. He was a young, Anglophone Westerner, tall in the way that used to be called willowy, with untidy shoulder-length hair; he was wearing colourful, roughly woven clothes of the kind that street vendors sell in the subway stations of cosmopolitan Western cities. I shall call him Mike.

Mike had acquired an interest in Indochina as an undergraduate and had eventually gone on to do a degree in area studies. He had spent several years in Vietnam and Cambodia and was fluent in the languages of both countries. He was good company in a friendly, easygoing way. He read Gabriel García-Márquez and *Granta*, avoided red meat, and believed in many admirable causes. Mike was deeply concerned about the welfare of the ethnic Vietnamese in Cambodia, and I was to learn later that be had been active in trying to pressure the UN into providing more protection for them. But for all that, when I asked him about the Strategic Investigation Teams, his answer was abrupt and immediate. 'I can't talk about that at all', he said.

I didn't want details, I told him. I just wanted to ask a few general questions. For example, could Cambodians always tell the difference between themselves and the Vietnamese?

'No', he said. 'Cambodians admit that there are situations in which they wouldn't be able to tell the difference.'

'What do you look for when you try to decide?' I asked.

'Sometimes its just glaringly obvious', he said. 'By that person's profession, by their linguistic abilities. By the way they look. But that's not such a good indicator. You can't just look. You have to talk to them, ask some questions, use whatever resources you have to try and determine what they are.'

When he first became interested in Indochina, I asked, had it ever occurred to him that from being a student of its languages and cultures he would one day find himself in a position where it was he who would draw the lines that demarcated them?

'When I accepted this job,' he said, 'I made a commitment to use my skills in it. I'm in a pretty unique kind of position and a difficult one too. There's no way anyone can expect to be right every time: to know someone's background 100 per cent. When I'm called upon to give an opinion, I always qualify it with whatever doubts I have. But I just accompany the teams. I'm only a translator.'

I pointed out that it was possible to take a different view: to argue that the military men who staffed the teams were merely the jailers and he the judge, since they were merely enforcing a set of rules, while it was he who represented the body of knowledge that gave those rules their force. His response was the same that decent, well-intentioned functionaries have given throughout this century in similar circumstances. He said, 'I'm just doing a job.'

Mike, like the majority of UNTAC's 'experts', had received his training in an area studies programme. I was often struck by the thought that even a decade ago an organization like

UNTAC would probably have turned to anthropology to furnish its advisers and experts. In fact, to the best of my knowledge, there was only one anthropologist working with the organization. The increasing self-reflexivity that is anthropology's redeeming grace has evidently tendered it unfit for the utilitarian tasks of governance that it once performed. But of course those functions have not disappeared: there is still an immense demand for practical kinds of knowledge whereby the non-West can be managed and dealt with. All that has happened is that that demand is now met by a different corridor within the academy.

Instrument of Containment

The UN, to its great credit, was extremely circumspect and scrupulous in its treatment of allegations about the presence of Vietnamese in Cambodia. Yet for those of us who look upon the UN as a bulwark against the wave of ethnic nationalism that is sweeping the world, the question remains: why should the world's largest and most important international organization be implicated in the task of defining a country's ethnic boundaries, even if only in a tangential way?

The answer, I think, is that there is an unspoken and unwritten agreement that underlies the UN's actions, not merely in Cambodia, but wherever it goes: an agreement that derives ultimately from what might be called the primal mandate of the UN itself. The UN represents the totality of the world's recognized nation-states, and the fundamental logic of its functioning is to recreate the image of its membership wherever it goes. Elections are, thus, only a step in restoring or conjuring up a nation-state, and wherever the demands of democracy or humanitarianism run contrary to the exigencies of the nation-state, it is the latter that will always win out.

Yet the entities that result from these efforts are clearly not nation-states in the traditional sense, since the nation-state is by definition sovereign and, so to speak, self-created

— an entity that has brought itself into being. The UN's very presence at the birth of these new entities is a clear contradiction of those precepts. Indeed, it could well be argued that, in the contemporary world, sovereignty resides precisely where the UN's peacekeepers do not: the reason why the UN is probably never going to intervene in Ulster or Tibet is because it will be excluded by actual, as opposed to nominal, sovereignty.

How then, are we to characterize the entities that will result from the UN's labours?

It is my belief that we are currently witnessing a fundamental change in the political institutions of this century, one that will probably result in a two-tier system of nation-states. In the first of those tiers, the boundaries of the nation-state, as traditionally understood, will become increasingly blurred; in the other, conversely, those boundaries will become increasingly rigid and will serve as a mechanism for the maintenance of a pattern of global order. Thus, the very institution that was (and is) so eagerly embraced by the peoples of the colonized world, as the embodiment of liberty, will become, effectively, the instrument of their containment.

This two-tier system will probably reflect global realities more accurately than did the international order of the Cold War era. But fundamentally the principles of that order will not be new. Throughout the period of Western expansion over the last two centuries, the nation-state has repeatedly supplied models of containment: we have only to think of the reservations of America or the Bantustans of South Africa. The transformation we are witnessing today may well be another step in the ascendancy of that pattern. What is novel in it perhaps is that now the peoples of the regions in which it is becoming ascendant are fully complicit in the taking of that step.

Notes

1. This quotation is from an UNTAC report entitled 'Field Trip: Phnom Penh, 7–12 January 1993; Full Report.' The author is anonymous.
2. This quotation is from an anonymously authored UNTAC document entitled 'Interview with Khat Sali, Sihanoukville (9–10/1/1992).'
3. This report is the anonymously authored UNTAC document 'Field Trip', quoted above and cited in note 1.

14 *The Fundamentalist Challenge*

WITH THE benefit of hindsight, I am ever more astonished by the degree to which, over the course of this century, religion has been reinvented as its own antithesis. At much the same time that one stream within modernism created a straw version of religion as a cloak of benighted ignorance that had to be destroyed with the weapons of literary, artistic, and scientific progressivism, another stream within this same movement created a no less fantastic version of religion as a bulwark against the dehumanization of contemporary life.

To a greater or lesser degree, most of us have felt the tug of both these currents. Indeed, it is hard to think of any contemporary, modern, or even not so modern thinker, writer, or artist who has not. Karl Marx, for instance, while writing his much-quoted sentence about religion being the opiate of the masses (itself not as dismissive as some of his followers have assumed), also wrote a less known passage describing religion as the heart of a heartless world.

These are commonplaces, of course. We all know the stories of modernist figures who have swum from one of these currents into the other: a narrative best exemplified by the career of W.H. Auden. At the heart of these stories is a moment, often an extended moment, of conversion, and it is this moment that puzzles me now — with the benefit of hindsight, as I said. It puzzles me because it seems to me increasingly that the intellectual pedigrees of most versions of religious extremism around the world today can be traced to similar moments of conversion.

Let me cite a few examples: Swami Vivekananda, the late-nineteenth-century thinker who is today claimed by Hindu extremists as a founding father, was famously a rationalist in the best positivist tradition, until he underwent a dramatic conversion. Or consider the Anagarika Dharmapala, who laid the foundations of Buddhist revivalism in Sri Lanka at the turn of the century. The Anagarika Dharmapala's early education was in Christian schools, and he is said to have learned the Bible by heart at an early age. He was reconverted to Buddhism by the American theosophist Henry Steel Olcott, who arrived in Sri Lanka in 1880. As with so many such figures, the first popular movement the Anagarika Dharmapala led was social rather than religious in nature — a temperance campaign.

In Iran, the figure who is thought to have played the most important part in the radicalization of Shiite youth in the recent past was neither a mullah nor an ayatollah but rather a Sorbonne-trained sociologist, Ali Shari'ati. In Shari'ati's writings, religion often assumes the aspect of a sociological instrument, a means to resist the versions of modernity he had witnessed in France.

Similarly the intellectual progenitors of religious extremism in Egypt, Hasan al-Banna and al-Sayyid Qutb, were not educated in traditional religious institutions. Both were graduates of the Dar al-Uluum, or House of Sciences, in Cairo, an institution that has been described as a 'modernist teacher training institute'. Al-Sayyid Qutb first made his name as a literary figure, a writer of fiction and critic who was actively involved in debates centred on questions of literary modernism in the Cairo of the 1930s and '40s. Like the Anagarika Dharmapala in Sri Lanka before him, he began his career in the educational bureaucracy. His bosses in Egypt's Ministry of Public Instruction sent him to America in 1948, apparently in the hope that he would be won over by American ways. His discovery of his religious mission is said to have occurred as he stood on the deck of the liner that was carrying him to New York. I have cited figures from

Hinduism, Buddhism, and Islam; many similar figures could be cited from the Jewish and Christian traditions.

What do these moments of conversion signify? In trying to answer that question, we find ourselves reaching reflexively for the terms that float by on one or the other side of the modernist stream. On the one shore we find terms or phrases such as 'atavism', 'medievalism', 'fear of uncertainty' coming all too readily to hand; on the other, our hands close upon 'resistance', 'alternative', 'search for community', 'thirst for meaning'.

To a greater or lesser degree, moments of conversion such as those I have referred to are all of these things, but they are also something else: they also mark a crossing from one current of modernism to another. It is all too easy to forget that these reinvented forms of religion are not a repudiation of, but a means of laying claim to, the modern world. That is why the advance-guard of these ideologies are never traditional religious specialists but rather young college graduates or engineering students — products, in other words, of secularly oriented, modernist institutions. It is for this reason that we find the same things valued on both shores but in diametrically opposed ways. Literature and art, for example, being regarded as the ultimate repository of value on one side, come to be excoriated on the other, in exact and equal measure, so that their destruction becomes a prime article of faith.

Where else are we to look for the sources of this antagonism except within the whirlpools that mark the meeting of these two currents? Certainly the conflict cannot be ascribed to religion in the broadest sense. For most of human history, religion and literature have been virtually inseparable, everywhere. I can think of non-religious ideologies that have thought of literature as an enemy; I know of no religion that has historically held that position. That is why we must be rigorous and unrelenting in our rejection of the claims of those religious extremists who try to invoke historical and religious precedents for their attacks on writers. These claims are offered in bad faith. In fact, the roots of this hostility lie in the eminently modern pedigree of their own moments of conversion. The religions they invoke do not begin with a positive content of faith; they have their beginnings in acts of negation.

I have been using the phrase 'religious extremism' with what may appear to be a reckless disregard for differences among the world's major religions. I do not do so unadvisedly. I do believe that the content of these ideologies is startlingly similar, across continents and cultures.

Consider, for example, that the rhetoric of religious extremism is everywhere centred on issues that would have been regarded as profane, or worldly, or largely secular a few generations ago: issues of state power, control of the bureaucracy, school curricula, the army, the law courts, banks, and other such institutions. Consider also that religious extremists are everywhere hostile to mainstream traditions of dissent within whatever religion they claim to be speaking for. Muslim extremists in the Middle East are contemptuous of the traditional Sufi tariqas that have so long been a mainstay within popular Islam; the political leadership of the Hindu extremist movement treats traditional mendicants and ascetics as a source of embarrassment. In both instances, this hostility has its roots in peculiarly bourgeois anxieties about respectability and rationality.

There is also much evidence to show that as the concerns of the major religions have grown more and more sociological, their doctrines and institutions have also increasingly converged. Yet while we speak of doctrine, we are still within a domain that is recognizably religious. But the truth is that in those areas of the world that are currently beset by religious turmoil, we very rarely hear anyone speak of doctrine or faith. In many of these areas, by a curious inversion, the language of religious hatred is not a religious language at all. The voices that spew hate invariably draw on more incendiary sources. One of these is the language of quantity, of number —

statistics, in other words, that famous syntax of falsehood. Such and such a group is growing too fast, they declare, its birth-rate is so and so; it will soon become a majority, overtake another group that has nowhere else to go; that group will then be swamped, washed into the sea by the rising tide of enemies within. Equally, these voices borrow the language of academic historiography. They produce archaeological data to prove that such and such a group has no right to be here, that they are invaders who arrived later than some other, more authentically located peoples, whose claim to the land is therefore greater.

One of the more curious elements of these bizarre but all too real discourses is what might be called the logic of competitive victimhood. Group X, incontestably a majority in its own area, will declare itself to be the real minority because it is outnumbered if the surrounding regions are taken into account. Its ideologues will cite this as the reason why, to preserve itself, it must drive members of Group Y off its territory: Group Y, which appears to be a minority, is actually a majority; the members of Group X are the real victims. And so on.

Most of these ideologies share similar discourses on women: what women should wear, how they should comport themselves, when and if they should reproduce. And all this, we are told, because scripture or custom has ordained it so. I remember very well an incident that dates back some fourteen years, to a time when I was living in a village in Egypt. One day a schoolboy of fifteen — one of the brightest and most likable in the village — said to me: 'Do you know what I did today? I gave my mother and the womenfolk in the house a stern talking-to. I told them that they could not go to the burial ground any more to pray at our family's tombs.'

I was taken aback by this. So far as I knew, the custom of visiting tombs was a very old one, and it served the additional function of providing women with a place to meet their kinfolk and friends. 'Why?' I asked the boy. 'What made you do this?'

'Because it is against our religion, of course,' he said. 'Visiting a grave is nothing but irrational superstition.'

It turned out, I later learned, that a schoolteacher with fundamentalist leanings had preached a fiery sermon in the mosque, urging the men of the village to put an end to this custom.

The image of that adolescent schoolboy lecturing his mother on what she could and could not do stayed with me for a long time. Where did he find that authority at the age of fifteen? Why did she allow him to speak to her like that? But wasn't he also right to do what he did? After all, is it not perhaps irrational to visit graves? But still, did she resent having to renounce her trips to the graveyard? I don't know. The outcome in any case was that she stayed at home. That is how religious extremism seems to work.

The issues around which these fundamentalist discourses are configured are not, of course, exclusively the concern of religious extremists. On the contrary, the concerns are precisely the same as those that animate certain kinds of conflict that have no religious referents at all: language conflicts, for example, or ethnic and tribal conflicts. In a sense, this is the most revealing aspect of these movements: that they all have recourse to the same language of difference — a language that is entirely profane, entirely devoid of faith or belief.

This was brought home to me very forcefully a couple of years ago when I was travelling in Cambodia. It so happened that the United Nations was then conducting a large-scale peace-keeping operation, and some 20,000 peace-keeping personnel from all over the globe had been deployed throughout the country. The principal obstacle to the peace was the Khmer Rouge, whose ideology had by that time been reduced to a nationalistic form of racism, directed at the Vietnamese and particularly the Vietnamese-speaking minority in Cambodia. A defector who had surrendered to UN officials a few months before the elections described his political training with the Khmer Rouge:

> As far as the Vietnamese are concerned, whenever we meet them we must kill them, whether they are militaries or civilians, because they are not ordinary civilians but soldiers disguised as civilians. We must kill them, whether they are men, women, or children, there is no distinction, they are enemies. Children are not militaries, but if they are born or grow up in Cambodia, when they will be adult, they will consider Cambodian land as theirs. So we make no distinction. As to women, they give birth to Vietnamese children.

The Khmer Rouge carried out several massacres of civilians during the peace-keeping process, most of them directed against small Vietnamese fishing communities.

I arrived in Cambodia in January 1993, just six or seven weeks after my own country, India, had faced what was perhaps its most serious political crisis since it gained independence in 1947. The crisis was precipitated by the demolition of a mosque in the city of Ayodhya by Hindu extremists. The demolition of the mosque was followed by a wave of murderous attacks upon Muslim-minority communities in India. In a series of pogroms in various Indian cities, thousands of Muslims were systematically murdered, raped, and brutalized by Hindu extremists. In many respects, the language of the Hindu extremists, with the appropriate substitutions, was identical to that of the Khmer Rouge in Cambodia.

It was against the background of these tragic events that I found myself one day in Siem Reap, in north-western Cambodia. In this town, famous for its proximity to the glorious temple complexes of Angkor Wat and Angkor Thom, I came upon a group of Indian doctors who were running a small field hospital for the UN. By virtue of the camaraderie that links compatriots in a faraway place, I was invited to join them for a meal at their hospital. The doctors received me with the greatest cordiality in their prefabricated dining room. But no sooner had I sat down than they turned to me, smiling cordially across the rice and daal, and one of them said: 'Mr Ghosh, can you think of a good reason why we Hindus should not demolish every mosque in India? After all, we are the majority. Why should we allow minorities to dictate what is right for us?' I had not noticed until then that my hosts were all Hindus, from various parts of India.

Their line of reasoning was, of course, far from unfamiliar to me: it was the standard majoritarian argument trotted out by Hindu extremists in India. But here, in this context, with the gunshots of the Khmer Rouge occasionally audible in the distance, it provoked an extra dimension of outrage. In the first place, these doctors were not extremists, in any ordinary meaning of the term. On the contrary, they were the personification of middle-class normality. Second, they were probably not religious in any but the most private sense. For them, most likely, religion was no more than a mark of distinction, defining the borders of what they believed to be a majority. In the course of the furious argument that followed, I was amazed to discover — though perhaps I should not have been — that these doctors actually harboured a lurking admiration for the Khmer Rouge, an admiration that was in no way diminished by the fact that we were then under Khmer Rouge fire.

I was amazed because I could not immediately understand why extremist Hindu beliefs should translate so fluently into sympathy for a group that had no religious affiliations at all, a group whose ideological genealogy ought to have inspired revulsion in these middle-class professional men. It only became obvious to me later, reading reports from Bosnia, Croatia, Sudan, Algeria, Sri Lanka, and other strife-torn lands, that for this species of thinking, religion, race, ethnicity, and language have no real content at all. Their only significance lies in the lines of distinction they provide. The actual content of the ideology, whether it manifests itself in its religious avatar or its linguistic or ethnic one, is actually the same in every case, although articulated through different symbols. In several instances — Sri Lanka, for example —

extremist movements have seamlessly shifted their focus from language to religion.

What then is this ideology that can travel so indifferently among such disparate political groups? I believe that it is an incarnation of a demon that has stalked liberal democracy everywhere throughout this century: an ideology that, for want of a better word, I shall call supremacism. It consists essentially in the belief that a group cannot ensure its continuity except by exerting absolute cultural and demographic control over a particular stretch of geography. The fascist antecedents of this ideology are clear and obvious. Some would go further and argue that nationalism of every kind must also be regarded as a variant of supremacism. This is often but not necessarily true. The non-sectarian, anti-imperialist nationalism of a Gandhi or a Saad Zaghloul was founded on a belief in the possibility of relative autonomy for heterogeneous populations and had nothing to do with asserting supremacy.

To return to where I began: it is my belief that extremist religious movements, whether in India or Israel or Egypt or the United States, are often supremacist movements, whatever their rhetoric. The movements that fit the pattern least perhaps are radical Muslim movements. Of all the world's religions, Islam remains today the least territorial, the least, as it were, nationalized. Yet it cannot be a coincidence that despite the critique of nationalism that is inherent in some branches of radical Islam, these movements have everywhere lapsed into patterns that are contained within the current framework of nation-states. Nor can it be a coincidence that in the Islamic world, as elsewhere, religious movements are at their most extreme in countries with large minority populations — Sudan and Egypt, for example. Indeed, such is the peculiar power of supremacist movements that they have actually conjured minorities into being where none actively existed before. Thus, in Algeria, Muslim extremists must now contend with an increasingly, assertive minority Berber population.

In principle, it is not unreasonable that a population should have the right to live under religious law, with the proper democratic safeguards. But in practice, in contemporary societies, when such laws are instituted they almost invariably become instruments of majoritarian domination. Consider, for example, the blasphemy laws enacted in Pakistan in the 1980s. A recently published Amnesty International report tells us that 'at present several dozen people are charged with blasphemy, in Pakistan.' The majority of these belong to the minority Ahmadiyya community. This sect, which considers itself Muslim, was declared heretical by the country's legislature, and its members were forbidden to profess, practice, or propagate their faith. According to Pakistani human rights activists, in a period of five years 108 Ahmadis were charged with blasphemy for practicing their faith. Over the last three years, according to the report, members of the Christian minority in Pakistan have also increasingly been charged with blasphemy. But here again, the meaning of blasphemy itself has changed. When a law such as this is available, it is unrealistic to expect that people will not use it in ways other than was intended. I quote from the report:

> In a number of cases, personal grudges against Christian neighbours seem to have led people to settle their disputes by bringing blasphemy charges. Anwar Masih, a Christian in Sammundri in Faisalabad district, had a quarrel with the local Muslim shopkeeper over a small debt and was subsequently charged with blasphemy. . . . A 13-year-old Christian boy in Punjab was reported to have said that he had had a fight with the eight-year-old son of a Muslim neighbour. 'It all started with some pigeons. The boys caught my pigeons and they didn't want to give them back to me. . . . The little boy with whom I had a fight said he saw me write [blasphemous words) on the mosque. . . . ' [The boy], who has never learned to read or write, and two adult Christians were charged with blasphemy, in May 1993.

How far we are here from a reverence for the spirit of scripture!

I would like to turn now to a novel which, more than anything I have read recently, has forced me to confront the questions that contemporary religious extremism raises for writers. This is the Bengali novel *Lojja* (Shame), by the Bangladeshi writer Taslima Nasrin. I believe that this book, deeply flawed in many respects, is nonetheless a very important novel and a work of considerable insight. It is also a work that is literally much misunderstood, because at the moment it is available to most of the world in an English translation that can only be described as appalling. As a result the book has received many slighting and dismissive notices in America and Europe, probably because reviewers have assumed uncritically that the translation provides an accurate indication of the book's quality. It happens that although I write in English, my own native language is Bengali, and having read the book in the original I know this assumption to be untrue. It seems more and more unlikely now that the book will ever get a fair reading, partly because it has become a pawn within the religious conflicts of the Indian subcontinent, and partly because Taslima Nasrin is herself now a global 'cause' for reasons that have little to do with her writing.

Lojja was apparently written at great speed, being completed in a couple of months. The book was later revised, but even in its revised version it remains a short novel — the new Bengali edition numbers 150 pages. The narrative is simple: through its protagonist, Suranjan Datta, it follows the fortunes of a Hindu family that finds itself engulfed in a wave of violence directed against the minority Hindu community in Bangladesh. The events it describes occur in the aftermath of the demolition of a mosque in Ayodhya on 6 December 1992. The narrative is punctuated throughout with paraphrased news reports, items from the files of human rights organizations, and other accounts detailing actual instances of violence. In particular it is a severe, because factual, indictment of certain groups of religious extremists in Bangladesh.

As is well known, the book caused an uproar when it was

published in Bangladesh in 1993. It also became an instant best seller on both sides of the border: that is, in Bangladesh as well as in the Bengali-speaking parts of India. A few months after its publication the government of Bangladesh, in response to the demands of religious extremists, declared a ban on the book and had it removed from circulation. Shortly thereafter, an extremist Muslim leader declared Taslima Nasrin an apostate and issued a death warrant against her. The warrant carried a large bounty. A few months later, in response to certain remarks Taslima Nasrin was alleged to have made in a newspaper interview in Calcutta, the government of Bangladesh charged her officially with the crime of offending religious sentiments and began criminal proceedings. Taslima Nasrin then went into hiding for a period of two months. Thanks to the international outcry that followed, she was allowed to leave Bangladesh in August 1994. She is currently living in Sweden. In her short career in exile she has continued to rock governments. Last October the French foreign ministry refused her a visa, a gesture that created such an outburst of public indignation that the ministry was soon forced to reverse its decision. What I have sketched here is perhaps only the beginning of Taslima Nasrin's story. Even as I write, a government prosecutor in Bangladesh is appearing before a court to demand that she be sentenced in absentia for the crime of blasphemy.

However, religious extremists were not the only people in Bangladesh who objected to *Lojja* when it first appeared. Many non-sectarian, liberal voices were also fiercely critical of the book. Their objections were important ones and must be taken into account because — and I cannot repeat this strongly enough — non-sectarian, broadly secularist voices do not by any means represent a weak or isolated strand of opinion in that country. Bangladeshi culture in particular, like Bengali culture in general, has a long and very powerful tradition of secularist thought; Taslima Nasrin is herself a product of this tradition. For all their visibility, the religious extremists represent a tiny minority of the population of Bangladesh. At present, for example, they control no more than two per cent of the country's legislature.

Of the criticisms directed at *Lojja* by liberal, non-sectarian Bangladeshis and Indians, perhaps the most important is the charge that the novel, by limiting its focus to Bangladesh, profoundly distorts the context of the violence it depicts. Taken literally, this is, I think, true. By concentrating on the events in Dhaka the book does indeed, by omission, distort the setting and causes of those events.

What then was this context? I shall try to sketch the chain of events as I see them, very briefly.

On 6 December 1992, several thousand Hindu supremacists tore down a 400-year-old mosque in Ayodhya, claiming that the structure was built upon the birthplace of their mythical hero Sri Rama. The Indian government, despite ample warning, was culpably negligent in not taking action to prevent the demolition. Thus, through CNN, the whole world witnessed the destructive frenzy of a mob of Hindu fanatics attacking an archaeological site, in the service of an utter delusion. (After all, a legendary world-bestriding hero can only be diminished if his birthplace comes to be confined to a circumscribed geographical location.)

The destruction of the mosque was followed by tension and general unrest, in Pakistan and Bangladesh as well as India. In India this quickly escalated into violence directed against Muslims by well-organized mobs of Hindus. Riots broke out in several major cities, and within two days 400 people had died. The overwhelming majority of the dead, as always in these situations in India, were Muslim. There is evidence that in many parts of the country the police cooperated with and even directed Hindu mobs. Within six days, according to the official reckoning, about 1,200 people had died. Reports from all over the country attest to the unprecedented brutality, the unspeakable savagery, of the violence that was directed against innocent Muslims by Hindu supremacists. A month later, there was a second wave of anti-Muslim violence centred primarily in Bombay and Surat. The violence now assumed the aspect of systematic pogroms, with crowds hunting out Muslims from door to door in particular neighbourhoods. I quote here a report from Surat, written by a Dutch observer:

> In a refugee camp which I visited a small boy, hardly six years of age, sits all alone in a corner staring in front of him. Before his eyes he has seen first his father and mother murdered by the mob, then his grandfather and grandmother, and in the end three of his brothers. He is still alive but bodily not unscathed with 16 stitches in his head and burns on his back. The men who did it thought he was dead when they had finished with him. . . . Page after page of my diary is filled with this sort of atrocity. Women between seven and 70 were up for grabs by male gangs roaming around the localities. . . . People were also thrown into the flames and roasted alive. A high-ranking official told me how he had seen furniture coming down over the balcony from the opposite multistoreyed apartment building: mattresses, chairs, and then to his horror small children as well.

Such was the nature of the horror that visited India in the winter of 1992, in the name of religion.

In Bangladesh and Pakistan, the destruction of the Ayodhya mosque also led to violence. Temples were attacked and destroyed in both countries. In Bangladesh, which has a substantial Hindu population, a great many Hindu shrines were destroyed and desecrated; Hindu-owned businesses were attacked and looted; many Hindu families were driven from their homes. Yet it must also be noted that despite all that happened in Bangladesh, there was no actual loss of life so far as I know. If accounts could be kept of such events, it would have to be said that the scale of violence in Bangladesh was small compared to what occurred in India.

But here we have to ask whether events such as these can be weighed at all on a scale of comparative horrors. For a minority family that is being harassed in Dhaka (or wherever), the horror of the situation is not mitigated by the knowledge that they are situated in the wings of the stage of violence, as it were, that far worse crimes are being visited upon minority groups in India. Equally, the terror of a middle-class Muslim family caught in a riot in Bombay is in no way lessened by the knowledge that there is greater violence still in Bosnia. To the Bosnian Serbs, in turn, the accounting of violence stretches back to the fourteenth century. To tinker with this calculus is really to enter into what I have called the logic of competitive victimhood: a discourse that ultimately serves only to fuel supremacism.

In inadvertently spotlighting events that were happening in the wings rather than centre stage, *Lojja* inevitably presents a partial view. As it happened, Hindu supremacists in India seized upon *Lojja* with undisguised glee. Pirated editions were quickly printed and the book was even distributed free by Hindu activists in an attempt to whip up anti-Muslim feeling. This in turn led to accusations that Taslima Nasrin was a willing dupe of Hindu supremacists in India, that she was in the pay of a Calcutta publishing house, and so on.

In fact, *Lojja* is unequivocal in its condemnation of Hindu supremacists. It simply does not give them as much space as it does their Muslim counterparts in Bangladesh, which is unavoidable given the book's setting. Just as important, Taslima Nasrin can hardly be held responsible for the uses to which her book is put. In passing into the public domain, a book also passes beyond its author's control. I know of no way that an author can protect his or her text against abuse of this kind. The only option really is not to write about such matters at all.

We who write fiction, even when we deal with matters of public significance, have no choice, no matter how lush or extravagant our fictions, but to represent events as they are refracted through our characters. Our point of entry into even the largest of events is inevitably local, situated in and focused on details and particulars. To write of any event in this way is necessarily to neglect its political contexts. Consider by way of example a relatively simple kind of event: a mugging, let us say, in the streets of New York. If we write of the mugging of a white man by a black man, do we not in some way distort the context of the event if we do not accommodate the collective histories which form its background? Conversely, if, in defiance of stereotypes, we were to make our mugger a white female bank executive, would we not distort an equally important context? But where would our search for contexts end? And would we not fatally disfigure the fictional texture of our work if we were to render all those broader contexts?

What then are the contexts that we, as writers of fiction, can properly supply? It seems to me that they must lie in the event itself, the scene, if you like: the aggressor's fear of his prey, the street lamps above, the paper clip that drops from the victim's pocket as he reaches for his money. It must be in some part the reader's responsibility to situate the event within broader contexts, to populate the scene with the products of his or her experience and learning. A reader who reads the scene literally or mean-spiritedly must surely bear some part of the blame for that reading.

Read by an attentive reader, *Lojja* succeeds magnificently. Through a richness of detail it creates a circumstance that is its own context, and in this sense is imaginatively available far beyond the boundaries of its location. I, for one, read *Lojja* not as a book about Hindus in Bangladesh but rather as a book about Muslims in India. It helped me feel on my own fingertips the texture of the fears that have prompted Muslim friends of mine to rent houses under false pretenses or to buy train tickets under Hindu names. In short, it has helped me understand what it means to live under the threat of supremacist terror.

Lojja can be read in this way because it is founded on a very important insight, one which directly illustrates my main point. Almost despite herself, Taslima Nasrin recognizes that religious extremism today has very little to do with matters of doctrine and faith, that its real texts are borrowed from sociology, demography, political science, and so on. For a book that is said to be blasphemous, *Lojja* surprisingly contains no scriptural or religious references at all. Even words such as 'Hindu' and 'Muslim' figure in it but rarely. The words Taslima Nasrin uses are, rather, 'minority' and 'majority'. There is nothing in *Lojja* that the most fastidiously devout reader could possibly object to, from a theological point of view. That it succeeded nonetheless in enraging extremist religious opinion in Bangladesh, and bolstering opinion within the opposite religious camp in India, is a sign that it cut through to an altogether different kind of reality. Yet it is a fact that, despite their outrage, the extremists could find no passage in it that could be indicted as blasphemous. That was why, perhaps, they later fell so gratefully on her throwaway remarks of doubtful provenance.

I would like to return now to some of the considerations with which I started. In particular I would like to go back to one of the images I offered at the beginning of this essay: that of W. H. Auden, breasting the modernist flow and crossing between currents. In offering this example I did not mean to suggest that Auden can in any way be associated with religious extremism as we know it today. To make such a suggestion would be plainly ludicrous. If there is an analogy here, it is a very limited one and it consists only in this: that a conversion such as Auden's to Christianity was — among many other things — also an act of dissent, an opting out of what might be regarded as the mainstream of modernist consciousness.

It is finally undeniable, I think, that some kinds of contemporary religious extremism also represent a generalized, nebulous consciousness of dissent, an inarticulate, perhaps inexpressible critique of the political and moral economy of today's world. But the question remains, even if this is true: why are these movements so easily pushed over the edge, why are they so violent, so destructive, and why is their thinking so filled with intolerance and hate?

Today, for the first time in history, a single ideal commands something close to absolute hegemony in the world: the notion that human existence must be permanently and irredeemably subordinated to the functioning of the impersonal mechanisms of a global marketplace. Realized in varying degrees in various parts of the world, this ideal enjoys the vigorous support of universities, banks, vast international corporations, and an increasingly interconnected global communications network. However, the market ideal as a cultural absolute, untempered by any other ethical, political, or spiritual ideals, is often so inhuman and predatory in its effects that it cannot but generate dissent. It is simply not conceivable that the majority of human beings will ever willingly give their assent to the idea that the search for profit should be the sole or central organizing principle of society.

By a curious paradox, the room for dissent has shrunk as the world has grown more free, and today, in this diminished space, every utterance begins to turn in on itself. This, I believe, is why we need to recreate, expand, and reimagine the space for articulate, humane, and creative dissent. In the absence of that space the misdirected and ugly energies of religious extremism will only continue to flourish and grow.

What then, finally, of religion itself? Must we resign ourselves to the possibility that religious belief has everywhere been irreversibly cannibalized by this plethora of political, sociological, and, in the end, profane ideas? It is tempting to say no, that 'real' Hindus, Buddhists, Christians, Jews, and Muslims continue to hold on to other values. Yet if it appears that the majority of the followers of a religion now profess ideas that are, as I have said, essentially political or sociological, then we must be prepared to accept that this is in fact what religion signifies in our time.

Still I, for one, have swum too long in pre-postmodernist

currents to accept that some part of the effort that human culture has so long invested in matters of the spirit will not, somehow, survive.

15 *The March of the Novel through History: the Testimony of my Grandfather's Bookcase*

As a child I spent my holidays in my grandfather's house in Calcutta, and it was there that I began to read. My grandfather's house was a chaotic and noisy place, populated by a large number of uncle, aunts, cousins, and dependants, some of them bizarre, some merely eccentric, but almost all excitable in the extreme. Yet I learned much more about reading in this house than I ever did in school.

The walls of my grandfather's house were lined with rows of books, neatly stacked in glass-fronted bookcases. The bookcases were prominently displayed in a large hall that served, among innumerable other functions, also those of playground, sitting room, and hallway. The bookcases towered above us, looking down, eavesdropping on every conversation, keeping track of family gossip, glowering upon quarrelling children. Very rarely were the bookcases stirred out of their silent vigil. I was perhaps the only person in the house who raided them regularly, and I was in Calcutta for no more than a couple of months every year. When the bookcases were disturbed in my absence, it was usually not for their contents but because some special occasion required their cleaning. If the impending event happened to concern a weighty matter like a delicate marital negotiation, the bookcases got a very thorough scrubbing indeed. And well they deserved it, for at such times they were important props in the little plays that were enacted in their presence. They let the visitor know that this was a house in which books were valued; in other words, that we were cultivated people. This is always important in Calcutta, for Calcutta is an oddly bookish city.

Were we indeed cultivated people? I wonder. On the whole I don't think so. In my memory my grandfather's house is always full — of aunts, uncles, cousins. I am astonished sometimes when I think of how many people it housed, fed, entertained, educated. But my uncles were busy, practical, and, on the whole, successful professionals, with little time to spend on books.

Only one of my uncles was a real reader. He was a shy and rather retiring man, not the kind of person who takes it upon himself to educate his siblings or improve his relatives' taste. The books in the bookcases were almost all his. He was too quiet a man to carry much weight in family matters, and his views never counted for much when the elders sought each other's counsel. Yet despite the fullness of the house and the fierce competition for space, it was taken for granted that his bookcases would occupy the place of honour in the hall. Eventually tiring of his noisy relatives, my book-loving uncle decided to move to a house of his own in a distant and uncharacteristically quiet part of the city. But oddly enough the bookcases stayed; by this time the family was so attached to them that they were less dispensable than my uncle.

In the years that followed, the house passed into the hands of a branch of the family that was definitely very far from bookish. Yet their attachment to the bookcases seemed to increase inversely to their love of reading. I had been engaged in a secret pillaging of the bookcases for a very long time. Under the new regime my depredations came to a sudden halt; at the slightest squeak of a hinge, hordes of cousins would materialize suddenly around my ankles, snapping dire threats.

It served no purpose to tell them that the books were being consumed by maggots and mildew, that books rotted when they were not read. Arguments such as these interested them not at all: as far as they were concerned the bookcases and their contents were a species of property and were subject to the same laws.

This attitude made me impatient, even contemptuous at the time. Books were meant to be read, I thought, by people who valued and understood them: I felt not the slightest remorse for my long years of thievery. It seemed to me a terrible waste that nonreaders should succeed in appropriating my uncle's library. Today I am not so sure. Perhaps those cousins were teaching me a lesson that was important on its own terms: they were teaching me to value the printed word. Would anyone who had not learned these lessons well be foolhardy enough to imagine that a living could be made from words? I doubt it.

In another way they were also teaching me what a book is, a proper book, that is, not just printed paper gathered between covers. However much I may have chafed against the regime that stood between me and the bookcases, I have not forgotten those lessons. For me, to this day, a book, a proper book, is and always will be the kind of book that was on the bookshelves.

And what exactly was this kind of book?

Although, so far as I know, no one had ever articulated any guidelines about them, there were in fact some fairly strict rules about the books that were allowed on to those shelves. Textbooks and schoolbooks were never allowed; nor were books of a technical or professional nature — nothing to do with engineering, or medicine, or law, or indeed any of the callings that afforded my uncles their livings. In fact, the great majority of the books were of a single kind; they were novels. There were a few works of anthropology and psychology, books that had in some way filtered into the literary consciousness of the time: *The Golden Bough*, for example, as well as the *Collected Works of Sigmund Freud*, Marx and Engels's *Manifesto*, Havelock Ellis and Malinowski on sexual behaviour, and so on.

But without a doubt it was the novel that weighed most

heavily on the floors of my grandfather's house. To this day I am unable to place a textbook or a computer manual upon a bookshelf without a twinge of embarrassment.

This is how Nirad Chaudhuri, that erstwhile Calcuttan, accounts for the position that novels occupy in Bengali cultural life:

> It has to be pointed out that in the latter half of the nineteenth century Bengali life and Bengali literature had become very closely connected and literature was bringing into the life of educated Bengalis something which they could not get from any other source. Whether in the cities and towns or in the villages, where the Bengali gentry still had the permanent base of their life, it was the mainstay of their life of feeling, sentiment and passion. Both emotional capacity and idealism were sustained by it. . . . When my sister was married in 1916, a college friend of mine presented her with fifteen of the latest novels by the foremost writers and my sister certainly did not prize them less than her far more costly clothes and jewellery. In fact, sales of fiction and poetry as wedding presents were a sure standby of their publishers. (155)

About a quarter of the novels in my uncle's bookcases were in Bengali — a representative selection of the mainstream tradition of Bengali fiction in the twentieth century. Prominent among these were the works of Bankim Chandra, Sarat Chandra, Tagore, Bibhuti Bhushan, and so on. The rest were in English. But of these only a small proportion consisted of books that had been originally written in English. The others were translations from a number of other languages, most of them European: Russian had pride of place, followed by French, Italian, German, and Danish. The great masterpieces of the nineteenth century were dutifully represented: the novels of Dostoevsky, Tolstoy, and Turgenev, of Victor Hugo, Flaubert, Stendhal, Maupassant, and others. But these were the dustiest books of all, placed on shelves that were lofty but remote.

The books that were prominently displayed were an oddly disparate lot — or so they seem today. Some of those titles can still be seen on bookshelves everywhere: Joyce, Faulkner, and so on. But many others have long since been forgotten: Marie Corelli and Grazia Deledda, for instance, names that are so little known today, even in Italy, that they have become a kind of secret incantation for me, a password that allows entry into the brotherhood of remembered bookcases. Knut Hamsun, too, was once a part of this incantation, but unlike the others his reputation has since had an immense revival — and with good reason.

Other names from those shelves have become, in this age of resurgent capitalism, symbols of a certain kind of embarrassment or unease — the social realists, for example. But on my uncle's shelves they stood tall and proud, Russians and Americans alike: Maxim Gorky, Mikhail Sholokhov, John Steinbeck, Upton Sinclair. There were many others, too, whose places next to each other seem hard to account for at first glance: Sienkiewicz (of *Quo Vadis?*), Maurice Maeterlinck, Bergson. Recently, looking through the mildewed remnants of those shelves, I came upon what must have been the last addition to that collection. It was Ivo Andrić's *Bridge on the Drina*, published in the sixties.

For a long time I was at a loss to account for my uncle's odd assortment of books. I knew their eclecticism couldn't really be ascribed to personal idiosyncrasies of taste. My uncle was a keen reader, but he was not, I suspect, the kind of person who allows his own taste to steer him through libraries and bookshops. On the contrary, he was a reader of the kind whose taste is guided largely by prevalent opinion. This uncle, I might add, was a writer himself, in a modest way. He wrote plays in an epic vein with characters borrowed from the Sanskrit classics. He never left India and, indeed, rarely ventured out of his home state of West Bengal.

The principles that guided my uncle's taste would have been much clearer to me had I ever had an interest in trivia. To the quiz-show adept, the link between Grazia Deledda, Gorky, Hamsun, Sholokhov, Sienkiewicz, and Andrić will be clear at once: it is the Nobel Prize for Literature.

Writing about the Calcutta of the twenties and thirties, Nirad Chaudhuri says:

> To be up to date about literary fashions was a greater craze among us than to be up to date in clothes is with society women, and this desire became keener with the introduction of the Nobel Prize for literature. Not to be able to show at least one book of a Nobel Laureate was regarded almost as being illiterate. (156)

But of course the Nobel Prize was itself both symptom and catalyst of a wider condition: the emergence of a notion of a universal 'literature', a form of artistic expression that embodies differences in place and culture, emotion and aspiration, but in such a way as to render them communicable. This idea may well have had its birth in Europe, but I suspect it met with a much more enthusiastic reception outside. I spent a couple of years studying in England in the late seventies and early eighties. I don't remember ever having come across a bookshelf like my uncle's: one that had been largely formed by this vision of literature, by a deliberate search for books from a wide array of other countries.

I have, however, come across many such elsewhere, most memorably in Burma in the house of the late Mya Than Tint, one of the most important Burmese writers of the twentieth century.

Mya Than Tint was an amazing man. He spent more than a decade as a political prisoner. For part of that time he was incarcerated in the British-founded penal colony of Cocos Island, an infamous outcrop of rock where prisoners had to forage to survive. On his release he began to publish sketches and stories that won him a wide readership and great popular esteem in Burma. These wonderfully warm and vivid pieces have recently been translated and published under the title *Tales of Everyday People.*

I met Mya Than Tint in 1995, at his home in Rangoon. The first thing he said to me was, 'I've seen your name somewhere.' I was taken aback. Such is the ferocity of Burma's censorship regime that it seemed hardly possible that he could have come across my books or articles in Rangoon. 'Wait a minute', Mya Than Tint said. He went to his study, fetched a tattered old copy of *Granta*, and pointed to my name on the contents page.

'Where did you get it?' I asked, open-mouthed. He explained, smiling, that he had kept his library going by befriending the ragpickers and papertraders who picked through the rubbish discarded by diplomats.

Looking through Mya Than Tint's bookshelves, I soon discovered that this determined refusal to be beaten into parochialism had its genesis in a bookcase that was startlingly similar to my uncle's. Knut Hamsun, Maxim Gorky, Sholokhov, all those once familiar names came echoing back to me, from Calcutta, as we sat talking in that bright, cool room in Rangoon.

I also once had occasion to meet the Indonesian novelist Pramoedya Ananta Toer, another writer of astonishing fortitude and courage. Of the same generation as Mya Than Tint, Pramoedya has lived through similar experiences of imprisonment and persecution. Unlike Mya Than Tint, Pramoedya works in a language that has only recently become a vehicle of literary expression, Bahasa Indonesia. Pramoedya is thus widely thought of as the founding figure in a national literary tradition.

At some point I asked what his principal literary influences were. I do not know what I had expected to hear, but it was not the answer I got. I should not have been surprised, however; the names were familiar ones — Maxim Gorky and John Steinbeck.

Over the last few years, unbeknown to itself, the world has caught up with Mya Than Tint and Pramoedya Ananta Toer. Today the habits of reading that they and others like them pioneered are mandatory among readers everywhere. Wherever I go today, the names that I see on serious bookshelves are always the same, no matter the script in which they are spelled: Garcia Marquez, Vargas Llosa, Nadine Gordimer, Michael Ondaatje, Marguerite Yourcenar, Günter

Grass, Salman Rushdie. That this is ever more true is self-evident: literary currents are now instantly transmitted around the world and instantly absorbed, like everything else. To mention this is to cite a jaded commonplace.

But the truth is that fiction had been thoroughly international for more than a century. In India, Burma, Egypt, Indonesia, and elsewhere this has long been self-evident. Yet curiously this truth has nowhere been more stoutly denied than in those places where the novel has its deepest roots; indeed it could be said that this denial is the condition that made the novel possible.

The novel as a form had been vigorously international from the start; we know that Spanish, English, French, and Russian novelists have read each other's work avidly since the eighteenth century. And yet, the paradox of the novel as a form is that it is founded upon a myth of parochiality, in the exact sense of a parish — a place named and charted, a definite location. A novel, in other words, must always be set somewhere: it must have its setting, and within the evolution of the narrative this setting must, classically, play a part almost as important as those of the characters themselves. Location is thus intrinsic to a novel: we are at a loss to imagine its absence no matter whether that place be Mrs Gaskell's Cranford or Joyce's Dublin. A poem can create its setting and atmosphere out of verbal texture alone; not so a novel.

We carry these assumptions with us much the same that we assume the presence of actors and lights in a play. They are both so commonplace and so deeply rooted that they preempt us from reflecting on how very strange they actually are. Consider that the conceptions of location that made the novel possible came into being at exactly the time when the world was beginning to experience the greatest dislocation it has ever known. When we read *Middlemarch* or *Madame Bovary* we have not the faintest inkling that the lives depicted in them are made possible by global empires (consider the contrast with that seminal work of Portuguese literature, De Camoens' *Lusiads*. Consider that when we read Hawthorne we have to look very carefully between the lines to see that the New England ports he writes about are sustained by a far-flung network of trade. Consider that nowhere are the literary conventions of location more powerful than in the literature of the United States, itself the product of several epic dislocations.

How sharply this contrasts with traditions of fiction that predate the novel! It is true, for example, that the city of Baghdad provides a notional location for the *One Thousand and One Nights*. But the Baghdad of Scheherazade is more a talisman, an incantation, than a setting. The stories could happen anywhere so long as our minds have room for an enchanted city.

Or think of that amazing collection of stories known as the *Panchatantra* or *Five Chapters*. These stories too have no settings to speak of, except the notion of a forest. Yet the *Panchatantra* is reckoned by some to be second only to the Bible in the extent of its global diffusion. Compiled in India early in the first millennium, the *Panchatantra* passed into Arabic through a sixth-century Persian translation, engendering some of the best known of Middle Eastern fables, including parts of the *One Thousand and One Nights*. The stories were handed on to the Slavic languages through Greek, then from Hebrew to Latin, a version in the latter appearing in 1270. Through Latin they passed into German and Italian. From the Italian version came the famous Elizabethan rendition of Sir Henry North, *The Morall Philosophy of Doni* (1570). These stories left their mark on collections as different as those of La Fontaine and the Grimm brothers, and today they are inseparably part of a global heritage.*

Equally, the stories called the *Jatakas*, originally compiled in India, came to be diffused throughout southern and eastern Asia and even further with the spread of Buddhism. The story, both in its epic form as well as its shorter version, was vital in the creation of the remarkable cultural authority that India enjoyed in the Asia of the Middle Ages; not until the

* C.E. Dimock, in *The Literature of India, an Introduction*, Chicago, Univ. of Chicago Press, 1974.

advent of Hollywood was narrative again to play so important a part in the diffusion of a civilization.

Everywhere these stories went they were freely and fluently adapted to local circumstances. Indeed, in a sense the whole point of the stories was their translatability — the dispensable and inessential nature of their locations. What held them together and gave them their appeal was not where they happened but how — the narrative, in other words. Or, to take another example, consider that European narrative tradition that was perhaps the immediate precursor of the novel: the story of Tristan and Isolde. By the late Middle Ages this Celtic narrative, which appears to have had its origins in Cornwall and Brittany, had been translated and adapted into several major European languages. Everywhere it went the story of Tristan and Isolde was immediately adapted to new locations and new settings. The questions of its origins and its original locations are at best matters of pedantic interest.

In these ways of storytelling, it is the story that gives places their meaning. That is why Homer leaps at us from signs on the New York turnpike, from exits marked Ithaca and Troy; that is why the Ayodhya of the Ramayana lends its name equally to a street in Banaras and a town in Thailand.

This style of fictional narrative is not extinct: far from it. It lives very vividly in the spirit that animates popular cinema in India and many other places. In a Hindi film, as in a kung fu movie, the details that constitute the setting are profoundly unimportant, incidental almost. In Hindi films, the setting of a single song can take us through a number of changes of costume, each in a different location. These films, I need hardly point out, command huge audiences on several continents and may well be the most widely circulated cultural artefacts the world has ever known. When Indonesian streets and villages suddenly empty at four in the afternoon, it is not because of Maxim Gorky or John Steinbeck: it is because of the timing of a daily broadcast of a Hindi film.

Such is the continued vitality of this style of narrative that it eventually succeeded in weaning my uncle from his bookcases. Toward the end of his life my book-loving uncle abandoned all of his old friends, Gorky and Sholokhov and Hamsun, and became a complete devotee of Bombay films. He would see dozens of Hindi films; sometimes we went together, on lazy afternoons. On the way home he would stop to buy fan magazines. Through much of his life he'd been a forbidding, distant man, an intellectual in the classic, Western sense; in his last years he was utterly transformed, warm, loving, thoughtful. His brothers and sisters scarcely recognized him.

Once, when we were watching a film together, he whispered in my ear that the star, then Bombay's reigning female deity, had recently contracted a severe infestation of lice.

'How do you know?' I asked.

'I read an interview with her hairdresser', he said. 'In *Stardust*.'

This was the man who'd handed me a copy of *And Quiet Flows the Don* when I was not quite twelve.

My uncle's journey is evidence that matters are not yet decided among different ways of telling stories: that if Literature, led by a flagship called the Novel, has declared victory, the other side, if there is one, has not necessarily conceded defeat. But what exactly is at stake here? What is being contested? Or to narrow the question: what is the difference between the ways in which place and location are thought of by novelists, and storytellers of other kinds?

The contrast is best seen, I think, where it is most apparent: that is in situations outside Europe and the Americas, where the novel is a relatively recent import. As an example, I would like to examine for a moment a novel from my own part of the world — Bengal. This novel is called *Rajmohun's Wife*, written in the early 1860s by the writer Bankim Chandra Chatterjee.

Bankim Chandra Chatterjee was a man of many parts. He was a civil servant, a scholar, a novelist, and a talented polemicist. He was also very widely read, in English as well as

Bengali and Sanskrit. In a sense his was the bookcase that was the ancestor of my uncle's.

Bankim played no small part in the extraordinary efflorescence of Bengali literature in the second half of the nineteenth century. He wrote several major novels in Bengali, all of which were quickly translated into other Indian languages. He was perhaps the first truly 'Indian' writer of modern times in the sense that his literary influence extended throughout the subcontinent. Nirad Chaudhuri describes him as 'the creator of Bengali fiction and . . . the greatest novelist in the Bengali language'. Bankim is also widely regarded as one of the intellectual progenitors of Indian nationalism.

Bankim Chandra was nothing if not a pioneer, and he self-consciously set himself the task of bringing the Bengali novel into being by attacking what he called 'the Sanskrit School'. It is hard today, looking back from a point of time when the novel sails as Literature's flagship, to imagine what it meant to champion such a form in nineteenth-century India. The traditions of fiction that Bankim was seeking to displace were powerful enough to awe its critics into silence. They still are: what modern writer, for example, could ever hope to achieve the success of the *Panchatantra*? It required true courage to seek to replace this style of narrative with a form so artificial and arbitrary as the novel; the endeavour must have seemed hopeless at the time. Nor did the so-called Sanskrit School lack for defendants. Bankim, and many others who took on the task of domesticating the novel, were immediately derided as monkey-like imitators of the West.

Bankim responded by calling for a full-scale insurrection. Imitation, he wrote, was the law of progress; no civilization was self-contained or self-generated, none could advance without borrowing. He wrote:

> Those who are familiar with the present writers in Bengali, will readily admit that they all, good and bad alike, may be classed under two heads, the Sanskrit and the English schools. The former represents Sanskrit scholarship and the ancient literature of the country; the latter is the fruit of Western

> knowledge and ideas. By far the greater number of Bengali writers belong to the Sanskrit school; but by far the greater number of good writers belong to the other. . . . It may be said that there is not at the present day anything like an indigenous school of writers, owing nothing either to Sanskrit writers or to those of Europe.

How poignantly ironic this passage seems a hundred years later, after generations of expatriate Indians, working mainly in England, have striven so hard to unlearn the lessons taught by Bankim and his successors in India. So successfully were novelistic conventions domesticated in the late nineteenth and early twentieth centuries that many Indian readers now think of them as somehow local, homegrown, comforting in their naturalistic simplicity, while the work of such writers as G.V. Desani, Zulfikar Ghose, Salman Rushdie, Adam Zameenzad, Shashi Tharoor, and others appears, by the same token, stylized and experimental.

Yet Bankim's opinions about the distinctiveness of Indian literature were much more extreme than those of his apocryphal Sanskrit School. In 1882 Bankim found himself embroiled in a very interesting controversy with a Protestant missionary, W. Hastie. The exchange began after Hastie had published a couple of letters in a Calcutta newspaper, *The Statesman*. I cannot resist quoting from one of these:

> Notwithstanding all that has been written about the myriotheistic idolatry of India, no pen has yet adequately depicted the hideousness and grossness of the monstrous system. It has been well described by one who knew it as 'Satan's masterpiece . . . the most stupendous fortress and citadel of ancient error and idolatry now in the world. . . .' With much that was noble and healthy in its early stages, the Sanskrit literature became infected by a moral leprosy which gradually spread like a corrupting disease through almost all its fibres and organs. The great Sanskrit scholars of Bengal know too well what I mean. . . . Only to think that this has been the principal pabulum of the spiritual life of the Hindus for about a thousand years, and the loudly boasted lore of their semi-deified priests! Need we seek elsewhere for the foul disease that has been

> preying upon the vitals of the national life, and reducing the people to what they are? 'Shew me your gods,' cried an ancient Greek apologist, 'and I will show you your men.' The Hindu is just what his idol gods have made him. His own idolatry, and not foreign conquerors has been the curse of his history. No people was ever degraded except by itself, and this is most literally so with the Hindus. (192–3)

Bankim responded by advising Mr. Hastie to 'obtain some knowledge of Sanskrit scriptures in the *original*'

> . . . [for] no translation from the Sanskrit into a European language can truly or even approximately represent the original. . . . The English or the German language can possess no words or expressions to denote ideas or conceptions which have never entered into a Teutonic brain. . . . A people so thoroughly unconnected with England or Germany as the old Sanskrit-speaking people of India, and developing a civilization and a literature peculiarly their own, had necessarily a vast store of ideas and conceptions utterly foreign to the Englishman or the German, just as the Englishman or the German boasts a still vaster number of ideas utterly foreign to the Hindu. . . . [Mr Hastie's position] is the logical outcome of that monstrous claim to omniscience, which certain Europeans . . . put forward for themselves. . . . Yet nothing is a more common subject of merriment among the natives of India than the Europeans' ignorance of all that relates to India. . . . A navvy who had strayed into the country . . . asked for some food from a native. . . . The native gave him a cocoanut. The hungry sailor . . . bit the husk, chewed it . . . and flung the fruit at the head of the unhappy donor. . . . The sailor carried away with him an opinion of Indian fruits parallel to that of Mr Hastie and others, who merely bite at the husk of Sanskrit learning, but do not know their way to the kernel within. . . .

He added: 'I cheerfully admit the intellectual superiority of Europe. I deny, however . . . that intellectual superiority can enable the blind to see or the deaf to hear.' (192–3)

By the time he wrote the passages quoted above Bankim was already an acclaimed novelist and a major figure in the Bengali literary world. But Bankim's experiments with the novel had begun some twenty years before, and his earliest efforts at novel writing were conducted in English. *Rajmohun's Wife* is the first known fictional work written by Bankim, and it was written in the early 1860s.

It will be evident from the above passages, abbreviated though they are, that Bankim wrote excellent English: his essays and letters are written in a style that is supple, light-handed, and effective. The style of *Rajmohun's Wife*, on the other hand, is deliberate, uncertain, and often ponderous. What intrigues me most about this book, however, are the long passages of description that preface several of the chapters, bookending, as it were, some extremely melodramatic scenes.

Here are some examples:

> The house of Mathur Ghose was a genuine specimen of mofussil magnificence united with a mofussil want of cleanliness.
>
> From the far-off paddy fields you could descry through the intervening foliage, its high palisades and blackened walls. On a nearer view might be seen pieces of plaster of a venerable antiquity prepared to bid farewell to their old and weather-beaten tenement. . . .
>
> A mazy suite of dark and damp apartments led from a corner of this part of the building to the inner *mahal*, another quadrangle, on all four sides of which towered double-storeyed verandahs, as before. . . . The walls of all the chambers above and below were well striped with numerous streaks of red, white, black, green, all colours of the rainbow, caused by the spittles of such as had found their mouths too much encumbered with paan, or by some improvident woman servant who had broken the *gola-handi* while it was full of its muddy contents. . . . Numerous sketches in charcoal, which showed, we fear, nothing of the conception of (Michael) Angelo or the tinting of Guido (Reni), attested the art or idleness of the wicked boys and ingenious girls who had contrived to while away hungry hours by essays in the arts of designing and of defacing wall. . . .
>
> A thick and massive door led to the 'godown' as the *mahal* was called by the males directly from outside. . . . (*Rajmohun's Wife* 52–3)

A kitchen scene:

> Madhav therefore immediately hurried into the inner apartments where he found it no very easy task to make himself heard in that busy hour of zenana life. There was a servant woman, black, rotund, and eloquent, demanding the transmission to her hand of sundry articles of domestic use, without however making it at all intelligible to whom her demands were addressed. There was another who boasted similar blessed corporal dimensions, but who thought it beneath her dignity to shelter them from view; and was busily employed broomstick in hand, in demolishing the little mountains of the skins and stems of sundry culinary vegetables which decorated the floors, and against which the half-naked dame never aimed a blow but coupled it with a curse on those whose duty it had been to prepare the said vegetables for dressing. (17)

The questions that strike me when I read these lengthy and laboured descriptions is: What are they for? For whom are they intended? Why did he bother to write them? Bankim must have known that this book was very unlikely to be read by anyone who did not know what the average Bengali landowner's house looked like — since by far the largest part of the literate population of Calcutta at that time consisted of landowners and their families. Similarly, anyone who had visited the Bengal of his time, for no matter how brief a period, would almost inevitably have been familiar with the other sights he describes: fishermen at work, cranes fishing, and so on.

Why then did Bankim go to the trouble of writing these passages? Did he think his book might be read by someone who was entirely unfamiliar with Bengal? The question is a natural and inevitable one, but I do not think it leads anywhere. For the fact of the matter is that I don't think Bankim was writing for anyone but himself. I suspect that Bankim never really intended to publish *Rajmohun's Wife*: the novel has the most cursory of endings as though he'd written it as an exercise and then thrown it aside once it had served its purpose. The book was not actually published until a decade or so after he'd stopped working on it. For Bankim, *Rajmohun's Wife* was clearly a rehearsal, a preparation for something else.

It is here, I think, that the answers lie. The passages of description in the book are not, in fact, intended to describe. Their only function is that they are there at all: they are Bankim's attempt to lay claim to the rhetoric of location, of place — to mount a springboard that would allow him to vault the gap between two entirely different conventions of narrative.

It is for a related reason, I think, that Bankim conducted his rehearsal in English rather than Bengali. To write about one's surroundings is anything but natural: to even perceive one's immediate environment one must somehow distance oneself from it; to describe it one must assume a certain posture, a form of address. In other words, to locate oneself through prose, one must begin with an act of dislocation. It was this perhaps that English provided for Bankim: a kind of disconnected soapbox on which he could test a certain form of address before trying it out in Bengali.

This still leaves a question. Every form of address assumes a listener, a silent participant. Who was the listener in Bankim's mind when he was working on *Rajmohun's Wife*? The answer, I think, is the bookcase. It is the very vastness and cosmopolitanism of the fictional bookcase that requires novelists to locate themselves in relation to it; that demands of their work that it carry marks to establish their location.

This then is the peculiar paradox of the novel: those of us who love novels often read them because of the eloquence with which they communicate a 'sense of place'. Yet the truth is that it is the very loss of a lived sense of place that makes their fictional representation possible.

Works Cited

Chatterjee, Bankim Chandra, *Essays and Letters*, in *Bankim Rachanavali*, Calcutta: Sahitya Samsad, n.d.

Rajmohun's Wife, in *Bankim Rachanavali*, ed. Jogesh Chandra Bagal, Calcutta: Sahitya Samsad, n.d.

Chaudhuri, Nirad, *Thy Hand, Great Anarch!* New York: Addison-Wesley, 1987.

Dimock, E., Edwin Gerow, C.M. Naim, A.K. Ramanujam, Gordon Roadarmel, J.A.B. van Buitenen, *The Literature of India, an Introduction*, Chicago: University of Chicago Press, 1974.

16 *The Greatest Sorrow: Times of Joy Recalled in Wretchedness*

... 'Nessun maggior dolore
che ricordarsi lempo felice
ne la miseria ...'

... 'There is no greater sorrow
than to recall our times of joy
in wretchedness ...'[1]

On 27 July this year, landing in Colombo's Katunayake airport, I saw at first hand how fragile a machine an aircraft is. My plane landed on a runway that was flanked with wreckage on either side. Through the scarred glass of my window, I spotted a blackened pile of debris that ended in the intact tail section of a plane. The shape of the vanished fuselage was etched into the tarmac like the outline of a cigar that has burnt itself slowly to extinction, leaving its ring standing in its ashes. Then there was another and still another, the charred remains lying scattered around the apron like a boxful of half-smoked Havanas arranged around the edges of an ebony table.

It was just four days since a small suicide squad of Tamil Tiger guerrillas had succeeded in entering Colombo's carefully guarded Katunayake airport. The strike was executed with meticulous precision and the guerrillas had destroyed some fourteen aircraft, virtually disabling Sri Lanka's civilian and military air fleets. It was till then perhaps the single most successful attack of its kind.

Thirty-six years had passed since I first landed at that airport, in a shuddering blunt-nosed Dakota. The aerodrome, as it was then spoken of, was a relic of an older war, in which Colombo had served as the nerve-centre of Lord Mountbatten's South-East Asia Command. I was nine then, a fresh entrant into that moment of childhood when we first begin to truly inhabit the world, in the particular sense of committing it to memory. I remember Colombo's red-tiled roofs, like stacks of hardbacked books spread open on a desk; I remember my school, Royal College, and the stairway where I first tasted blood on my lip; I remember afterschool cricket matches on Layard's Road and wickets knocked over by kabara-goyas; I remember marshmallow ice cream at Elephant House and the pearly insides of mangosteens; I remember the palm trees at Hikkaduwa leaning like dancers over the golden sands; I remember Elephant's Pass and the road to Jaffna, as narrow as the clasp between a necklace and its pendant; I remember at Pollonaruwa, a cobra coiled on the floor of a rest-house, looking up as though in surprise at my silhouette in the doorway; I remember a train on a slope, its smoke mingling with the mists of Nuwara Eliya.

Such was the paradise from which I was abruptly torn, when I arrived upon the threshold of adolescence. In the summer of 1967, when I had reached the age of eleven I was sent away to be educated at the other end of the subcontinent, in Dehra Dun, which was said to be one of the most picturesque places in India. But for me this sub-Himalayan valley proved to be anything but arcadia: I found myself imprisoned in a walled city of woe, with five hundred adolescents who had been herded together to be instructed in the dark arts of harrowing their peers. That it was my parents who were the agents of my expulsion from Paradise was not the least part of the bewildering pain of my banishment. It was in that sub-Himalayan purgatory that I learnt what it was to recall a time of joy in wretchedness. Now, in the recollection of that emotion, I have come to recognize a commonality with many, perhaps most, Sri Lankans — indeed, with everyone who remembers what it was to live in Serendib before the Fall.

Michael Ondaatje writes:

> The last Sinhala word I lost,
> was vatura.
> The word for water.
> Forest water. The water in a kiss. The tears
> I gave to my ayah Rosalin on leaving
> the first home of my life
>
> More water for her than any other
> that fled my eyes again
> this year, remembering her,
> a lost almost-mother in those years
> of thirsty love
>
> No photograph of her, no meeting
> since the age of eleven,
> not even knowledge of her grave.
>
> Who abandoned who, I wonder now.[2]

These lines look back — as do I when I think of Sri Lanka — to a childhood long past. But the poem was published recently, in Canada, and I doubt that it would have sounded this exact note had it been written at any other time and in any other circumstances. This is not merely a eulogy for Rosalin: it is an elegy of homecoming spoken in a voice that has been orphaned not just by the loss of an almost-mother, but by history itself. It is a lament that mourns the passing of the Paradise that made Rosalin possible.

At the other end of the subcontinent lies another land devastated by the twin terrors of armed insurgency and state repression: Kashmir, of which an Emperor famously said:

> If there is a paradise on earth,
> It is this, it is this, it is this

In the mid-nineteen nineties, at about the same time that Michael Ondaatje was writing his elegy to Rosalin, the Kashmiri poet Agha Shahid Ali, was writing his great poem 'The Last Saffron'. The poem begins:

> I will die, in autumn, in Kashmir,
> and the shadowed routine of each vein
> will almost be news, the blood censored,
> for the *Saffron Sun* and the *Times of Rain*.

The poem ends with these verses:

> Yes, I remember it,
> the day I'll die, I broadcast the crimson,
>
> so long ago of that sky, its spread air,
> its rushing dyes, and a piece of earth
>
> bleeding, apart from the shore, as we went
> on the day I'll die, past the guards, and he,
>
> keeper of the world's last saffron, rowed me
> on an island the size of a grave. On
>
> two yards he rowed me into the sunset,
> past all pain. On everyone's lips was news
>
> of my death but only that beloved couplet,
> broken, on his:
>
> 'If there is a paradise on earth
> It is this, it is this, it is this.[3]

If the twin terrors of insurgency and repression could be said to have engendered any single literary leitmotif, it is surely the narrative of the loss of Paradise. Nowhere is this story more precisely chronicled than in Shyam Selvadorai's 1994 novel, *Funny Boy.* The novel is set in Colombo, in the turmoil of the early 1980s, when long-simmering tensions between Sri Lanka's Sinhala-dominated government and the minority Tamil population exploded into a savagely violent conflict. The narrator is a teenage boy from a wealthy Tamil family and the novel's final chapter recounts the events of

July 1983, when a terrorist attack upon the Sri Lankan army triggered massive reprisals against the Tamils of Colombo.

In *Funny Boy* the destruction of Paradise is assigned precise dates and an exact span of time: it starts at 9.30 a.m. on 25 July 1983. It is only a few hours since the novel's teenage narrator and his family have learned that 'there [is] trouble in Colombo': the night before a mob has gone wild after a funeral for thirteen slain soldiers, many Tamil houses have been burned. At 9.30 a.m. the family begins to ready itself for a hasty departure from their own house. 'We are supposed to bring a few clothes and one other thing that is important to us. I can't decide which thing to take.' But the boy's mother has already decided; not the least of her provisions for the uncertainties of the future is the preparation for the coming age of sorrow: 'Amma is taking all the family albums. She says that if anything happens they will remind us of happier days.'

All through the day, the family waits in the once-beloved home that has now become a prison. As the hours pass, the narrator seeks consolation in his journal, recording rumours and reports. He hears that the government has distributed electoral lists to help the mobs locate Tamil homes; he is hugely relieved when he is told that a curfew has been declared, and is therefore doubly dismayed to learn that the announcement has made no difference, the mob is still on the rampage. He hears of the police and army watching in silent indifference as a Tamil family is burned alive in a car. At 11.30 p.m. the boy writes: 'The waiting is terrible. I wish the mob would come so that this dreadful waiting would end.'

The next entry is written a little more than half a day later, but in that brief span of time the world has become a different place. Nothing will ever be the same again, the boy's childhood has become a place apart; this is the moment when history, the connection between time past and time ahead, has ended and memory has become an island that is severed for ever from the present and the future. 'July 26,

12.30 p.m.: I have just read my last entry and it seems unbelievable that only thirteen hours ago I was sitting on my bed writing in this journal. A year seems to have passed since that time. Our lives have completely changed. I try and try to make sense of it, but it just won't work.'

What has happened is this: the long wait has come to an end soon after the writing of the penultimate journal entry. On hearing the chants of an approaching mob, the family has taken refuge in a Sinhala neighbour's house. Huddled in a storeroom, they have listened, as their house is burnt to the ground.

The morning after, they have looked over the remains of the house: the sight has made little impression; it is almost incomprehensible; the boy notes that his vinyl records have dissolved into black puddles, that the furniture has cracked open to reveal the whiteness of common wood. 'I observed all this with not a trace of remorse, not a touch of sorrow for the loss and destruction around me. Even now I feel no sorrow. I try to remind myself that the house is destroyed, that we will never live in it again, but my heart refuses to understand this.' It is only later, on being told of the destruction of his grandparents' home, that he is able to grieve: '. . . I thought about childhood spend-the-days and all the good times we had there. These thoughts made me cry. I couldn't cry for my own house, but it was easy to grieve for my grandparents' house.' A precocious prescience has led the boy to grasp the precise nature of his grief: he ascribes it not to the immediacy of his own experience, but to the memory of better times — to that act of remembrance than which, as Dante's Francesca da Rimini tells us, there is 'no greater sorrow': that is to say, in the recollection of better times.

This depiction of the violence of 1983 — and to my mind *Funny Boy* is one of the most powerful and moving accounts of those events — was published in 1994 in Canada, where Shyam Selvadorai's family had settled after leaving Sri Lanka. I draw attention to this only to underscore two facts: that *Funny Boy* was written by a recent immigrant to North

America and that it is an act of recollection that tells the story of a departure. These facts appear unremarkable, yet there is to my mind a puzzle here and it lies in this: an immigrant's story is usually a narrative of arrival, not departure. And nowhere is this more true than in North America.

North America is famously peopled by immigrants, and nowhere else on earth is the experience of immigration so richly figured as it is here: in popular culture, literature, film and indeed every aspect of public life. In photography, the emblematic image of this experience is that of a family of immigrants standing on the deck of the ship that has brought them across the Atlantic. In these pictures the immigrants' eyes are always turned in the direction of the waiting shore; towards the Statue of Liberty and the towers of the shining city ahead. Many of these immigrants have suffered terrible hardships, yet we would search in vain for similarly powerful images taken at the hour when they boarded the ship: that moment holds only passing interest in this story. This is because, classically, narratives of immigration into North America are stories of arrival, not departure; stories of suffering but not sorrow or regret; they are stories of hope, founded on a belief in the redemptive power of the land ahead. The vitality of these stories derives in no small part from the obvious parallels with the Biblical story of the Promised Land, which is, of course, equally a story of hope and of arrival. Those who followed Moses out of Egypt did not linger to cast glances of melancholy longing upon the Nile. They looked only ahead; their memory of Egypt was of unmitigated suffering; there were no times of joy there to be recalled in wretchedness. The mark of an exodus lies in the direction of these eyes, looking ahead towards the far shore, confident in the belief that the bonds of community will not perish in the process of migration. But this is not the direction in which Selvadorai's narrator has turned his gaze. Here is the novel's penultimate sentence: 'When I reached the top of the road, I couldn't prevent myself from turning back to look at the house one last time.' And this is how he ends his story, with the narrator looking back, through the rain, at the charred remains of a home that was once filled with happiness.

It is the direction of the gaze that identifies this as a story not of an exodus, but of a dispersal; the story of an irrevocable sundering of the dual bonds that tie members of a community to each other and to other like communities. In the experience of an exodus there is an unspoken ambiguity: the sufferings of displacement are tinged with the hope of arrival and the opening of new vistas in the future. A dispersal offers no such consolation: the pain that haunts it is not that of remembered oppression; it is rather that particular species of pain that comes from the knowledge that the oppressor and the oppressed were once brothers. It is this species of pain, exactly, that runs so poignantly through the literature that resulted from the Partition of the Indian subcontinent in 1947. For we know, from that line of Boëtius which Dante was later to give to Francesca da Rimini, that among fortune's many adversities the most unhappy kind is to nurture the memory of having once been happy.[4]

This is where recollection turns its back on history, for it is the burden of history to make sense of the past, while the memory of dispersal is haunted always by the essential inexplicability of what has come to pass; by the knowledge that there was nothing inevitable, nothing pre-destined about what has happened; that far from being primordial, the enmities that have led to the sufferings of the present are new and unaccountable; that there was a time once, when neither protagonist saw the other as an adversary — a time that will be irrevocably lost with the dissolution of the history that made it possible for many parts to be a whole.

That which I, in the fever of my pride, am struggling to put into words, has been much better said in Agha Shahid Ali's poem, 'Farewell':

> At a certain point I lost track of you.
> You needed me. You needed to perfect me:
> In your absence you polished me into the Enemy.

Your history gets in the way of my memory.
I am everything you lost. Your perfect enemy.
Your memory gets in the way of my memory . . .

There is nothing to forgive. You won't forgive me.
I hid my pain even from myself; I revealed my pain
only to myself.
There is everything to forgive. You can't forgive me.
If only somehow you could have been mine,
what would not have been possible in the world?[5]

There is nothing arbitrary then about the ending of Selvadorai's novel — the story ends here because it must. To carry it any further would be to link it to the present and the future, to imply the possibility of a consolation. And this of course, the writer could not do, for the reason why there is no greater sorrow than the recalling of times of joy, is precisely that this is a grief beyond consolation.

In 1983, at the time of the Colombo riots, I was hard at work on my first novel, *The Circle of Reason*. I was living in New Delhi, where I had succeeded in finding a minor appointment at Delhi University. Some of my colleagues and mentors at the University — Veena Das and Ashish Nandy for example — had close connections with human rights activists in Sri Lanka. They were thus able to acquire many of the documents, records and testimonies that were produced by Sri Lankan researchers. Newspaper accounts of the riots were shocking enough, but the picture that emerged from these independent reports was more menacing still. They left no doubt that some parts of the machinery of state had been used to target a minority population. I don't remember whether we asked ourselves what would happen if this pattern were to spread through the subcontinent. The question was perhaps too grim to pose in an India that was beset by insurgency, calamity and terror.

A year later with Indira Gandhi's assassination, the tide

crested on our own doorsteps. I remember that day graphically: I remember taking the bus across Delhi; I remember the eerie silence in the University; I remember the evil that gleamed in the eyes of the thugs who began to attack Sikhs wherever they could find them. I have written about these events in detail elsewhere and will limit myself here to noting only the close parallels between the patterns of violence in Colombo in 1983 and in New Delhi in 1984. In both instances, inexcusable crimes were committed by insurgent groups in the name of freedom; in both cases, the information-gathering function of government was turned to the sinister purpose of targeting minority populations; in both there were clear instances of collusion between officials and criminals.

Through the riots and their aftermath, I, like many of my friends and colleagues, worked with a citizen's relief organization called the Nagarik Ekta Manch.[6] After the immediate crisis was over I returned to the manuscript I was working on. This novel, *The Circle of Reason*, was the story of a journey, and its central section told the story of a group of immigrants — South Asian and Middle Eastern — living in a fictitious oil-rich sheikhdom in the Gulf. Looking back today, it strikes me that *The Circle of Reason* could, within the parameters that I have used here, be identified as an exodus novel, a story of migration in the classic sense of having its gaze turned firmly towards the future. The book ended with the words: 'Hope is the beginning'.

I was working on the last part of the book in 1984 when the riots broke out. After the violence it was a struggle to bring the manuscript to a conclusion: my attention had turned away from it. Unlike Shyam Selvadorai, unlike the Sikhs of New Delhi, I was not in the position of a victim during the riots of 1984. But the violence had the effect of bringing to the surface of my memory events from my own childhood, when I had indeed been in a similar situation.

Somehow I did manage to finish *The Circle of Reason*, and soon afterwards I started the novel that would eventually be published as *The Shadow Lines*. When I began to work on the manuscript, I found that the book was following a pattern of growth that was exactly the opposite of its predecessor's. *The Circle of Reason* had grown upwards, like a sapling rising from the soil of my immediate experience; *The Shadow Lines* had its opening planted in the present, but it grew downwards, into the soil, like a root system straining to find a source of nourishment.

It was in this process that I came to examine the ways in which my own life had been affected by civil violence. I remembered stories my mother had told me about the Great Calcutta killing of 1946; I remembered my uncles' stories of anti-Indian riots in Rangoon in 1930 and 1938. At the heart of the book, however, was an event that had occurred in Dhaka in 1964, the year before my family moved to Colombo: in the unlit depths of my memory there stirred a recollection of a night when our house, flooded with refugees, was besieged by an angry mob.[7] I had not thought of this event in decades, but after 1984 it began to haunt me: I was astonished by how vivid my memories were and how fully I could access them once I had given myself permission to do so. But my memories had no context: I had no way of knowing what had happened, whether it was an isolated incident, particularly to the neighbourhood we were living in, or whether it had implications beyond. I decided to find out what had happened. I went to libraries and sifted through hundreds of newspapers and in the end, through perseverance, luck and guesswork I did find out what had happened. The riots of my memory were not a local affair: they had engulfed much of the subcontinent. The violence had been set in motion by the reported theft of a holy relic from the Hazratbal mosque in Srinagar. Although Kashmir was unaffected, other parts of the subcontinent had gone up in flames. The rioting had continued for the better part of a week, in India as well as the two wings of Pakistan.

The process by which I came to learn of this was itself to become a pivotal part of the narrative of *The Shadow Lines*. While searching for evidence of the riots, I came across dozens of books about the Indo-Chinese war of 1962. This was an event that had evidently created a torrent of public discourse. Yet the bare fact is that this was a war that was fought in a remote patch of terrain, far removed from major population centres, and it had few repercussions outside the immediate area. The riots of 1964 on the other hand, had affected many major cities and had caused extensive civilian casualties. Yet there was not a single book devoted to this event: a cursory glance at a library's bookshelves was enough to establish that in historical memory a small war counts for much more than a major outbreak of civil violence. While the riots were under way, they had received extensive and detailed coverage. Yet, once contained, they had vanished instantly, both from public memory and the discourse of history. Why was this so? Why is it that civil violence seems to occur in parallel time, as though it were outside history? Why is it that we can look back upon these events in sorrow and outrage and yet be incapable of divining any lasting solutions or any portents for the future?

Inasmuch as I addressed these conundrums in *The Shadow Lines*, it was in these words:

> Every word I write about those events of 1964 is the product of a struggle with silence. It is a struggle that I am destined to lose — have already lost — for even after all these years I do not know where within me, in which corner of my world, this silence lies. All I know of it is what it is not. It is not, for example, the silence of a ruthless state — nothing like that: no barbed wire, no check-points to tell me where its boundaries lie. I know nothing of this silence except that it lies outside the reach of my intelligence, beyond words — that is why this silence must win, must inevitably defeat me, because it is not a presence at all; it is simply a gap, a hole, an emptiness in which there are not words.
>
> The enemy of silence is speech, but there can be no speech without words, and there can be no words without meanings — so it follows inexorably, in the manner of syllogisms, that when we try to speak of events of which we do not know the meaning, we must lose ourselves in the silence that lies in the

> gap between words and the world. . . . Where there is no meaning, there is banality, and that is what this silence consists in, that is why it cannot be defeated — because it is the silence of an absolute, impenetrable banality.

I can still feel the sorrow and outrage that provoked these words — emotions that owed much more to the events of 1984 than to my memories of 1964. Just as terrible as the violence itself was the thought that so many lives had been expended for nothing, that this terrible weight of suffering had created no discernibly new trajectory in the history or politics of the region. When we grieve for the appalling loss of life in World War II, our sorrow is not compounded by the thought that the war has changed nothing: we know that it has changed the world in very significant ways, has created a new epoch. But in the violence of 1984 — to take just one example — it was impossible to see any such portents. It was hard to see how a further partitioning of the subcontinent could provide a solution, on the contrary it would create only a new set of minorities and new oppressions. In effect, it would amount only to a re-casting of the problem itself, in a different form. In the absence of such meanings, there seemed to be no means of representing these events except in outrage and in sorrow.

It follows then that the reason why I — and many others who have written of such events — are compelled to look back in sorrow is because we cannot look ahead. It is as though the events of the immediate past have made the future even more obscure than it is usually acknowledged to be. Now, close on two decades later, I find myself asking: Why is this so? Why was it that in the 1980s, history itself seemed to stumble and come to a standstill?

The past, as Faulkner famously said, is not over, in fact the past is not even the past. One of the paradoxes of history is that it is impossible to draw a chart of the past without imagining a map of the present and the future. History, in other words, is never innocent of teleologies, implicit or otherwise. Ranajit Guha, in a recent lecture on Hegel and the writing of history in South Asia, says: 'It is the state which first supplies a content, which not only lends itself to the prose of history but actually helps to produce it.'[8] In other words, the actions of the state provide that essential element of continuity that makes time, as a collective experience, thinkable, by linking the past, the present and the future. The state as thus conceived is not merely an apparatus of rule but 'a conscious, ethical institution', an instrument designed to conquer the 'unhistorical power of time'. In other words, since the nineteenth century, and perhaps even earlier, it is the State which has provided the grid on which history is mapped.

It was perhaps this politically insignificant but epistemologically indispensable aspect of time's continuity that was most vitally damaged by the conflagrations of the 1980s. Even before then, it had often been suspected that elements of the state's machinery had been colluding in the production of communal violence: after the violence of the eighties this became established as a fact. It became evident that certain parts of the state had been absorbed — had indeed become sponsors — of criminal violence. No longer could the state be seen as a protagonist in its own right. It is for this reason that I have used the self-contradictory phrase 'civil violence' here, in preference to other more commonly used terms: because these events signalled the collapse of the familiar categories of 'state' and 'civil society'.[9]

The flames created by our recent past are so plentiful that only poets noticed the unsung death of a teleology. 'Everything is finished, nothing remains,' writes Agha Shahid Ali of a poet who returns to Kashmir in search of the keeper of a destroyed minaret.

> 'Nothing will remain, everything's finished,
> I see his voice again: 'This is a shrine
> of words. You'll find your letters to me. And mine
> to you. Come soon and tear open these vanished
> envelopes.' . . .

This is an archive. I've found the remains
of his voice, that map of longings with no limit.[10]

Buried within the poet's 'shrine of words', lies a map: a chart 'of longings without limit'. It is not the fall of the minaret but the loss of the map that is the true catastrophe, it is this loss that evokes the words 'Nothing will remain, everything's finished'.

Shahid's is not the only lost map: in 'The Story' Michael Ondaatje invokes another.

For his first forty days a child
is given dreams of previous lives.
journeys, winding paths,
a hundred small lessons
and then the past is erased.

Some are born screaming,
some full of introspective wandering
into the past — that bus ride in winter,
the sudden arrival within
a new city in the dark.
And those departures from family bonds
leaving what was lost and needed.
So the child's face is a lake
of fast moving clouds and emotions.

A last chance for the clear history of the self.
All our mothers and grandparents here,
our dismantled childhoods
in the buildings of the past.

Some great forty-day daydream
before we bury the maps.

The old maps are gone and two of the finest poets of our time, Michael Ondaatje and Agha Shahid Ali, exiles from twinned Edens, have borne witness to their loss; gone are Michael's 'forty-day daydream' and Shahid's 'longings without limit'. Writers who look back, in the wake of that loss can only build shrines to that past. And yet the mystery of the sorrow that is entombed in their work is that their grief is not just for a time remembered: they grieve also for the loss of the map that made the future thinkable.

Is there then another map to replace those that have been buried in the rubble of our daydreams? Once, six years ago, I thought I had a glimpse of one: this is how it came about. I had spent a sleepless night at a guerrilla camp in the thickly forested mountains of the Burma-Thailand border. The Myanmar army was entrenched a few miles away, fighting a fierce engagement with Karenni insurgents. My hosts had handed me a makeshift pillow, of a book wrapped in a towel. The bundle came undone at some point during the night and I discovered, switching on my flashlight, that the book was called *The Transformation of War*. It was written by a military historian called Martin Van Creveld. I began to read and was still reading hours later. The next day, I wrote in my diary: 'I am appalled by Van Creveld's vision of the future, yet over here, it makes more sense than anything I have read about this kind of conflict. Van Creveld is arguing that modern weaponry has been rendered obsolete by its very effectiveness. The destructiveness of these weapons is such as to make conventional military-based conflict impossible: hence fighting will increasingly take the form of low-intensity conflict, based upon "close intermingling with the enemy". Civilians will be in the front lines of the conflict; they will be the focus of attack and conventional distinctions between army, state and civil society will break down. Groups such as private mercenary bands commanded by warlords and even commercial organs will become the main combatants: "future war-making entities will probably resemble the Assassins, the group which, motivated by religion and allegedly supporting itself on drugs, terrorized the Middle East for . . . centuries." '

Till then I had taken for granted a pattern of the world that divided the globe between a large number of nation-states. Now suddenly it was as though a bucket had been upended on the map, making the colours run. The camp and the disputed territory around it was no longer on no-man's land; it was a reality in its own right, one that extended in an unbroken swathe through northern Burma and north-east India, to western China and Kashmir, Afghanistan, Central Asia and the Caucasus. In this immense stretch of territory Van Creveld's vision was not just one of many possible forks in the road: it was a turn already taken. Nor could I any longer regard Myanmar and its brutally despotic regime as an aberration, a holdover from a pre-empted past. I was forced to ask myself whether that country might not hold some portents for the future. Burma is a country to which terrorism and insurgency came exceptionally early: within a few months of independence, in 1948, the Rangoon government was besieged by sixteen rebellions. Accounts of life in Burma in the 1950s are replete with tales of derailed trains, bombs in stations, sudden ambushes and the like. Within a few years civil society collapsed and there followed an absolute militarization of political life: the results are well-known. That this could happen elsewhere did not seem improbable.

Not unaware of the world's discontents, I took Van Creveld's vision seriously and tried to incorporate his warnings into my everyday life. I made a point, for example, of not trying to shield my children from news of violence and terror. Yet no matter how carefully we prepare ourselves for the future, the reality is always far in excess of our imaginings.

On the morning of 11 September, I was sitting at my desk in my house in Brooklyn, when my wife called, from her office in mid-town Manhattan, to tell me about the attacks on the World Trade Center. My ten-year old daughter, Lila, was at school, a couple of miles away and my eight-year-old son was at home: this was to have been his first day in a new school and I was scheduled to take him there later that morning. But instead, we rushed out together to fetch Lila home from her school, in Brooklyn Heights.

Downtown Brooklyn was choked with people and in the distance we saw a plume of dust rising into the clear blue sky, darkening the horizon like a thundercloud. Everyone was heading away from the river; only the two of us seemed to be walking towards the darkness in the distance. I held my son's hand and walked as fast as I could. On arriving in Brooklyn Heights, we found Lila in the basement of her school. Her eyes were bright and she was eager to tell me what had happened. 'Where were you?' she said. 'I saw it all. From the window of our history class we had a clear view.'

We stepped out and joined the great wave of dust-caked evacuees that was pouring over the Brooklyn Bridge. I held my childrens' hands and tried to think of words of reassurance, something that would re-attach the moorings that had come undone that morning and restore their sense of safety. But words are not to be had for the asking and I could think of none.

Since then I have come to recognize that there is very little I can say to broaden my children's understanding of what they saw that day. As a writer I have tried to live by the credo that nothing human should be alien to me. Yet, my imagination stops short as I try to think of the human realities of what it must mean to plan a collective suicide over a span of years or to stand in a check-in line with people whose murder has already been decided on; of what it takes to speak of love on a cellphone moments before one's death or to reach for a stranger's hand as one leaps from the topmost floor of a skyscraper. These are new dimensions of human experience and I realize that they will become a part of the generational gap that separate me from my children: their imagining of the world will be different from mine and that very difference will create a new reality. From my own childhood I remember a day when I stared at a newspaper, mesmerized by a picture of a Buddhist monk burning at a crossroads in Saigon. At that time, this too represented a new addition to the armoury of human motivation: this was the moment that inaugurated the era of political suicide in the modern world. Since then such suicides have become so commonplace as often to go unreported. They have become a part of the unseen foundations of our awareness, present but unnoticed, like the earth beneath a basement.

The thickening crust of our awareness is both a sign and reminder of our unwitting complicity in the evolution of violence: if that which mesmerized us yesterday ceases to interest us today, then it follows that the act which will next claim our attention will be even more horrific, even more resistant to yesterday's imagination, than the last. The horror of these acts is thus exactly calibrated to the indifference upon which they are inflicted. Their purpose is not warlike, in the sense of achieving specific ends through violence; their purpose is horror itself.

In one of its aspects terror represents an epistemic violence; a radical interruption in the procedures and protocols that give the world a semblance of comprehensibility. This is why it causes not just fear and anger, but also long-lasting confusion and utterly disproportionate panic; it tears apart the stories through which individuals link their lives to a collective past and present. Everyday life would be impossible if we did not act upon certain assumptions about the future, near and distant; about the train we will catch tomorrow, as well as the money we pay into our pensions. Not the least of the terror of a moment such as that of 11 September is that it reveals the future to be truly what it is: unknown, unpredictable and utterly inscrutable. It is this epistemic upheaval that Michael Ondaatje and Agha Shahid Ali point to when they mourn the maps of our longings and our forty-day daydreams: the pure intuition of poetry had led them to an awareness of this loss long before the world awakened to the knowledge that 'nothing will be the same again'.

On 11 October, a month after the attacks on the World Trade Center, *The New Yorker* organized an evening of readings to raise money for the victims. I was one of those invited to read and I chose to read two of Shahid's poems. Several of the other readers chose texts that hearkened back to the wars of the twentieth century: Winston Churchill on World War I; Remarque on the trenches of the western front; Auden on the declaration of war in September, 1939. When it was my turn to read, I was struck by the sharpness of the contrast between Shahid's voice and those of the poets of the last century; by the vividness of emotion; by the almost-palpable terror that comes of having looked into the obscurity of a time that will not permit itself to be mapped with the measures of the past. It was as though news of times to come had been carried to the capital of the world by a messenger from a half-forgotten hinterland. Time had turned on itself: the backward had preceded the advanced; the periphery had visited the present before the centre; the 'half-made' world had become the diviner of the fully-formed.

Yet the message itself was neither a presaging nor a prediction; it lay merely in the acknowledgement of the loss of a map. But to be aware of the death of a teleology is not to know of what will take its place. The truth is that on the morning of 11 September I had nothing to say to my children that had not been said in Michael Ondaatje's poem, 'The Story':

> With all the swerves of history
> I cannot imagine your future . . .
>
> I no longer guess a future.
> And do not know how we end
> nor where.
>
> Though I know a story about maps, for you.

Notes

1. Canto V, lines 121–3, Dante Alighieri, *The Inferno*, trans R. & J. Hollander, Doubleday, New York, 2000.
2. From 'Wells', in *Handwriting*, Michael Ondaatje, Knopf, New York, 1999, p. 50.
3. From 'The Last Saffron' in *The Country Without a Post Office*, Agha Shahid Ali, W. W. Norton & Co., New York, 1997.
4. Those lines of Dante's from which the title of this essay is taken, is

thought to be based on a passage from Boëtius' *The Consolation of Philosophy*, 'among fortune's many adversities the most unhappy kind is once to have been happy' (R. & J. Hollander, *The Inferno*, p. 99).

5. From 'Farewell', in *The Country Without a Post Office*, Agha Shahid Ali, pp. 22–3.
6. See 'The Ghosts of Mrs Gandhi'.
7. I have described this event in detail in my book, *In An Antique Land*, Ravi Dayal, Delhi, 1992, pp. 204–10.
8. Ranajit Guha, *History at the Limit of World History*, lecture III.
9. It is not without interest that the corresponding administrative term — handed down from the Raj — is 'civil disturbance'.
10. *The Country Without a Post Office*, pp. 48–51.

17 *The Hunger of Stones*
(a translation of 'Kshudhita Pâshân' *by Rabindranath Tagore)*

WE MET him on the train, my cousin and I, on our way back to Calcutta after a trip around the country during the Puja holidays. At first we took him for a north Indian Muslim, because of the way he was dressed. As for his conversation, it left us utterly baffled. He held forth on every conceivable subject, and with such confidence that you would think the Creator himself never moved a finger except on his advice. We'd had no idea that there were so many unheard-of goings-on in the world: that the Russians had advanced so far, that the British had so many hidden designs, that there was so much trouble brewing amongst our own rajas and maharajas — we had been entirely at peace with the world till then, not having known anything about all this. But then, as our new-found friend said with a tight little smile, 'There happen more things in heaven and earth, Horatio, than are reported in your newspapers.' We were real innocents: this was the first time we had been away from home. He held us spell-bound: on the slightest of pretexts, he would switch from lecturing us on science to expounding the Vedas or reciting Persian poetry — and since we knew nothing about science or the Vedas or Persian poetry, our awe of him increased with every word he uttered. My cousin, who was a theosophist, was even convinced that he had some sort of supernatural power — some magnetism or divine force, or an astral body, or something of the kind. He hung upon the lightest word from this unusual man with the rapt attention of a devotee, even jotting down notes in secret. I felt the great man too knew what was going on and, although he didn't let on, he was not in the least bit displeased.

When we got to the station where we were to change trains, we went off to the waiting-room together. It was half past ten. We learnt there was a long wait ahead: our train had been delayed for some reason or the other. I made up a bed for myself on one of the tables, hoping to catch some sleep. But just then the great man launched upon a story.

There was not to be any sleep for me that night.

When I went to work for the Nizam's government in Hyderabad, having quit my job in Junagadh State because of certain disagreements over administrative matters, my new employers chose to send me, because of my youth and good health, to the outlying town of Barich to handle the collection of cotton revenues.

Barich stands upon a very romantic site. Beneath a range of lonely mountains, the fast-flowing river Shusta (from the Sanskrit *svachchhatoa*, limpid) runs like a nimble dancer through towering forests along its winding, rippling course. Right on its banks, looming in solitude at the foot of the mountains, at the top of a flight of one hundred and fifty stone steps, rises a palace built of white marble. There is no habitation anywhere near by. The village and the cotton market of Barich are a good distance away.

Some two hundred and fifty years ago, Shah Mahmud II had built this palace here, upon this remote and lonely site, as his house of pleasure. At that time, secluded deep within the mansion's cool moist interior, rosewater flowed from fountains in the bathing-chambers; and young Persian women, their hair loosened before their bath, sat on smooth wet stone seats with their bare feet in the clear water of the pool, strumming sitars and singing ghazals of the vineyard.

The fountains are silent now; there are no songs, and no fair footsteps resound on the white marble. Today the palace serves as an enormous empty residence for lonely womanless revenue-collectors like myself. An elderly clerk in my office, Karim Khan, warned me repeatedly against living in that palace. 'Go there during the day if you must,' he said, 'but don't on any account spend the night there.' I laughed. My servants said they would work there during the day but would not spend the night. I agreed. The palace's reputation was such that even thieves would not go there at night.

At first the emptiness of that abandoned marble mansion bore down on me like a crushing weight. I spent as much time away as I could, working through the day without a pause; and when I went back at night, I would fall asleep at once in exhaustion.

But before a week had passed, the house began to assail me like a strange addiction. It is hard to describe the state I was in, and just as hard to make it sound credible. The palace was like a living thing, slowly ingesting me in its entrails.

Perhaps the process had started the moment I set foot in the place; but I still remember, perfectly clearly, the day when I first became aware of the way it was working on me.

The hot weather was just beginning to set in, so the market was slow and I didn't have much to do. It was a little before sunset; I was sitting by the river, at the bottom of the great flight of steps, relaxing in a long-armed chair. The river was running low then: a broad stretch of sand had appeared on the far shore and was glowing with the colours of the sunset sky; on this side, close at hand, pebbles glistened on the steps that lay beneath the clear shallow water. It was very still that day. The air was heavy with the thick scent of wild basil, mint and fennel wafting down from the nearby mountains.

The moment the sun slipped below the mountain-tops, a low dark curtain descended upon the stage of the day. Because the hilly terrain shut out the last light of the sun, twilight was of short duration here. Toying with the idea of going for a ride,

I had half-risen from my chair when I heard a footstep on the steps behind me. I turned to look: there was no one there.

My hearing had played a trick on me, I decided; but no sooner had I sat down than I heard a sound again, a number of footsteps this time, running quickly down the stairs. I was transfixed, seized by an excited delight not unmixed with a tinge of fear. There was nothing in front of me, no discernible form; yet I knew, as well as if I could see them, that a group of high-spirited young women had just stepped into the river to bathe at the end of the hot summer's day. Even though there was not so much as a whisper anywhere that evening, neither in the mountains, the river nor the house, I still heard the bathers perfectly clearly as they swept past me one after another, laughing and chattering like a playful mountain stream. They did not notice me: I seemed to be just as invisible to them as they were to me. The river was as calm as ever, but I still felt clearly that the waters were being stirred by many braceleted arms, as the women laughed and splashed water on each other, and their feet sent the water-drops arcing through the air like fistfuls of pearls.

A great ferment of excitement was stirring within me now: whether it grew out of fear or joy or curiosity I cannot say. I began to wish I could see everything properly, but there was nothing to see; I thought, if only I listened carefully, I would be able to hear everything they were saying — but no matter how intently I listened, all I could hear was crickets chirping in the forest around me. I thought: swinging in front of me is a dark curtain, two and a half centuries old. Let me pick up a corner of it and cast an apprehensive glance inside: I would see a great gathering of people. But there was nothing visible in that inky darkness.

Suddenly the pall of stillness was swept aside by a gust of wind. The Shusta's surface was quickly teased into wavelets, like the braids of a heavenly nymph, and the shadowy evening forest gave a deep sigh, as if waking from a bad dream. Dream or reality, the unseen mirage from two hundred and fifty years ago that had presented itself before me vanished in the twinkling of an eye. The magical creatures that had brushed past me with swift disembodied steps and shrill silent laughter to plunge into the Shusta did not make their way back, wringing the water from their dripping clothes. They vanished in that single breath of spring, as a whiff of perfume is lost upon the breeze.

Then, all of a sudden, I had a fright. I began to wonder whether the muse of poetry had chosen to descend on me, finding me off my guard in that desolate place — perhaps I, who had to sweat for my living by collecting cotton-revenues, had suddenly been doomed to the curse of poesy. I thought to myself, I must make sure to eat properly: it's when your stomach's empty that obstinate sicknesses of all kinds crowd in on you. I called my cook and ordered a truly Mughal dinner, rich and spicy.

Next morning the episode began to seem ridiculous. I clapped a sola-topee on my head like an Englishman, and went rattling off to work in the best of spirits, driving the trap myself. I expected to be home late that day, as I had my quarterly report to write. But no sooner did evening come than I began to feel that the house was summoning me back. Who summoned me, I cannot say; but I kept thinking, it won't do to stay any longer, everybody will be waiting. I left my report unfinished, put on my sola-topee, and drove back to that great silent palace below the mountains, startling the lonely twilit tree-lined path with the rumbling of my wheels.

At the top of the palace's main stairway was an enormous room. Three rows of monumental columns held up the ceiling on intricately carved arches. The very emptiness of that vast room sent its echoes resounding through the house all day and all night. It was still early in the evening, so no lamps had been lit yet. The moment I pushed the door open and entered the great room, I had the distinct feeling that I had caused an uproar — that a large gathering had suddenly broken up, and people were tumbling through the windows and out of the doors, fleeing where they could in every direction, down the terraces and corridors. In my astonishment, seeing nothing anywhere, I stayed exactly where I was. A rapture stole over my body; the mild scent of vanished perfumes and pomades, relics from another epoch, wafted past my nostrils. Standing there in that great dark empty room, amongst those long rows of ancient columns, I heard the gurgling of fountains upon the marble floor and the sound of sitars playing an unknown tune. Somewhere, a copper gong was striking the hour; from somewhere else came the ringing sound of anklets and gold jewellery; musical instruments were playing far away; crystal chandeliers tinkled in the breeze; bulbuls sang in cages on the terrace, and the palace cranes called in the garden, the whole weaving a ghostly music around me.

I was in such a trance that I began to imagine that this ineffable, unattainable, unreal setting was the only reality on earth, that everything else was a mirage. That I was the person I was — So-and-so, eldest son of the late So-and-so, who earned a salary of four hundred and fifty rupees collecting cotton-revenues, who went to his office every morning in a trap wearing a sola-topee and a short jacket — all this seemed such an absurd, unfounded lie that I began to shout with laughter, standing in the middle of that great silent room.

At that moment, my Muslim servant entered the room with a lighted kerosene lamp. Whether he thought me mad or not I do not know, but as for myself I recalled at once who I was, that I was indeed the worthy Mr So-and-so, son and heir of the late So-and-so. I also bethought myself that only seers and poets can tell whether, in this world or beyond it, water can really spout endlessly from invisible fountains, and unending melodies sound on illusory sitars; but it was certain that I earned four hundred and fifty rupees a month collecting taxes in the cotton markets of Barich. The thought of my recent trance began to seem ridiculous; sitting down at my lamplit camp-table, with a newspaper in my hands, I soon succumbed to laughter.

After a meal of rich Mughlai food, having read my newspaper, I took myself off to the small corner room that served as my chamber, put out the lamp and lay down on my bed.

A brilliant star shone through an open window: perched high above the dark forested Aravalli mountains, from its exalted place in the sky millions of leagues away, it fixed its gaze upon the humble Mr Tax-Collector on his humble camp-cot. Diverted by this odd conceit, I soon drifted off to sleep: for how long I cannot say, but suddenly I felt myself shiver, and I was awake again. It was not as though there had been any sound in the room, or that anyone had entered it. But by that time, the dim glow of the waning moon was creeping in diffidently through the open window, while the star that had gazed so fixedly upon me had dipped beneath the gloomy mountains.

I could not see anybody in the room. But I had a clear sense that someone was nudging me, ever so gently. The moment I sat up, five beringed fingers beckoned and, without a word being said, gestured to me to follow cautiously behind.

I rose stealthily to my feet. I knew there was no living soul but me in that immense hundred-chambered palace, filled with a great emptiness, with sleeping sounds and waking echoes; yet with every step I took along those deserted, echoing corridors, I was stricken with fear, terrified that somebody would awaken suddenly. Most of the rooms in the palace were kept shut, and I had never ventured to enter any of them. I cannot clearly tell where I went that night, following that invisible, beckoning figure with silent step and hushed breath. I could not begin to count the dark narrow passages, the broad corridors, the still sombre council-hall and small hidden airless chambers through which we made our way.

Even though I had not set eyes on my guide, my mind was not entirely ignorant of her appearance. She was from Arabia: her firm rounded arm, looking as if it were carved from marble, showed below her broad sleeve, a fine veil hung down from her cap across her face, and a curved dagger glinted in her waistband.

It seemed to me that a night from the Thousand and One Nights had transported itself here from the realms of fiction;

that I was stealing through the narrow unlit alleyways of the sleeping city of Baghdad on a dark night, on my way to some perilous assignation.

All of a sudden, my guide came to a halt and gestured towards the bottom of an indigo curtain. There was nothing there, but the blood froze in my veins. I sensed that at the foot of the curtain, swathed in a robe of silk brocade, lay the drowsing form of a gigantic Kafir eunuch, his legs outstretched, a drawn sword resting on his lap. My guide stepped lightly over his legs and lifted up a corner of the curtain.

A part of a room was visible inside, its floor covered with a Persian rug. There was a seated figure too, but all that could be seen of her was the lower part of a pair of loose saffron-coloured leggings and two beautifully-shaped feet in gold-worked slippers, resting on a cushion of pink velvet. On a table beside her, arranged on a blue crystal platter, were apples, pears, oranges and bunches of grapes; and beside them, as though in expectation of a visitor, two wine-glasses and a gold-encrusted decanter. An intoxicating scent of incense drifted from the room and overcame me.

Heart pounding, I raised a foot to climb over the eunuch's outstretched legs when he suddenly awoke, his naked sword falling to the floor with a clatter.

I started at the sound of a piercing shout, and found myself sitting on my camp-cot, drenched in sweat. The waning moon had turned pale in the first light of dawn, like a sick man after a sleepless night; and crazy old Meher Ali was marching down the empty road as was his custom, shouting, 'Stay away, stay away.'

Thus untimely ended the first of my Arabian nights — with a thousand left, yet remaining.

A strange feud now arose between my days and my nights. By day, I would take my weary body off to work, heaping curses upon my beguiling nights full of empty dreams. But once evening had set in, it was my workaday daytime existence that seemed trivial, false and absurd.

Once evening came, I would feel myself caught in a web

of rapture. I would become a different being, a character in an unrecorded history of centuries ago. My short English jacket and my tight pantaloons would begin to seem oddly incongruous; with the greatest care, I would put on a red velvet fez, loose leggings, a flowered shirt and a long silk achkan, with a coloured attar-scented handkerchief. Then, putting away my cigarettes, I would light a great hubble-bubble filled with rosewater, and sink into a high upholstered sofa. And thus I would sit, as though I were waiting in the most eager suspense for some extraordinary night-time tryst.

As the darkness gathered around me, strange things would happen that are impossible to describe. It was as though the pages of some extravagant romance were blowing through the strange rooms of that vast palace on sudden gusts of summer breeze — episodes that could be followed only to a certain point and no further. Setting out in pursuit of those swirling fragments, I would wander from room to room all through the night.

Whirling through those disjointed dreams — gusts of wind moist with scented waters, whiffs of henna and snatches of sitar music — I would sometimes catch fleeting glimpses of a woman, like flashes of lightning. Hers were the saffron leggings, the soft pink feet shod in upturned gold-worked sandals. Her breasts were tightly bound in a flowered bodice with gold braid, and a fringe of gold hung from her red cap to veil her forehead and cheeks.

I was besotted with her: it was to meet her that I would roam every night among the alleyways of that labyrinthine dreamworld, in the subterranean realm of sleep.

Sometimes, standing before my wide candle-flanked mirror, changing into my princely night-time attire, I would catch sight of her, that Persian woman, reflected back at me beside my own mirror-image, bending her neck, glancing passionately, painfully, sensually out of her great dark eyes, hinting with full red lips at some unspoken utterance, pirouetting with her slim youthful figure in a light graceful dance — and then, in a trice, melting into the glass in a shower of incandescence from her pain and desire and rapture, laughter and sidelong glances and shimmering jewellery. Then a strong wind, redolent of all the scents of the forest, would blow out my candles; I would abandon my elaborate costume, close my eyes, and stretch out my ecstatic body on the bed in the corner of my dressing-room. In the breezes that blew over me, in all the mingled scents borne from the Aravalli hills, I would discover many kisses, many caresses, many a touch of a soft hand floating in that solitary darkness. I would hear murmuring voices, feel the warmth of perfumed breath upon my forehead and the gentle scented touch of a woman's kerchief blown across my cheek, again and again. It was as though a bewitching she-serpent was binding me in her intoxicating coils: with deep sighs, my benumbed body would sink into a heavy sleep.

One evening, I thought of going out for a ride. I have no idea who it was that kept dissuading me, but I paid no heed. My sola-topee and short jacket were hanging from a wooden rack. Just as I was about to change into them, a sudden whirlwind swept down, carrying the sand of the Shusta and dead leaves from the Aravallis like a pennant, and bore away my jacket and my hat. They went cartwheeling through the air: a sweet chorus of laughter swirled along with them, rising through several octaves, sounding every note on the scale of derision, until finally it dissolved into the sunset.

I did not go riding that day; and never again did I wear my absurd little English jacket and sola-topee.

That very midnight, sitting up suddenly on my bed, I heard the sound of weeping — racking, broken-hearted sobs. It was as though beneath my bed, beneath the floor, among the foundations of this vast mass of stone, a voice was calling out from a dark and musty grave, crying: 'Take me away, give me my deliverance; break down the doors of this rooted illusion, this deep sleep, this futile dream. Put me on your horse, take me in your embrace — carry me away through the forest, over the mountains, across the river into your own sunlit room. Give me my deliverance!'

I! But who was I? How could I save her? What lovely creature of desire was I to draw out of the flowing, whirling torrent of dreams in which she was immersed? Where did you live and when, you other-worldly beauty? Where were you born, in which palm-fringed oasis, by which desert stream? What desert-dwelling nomad woman brought you into this world? What Bedouin raider plucked you from your mother's arms like a tender flower from its parent creeper, and carried you off on his lightning-swift horse across the searing sands to the slave market before some royal palace? What servant of the emperor counted out his gold upon seeing your first bashful bloom of youth, transported you across the seas, and then carried you on a litter of gold as a gift for his master's harem? And what then was your history? The sound of the sarangi, the tinkling of ankle-bells, the golden wine of Shiraz — and interspersed among them, the glint of a dagger, the sting of poison, a wounding glance. Limitless wealth, perpetual imprisonment.

Diamonds glitter on the bracelets of slave-girls as they wave their fans on either side; the Shah-en-shah Badshah lies beneath those gleaming feet, beside those pearl-embroidered slippers; a gigantic Ethiopian stands at the door, drawn sword in hand, like a messenger of death in angel's dress. And then that rich, envy-spuming, blood-soaked, intrigue-ridden torrent sweeps over you, fearsomely bright — to what abyss of cruel death, my fragile sprig of the desert, or still more cruel shore of noble living?

Then Meher Ali began to shout: 'Stay away, stay away. It's a lie, all of it's a lie.' Opening my eyes, I saw that it was morning: a messenger from my office handed me the day's mail, and the cook came to ask what meals he should prepare that day.

I told myself, 'It won't do to live here any longer.' That very day I packed my things and moved into my office. The old clerk, Karim Khan, smiled wryly upon seeing me. His smile annoyed me. Without responding, I began on the day's work.

As the day wore on, my mind began to wander. It was as though I had an appointment to keep. The cotton-revenue accounts lost their urgency, indeed the affairs of the Nizam's entire estate dwindled into insignificance. Everything that was actual and current, everything happening around me — people coming and going, eating and working — seemed utterly mean, trivial, devoid of sense.

Flinging my pen aside, I shut my enormous account-book and leapt into my trap. It seemed to halt of its own accord at the gates of that great marble palace at the very point of dusk. I raced up the staircase to the vast room at the top.

Everything was quiet today, as though the chamber had taken offence and was sulking. I was stricken with remorse — but to whom could I express it, of whom could I ask pardon? I wandered vacantly from room to room, wishing that I had an instrument in my hands so that I could sing to one absent: 'O flame, the moth that tried to fly away from you has come back to die. Give it its absolution, set its wings alight and turn it to ashes.'

Then, suddenly, I felt a couple of teardrops falling on my cheek. The sky above the Aravallis had been heavy with rain-filled clouds that day. The darkness-shrouded forest and the Shusta's inky waters were still with fearful expectation. Suddenly, the water, the earth and the sky quivered, all at once; and a howling storm burst forth out of the distant forest like a madman that had burst his chains, baring its teeth in lightning-flashes. The palace's empty cavernous rooms began to shriek in torment, beating their doors wildly in the wind.

All my servants were at the office that day, and there was nobody at hand to light the lamps. Thus it happened that there, in the impenetrable darkness of that room, on that overclouded, moonless night, I sensed, with perfect clarity — a woman, lying face down on a rug beside the bed, tugging at her unbound hair with clenched fists, blood pouring from her ivory forehead: sometimes bursting into fierce arid laughter, sometimes into heart-rending sobs, tearing away her dress and beating upon her bared breasts with both hands — and all the while, driven by the roaring wind, sheets of rain poured in through an open window, drenching her entire body.

Neither the storm nor the weeping stopped that night. I spent those hours wandering in the dark from room to room, grieving helplessly. There was no one anywhere; no one to whom I could offer solace. Whose was this dreadful sorrow? What was it that lay behind such a perturbation?

Then there came the lunatic's cry: 'Stay away! Stay away! It's a lie, all of it's a lie.'

I saw that it was dawn. Meher Ali was making his rounds and shouting out his cry as usual, even on this unpropitious morning. It occurred to me then that perhaps Meher Ali too had once lived like me in this palace. Emerging deranged by the experience, he returned each morning even now to wander around the palace, still held in thrall by the great stone monster.

Right then, in the pouring rain, I ran up to the crazy old fellow and asked: 'Meher Ali, what is it that's a lie?'

He thrust me aside without an answer and went on his way, circling around and around in a mesmeric trance, like a bird caught in the hypnotic spell of a python's gaze. But over and over again, as though his life depended on it, he kept warning himself: 'Stay away! Stay away! It's a lie, all of it's a lie.'

I left for my office at once, careering like a madman through the storm. I summoned Karim Khan and demanded: 'Tell me clearly, what does all this mean?'

The gist of what the old man said is this. There was a time once when many flames of unfulfilled desire and demented lust had teemed and flared inside that palace. Every block of stone within it is still hungry, still athirst, from the curse of that anguished and frustrated longing. Whenever they find a living human being within their grasp, they seek to devour him like ravening demons. Of all the people who had spent three nights in that place, Meher Ali was the only one who had emerged alive, although he too had lost his reason. No one else has ever been able to elude its grasp.

I asked: 'Is there no way to save me?'

The old man said: 'Only one, and a very difficult way it is too. I'll tell you what it is — but to do that I must first tell you the old story of the Persian slave-girl in that rose-garden. In all the world there has never been another tale so strange or so affecting . . .'

Just then the porters came to inform us that our train was pulling into the station. So soon? By the time we had repacked our bedrolls, the train had arrived. An Englishman, just up from sleep, thrust his head out of a first-class compartment to read the name of the station. Spotting our fellow-traveller, he cried out 'Hullo' and invited him into his compartment. Ours on the other hand was a second-class carriage. So we never learnt who the gentleman was, nor did we get to hear the end of his story.

I said, 'The man took us for fools and had a good laugh at our expense. The story was all made up from beginning to end.'

The argument that followed led to a lifelong rupture between me and my theosophist cousin.

18 'The Ghat of the Only World': Agha Shahid Ali in Brooklyn

THE FIRST time that Agha Shahid Ali spoke to me about his approaching death was on 25 April 2001. The conversation began routinely. I had telephoned to remind him that we had been invited to a friend's house for lunch and that I was going to come by his apartment to pick him up. Although he had been under treatment for cancer for some fourteen months, Shahid was still on his feet and perfectly lucid, except for occasional lapses of memory. I heard him thumbing through his engagement book and then suddenly he said: 'Oh dear. I can't see a thing.' There was a brief pause and then he added: 'I hope this doesn't mean that I'm dying . . .'

Although Shahid and I had talked a great deal over the last many weeks, I had never before heard him touch on the subject of death. I did not know how to respond: his voice was completely at odds with the content of what he had just said, light to the point of jocularity. I mumbled something innocuous: 'No Shahid — of course not. You'll be fine.' He cut me short. In a tone of voice that was at once quizzical and direct, he said: 'When it happens I hope you'll write something about me.'

I was shocked into silence and a long moment passed before I could bring myself to say the things that people say on such occasions. 'Shahid you'll be fine; you have to be strong . . .'

From the window of my study I could see a corner of the

building in which he lived, some eight blocks away. It was just a few months since he moved there: he had been living a few miles away, in Manhattan, when he had a sudden blackout in February 2000. After tests revealed that he had a malignant brain tumour, he decided to move to Brooklyn, to be close to his youngest sister, Sameetah, who teaches at the Pratt Institute — a few blocks away from the street where I live.

Shahid ignored my reassurances. He began to laugh and it was then that I realized that he was dead serious. I understood that he was entrusting me with a quite specific charge: he wanted me to remember him not through the spoken recitatives of memory and friendship, but through the written word. Shahid knew all too well that for those writers for whom things become real only in the process of writing, there is an inbuilt resistance to dealing with loss and bereavement. He knew that my instincts would have led me to search for reasons to avoid writing about his death: I would have told myself that I was not a poet; that our friendship was of recent date; that there were many others who knew him much better and would be writing from greater understanding and knowledge. All this Shahid had guessed and he had decided to shut off those routes while there was still time.

'You must write about me.'

Clear though it was that this imperative would have to be acknowledged, I could think of nothing to say: what are the words in which one promises a friend that one will write about him after his death? Finally, I said: 'Shahid, I will; I'll do the best I can.'

By the end of the conversation I knew exactly what I had to do. I picked up my pen, noted the date, and wrote down everything I remembered of that conversation. This I continued to do for the next few months: it is this record that has made it possible for me to fulfil the pledge I made that day.

I knew Shahid's work long before I met him. His 1997 collection, *The Country Without a Post Office*, had made a powerful impression on me. His voice was like none I had ever heard before, at once lyrical and fiercely disciplined, engaged and yet deeply inward. Not for him the mock-casual almost-prose of so much contemporary poetry: his was a voice that was not ashamed to speak in a bardic register. I knew of no one else who would even conceive of publishing a line like: 'Mad heart, be brave.'

In 1998, I quoted a line from *The Country Without a Post Office* in an article that touched briefly on Kashmir. At the time all I knew about Shahid was that he was from Srinagar and had studied in Delhi. I had been at Delhi University myself, but although our time there had briefly overlapped, we had never met. We had friends in common however, and one of them put me in touch with Shahid. In 1998 and 1999 we had several conversations on the phone and even met a couple of times. But we were no more than acquaintances until he moved to Brooklyn the next year. Once we were in the same neighbourhood, we began to meet for occasional meals and quickly discovered that we had a great deal in common. By this time of course Shahid's condition was already serious, yet his illness did not impede the progress of our friendship. We found that we had a huge roster of common friends, in India, America, and elsewhere; we discovered a shared love of rogan josh, Roshanara Begum and Kishore Kumar; a mutual indifference to cricket and an equal attachment to old Bombay films. Because of Shahid's condition even the most trivial exchanges had a special charge and urgency: the inescapable poignance of talking about food and half-forgotten figures from the past with a man who knew himself to be dying, was multiplied, in this instance, by the knowledge that this man was also a poet who had achieved greatness — perhaps the only such that I shall ever know as a friend.

One afternoon, the writer Suketu Mehta, who also lives in Brooklyn, joined us for lunch. Together we hatched a plan for an adda — by definition, a gathering that has no agenda, other than conviviality. Shahid was enthusiastic and we began to meet regularly. From time to time other writers would join us. On one occasion a crew arrived with a television camera. Shahid was not in the least bit put out: 'I'm *so* shameless; I just *love* the camera.'

Shahid had a sorcerer's ability to transmute the mundane into the magical. Once I accompanied Iqbal, his brother, and Hena, his sister, on a trip to fetch him home from hospital. This was on 21 May: by that time he had already been through several unsuccessful operations. Now he was back in hospital to undergo a surgical procedure that was intended to relieve the pressure on his brain. His head was shaved and the shape of the tumour was visible upon his bare scalp, its edges outlined by metal sutures. When it was time to leave the ward a blue-uniformed hospital escort arrived with a wheelchair. Shahid waved him away, declaring that he was strong enough to walk out of the hospital on his own. But he was groggier than he had thought and his knees buckled after no more than a few steps. Iqbal went running off to bring back the wheelchair while the rest of us stood in the corridor, holding him upright. At that moment, leaning against the cheerless hospital wall, a kind of rapture descended on Shahid. When the hospital orderly returned with the wheelchair Shahid gave him a beaming smile and asked where he was from. Ecuador, the man said, and Shahid clapped his hands gleefully together. 'Spanish!' he cried, at the top of his voice. 'I always wanted to learn Spanish. Just to read Lorca.'

At this the tired, slack-shouldered orderly came suddenly to life. 'Lorca? Did you say Lorca?' He quoted a few lines, to Shahid's great delight. 'Ah! "La Cinque de la Tarde" ', Shahid cried, rolling the syllables gleefully around his tongue. 'How I love those words. "La Cinque de la Tarde" '! That was how we made our way through the hospital's crowded lobby: with Shahid and the orderly in the vanguard, one quoting snatches of Spanish poetry and the other breaking in from time to time with exultant cries of, 'La Cinque de la Tarde, La Cinque de la Tarde . . . '

Shahid's gregariousness had no limit: there was never an evening when there wasn't a party in his living room. 'I love it that so many people are here', he told me once. 'I love it that people come and there's always food. I love this spirit of festivity; it means that I don't have time to be depressed.'

His apartment was a spacious and airy split-level, on the seventh floor of a newly-renovated building. There was a cavernous study on the top floor and a wide terrace that provided a magnificent view of the Manhattan skyline, across the East River. Shahid loved this view of the Brooklyn waterfront slipping, like a ghat, into the East River, under the glittering lights of Manhattan.

The journey from the foyer of Shahid's building to his door was a voyage between continents: on the way up the rich fragrance of rogan josh and haak would invade the dour, grey interior of the elevator; against the background of the songs and voices that were always echoing out of his apartment, even the ringing of the doorbell had an oddly musical sound. Suddenly, Shahid would appear, flinging open the door, releasing a great cloud of *heeng* into the frosty New York air. 'Oh, how *nice*,' he would cry, clapping his hands, 'how *nice* that you've come to see your little Mos-lem!' Invariably, there'd be some half-dozen or more people gathered inside — poets, students, writers, relatives — and in the kitchen someone would always be cooking or making tea. Almost to the very end, even as his life was being consumed by his disease, he was the centre of a perpetual carnival, an endless mela of talk, laughter, food and, of course, poetry.

No matter how many people there were, Shahid was never so distracted as to lose track of the progress of the evening's meal. From time to time he would interrupt himself to shout directions to whoever was in the kitchen: 'yes, now, add the dahi now.' Even when his eyesight was failing, he could tell from the smell alone, exactly which stage the rogan josh had reached. And when things went exactly as they should, he would sniff the air and cry out loud: 'Ah! Khana ka kya mehek hai!'

Shahid was legendary for his prowess in the kitchen, frequently spending days over the planning and preparation of a dinner party. It was through one such party, given while he was in Arizona, that he met James Merrill, the poet who was to radically alter the direction of his poetry: it was after this encounter that he began to experiment with strict, metrical patterns and verse forms such as the canzone and the sestina. No one had a greater influence on Shahid's poetry than James Merrill: indeed, in the poem in which he most explicitly prefigured his own death, 'I Dream I Am At the Ghat of the Only World', he awarded the envoy to Merrill: 'SHAHID, HUSH. THIS IS ME, JAMES. THE LOVED ONE ALWAYS LEAVES.'

'How did you meet Merrill?' I asked Shahid once.

'I heard he was coming down for a reading and I told the people in charge that I wanted to meet him. They said, "then why don't you cook for him?" So I did.' Merrill loved the food and on learning that Shahid was moving to Hamilton College in upstate New York, he gave him his telephone number and asked him to call. On the occasion of Shahid's first reading at the Academy of American Poets, Merrill was present: a signal honour considering that he was one of America's best-known poets. 'Afterwards,' Shahid liked to recall, 'everybody rushed up and said, "Did you know that Jim Merrill was here?" My stock in New York went up a thousand-fold that evening.'

Shahid placed great store on authenticity and exactitude in cooking and would tolerate no deviation from traditional methods and recipes: for those who took short cuts, he had only pity. He had a special passion for the food of his region, one variant of it in particular: 'Kashmiri food in the Pandit style'. I asked him once why this was so important to him and he explained that it was because of a recurrent dream, in which all the Pandits had vanished from the valley of Kashmir and their food had become extinct. This was a nightmare that haunted him and he returned to it again and again, in his conversation and his poetry.

> At a certain point I lost track of you.
> You needed me. You needed to perfect me:
> In your absence you polished me into the Enemy.
> Your history gets in the way of my memory.
> I am everything you lost. Your perfect enemy.
> Your memory gets in the way of my memory . . .
>
> There is nothing to forgive. You won't forgive me.
> I hid my pain even from myself; I revealed my pain only to
> myself.
> There is nothing to forgive. You won't forgive me.
> If only somehow you could have been mine,
> what would not have been possible in the world?[1]

Once, in conversation, he told me that he also loved Bengali food. I protested: 'But Shahid, you've never even been to Calcutta.'

'No', he said. 'But we had friends who used to bring us that food. When you ate it you could see that there were so many things that you didn't know about, everywhere in the country . . .'

This was at a time when his illness had forced him into spending long periods in bed. He was lying prone on his back, shielding his eyes with his fingers. Suddenly he broke off and reached for my hand. 'I wish all this had not happened', he said. 'This dividing of the country, the divisions between people — Hindu, Muslim, Muslim, Hindu — you can't imagine, how much I hate it. It makes me sick. What I say is: why can't you be happy with the cuisines and the clothes and the music and all these wonderful things?' He paused and added softly, 'At least here we have been able to make a space where we can all come together because of the good things.'

Of the many 'good things' in which he took pleasure, none was more dear to him than the music of Begum Akhtar. He had met the great ghazal singer when he was in his teens, through a friend, and she had become an abiding presence and influence in his life. In his apartment there were several shrine-like niches that were filled with pictures of the people he worshipped: Begum Akhtar was one of these, along with his father, his mother and James Merrill. 'I loved Begum Akhtar', he told me once. 'In other circumstances you could have said that it was a sexual kind of love — but I don't know what it was. I loved to listen to her, I loved to be with her, I couldn't bear to be away from her. You can imagine what it was like. Here I was in my mid-teens — just sixteen — and I couldn't bear to be away from her.'

His love of Begum Akhtar was such as to spill over into a powerful sense of identification. He told me once that the singer Sheila Dhar, who had known Begum Akhtar well, had told him that he even bore a resemblance to Begum Akhtar: 'It's something about our teeth and mouth.'

I said: 'I don't see a resemblance between you and Begum Akhtar.'

He directed a wounded glance at me. 'Yes there is,' he said, 'Sheila Dhar told me so.'

'Well,' I quickly corrected myself, 'she knew Begum Akhtar, so I think she knows more about it than I do.'

He nodded. 'Yes', he said. 'It's something about the teeth. Her teeth were a little prominent (*dant agey they*) — so are mine.'

It may well have been this relationship with Begum Akhtar that engendered his passion for the ghazal as a verse form. Yet, ardent advocate though he was of the form, he had little time for the gushing ardour of some of its contemporary American fans: 'Imagine me at a writer's conference where a woman kept saying to me, "Oh, I just love guh-zaals, I'm gonna write a lot of g'zaals," and I said to her, in utter pain, "OH, PLEASE DON'T!" '[2] Always the disciplinarian in such matters, he believed that the ghazal would never flourish if its structure were not given due respect: 'Some rules of the ghazal are clear and classically stringent.

The opening couplet (called *matla*) sets up a scheme (of rhyme called *qafia*; and refrain — called *radif*) by having it occur in both lines — the rhyme *immediately* preceding the refrain — and then this scheme occurs only in the second line of each succeeding couplet. That is, once a poet establishes the scheme — with total freedom, I might add — she or he becomes its slave. What results in the rest of the poem is the alluring tension of a slave trying to master the master.'[3] Over a period of several years he took it on himself to solicit ghazals from a number of poets writing in English. The resulting collection, *Ravishing Disunities: Real Ghazals in English*, was published in 2000. In establishing a benchmark for the form it has already begun to exert a powerful influence: the formalization of the ghazal may well prove to be Shahid's most important scholarly contribution to the canon of English poetry. His own summation of the project was this: 'If one writes in free verse — and one should — to subvert Western civilization, surely one should write in forms to save oneself from Western civilization?'[4]

For Shahid, Begum Akhtar was the embodiment of one such form, not just in her music, but in many other aspects of her being. An aspect of the ghazal which he greatly prized was the latitude it provided for wordplay, wit and *nakhra*: Begum Akhtar was a consummate master of all of these. Shahid had a fund of stories about her sharpness in repartee. On one occasion he had accompanied her to the studios of All India Radio for a recording session. On the way in they met a famous singer, a man who was reputed to be having an affair with his dhobin. Begum Akhtar greeted the Ustad with a deep salaam, as befitted by his standing in the world of music. But then, in passing, she tossed off the line: 'Arrey Khan-sahib, what a very clean kurta you're wearing today.' Later, once out of the maestro's sight, they fell over laughing.

Shahid was himself no mean practitioner of repartee. On one famous occasion, at Barcelona airport, he was stopped by a security guard just as he was about to board a plane. The guard, a woman, asked: 'What do you do?'

'I'm a poet', Shahid answered.

'What were you doing in Spain?'

'Writing poetry.'

No matter what the question, Shahid worked poetry into his answer. Finally, the exasperated woman asked: 'Are you carrying anything that could be dangerous to the other passengers?' At this Shahid clapped a hand to his chest and cried: 'Only my heart.'

This was one of his great Wildean moments, and it was to occasion the poem 'Barcelona Airport'. He treasured these moments: 'I long for people to give me an opportunity to answer questions', he told me once. On 7 May I had the good fortune to be with him when one such opportunity presented itself. Shahid was teaching at Manhattan's Baruch College in the Spring semester of 2000 and this was to be his last class — indeed the last he was ever to teach. The class was to be a short one for he had an appointment at the hospital immediately afterwards. I had heard a great deal about the brilliance of Shahid's teaching, but this was the first and only time that I was to see him perform in a classroom. It was evident from the moment we walked in that the students adored him: they had printed a magazine and dedicated the issue to him. Shahid for his part, was not in the least subdued by the sadness of the occasion. From beginning to end, he was a sparkling diva, Akhtar incarnate, brimming with laughter and *nakhra*. When an Indian student walked in late he greeted her with the cry: 'Ah my little subcontinental has arrived.' Clasping his hands, he feigned a swoon. 'It stirs such a tide of patriotism in me to behold another South Asian!'

Towards the end of the class a student asked a complicated question about the difference between plausibility and inevitability in a poem. Shahid's eyebrows arched higher and higher as he listened. At last, unable to contain himself, he broke in. 'Oh you're such a *naughty* boy', he cried, tapping the table with his fingertips. 'You always turn *everything* into an abstraction.'

But Begum Akhtar was not all wit and *nakhra*: indeed,

the strongest bond between Shahid and her was, I suspect, the idea that sorrow has no finer mask than a studied lightness of manner. Shahid often told a story about Begum Akhtar's marriage: although her family's origins were dubious, her fame as a beauty was such that she received a proposal from the scion of a prominent Muslim family of Lucknow. The proposal came with the condition that the talented young singer would give up singing: the man's family was deeply conservative and could not conceive of one of its members performing on stage. Begum Akhtar — or Akhtaribai Faizabadi, as she was then — accepted, but soon afterwards her mother died. Heartbroken, Akhtaribai spent her days weeping on her grave. Her condition became such that a doctor had to be brought in to examine her. He said that if she were not allowed to sing she would lose her mind: it was only then that her husband's family relented and allowed her to sing again.

Shahid was haunted by this image of Begum Akhtar, as a bereaved and inconsolable daughter, weeping on her mother's grave; it is in this grief-stricken aspect that she is evoked again and again in his poems. The poem that was his farewell to the world, 'I Dream I Am At the Ghat of the Only World', opens with an evocation of Begum Akhtar:

> A night of ghazals comes to an end. The singer
> departs through her chosen mirror, her one diamond
> cut on her countless necks. I, as ever, linger.

It was Shahid's mother who had introduced him to the music of Begum Akhtar: 'With her I'd heard — on 78 rpm — *Peer Gynt* . . . / and Ghalib's grief in the voice of Begum Akhtar'.[5] In Shahid's later poems, Begum Akhtar was to become an image for the embodiment of his own sorrow after his mother's death. Shahid's mother, a woman of striking beauty, happened to have a close, indeed startling, resemblance to Begum Akhtar: Shahid's walls were hung with many pictures of both and I would frequently mistake the one for the other. What then of Shahid's belief that he resembled

Begum Akhtar? There is a mystery here that I am content to leave untouched.

Shahid was born in New Delhi in 1949. Later, in one of the temporal inversions that marked his poetry, he was to relive his conception in his poem *A Lost Memory Of Delhi*:

> I am not born
> it is 1948 and the bus turns
> onto a road without name
>
> There on his bicycle
> my father
> He is younger than I
>
> At Okhla where I get off
> I pass my parents
> strolling by the Jamuna River[6]

Shahid's father's family was from Srinagar in Kashmir. They were Shia, who are a minority amongst the Muslims of Kashmir. Shahid liked to tell a story about the origins of his family: the line was founded, he used to say, by two brothers who came to Kashmir from Central Asia. The brothers had been trained as hakims, specializing in Yunani medicine, and they arrived in Kashmir with nothing but their knowledge of medical lore: they were so poor that they had to share a single cloak between them. But it so happened that the then Maharajah of Kashmir was suffering from terrible stomach pains, 'some kind of colic'. Learning that all the kingdom's doctors had failed to cure the ailing ruler, the two brothers decided to try their hand. They gave the Maharajah a concoction that went through the royal intestines like a plunger through a tube, bringing sudden and explosive relief. Delighted with his cure, the grateful potentate appointed the brothers his court physicians: thus began the family's prosperity.

'So you see', Shahid would comment, in bringing the story to its conclusion. 'My family's fortunes were founded on a fart.'

By Shahid's account, his great-grandfather was the first Kashmiri Muslim to matriculate. The story went that to sit for the examination, he had had to travel all the way from Srinagar to Rawalpindi in a tonga. Later, he too became an official at the court of the Maharajah of Kashmir. He had special charge of education, and took the initiative to educate his daughter. Shahid's grandmother was thus one of the first educated women in Kashmir. She passed the matriculation examination, took several other degrees, and in time became the Inspector of Women's Schools. She could quote poetry in four languages: English, Urdu, Farsi and Kashmiri. Shahid's father, Agha Ashraf Ali, continued the family tradition of public service in education. He taught at Jamia Millia University in New Delhi and went on to become the principal of the Teacher's College in Srinagar. In 1961, he enrolled at Ball State Teacher's College, in Muncie, Indiana, to do a Ph.D. in Comparative Education. Shahid was twelve when the family moved to the US and for the next three years he attended school in Muncie. Later the family moved back to Srinagar and that was where Shahid completed his schooling. But it was because of his early experience, I suspect, that Shahid was able to take America so completely in his stride when he arrived in Pennsylvania as a graduate student. The idea of a cultural divide or conflict had no purchase in his mind: America and India were the two poles of his life and he was at home in both in a way that was utterly easeful and unproblematic.

Shahid took his undergraduate degree at the University of Kashmir, in Srinagar. Although he excelled there, graduating with the highest marks in his class, he did not recall the experience with any fondness. 'I learned nothing there', he told me once. 'It was just a question of ratto-maroing.' In 1968 he joined Hindu College in Delhi University to study for an M.A. in English literature. Once again he performed with distinction and went on to become a lecturer at the same college. It was in this period that he published his first collection of poems, with P. Lal of the 'Writer's Workshop' in Calcutta.

Shahid's memories of Delhi University were deeply conflicted: he became something of a campus celebrity but also endured rebuffs and disappointments that may well have come his way only because he was a Muslim and a Kashmiri. Although he developed many close and lasting friendships he also suffered many betrayals and much unhappiness. In any event, he was, I think, deeply relieved when Penn State University in College Park, Pennsylvania, offered him a scholarship for a Ph.D.

His time at Penn State he remembered with unmitigated pleasure: 'I grew as a reader, I grew as a poet, I grew as a lover.' He fell in with a vibrant group of graduate students, many of whom were Indian. This was, he often said, the happiest time of his life. Later Shahid moved to Arizona to take a degree in creative writing. This in turn was followed by a series of jobs in colleges and universities: Hamilton College, the University of Massachusetts at Amherst, and finally, the University of Utah in Salt Lake City, where he was appointed professor in 1999. He was on leave from Utah, doing a brief stint at New York University, when he had his first blackout in February 2000.

After 1975, when he moved to Pennsylvania, Shahid lived mainly in America. His brother was already there and they were later joined by their two sisters. But Shahid's parents continued to live in Srinagar and it was his custom to spend the summer months with them there every year: 'I always move in my heart between sad countries.'[7] Travelling between the United States and India he was thus an intermittent but first hand witness (*shahid*) to the mounting violence that seized the region from the late 1980s onwards:

> It was '89, the stones were not far, signs of change
> everywhere (Kashmir would soon be in literal
> flames) . . .[8]

The steady deterioration of the political situation in Kashmir — the violence and counter-violence — had a powerful effect on him. In time it became one of the central subjects of his work: indeed, it could be said that it was in writing of Kashmir that he created his finest work. The irony of this is that Shahid was not by inclination a political poet. I heard him say once: 'If you are from a difficult place and that's all you have to write about then you should stop writing. You have to respect your art, your form — that is just as important as what you write about.' Another time, I was present at Shahid's apartment when his long-time friend, Patricia O'Neill, showed him a couple of sonnets written by a Victorian poet. The poems were political, trenchant in their criticism of the British Government for its failure to prevent the massacre of the Armenians in Turkey. Shahid glanced at them and tossed them off-handedly aside: 'These are terrible poems.' Patricia asked why, and he said: 'Look, I already know where I stand on the massacre of the Armenians. Of course I am against it. But this poem tells me nothing of the massacre; it makes nothing of it formally. I might as well just read a news report.'

Anguished as he was about Kashmir's destiny, Shahid resolutely refused to embrace the role of victim that could so easily have been his. Had he not done so, he could no doubt have easily become a fixture on talk shows, news programmes and op-ed pages. But Shahid never had any doubt about his calling: he was a poet, schooled in the fierce and unforgiving arts of language. Such as they were, Shahid's political views were inherited largely from his father, whose beliefs were akin to those of most secular, left-leaning Muslim intellectuals of the Nehruvian era. Although respectful of religion, he remains a firm believer in the separation of politics and religious practice.

Once, when Shahid was at dinner with my family, I asked him bluntly: 'What do you think is the solution for Kashmir?' His answer was: 'I think ideally the best solution would be absolute autonomy within the Indian Union in the broadest sense.' But this led almost immediately to the enumeration of a long list of caveats and reservations: quite possibly, he said, such a solution was no longer possible, given the actions of the Indian state in Kashmir; the extremist groups would never accept the 'autonomy' solution in any case and so many other complications had entered the situation that it was almost impossible to think of a solution.

The truth is that Shahid's gaze was not political in the sense of being framed in terms of policy and solutions. In the broadest sense, his vision tended always towards the inclusive and ecumenical, an outlook that he credited to his upbringing. He spoke often of a time in his childhood when he had been seized by the desire to create a small Hindu temple in his room in Srinagar. He was initially hesitant to tell his parents, but when he did they responded with an enthusiasm equal to his own. His mother bought him *murtis* and other accoutrements and for a while he was assiduous in conducting pujas at this shrine. This was a favourite story. 'Whenever people talk to me about Muslim fanaticism,' he said to me once, 'I tell them how my mother helped me make a temple in my room. "What do you make of that?" I ask them.' There is a touching evocation of this in his poem, 'Lenox Hill': *and I, one festival, crowned Krishna by you, Kashmir/ listening to my flute.*

I once remarked to Shahid that he was the closest that Kashmir had to a national poet. He shot back: 'A national poet, maybe. But not a *nationalist* poet; please not that.' If anything, Kashmir's current plight represented for him the failure of the emancipatory promise of nationhood and the extinction of the pluralistic ideal that had been so dear to intellectuals of his father's generation. In the title poem of *The Country Without a Post Office*, a poet returns to Kashmir to find the keeper of a fallen minaret:

> 'Nothing will remain, everything's finished,'
> I see his voice again: 'This is a shrine
> of words. You'll find your letters to me. And mine
> to you. Come soon and tear open these vanished
> envelopes.' . . .
>
> This is an archive. I've found the remains
> of his voice, that map of longings with no limit.[9]

The pessimism engendered by the loss of these ideals — *that map of longings with no limit* — resulted in a vision in which, increasingly, Kashmir became a vortex of images circling around a single point of stillness: the idea of death. In this figuring of his homeland, he himself became one of the images that were spinning around the dark point of stillness — both Sháhid and Shahīd, witness and martyr — his destiny inextricably linked with Kashmir's, each prefigured by the other.

> I will die, in autumn, in Kashmir,
> and the shadowed routine of each vein
> will almost be news, the blood censored,
> for the *Saffron Sun* and the *Times of Rain* . . .

Among my notes is a record of a telephone conversation on 5 May. The day before he had gone to the hospital for an important test: a scan that was expected to reveal whether or not the course of chemotherapy that he was then undergoing had had the desired effect. All other alternative therapies and courses of treatment had been put off until this report.

The scan was scheduled for 2.30 in the afternoon. I called his number several times in the late afternoon and early evening — there was no response. I called again the next morning and this time he answered. There were no preambles. He said: 'Listen Amitav, the news is not good at all. Basically they are going to stop all my medicines now — the chemotherapy and so on. They give me a year or less. They'd suspected that I was not responding well because of the way I look. They will give me some radiation a little later. But they said there was not much hope.'

Dazed, staring blankly at my desk, I said: 'What will you do now Shahid?'

'I would like to go back to Kashmir to die.' His voice was quiet and untroubled. 'Now I have to get my passport, settle my will and all that. I don't want to leave a mess for my siblings. But after that I would like to go to Kashmir. It's still such a feudal system there and there will be so much support — and my father is there too. Anyway, I don't want my siblings to have to make the journey afterwards, like we had to with my mother.'

Later, because of logistical and other reasons, he changed his mind about returning to Kashmir: he was content to be laid to rest in Northampton, in the vicinity of Amherst, a town sacred to the memory of his beloved Emily Dickinson. But I do not think it was an accident that his mind turned to Kashmir in speaking of death. Already, in his poetic imagery, death, Kashmir, and Sháhid/Shahīd had become so closely overlaid as to be inseparable, like old photographs that have melted together in the rain.

Yes, I remember it,
the day I'll die, I broadcast the crimson,

so long ago of that sky, its spread air,
its rushing dyes, and a piece of earth

bleeding, apart from the shore, as we went
on the day I'll die, post the guards, and he,

keeper of the world's last saffron, rowed me
on an island the size of a grave. On

two yards he rowed me into the sunset,
past all pain. On everyone's lips was news

of my death but only that beloved couplet,
broken, on his:

'If there is a paradise on earth
It is this, it is this, it is this.'

Shahid's mother, Sufia Nomani, was from Rudauli in Uttar Pradesh. She was descended from a family that was well-known for its Sufi heritage. Shahid believed that this connection influenced her life in many intangible ways; 'she had the grandeur of a Sufi', he liked to say.

Although Shahid's parents lived in Srinagar, they usually spent the winter months in their flat in New Delhi. It was there that his mother had her first seizure in December 1995. The attack was initially misdiagnosed and it was not till the family brought her to New York's Lenox Hill Hospital, in January 1996, that it was confirmed that she had a malignant brain tumour. Her condition was so serious that she was operated on two days after her arrival. The operation did not have the desired effect and resulted instead in a partial paralysis. At the time Shahid and his younger brother lqbal were both teaching at the University of Massachusetts in Amherst. His sister, Hena, was working on a Ph.D. at the same institution. The siblings decided to move their mother to Amherst and it was there that she died on 24 April 1997. In keeping with her wishes, the family took her body back to Kashmir for burial. This long and traumatic journey forms the subject of a cycle of poems, 'From Amherst to Kashmir', that was later included in Shahid's 2001 collection, *Rooms Are Never Finished.*

During the last phase of his mother's illness and for several months afterwards, Shahid was unable to write. The dry spell was broken in 1998, with 'Lenox Hill', possibly his greatest poem. The poem was a canzone, a form of unusual rigour and difficulty (the poet Anthony Hecht once remarked that Shahid deserved to be in the Guinness Book of records for having written three canzones — more than any other poet). In 'Lenox Hill', the architectonics of the form creates a soaring superstructure, an immense domed enclosure, like that of the great mosque of Isfahan or the mausoleum of Sayyida Zainab in Cairo: a space that seems all the more vast because of the austerity of its proportions. The rhymes and half-rhymes are the honeycombed arches that thrust the dome towards the heavens, and the metre is the mosaic that holds the whole in place. Within the immensity of this bounded space, every line throws open a window that beams a shaft of light across continents, from Amherst to Kashmir, from the hospital of Lenox Hill to the

Pir Panjal Pass. Entombed at the centre of this soaring edifice lies his mother:

> . . . Mother,
> they asked me, *So how's the writing?* I answered *My mother*
> *is my poem.* What did they expect? For no verse
> sufficed except the promise, fading, of Kashmir
> and the cries that reached you from the cliffs of Kashmir
>
> (across fifteen centuries) in the hospital. *Kashmir,*
> *she's dying!* How her breathing drowns out the universe
> as she sleeps in Amherst.

The poem is packed with the devices that he had perfected over a lifetime: rhetorical questions, imperative commands, lines broken or punctuated to create resonant and unresolvable ambiguities. It ends, characteristically, with a turn that is at once disingenous and wrenchingly direct.

> For compared to my grief for you, what are those of Kashmir,
> and what (I close the ledger) are the griefs of the universe
> when I remember you — beyond all accounting — O my
> mother?

For Shahid, the passage of time produced no cushioning from the shock of the loss of his mother: he re-lived it over and over again until the end. Often he would interrupt himself in mid-conversation: 'I can't believe she's gone; I still can't believe it.' The week before his death on waking one morning, he asked his family where his mother was and whether it was true that she was dead. On being told that she was, he wept as though he were living afresh through the event.

In the penultimate stanza of 'Lenox Hill', in a breathtaking, heart-shopping inversion, Shahid figures himself as his mother's mother:

> 'As you sit here by me, you're just like my mother,'
> she tells me. I imagine her: a bride in Kashmir,
> she's watching at the Regal, her first film with Father.
> If only I could gather you in my arms, Mother,

I'd save you — now my daughter — from God. The universe
opens its ledger. I write: How helpless was God's mother!

I remember clearly the evening when Shahid read this poem in the living room of my house. I remember it because I could not keep myself from wondering whether it was possible that Shahid's identification with his mother was so powerful as to spill beyond the spirit and into the body. Brain cancer is not, so far as I know, a hereditary disease, yet his body had, as it were, elected to reproduce the conditions of his mother's death. But how could this be possible? Even the thought appears preposterous in the bleak light of the Aristotelian distinction between mind and body, and the notions of cause and effect that flow from it. Yet there are traditions in which poetry is a world of causality entire unto itself, where metaphor extends beyond the mere linking of words, into the conjugation of a distinctive reality. In Shahid's last months I thought often of the death of Babar, who was not just the first of the Mughal Emperors, but also a poet and writer of extraordinary distinction.

Shahid thought of his work as being placed squarely within a modern Western tradition. Yet the mechanics of his imagination — dreams, visions, an overpowering sense of identity with those he loved — as well as his life, and perhaps even his death, were fashioned by a will that owed more perhaps to the Sufis and the Bhakti poets than to the modernists. In his determination to be not just a writer of poetry but an embodiment of his poetic vision, he was, I think, more the heir of Rumi and Kabir than Eliot and Merrill.

The last time I saw Shahid was on the 27th of October, at his brother's house in Amherst. He was intermittently able to converse and there were moments when we talked just as we had in the past. He was aware, as he had long been, of his approaching end and he had made his peace with it. I saw no trace of anguish or conflict: surrounded by the love of his family and friends, he was calm, contented, at peace. He had said to me once, 'I love to think that

I'll meet my mother in the after-life, if there is an after-life.' I had the sense that as the end neared, this was his supreme consolation. He died peacefully, in his sleep, at 2 a.m. on 8 December.

Now, in his absence, I am amazed that so brief a friendship has resulted in so vast a void. Often, when I walk into my living room, I remember his presence there, particularly on the night when he read us his farewell to the world: 'I Dream I Am At the Ghat of the Only World.' I remember how he created a vision of an evening of ghazals, drawing to its end; of the be-diamonded singer vanishing through a mirror; I remember him evoking the voices he loved — of Begum Akhtar, Eqbal Ahmed and James Merrill — urging him on as he journeys towards his mother: *'love doesn't help anyone finally survive'*. Shahid knew exactly how it would end and he was meticulous in saying his farewells, careful in crafting the envoy to the last verses of his own life.

Notes

1. From 'Farewell', in *The Country Without a Post Office*, Agha Shahid Ali, W.W. Norton & Co., New York, 1997, pp. 22–3.
2. *Ravishing Disunities: Real Ghazals in English*, ed. Agha Shahid Ali, Wesleyan University Press, 2000, introduction, p. 1.
3. Ibid., p. 3.
4. Ibid., p. 13.
5. 'I Dream I Am At the Ghat of the Only World', *Rooms Are Never Finished*, Norton, 2001.
6. I would like to thank Daniel Hall for bringing this poem to my attention.
7. 'I Dream I Am At the Ghat of the Only World', *Rooms Are Never Finished.*
8. 'Summers of Translation', *Rooms Are Never Finished.*
9. 'The Country Without a Post Office', pp. 48–51, *The Country Without a Post Office.*
10. From 'The Last Saffron' in *The Country Without a Post Office.*

[illegible] from the [illegible] of the [illegible] I had the sense that [illegible] the end [illegible] this was [illegible] supreme consolation. He died peacefully in his sleep [illegible] 2 a.m. on 28 December.

Now, in his absence, I am amazed that [illegible] friendship [illegible] in so vast a space. Often [illegible] I walk into my living room. I remember his presence there, particularly on the night when he [illegible] the words 'I Dream [illegible] At the Ghat of the Only World', I remember how he [illegible] a vision of an evening of [illegible] of the [illegible] diamonded [illegible] I remember him evoking the voices [illegible] Mistry, Iqbal Ahmad and James Merrill [illegible] him on as he journeys towards [illegible]. [illegible] I knew exactly how it would end and he was meticulous in [illegible] he [illegible] to the last [illegible] of his own life.

Notes

1. [illegible], in *The Country Without a Post Office*, Agha Shahid Ali, W.W. Norton & Company, [illegible], pp. [illegible].
2. [illegible], *Ravishing DisUnities: Real Ghazals in English*, Agha Shahid Ali, Wesleyan University Press, 2000, Introduction, p. [illegible].
3. Ibid.
4. Ibid.
5. 'I Dream I Am At the Ghat of the Only World', [illegible], 2001.
6. I would like to thank [illegible] Hall for bringing this poem to my attention.
7. 'I Dream I Am At the Ghat of the Only World', [illegible] Would [illegible].
8. [illegible].
9. 'The Country Without a Post Office', pp. [illegible].
10. [illegible].

together.[3] Hinduism, too, is not short of similar attitudes. Tourist information for Hindu Nepal warns foreigners to avoid public kissing and cuddling, 'especially between men and women'.[4] The radical Hindu political group Shiv Shena has created its own Valentine's Day traditions in India: heterosexual couples whom the activists deem too intimate in public have their faces blackened and their hair forcibly cut, while businesses that celebrate Valentine's Day have been vandalized.[5]

As far as Christianity is concerned, Jesus himself insisted that it is possible to be guilty of sexual unfaithfulness without physical contact: 'But I say unto you, That whosoever looketh on a woman to lust after her hath committed adultery with her already in his heart.'[6] According to Thomas Aquinas, historically speaking probably the most important Roman Catholic theologian, touching and kissing between people of different sexes are not mortal sins in themselves but, depending on the motivation, can easily become so.[7] There is a long tradition within Christianity that unfulfilled desire can in itself be a sexual sin. When Christian missionaries went forth and preached that such sexual thoughts were sinful, it was an utterly novel concept to many of the peoples they came in contact with.[8]

It is in the same spirit that Muhammad believed that looking at forbidden things, or looking at someone with desire, was adultery of the eye and talking about forbidden things, or about what one desires, was adultery of the tongue.[9] There is also adultery of the ear when people listen to things of a sexual nature, and adultery of the hand when people touch what they are lusting after. Rather less sublime, perhaps, is adultery of the feet, which means walking to the place where one is planning to commit adultery.[10] Muhammad does, however, seem to be more tolerant of human desire than Jesus, so long as it remains unfulfilled: he does not propose any religious consequences for unfulfilled desires.

Desire per se is also a problematical sexual category for Buddhism, but here it is a matter of desire in itself being a greater challenge than sex in itself. The problem with desire is linked to all the senses, each of which in its own way holds us back in passion. As with other religions, however, Buddhism also sometimes operates with an extended concept of sex: the mere fact that men enjoy looking at women, even just pictures of them, is sometimes understood to be a sexual act.[11]

of very diverse religious convictions. All this needs to be kept in mind when we study the relationship between the different religions and sex.

But What is Sex?

In any consideration of the attitudes various religions take to sex, it is relevant to have a clear idea of what actually constitutes sex, and that is not always easy. According to the *Oxford English Dictionary*, sex means 'sexual activity, specifically sexual intercourse'. A more common understanding of sex is that it is an activity involving the sexual organs and some level of excitement. When we move into the field of religion we do not find any particularly precise understanding of what sex is: rather the reverse. All religions recognize that heterosexual vaginal intercourse is sex, but once we go beyond that we find that the limits of what is understood as sex vary enormously between different religions and, indeed, within any one religion.

In the history of religion a great deal of effort has been put into regulating what are commonly considered to be sexual frontier zones. In Judaic law, for instance, the concept of *yichud* refers to the necessity of keeping unmarried men and women physically separate. Even though this principle is no longer as widespread as it was, it nevertheless appears in new forms. Separate buses for men and women are becoming more common as a result of the demands of ultra-Orthodox or Haredi Jews, and on a number of routes where such segregated buses do not yet exist, women have to sit at the back of the bus in order to prevent the fundamentally indecent behaviour represented by contact between the sexes. Women have occasionally been beaten up by ultra-Orthodox men, because they refuse to sit at the back of the bus.[1] Similar ordinances to keep men and women apart are to be found in conservative parts of Islam. The Afghan Taliban legislation forbidding women to move outside the home without a male chaperone represents a more extreme example. More often it is about states letting women be restricted in this manner by their families. But men are targeted, too: in the winter of 2008 57 young men were arrested in a shopping centre in Mecca for wearing indecent clothes, playing loud music and dancing because they were allegedly behaving in this manner to attract the attention of women.2 In the autumn of 2008 a group of imams in Oslo turned up at public Norwegian-Somali festivities, protesting loudly against men and women who were not family relations being present